ATLA BIBLIOGRAPHY SERIES
edited by Dr. Kenneth E. Rowe

THE PARABLES OF JESUS

A History of Interpretation and Bibliography

by

Warren S. Kissinger

ATLA Bibliography Series, No. 4

The Scarecrow Press, Inc.,
Metuchen, N.J. & London,
and
The American Theological Library Association
1979

Library of Congress Cataloging in Publication Data

Kissinger, Warren S   1922-
    The parables of Jesus.

        (ATLA bibliography series ; no. 4)
        Includes index.
        1.   Jesus Christ--Parables.   2.   Jesus Christ--
Parables--Bibliography.   I.   Title.   II.   Series: Ameri-
can Theological Library Association.   ATLA bibliography
series ; no. 4.
BT375. 2. K56   226'. 8'06   78-23271
ISBN 0-8108-1186-3

To my parents

Howard Kissinger
and
Anna (Stauffer) Kissinger

with fond memories and gratitude

EDITOR'S NOTE

The American Theological Library Association Bibliography series is designed to stimulate and encourage the preparation of reliable bibliographies and guides to the literature of religious studies in all of its scope and variety. Compilers are free to define their field, make their own selections, and work out internal organization as the unique demands of the subject indicate. We are pleased to publish this guide to the literature of the Parables as number four in our series.

Warren S. Kissinger studied theology at Yale Divinity School and at the Lutheran Theological Seminary in Gettysburg, Pa. , and library science at Drexel University in Philadelphia. An ordained minister in the Church of the Brethren, he has served several pastorates in Pennsylvania, taught religion at Juniata College in Huntingdon, Pa. , and currently serves as subject cataloger in religion at the Library of Congress.

Kenneth E. Rowe, Editor
Drew University Library
Madison, New Jersey 07940

FOREWORD

Research on the parables of Jesus has entered a decisive new stage. Adolf Jülicher's work represents the watershed between pre-modern (allegorical) interpretation of the parables and the modern, historical-critical approach. C. H. Dodd and Joachim Jeremias accepted Jülicher's negative view of allegory and then rejected his broadest principle of moral application in favor of a strictly historical interpretive context; that context was taken to be eschatological and, for Jeremias, polemical. A general moral point was exchanged for a particular historical point. In spite of differences, Dodd and Jeremias remain firmly in the tradition of Jülicher.

More recent interpreters are greatly in debt to Jeremias, Dodd, and Jülicher. Yet contemporary work on the parables views the parables in their literary and aesthetic dimensions and reads them as root metaphors. The parables of Jesus are taken to found a new symbol system, out of which Christianity with its variety of secondary and syncretic languages grew. As metaphors, the parables transcend the context into which Jesus spoke them, just as a great painting or musical composition overflows its historical context. For this reason, current parable interpretation is a serious modifiction of the Jülicher-Dodd-Jeremias tradition and links up, remotely, with the older allegorical approach. Nevertheless, recent leaders of the new mode of parable interpretation insist on the rights of historical criticism while tempering those rights with literary criticism, structuralism, and interpretation theory. It may be said that the new phase of parable interpretation is as distinct from its immediate scholarly antecedents as Jülicher was from his.

It is thus entirely appropriate and even timely that Warren Kissinger should have provided an important new research tool for parable study. His history of parable interpretation should serve to deepen reflection on the parables, and his account of recent developments, because it is perceptive, lucid, and comprehensive, will serve generalist and

specialist alike.   Indeed, his sketch will be a special boon to
students.   In addition, the author has prepared an extensive
bibliography which will of necessity become a reference work
for every serious student of the parables.   The appearance
of this volume will do much to stimulate the next round of
advances and will thus contribute to its own obsolescence.
Such is the reward of productive scholarship.

Robert W. Funk
University of Montana
1 February 1978

CONTENTS

Part II.   The Bibliography

INTRODUCTION

Anyone who has ever attended Sunday school knows that a parable is "an earthly story with a heavenly meaning." Thus Jesus, who was a master parable-teller, used "earthly stories" to point his hearers to "heavenly meanings." This definition of parable portrays Jesus' skill in using the commonplace and the events of everyday to illumine the mysteries of the Kingdom of God and to confront persons with the reality of their situation and their need for renewal. However, it gives no indication of the fact that interpreters of the parables have diverged widely in both their understanding of the "earthly story" and the "heavenly meaning."

The term parabolē, from which "parable" is derived, means a comparison or analogy. It was the word generally chosen by the translators of the Septuagint for the Hebrew word mashal which was derived from a verb meaning "to be like." There are many examples of the mashal in the Old Testament as well as in rabbinic literature. Many of these, as in the Wisdom Literature, are in the form of proverbial sayings. Moreover, there are also extended meshalim which approximate the parables found in the Gospels. But while the parables of Jesus have antecedents in the Old Testament and in rabbinic literature, they represent a particular kind of literary genre unlike that found in the earlier writings. Indeed, as far as the biblical canon is concerned, the Gospel parables are virtually a new and highly original form, in reference both to purpose and to content. Jesus' teaching reflects a unique creativity and freshness when compared with the nearest approach to it elsewhere in the Bible.

In any discussion about the nature and the meaning of parables, the problem of terminology is central. A parable is a figurative form of speech and may be a simile or a metaphor. In both one thing is compared with another; in the former this comparison is formally expressed, while in the latter it is effected by transferring to the one the designation of the other. When a simile depicts familiar scenes

and relationships and is presented in some detail, we have
what might be termed a "similitude." When a similitude is
expanded into a story like the Good Samaritan or the Rich
Man and Lazarus, the term often used is "example-story,"
following Adolf Jülicher's Beispielerzählungen. Another form
which played a key role in parable interpretation for many
centuries was allegory. Allegory differs from similitude in
that instead of setting one thing by the side of another, it
substitutes one thing for another. It must be interpreted
point by point and feature by feature because everything
represents something else. Its secret code must be unraveled so that its intent and message can be discerned. Discussions about the above terminology have occupied a prominent place in the history of parable research.

The parables of Jesus are confined to the Synoptic
Gospels, and there is general agreement that the Fourth
Gospel contains few if any parables. As for the distribution
of the parables, Luke contains the most, Matthew the second most, and Mark the fewest. There are a large number
of parables which are common to Luke and Matthew, and following the widespread acceptance of critical scholarship, the
source of these parables is designated "Q." As to the number of parables, the count will vary quite widely depending
on how many of Jesus' short figurative sayings are included.
The numbers have ranged from a low of about 30 to a high
of 60 or more.

The parables pose a wide range of critical problems
which are reflected in the history of their interpretation.
One of the most persistent relates to allegorization. Are the
parables a "secret code" which needs to be deciphered? Or
are they free from allegorical elements? Are they example-
stories designed to teach moral lessons? Does a given parable make only one point? Or can there be a number of
points? What about the authenticity of the parables? Do
they represent our best approach to the historical Jesus?
Or have they been so modified in the course of transmission
that we cannot "hear the voice of Jesus" in them? To what
degree can we reconstruct the historical context out of which
the parables arose? And do they afford us insights into the
sociology, the economics, the politics, the daily life of first-
century Palestine? What part did eschatology play in their
origin and in their subsequent interpretation? Can the parables "speak for themselves" or must one become schooled
in contemporary philosophy or literary criticism in order to
rightly understand them? On these and other issues parable

scholars have disagreed. Moreover, the problems are far from solved, and today parable research is proving to be perhaps the most creative and dynamic area of biblical research.

The history of parabolic interpretation might be divided into segments depending upon the prevailing methodology and emphases. Thus from the patristic period to the end of the 19th century the allegorical interpretation of the parables (with few exceptions) prevailed. With the appearance of Adolf Jülicher's Die Gleichnisreden Jesu in 1888 and 1899 there dawned a new day in parable research. Jülicher categorically rejected allegorization and insisted that the essence of the parable was similitude. He further maintained that a parable's purpose was to make one central point which should be understood in terms of a general moral truth. Jülicher's work resulted in a revision of current and traditional views, and subsequent scholars had to reckon with his conclusions.

The next "epoch" in this history centers around C. H. Dodd and Joachim Jeremias whose major works on the parables were published in 1935 and 1947 respectively. Their prime concern was to recover the actual situation in the life and ministry of Jesus out of which the parables came. The parables had their setting in the ministry of Jesus which must be seen as an eschatological "crisis" through which God would visit and redeem His people.

In the late 1960s and early 1970s a number of scholars began to move in new directions insofar as parable research was concerned. Some took issue with Dodd and Jeremias for being too restrictive and one-sided in their concentration on the original setting and purpose of the parables in Jesus' ministry. They had failed to give attention to the existential and literary dimensions of the parables. Consequently, there developed a movement led by the students of Rudolf Bultmann (particularly Ernst Fuchs) known as the "new hermeneutic" which had a marked influence upon parable interpretation. This new phase of the history moved away from Bultmann's skepticism concerning the historical Jesus. The exponents of the new hermeneutic saw in the parables an authentic core of Jesus' teaching and an "implicit" Christology which formed the basis of the early Christian kerygma. Thus the continuity between the Jesus of history and the Christ of faith was affirmed by a new emphasis upon the authenticity of the parables.

A second concern of the new hermeneutic centered upon the existential implications of the parables. Drawing upon motifs from Bultmann and Martin Heidegger, they viewed the parables as language events which have the capacity of confronting one with the necessity of decision, of coming to authentic existence, of generating fresh relevance in today's situation.

Another trend in current parable research focuses upon their literary form. It is not enough to interpret the parables in ideational, theological, moral, or historical terms. One must reckon with the fact that the text is inseparably related to the form and purpose of its language. This approach to the parables is evidenced in the work of such exegetes as Geraint V. Jones, Robert W. Funk, Dan Otto Via, Jr., Dominic Crossan, and others. This cross fertilization between New Testament research and literary studies has always been a feature of Amos Wilder's work, and he has had a prominent influence upon much contemporary American parable scholarship. This new movement is particularly concerned with the nature and function of metaphorical language, with the internal dynamic of narrative and of its ability to engage the hearer as participant. It appears to be a proliferating movement and one which shows promise for future exegesis of the parables. In addition to the monographs that have been written, creative work has been progressing through the Society of Biblical Literature Seminars on the Parables in which the leading American parable scholars participate. One can conclude that the current trend in parable interpretation reflects a decreasing emphasis upon historical, moralistic, and theological concerns and an increasing emphasis upon the literary-critical, existentialist analysis of the parabolic speech of Jesus.

In view of the extensive bibliography on the parables, works on the history of their interpretation are relatively few. To my knowledge there is no single monograph devoted entirely to the history of parable interpretation. The best-known and most detailed discussion is found in Part I of Jülicher's Die Gleichnisreden Jesu. His survey covers more than one hundred pages and treats many interpreters from the patristic period to his own time.

Christian A. Bugge's volume on the parables which was published in 1895 is a type of history of interpretation since in his analysis of individual parables he includes selections from the Church Fathers and medieval exegetes. The same method is followed in Section III of J. C. B. Jansen's Barmhartige Samaritan in Rovershanden? (1974). This work is on the parable of the Good Samaritan, and Jansen includes "models" of interpretation, consisting of selections from the Reformation to the present time.

A number of other works have sizable portions devoted to a history of interpretation. A. M. Hunter's Interpreting the Parables (1960) includes a good overview of the story of parable interpretation from the patristic to the modern periods. Geriant V. Jones' The Art and Truth of Parables (1964) includes an admirable survey of parable research before and after Jülicher. He deals with a number of lesser-known exegetes as well as those most usually cited. Leone Algisi in his Gesù e le sue parabole (1963) has two sections on ancient and modern interpretation. David M. Granskou's Preaching on the Parables (1972) surveys the history of parable interpretation beginning with Jülicher. Jack D. Kingsbury includes a brief section on modern trends in parable interpretation in The Parables of Jesus in Matthew 13 (1969). One of the finest surveys of the history of parable research is to be found in Norman Perrin's Jesus and the Language of the Kingdom: Symbol and Metaphor in New Testament Interpretation (1976). This volume is noteworthy for its treatment of recent parable interpretation, and particularly of current American scholarship on the parables.

In addition to the above, there is a two-volume study of the parables in Ireneus (Antonio Orbe, Parábolas evangélicas en San Ireno, 1972). Hans Gunther Klemm deals with the exegesis of the parable of the Good Samaritan in the 16th and 17th centuries in Das Gleichnis vom Barmherzigen Samariter (1973). The history of interpretation of the parable of the Talents in the patristic and medieval periods and in Calvin is discussed by Mario Miegge in I talenti messi a profitto (1969). Paolo Siniscalco discusses the interpretation of the Good Samaritan, the Lost Coin, and the Prodigal Son in the patristic period in Mito e storia della salvezza (1971). He traces the interpretation through Gnosticism, Irenaeus, Clement of Alexandria, Tertullian, and Origen.

A number of journal articles deal with various areas of the history of parable interpretation. Turning first to the patristic period, M. F. Wiles in "Early Exegesis of the Parables" (1958) has dealt with Ante-Nicene interpretation. Dominique Sanchis and H. Rondet analyze Augustine's treatment of the Good Samaritan and the Pharisee and the Publican respectively in "L'Exégèse augustinienne de la parabole du bon samaritain" (1961), and "La Parabole du Pharisien et du Publicain dan l'oeuvre de S. Augustin" (1963). M. Alexandre has dealt with Gregory of Nyssa on the parable of the Rich Man and Lazarus, "L'Interpretation de Luc 16, 19-13 chez Grégoire de Nysse" (1972), and P. Siniscalco on Irenaeus' understanding of the parable of the Prodigal Son, "La parabola del figlio prodigo in Ireneo" (1967). Porphyry's criticism of the parables is described by M. Gronewald in "Porphyrios Kritik an den Gleichnissen des Evangeliums" (1968).

Coming to the modern period, David Eaton and H. G. Klemm have written articles on Jülicher--"Professor Jülicher on the Parables of Jesus" (1899), and "Die Gleichnisauslegung Adolf Jülichers im Bannkreis der Fabeltheorie Lessings" (1969). P. Bonnard and C. Svanholm treat the period from Jülicher to Jeremias in "Qù en est la question des paraboles évangéliques? De Jülicher (1888) à Jeremias (1947)" (1967), and "Hovedprobleme i forlolkningen av Jesus Lignelser in den Nyere Teologi fra Jülicher av" (1953). In a series of three articles, James C. Little has surveyed the 20th century, "Parable Research in the Twentieth Century" (1976). In the Kümmel Festschrift, Rudolf Bultmann analyzes mostly German interpretations of the Sower parable since Jülicher.

Contemporary interpretation of the parables has been ably described by such scholars as E. C. Blackman, "New Methods of Parable Interpretation" (1969); Jack D. Kingsbury, "Major Trends in Parable Interpretation" (1971), and Parables of Jesus in Current Research" (1972); Norman Perrin, "The Modern Interpretation of the Parables of Jesus and the Problem of Hermeneutics" (1971); Wilfred J. Harrington, "Parables in Recent Study, 1960-1971" (1972); Charles E. Carlston "Changing Fashions in Interpreting the Parables" (1974). In addition to these broader surveys, Roy B. Ward has written on C. H. Dodd, "C. H. Dodd and the Parables of Jesus" (1970); and Jack D. Kingsbury and A. C. Thiselton on Ernest Fuchs, "Ernst Fuchs' Existentialist Interpretation of the Parables" (1970) and "Parables as Language Event; Some Comments on Fuchs' Hermeneutics in the Light of Linguistic Philosophy" (1970). D. Gewalt has given attention to contemporary interpretation of the parable of the Last Judgment in "Matthäus 25, 31-46 im Erwartungshorizont heutiger Exegese" (1973). Writing in 1951, F. W. Beare dealt with the history of interpretation of the parable of the Marriage Feast, "The Parable of the Guests at the Banquet: A Sketch of the History of Its Interpretation. "

About the Present Work

In the first part of this volume I have attempted to survey the history of parable interpretation from the period of the Church Fathers to the present. Any undertaking of this scope must of necessity be selective in its treatment. This is true because of the sheer volume of material on the parables. But the selective process is also dependent upon such other factors as the author's theological orientation, his ecclesiastical affiliation, his language facility, his vocational interests, his access to source materials, etc. Consequently, this work reflects certain accents and procedures which would differ from those of another person approaching the same task.

A number of interpreters and their works which are not included in this study should be mentioned because they too have played a part in the story of parable exegesis. In the 17th century following the Reformation there developed a movement known as Protestant scholasticism. During this period there arose a method of biblical interpretation sometimes known as the "historico-prophetical" school. Its best-known exponents were Campegius Vitringa (1659-1722) and Johannes Cocceius (1603-1669), who for a time were colleagues at the University of Franeker. Vitringa presented some lectures on the parables at the university. He held that personages of the parables applied to historical figures or contemporary institutions. For example, he said that the pearl of great price was the Church of Geneva. This "school" of interpretation emphasized scriptural prophecies by relating them to historical events. A concern for biblical typology also characterized their exegesis.

Prior to Jülicher the most scholarly and comprehensive study of the parables was a two-volume work by C. E. van Koestveld entitled De Gelijkenissen van den Zaligmaker (1869). Geriant V. Jones notes that van Koestveld anticipated principles of interpretation evidenced in more recent scholarship such as a rejection of allegorization, the parables' historical relevance, and their eschatological significance. Jones observes further that had van Koestveld written in German instead of Dutch, he would have doubtless acquired a prestige equal to that of Jülicher, whose admiration for him was by no means exaggerated.

Norman Perrin has pointed out that there is perhaps no plainer example of the exegete's presuppositions affecting

his exegesis than in parable interpretation. Here one's theological position, fundamental concerns, and methodological
presuppositions can play a surprisingly large role in the way
in which the parables are finally understood. Leonhard Ragaz's Die Gleichnisse Jesu: Seine sozial Botschaft (1944) is a
case in point. Ragaz was a Christian socialist who believed
that the teachings of Jesus had radical social implications,
and this orientation is reflected in his interpretation of the
parables. For Ragaz they were inordinately revolutionary
because they pointed to the "revolution of the world through
God." They were "Jesus' social message," or they embodied
the social meaning of Jesus' message. The parables are
about the Kingdom of God, which has nothing to do with theology and dogma; they manifest the secularity (Weltlichkeit) of
the Kingdom which has to do not with religion but with the
world and nature. Moreover, like Israel's prophets, Jesus
understood the Kingdom of God in terms of social justice.
So Ragaz finds in the parables motifs that are congenial with
his Christian socialism.

As noted above, Jack D. Kingsbury has contributed
several articles dealing with the history of modern parable
interpretation. He has also written a noteworthy volume on
the parables of Jesus in Matthew 13. The uniqueness of this
work is that Kingsbury analyzes these parables according to
the methods of redaction-criticism. His premise is that,
just as Jesus employed parables to meet the demands of his
own situation, so Matthew employed parables that had come
down to him to meet the demands of the situation of the
church to which he belonged. Matthew placed the parables
of chapter 13 in the service of his age and theology, and
these parables, when studied within the context of his gospel,
will likewise reflect this age and theology. Accordingly, the
study of these parables must begin with Matthew's gospel itself, rather than with some preconceived theory or methodology. In a word, the parables of Matthew 13 afford us an
avenue into Matthew's theology and into the dynamics of the
composition of his gospel.

Raymond E. Brown in reviewing modern Catholic parable scholarship notes that it has been relatively modest.
Many of the numerous Catholic books on the parables simply
dealt with allegorical material in the Church Fathers and
contented themselves with explaining some of the obscure details of the stories. The most serious study of the parables
by a Catholic is Leopold Fonck's Die Parabeln des Herrn im
Evangelium exegetisch und praktisch erlautert (1904, 2. Aufl.).

Brown says that in spite of its erudition it failed completely
in the critical task of distinguishing between Jesus and the
evangelists. Other noteworthy Catholic works are Denis
Buzy's Les Paraboles (1932) and Maxim Hermaniuk's La Parabole evangelique (1947) which served to correct Jülicher's
overly-ambitious distinction between parable and allegory.
Brown states further that since World War II Catholic scholars
have been producing excellent studies on the parables as a
whole or on individual parables. Those whom he singles out
are L. Cerfaux, M. De Goedt, J. Dupont, A. George, M.
Didier, E. Siegman. Even so, Brown concludes: "There
has been no complete modern treatment of the parables by a
Catholic--a treatment that would give both Catholic theologians
and parish priests a thorough treatment of each parable and
a firm guide in approaching parable exegesis" [Heinrich Kahlefeld, Parables and Instructions in the Gospels, trans. Arlene Swidler (New York: Herder and Herder, 1966), pp9-10].

An area which has had a significant influence upon parable research is rabbinic studies. The major works are by
Christian Bugge and Paul Fiebig, together with the extensive
volumes of Strack-Billerbeck (Kommentar zum neuen Testament aus Talmud und Midrash). Although there are similarities between the rabbinic parables and those of Jesus, these
studies have served to confirm the uniqueness of Jesus' parables rather than their indebtedness to the rabbinic literature.
The rabbinic meshalim are generally considered later than
the parables of Jesus, with only one (attributed to Hillel)
thought to date from the pre-Christian era.

In 1945 the allegedly Gnostic Gospel according to Thomas, together with some other books, were discovered in Up-
per Egypt. This discovery was to have an important bearing
upon parable research because 30 of the Gospel's 115 logia
are definitely parables or parabolic sayings. Only four of
these are not in the Gospels, and the rest closely resemble
the Synoptic Gospel parables. The comparison between the
parables found in the Gospel of Thomas and in the Synoptic
Gospels poses some complex critical problems on which scholars disagree. Certain of the logia in the Gospel of Thomas
may be more original than the Synoptic sayings and may have
undergone modification in the interests of Gnosticism. Geriant V. Jones observes, however, that all the logia with Synoptic parallels are given a curious slant and an idiom alien to
that of the Gospels. He concludes that the literary and artistic level of the parables of Thomas is much lower than
that of the Gospel parables and that they do not confront the

audience with a sense of crisis and urgency. [For Jones'
description and evaluation of the Gospel of Thomas parables,
see Geriant V. Jones, The Art and Truth of the Parables
(London: S. P. C. K., 1964), pp230-40.] Scholars will continue to discuss and to disagree over questions about the
origin, the relationship to the Synoptic parables, and the authenticity of the parables in the Gospel of Thomas. But now
for the first time parallels to the Synoptic parables are available which probably go back in time to a period less than a
century after the parables were given.

The Bibliography

        Part II of this volume comprises an extensive bibliog-
raphy on the parables, primarily in the Western European
languages. The first section deals with the parables as a
whole while the second lists works on individual parables or
on studies devoted to words or smaller segments of a given
parable. In addition to the monographic literature, audio-
visual material is included. The bibliography does not include works dealing with such areas as literary criticism,
structuralism, existentialism, hermeneutics, biblical criticism,
etc., all of which have a bearing on parable interpretation.
Nor, with few exceptions, does it include references to re-
views of books on the parables. Neither does it contain commentaries or other interpretative works on the Gospels.

        The bibliography on the parables compiled by John Do-
minic Crossan is worthy of note [see Semeia 1 (1974), 236-73].
He calls it a "basic bibliography for parables research." It
is divided into two parts, the Traditiocritical Bibliography for
Parable Research, and the Structuralism Bibliography for Parable Research. Part 1 lists introductory and general studies,
surveys of research, grouped parables, and individual parables.
These works are restricted almost exclusively to the period
after 1956. Part 2 gives a basic bibliography for structuralist theory, method, and practice, followed by works on structuralism as applied to the Bible, and finally by specific structuralist works on the parables themselves. Crossan's bibliography also includes a good section on the Gospel of Thomas.

        The question as to the number of parables and their
names or designations involves some arbitrary decisions. A
list of parables and their location in the Gospels follows this
Introduction. I have attempted to provide see references
from various names by which a given parable may be known

to the name which I have chosen to use both in this list and in the index.

I wish to acknowledge my gratitude to the librarians who so ably assisted me in my research, and particularly to Margaret Whitelock of the Speer Library, Princeton Theological Seminary. I am particularly indebted to numerous colleagues at the Library of Congress, especially Theodore Wiener and Tasso Sporidi, for their help with various vocabulary and linguistic problems. Finally, I thank my family for their encouragement and support and their patience and understanding during the long hours of researching, writing, and compiling this work.

Warren S. Kissinger
University Park, Maryland
January 1978

LIST OF PARABLES
(L = Luke; Mrk = Mark; Mt = Matthew)

Asking Son (Mt7:9-10, L11: 11-12)

Barren Fig Tree (L13:6-9)

Blind Leading the Blind (Mt15:14, L6:39)

Bread and the Stone see Asking Son

Budding Fig Tree (Mt24:32, Mrk13:28, L21:29-30)

Building of the Tower see Tower Builder

Burglar (Mt24:43-44, L12: 39-40)

Callous Judge see Unjust Judge

Campaign Planner see Warring King

City on the Hill (Mt5:14)

Costly Pearl see Pearl

Darnel see Tares

Defendant (Mt5:25-26, L12: 57-59)

Disobliging Neighbor see Friend at Midnight

Dives and Lazarus see Rich Man and Lazarus

Divided House (Mt12:25-26, Mrk3:23-26, L11:17-18)

Divided Kingdom [Realm] see Divided House

Doctor and the Sick (Mrk2: 17)

Doorkeeper see Watchman

Dragnet (Mt13:47-50)

Empty House (Mt12:43-45, L11: 24-26)

Faithful and the Unfaithful Stewards [Servants] see Servant in Authority

Farmer and His Man see Master and the Servants

Fig Tree see Barren Fig Tree; Budding Fig Tree

Friend at Midnight (L11:5-8)

Going to War see Warring King

Good Samaritan (L10:30-37)

Great Feast see Marriage Feast

Great Supper see Marriage Feast

Guests Who Made Excuses see Marriage Feast

Hand to the Plow (L9:62)

Hid [Hidden] Treasure (Mt13: 44)

House on the Rock and the House on the Sand see Two Builders

Householder (Mt13:52)

Importunate Friend see Friend at Midnight

Importunate Widow see Unjust Judge

King at War see Warring King

Laborers and the Harvest (Mt9:37-38, L10:2)

Part I

History of Interpretation

1   IRENAEUS

The major extant work of Irenaeus is Adversus Haereses (Against Heresies) which presents a detailed attack against
Gnosticism, especially the system of Valentinus. While he
does not discuss the parables in any systematic fashion, Irenaeus does comment on a general method of parable interpretation and makes numerous references to individual parables.

In Adversus Haereses, Book II, chapter xxvii, Irenaeus
deals with the "proper mode of interpreting parables and obscure passages." The view of scriptural interpretation reflected here is that the Bible can be easily understood by anyone endowed with a sound mind and devoted to piety and the
love of truth. Consequently, one's understanding of the parables should be free from ambiguous expressions. Irenaeus
maintains that such a reasonable and unambiguous approach
to the parables will enable one to arrive at an understanding
of them which is clear and seemingly obvious to everyone.
Moreover, this method will avoid the dangers of subjectivity
whereby everyone follows his own inclinations and thereby
distorts the parables. Subjectivism leads further to various
systems of truth and antagonistic doctrines which are completely
at variance with the holistic and harmonious method which
Irenaeus espouses. Furthermore, such a false procedure
places one in the position of always inquiring, but never finding because he has rejected the "very method of discovery."
In dire tones, Irenaeus states that such persons are like
those in Jesus' parable whose lamps were untrimmed and not
burning with the brightness of a steady light. Consequently,
because they obscure the interpretation of the parables, "for-
saking him who by his plain announcements freely imparts
gifts to all who come to him," they shall be excluded from
his marriage-chamber. Since everyone can "clearly, unambig-
uously, and harmoniously" understand the entire Scriptures,
those who misinterpret the parables "put fetters upon themselves," and each one imagines that he has found a God of

1

his own through his obscure interpretation. The end result
of this subjectivism is the view that Jesus intended the parables only for certain of his disciples who could comprehend
them, and who understood what was intended by him through
means of arguments and enigmas. Irenaeus is certain that
though the parables can be variously interpreted, nevertheless,
their message is clear and open to anyone who approaches
them in a reasonable fashion. Those who reject this method
"eagerly throw themselves into danger, and act as if destitute
of reason." Referring to the parable which concludes the
Sermon on the Mount (Matt. 7:24-27), Irenaeus says that such
a course of conduct can only be likened to one who builds his
house not upon a rock but upon the shifting sand where its
overthrow is certain.

With the foregoing as a background, let us now examine
Irenaeus' treatment of several parables to see whether he follows the literal and unambiguous method of exegesis which he
proposed.

In IV, xxvi, 1 Irenaeus makes reference to the parable
concerning the Kingdom of Heaven being like the Hid Treasure.
He says that if anyone reads the Scriptures "with attention"
he will find that "Christ is the treasure which was hid in the
field." Referring to the parable of the Sower, Irenaeus observes that the field is the world (Matt. 13:38). Therefore
Christ is the treasure which is hid both in the world and in
the Scriptures. Irenaeus now departs from his previous insistence that the parables are clear to everyone. To the
Jews the incarnation of Christ is like a fable because they do
not possess the necessary explanation regarding Christ's advent. But to Christians, while Christ is the treasure hid in
a field, the truth about him is brought to light by the cross.

In commenting on the parable of the king who gave a
marriage feast for his son, Irenaeus has some interesting
things to say about the "wedding garments." The wedding
garment is the Holy Spirit resting upon us. Those who have
been called to God's supper, yet have not received the Holy
Spirit because of their wicked conduct, shall be "cast into outer
darkness" [IV, xxxvi, 6].

Irenaeus interprets the parable of the Laborers in the
Vineyard in a way that is far removed from his stated principles. The householder is God and the various times at
which the laborers were hired has a unique significance.
Those called in the beginning refers to the creation of the

world. Others were called in the intermediate period following the creation, while the remainder were called in the end of time. This means that there are many workmen in their generations, but only one householder who calls them together. The "one vineyard" shows that there is but one righteousness, and one dispensator, for there is one Spirit of God who arranges all things. Irenaeus continues with his allegorization by saying that there is one hire because each laborer received a penny. The penny carried the royal image and superscription, "the knowledge of the Son of God, which is immortality." Irenaeus concludes his exposition of this parable with the observation that the householder began by giving pay to those hired last because in the last times when the Lord was revealed, he presented himself to all as their reward [IV, xxxvi, 7].

Concerning the son who said that he would go but did not in the parable of the Two Sons, Irenaeus refers to Psalms and Romans which state: "Every man is a liar," and "To will is present with him, but he finds not means to perform it" [IV, xxxvi, 8].

In this same section reference is made to the man in the parable of the Fig Tree who said that he had sought fruit on the tree for three years but did not find any. For Irenaeus this suggests the advent of the Lord to which the prophets pointed. Through the prophets the Lord came from time to time, seeking the fruit of righteousness which he did not find [IV, xxvi, 8].

Turning to the parable of the Tares, Irenaeus identifies the devil as the one who sowed tares in the midst of the wheat while men slept. The enemy was envious of God's workmanship and attempted to turn God's workmanship against Him. For this reason the enemy was banished from God's presence. But He took compassion on man and He turned the enmity by which the devil sought to make man the enemy of God against the author. Consequently, this enmity was sent upon the serpent [IV, xi, 3].

In a section devoted to the relationship of the Holy Spirit and Jesus, Irenaeus makes reference to the parable of the Good Samaritan. He observes that while man has an accuser he also has an Advocate. The Lord has commended man to the Holy Spirit. Man had "fallen among thieves," but God has compassion upon him and "bound up his wounds, giving two royal denaria; so that we, receiving by the Spirit the image and superscription of the Father and the Son, might cause the denarium entrusted to us to be fruitful, counting out the increase to the Lord" [III, xvii, 3].

In the foregoing description of Irenaeus' treatment of the parables we see him in the process of developing an apologetic for the Christian faith. He is the first of the outstanding post-New Testament theologians, and stresses such themes as the authority of the Bible, especially the four Gospels; the unity of the Father and the Son in the work of revelation and redemption; and the fullness of the Incarnation of Christ.

As we have noted, he is an inveterate critic of the Valentinians. In his attack upon them he refers to the parables at times to refute their "heresy." At one point he refers to the parable of the Leaven and denounces the Valentinians for misusing it. He says that according to their teaching the woman represented Sophia; the three measures of meal, the three kinds of men--spiritual, animal, and material; while the leaven denoted the Savior himself [I, viii, 3]. Irenaeus follows this observation with an esoteric discussion of the spiritual and the material.

In Irenaeus we have observed his use of allegory in spite of his insistence that the parables are clear and that their message is evident to any rational person. But his use of the allegorical method is modest and restrained in comparison with those to whom we now turn.

2   TERTULLIAN

Tertullian does not refer to the parables nearly as often as does Irenaeus. However, he singles out three parables for special and rather lengthy interpretation--the Lost Sheep, the Lost Coin, and the Prodigal Son.

Like Irenaeus, Tertullian proposes "certain general principles of parabolic interpretation." One must not make the parables the sources from which subject-matters are devised. Rather the subject-matters are the sources for interpreting the parables. Furthermore, one should not work hard to "twist all things in the exposition" and should "take care to avoid all contradictions" [On Modesty, chap. IX]. In his work against Marcion, Tertullian implies at one point that the parables are bearers of concepts that are not readily understood and open to everyone and that such language was

promised by the Creator. But in contrast to the parables there is a direct mode of speaking which is characterized by Christ's frequent admonition: "He that hath ears to hear, let him hear" [Against Marcion, Book IV, chap. xix].

In his treatise On Repentance Tertullian refers to the parables of the Lost Sheep, the Lost Coin, and the Prodigal Son as "examples from Scripture to prove the Lord's willingness to forgive." His analysis here is fairly conventional. The woman who finds the lost coin is joyful, and this is an example of a restored sinner. The one little ewe which strayed from the shepherd's flock was more dear than the flock. The ewe was earnestly sought, and the one is longed for instead of all. Likewise, the father of the prodigal receives him repentant after his indigence, slays the fatted calf, and expresses his joy with a banquet. "Who is that father to be understood by us to be? God, surely: no one is so truly a Father; no one so rich in paternal love." Just so, God will receive each of us even though we have sinned like the prodigal, and He will rejoice more than over the sobriety of the elder brother. However, all this is contingent upon our repentance and our confession of sins because confession shows that we are ready to make satisfaction [On Repentance, chap. VIII].

In Against Marcion, Book IV, chap. xxxii Tertullian adopts a somewhat freer understanding of the parables of the Lost Sheep and the Lost Coin. His intention now is "to show that the parables of the Lost Sheep and the Lost Drachma have no suitable application to the Christ of Marcion." He begins with a series of rhetorical questions, asking who sought after the lost sheep and the lost coin. "Was it not the loser? Was it not he who once possessed them? Who, then, was that?" Tertullian answers that neither parable has anything to do with man since neither the sheep nor the coin belongs to man, but are the sole property of the Creator. But this is also the case with man; he likewise belongs to God. It was not man who lost either the sheep or the coin because he did not possess them in the first place. Neither did man seek them because he had not lost them. Just so he did not find them because he did not seek them, and he did not rejoice because man did not find them. Tertullian concludes that to rejoice over the sinner's repentance, i.e., the recovery of lost man, is the attribute of God along whose wish is that the sinner should repent rather than die.

The most lengthy interpretation of the above three

parables is in On Modesty, chaps. VII-IX, and it is here without doubt that Tertullian resorts to allegorization. He first
raises the question as to whether a Christian or a heathen
was the object of restoration in the parables of the Lost Sheep
and the Lost Coin. These parables refer to the heathen in
view of the Pharisees' criticism of Jesus' eating with "heathen
publicans and sinners." The Jews are in the parable of the
Lost Sheep because they were "indignant at the hope of the
heathens." They were the ones who were "righteous" and
"had no need of repentance." He set them therefore in the
parable ... that they might blush the more when they heard
that repentance was necessary to others, and not to themselves."

Tertullian takes up the arguments of those who say that
the parables refer to Christians instead of the heathen. In
the course of his defense he gives examples of his opponents'
allegorizing. For example, the house where the coin was
lost is the church; the lamp which aided the search is God's
word. He persists in his claim that the ewe and the drachma
refer to the heathen and that they cannot possibly apply to the
Christian.

Turning to the parable of the Prodigal Son, Tertullian
continues to refute the interpretation of those who try to find
the Christian in the parable. They say that the elder brother
symbolizes the Jew while the younger represents the Christian.
The basic fallacy of these heretics is that they have used the
parables to buttress their doctrines and have made their doctrines conform to their understanding of the parables. Before
giving the "correct" understanding of the parable of the Prodigal Son, Tertullian sets forth his general principles of parabolic interpretation as described above.

Tertullian's opponents had suggested that the Christian
was the younger son and the Jew the elder brother. It is
the other way around. The one who "perishes" and the one
who is "safe and sound" is "he who knows the Lord." The
"substance" which the prodigal squandered is one's origin in
God and "wisdom and natural power of Godward recognition."
Because of his sensuous living the younger son was compelled
to hand himself over to a citizen in the far country. Tertullian observes that this citizen was the "prince of this age" or
the devil. The devil set him over swine, "to feed that flock
familiar to demons, where he would not be master of a supply
of vital food, and at the same time would see others (engaged)
in a divine work, having abundance of heavenly bread." Retur-

ning to his father, the prodigal receives again the pristine garment--"the condition which Adam by transgression had lost." He receives the ring which symbolizes baptism and publicly seals the agreement of faith. The banquet and the fatted calf which he thenceforth feeds upon are the Lord's body or the Eucharist. Such is the authentic meaning of the parable, and from it there follow further insights, particularly concerning the Jews.

In the persons of "publicans and sinners" the Pharisees mourned over the prodigal returning from the world to the Father. Thus the Jews have assumed the elder brother's envy, not because they were innocent and obedient to God, but because "they envied the nation's salvation." Moreover, the Jew groans over the first calling of the Christian and not over the second restoration because that takes place in churches and is not open to the Jews.

Tertullian charges his opponents with sinister motives in their "perversion" of the three parables. Their attempt to find the Christian sinner in the parables is motivated by their desire to endow adultery and fornication with the possibility of remission. But if this be true, then one must regard other crimes of equal seriousness as remissible. It is an either-or situation--either regard all crimes as forgivable, or adultery and fornication as not forgivable. The result of their misinterpretation is that not only adulterers and fornicators, "but idolaters, and blasphemers, and renegades, and every class of apostates, will by this parable make satisfaction to the Father."

With Tertullian, allegorization continues apace, and he appears to have read far more into the parables than they can bear. He, however, concludes: "I think that I have advanced interpretations more consonant with the subject-matter of the parables, and the congruity of things, and the preservation of disciplines."

3   CLEMENT OF ALEXANDRIA

During the latter part of the second century there developed a theological School at Alexandria. Its first known teacher and head was Pantaenus. Clement of Alexandria was a pupil of Pantaenus whom he succeeded in A. D. 190. The School rose to its highest influence under Clement and Origen. The Alexandrians attempted to harmonize Christian theology and the Scriptures with hellenic philosophy. The Alexandrian exegesis of Scripture was strongly drawn to mystical and allegorical exposition, in contrast with the more literal and historical method of Antioch.

Clement came under the influence of Gnosticism and this may be reflected in his understanding of Jesus' intention in speaking in parables. He speaks about the mystery and the hidden wisdom of God which is in Christ and which he makes known in parables. Clement states that the Savior himself seals these things when he says: "To you it is given to know the mysteries of the Kingdom of Heaven" (Matt. 13:11; Mark 4:11; Luke 8:10). This was Jesus' response to his disciples' question as to why he spoke to them in parables. To further buttress his contention, Clement refers to Psalm 78:2 and understands this to be a prophecy concerning Christ. "He will open his mouth in parables, and will utter things kept secret from the foundation of the world" [The Stromata, V, 12]. This same theme recurs when Clement contends that the holy mysteries of the prophecies are veiled in the parables and are preserved for certain chosen persons who are endowed with knowledge and faith. "For the style of the Scriptures is parabolic." Clement maintains that the parables have hidden meanings which lie behind what appears to be the principal subject, and are evident only to those who are chosen to understand. "Or, as some say, a mode of speech presenting with vigor, by means of other circumstances, what is the principal subject." Clement adds that the parabolic style, which is of great antiquity, abounded most in the prophets. This was so that the Holy Spirit might show that the philosophers among the Greeks, and the wise men among the Barbarians were ignorant of the future coming of the Lord, and of the mystic teaching which he was to deliver. He maintains that it was Christ who spoke in parables through both prophecy and law. He arrives at this conclusion by means of an interesting exegesis of Matthew 13:34 and John 1:3. Jesus spoke in parables and without a parable he did not speak anything to his hearers. Turning to John 1:3 Clement concludes that since "all things were made by him...," consequently, prophecy and law were by him, and were spoken by him in parables [ibid., VI, 15].

Clement comments further on the veiled character of the parables by referring to Matthew 13:13 where Jesus says that he speaks to them in parables because seeing they do not see, and hearing they do not hear, nor do they understand. One cannot say that the Lord caused the ignorance because this would be impious. However, "he prophetically exposed this ignorance, that existed in them, and intimated that they would not understand the things spoken" [ibid., I, 1].

Turning to Clement's interpretation of various parables, one can readily appreciate his bent toward allegorization in view of the foregoing observations. His treatment of the parable of the Mustard Seed is most interesting. Clement centers his attention on the taste and medicinal qualities of mustard. Furthermore, mustard "represses bile, that is, anger, and checks inflammation, that is, pride." The mustard seed is the word upon which the soul's welfare is dependent. Moreover the word has grown to such size as to become a tree which is the "Church of Christ established over the whole earth." It has filled the world so that the fowls of the air dwelt in its branches. And who are the fowls of the air? They are the divine angels and lofty souls [Fragments from the Hypotyposes, IV].

Clement uses the same freedom of interpretation with the parable of the Costly Pearl. The pearl which is transparent and "of purest ray" is Jesus "whom of the lightening flash of divinity the Virgin bore." The pearl is produced in the flesh of the oyster in the oyster shell, and though it appears to be a moist and transparent body, it is full of light and spirit. This, for Clement, becomes an analogy of the incarnation. The incarnate Word sends his rays through a body which is luminous and moist [ibid., V].

Concerning differences in virtue according to merit and rewards, Clement makes reference to the parable of the Laborers in the Vineyard. The text here is mutilated and corrupt, but according to the translation completed and amended by Heinsius, Jesus indicated the differences in virtue by the hours unequal in number and by the equal reward given to each laborer. The penny which each was given is salvation and also indicates the equality of justice. The parable teaches further that the laborers shall work in accordance with the appropriate mansions of which they have been deemed worthy as rewards [The Stromata, IV, 6].

In the parable of the Leaven, Clement finds an example of Jesus' concealment of the mysteries of the Kingdom. But he also makes this additional observation and application of the parable: "For the tripartite soul is saved by obedience, through the spiritual power hidden in it by faith; or because the power of the word which is given to us, being strong and powerful, draws to itself secretly and invisibly every one who receives it, and keeps it within himself, and brings his whole system into unity" [ibid., V, 12].

Clement makes a brief reference to the parable of the Tares in an attempt to answer the objection to join the church on account of the diversity of heresies. He maintains that the "tares among the wheat" is a prophecy of Jesus that "heresies should be sown among the truth" [ibid., VII, 15].

The parable of the Good Samaritan was given by Jesus in answer to the lawyer's question as to who was his neighbor. This followed the lawyer's recitation of the great commandment as a precondition for gaining eternal life. Clement comments on the two commandments, and in reference to the second, retells the parable of the Good Samaritan without any attempt at allegorization [Who Is the Rich Man That Shall Be Saved? XXVIII].

It is the parable of the Prodigal Son to which Clement gives his most sustained attention and upon which he exercises his genius for allegorization. He delivers an oration or sermon on the parable in which he presents two interpretations, the second of which seems to be addressed to those schooled in hellenistic philosophy.

The "best robe" which the father puts on the prodigal is the robe of immortality. The ring is a royal signet and divine seal which is the "impress of consecration, signature of glory, pledge of testimony." Here Clement quotes John 3:23: "He hath set to his seal that God is true."

Clement gives an extraordinary exposition on the shoes which the prodigal received. The shoes are not the ordinary kind which wear out, but are such that are imperishable and suited for the journey to heaven. They adorn the heavenly path and are unlike those put on unwashed feet, but are like those put on feet washed by Christ. Moreover, the sinful soul is cramped and bound by many shoes. "For each man is cramped by the cords of his own sins." But the shoes which the servant gave to the prodigal do not impede or drag to the earth. Rather, they are "buoyant and ascending, and waft to heaven, and serve as such a ladder and chariot as he requires who has turned his mind towards the Father."

The fatted calf which is killed can also be spoken of as a lamb, but not literally. Consequently, Christ is the fatted calf--the "Lamb of God who taketh away the sin of the world" (John 1:29). But the fatted calf which forms the basis for the feast celebrating the prodigal's return is the Eucharist. Christ was wholly devoted and consecrated to God, "so well grown, and to such excessive size, as to reach and extend over all, and to fill those who eat him and feed upon him. For he is both flesh and bread, and has given himself as both to us to be eaten." After some further remarks about the elder brother and the Father, Clement concludes his exposition.

There follows a second interpretation of the parable which purports to be the "strict meaning of the parable." Some interpreters of Clement feel that this "new exposition" is by another and later hand. Be that as it may, the analysis now moves in a different direction. Allegorization is still evident, but the emphasis turns to the rational and the moral. The parable shows that the exercise of the faculty of reason has been accorded to each person. What the prodigal asks from his father as his portion is a state of mind endowed by reason. The gift of reason is given to all for the pursuit of what is good, and the avoidance of what is bad. But what actually happens is that many misuse their knowledge and consequently turn toward evil practices. Thus the substance of reason is wickedly wasted. The squandering and perversion of the right use of reason--this is what Christ represents in the parable. The younger brother presents the tragic sight of a rational creature whose reason has been darkened. But such a life of profligacy is also an example of making a wicked use of what had been given, and especially of the benefits of baptism which had been entrusted to him. For when the Father ordered the "best robe," this was the prodigal's the moment he obtained baptism. The remission of sins and the blessings of baptism he obtained immediately when he touched the font. So the parable presents a picture of both the misuse and the regaining of the blessings of baptism.

The ring that is put on his hand is now the mystery of the Trinity which is the "seal impressed on those who believe." The shoes are put on his feet for "the preparation of the gospel of peace" (Eph. 6:15), and the whole course that leads to good actions. With a stirring moral challenge, this most imaginative exposition of the parable of the Prodigal Son is concluded, and we turn to Clement's successor as head of the Alexandrian School.

4   ORIGEN

Without question, Origen was the first great interpreter of Scripture in the Church, and was one of the most prolific writers among the Church Fathers. Like Clement, and in keeping with the Alexandrian exegesis, he regarded Scripture as an inspired and infallible repository of truth. However, this truth was not readily evident to the average reader because it required spiritual discernment to understand its hidden and mystical import.

Origen advocates an approach to Scripture which finds an analogy in the human person. "For as man consists of body, and soul, and spirit, so in the same way does Scripture, which has been arranged to be given by God for the salvation of men" [De Principiis, IV, i, 11]. Scripture therefore has three dimensions. There is the bodily or the obvious, historical, or literal sense. Next there is the soul, the psychical or moral sense which can serve to edify the pious. But the highest is the spiritual by which one can ascertain the "true" meaning. For Origen the Scriptures are full of mysteries and hidden truths. The highest task of the interpreter is to unveil these obscure secrets. In his commentary on John, Origen writes:

> What we have now to do is to transform the sensible gospel into a spiritual one. For what would the narrative of the sensible gospel amount to if it were not developed to a spiritual one? It would be of little account or none; any one can read it and assure himself of the facts it tells--no more. But our whole energy is now to be directed to the effort to penetrate to the deep things of the meaning of the gospel and to search out the truth that is in it when divested of types [Commentary on John, I, 10].

It is this "spiritual" or "heavenly" sense of Scripture which intrigues Origen and which engages his interest. Consequently, one can readily appreciate Origen's attraction to the allegorical method of scriptural interpretation. Turning to the parables, we see Origen in his "best exegetical form" which is probably "unexcelled" in the history of parable interpretation.

Although much of Origen's commentary on Matthew has not survived, we are fortunate in having part of the section on the parables of the Kingdom of Heaven in Matthew 13.

Origen raises the question as to whether they are to be called parables or similitudes, and he contrasts the two terms. The similitude seems to be generic, while the parable is specific. The similitude is the highest genus of the parable and it contains the parable, which is one of its species [Commentary on Matthew, X, 4]. Origen infers that Jesus spoke to the multitudes in parables, but to the disciples in similitudes. He quotes Matthew 13:11 where Jesus tells the disciples that the secrets of the Kingdom of Heaven have been given to them, but to the others he speaks in parables. Consequently, the similitude is a higher genus because it conveys the "secrets of the Kingdom" which are reserved for the chosen few, while parables are addressed to the multitudes [ibid., X, 16].

Beginning with the exposition of the parable of the Tares, Origen suggests that the good seed refers to the children of the Kingdom who have been sown by God the Word. But while men are asleep, not acting according to Jesus' admonition to watch and pray that they enter not into temptation, the devil sows what are called tares--i.e., evil opinions. The field is not the church, but the whole world where the son of man sowed the good seed, but the devil sowed tares--i.e., evil words. The end or the harvest is coming when the angels who have been appointed for this work will gather up the bad opinions which have grown upon the soul as well as anything which causes iniquity, and cast them into the burning furnace of fire.

In his explanation of the parable, Jesus says that after the destruction of the wicked, "the righteous will shine like the sun in the Kingdom of their Father." Then he adds: "He who has ears let him hear" (Matt. 13:43). Here Origen detects that Jesus may be indicating that there is indeed a hidden meaning in the entire parable, but particularly in the shining of the righteous like the sun. While it may appear that the parable is perfectly clear so that anyone can understand it, the fact is that "even the things connected with the interpretation of the parable stand in need of explanation." Origen goes to Daniel 12:3 for the key to explain Jesus' reference to the shining of the righteous. "And those who are wise shall shine like the brightness of the firmament; and those who turn many to righteousness, like the stars for ever and ever." Paul is saying the same thing as Daniel when he speaks about one glory of the sun, another of the moon, another of the stars (I Cor. 15:41-42). While one may speak about the difference of light among the righteous now, after wickedness is destroyed by fire, then the righteous becoming one light of the sun shall

shine in the Kingdom of their Father.   But they will not "shine
for themselves" but for "those below them. "   The light of
Jesus' disciples shines now before others, but after the consummation "they shall shine as the Son in the Kingdom of their
Father" [ibid. , X, 1-3].

The parable of the Hid Treasure, Origen says, is the
first of three which are not parables, but similes.   Those before were spoken to the multitudes, but these three to the
disciples so that they might know the "mysteries of the Kingdom of Heaven. "

How is this parable to be understood?   The field is the
Scripture which was planted with what is manifest in the words
of the history, and the law, and the prophets, and the rest of
the thoughts.   The treasure in the field is that which lies behind and under that which is manifest, viz. Christ, "in whom
are hid all the treasures of wisdom and knowledge" (Col. 2:3).

Origen offers an alternate interpretation and observes
that some might say that the field is that which is full and
which the Lord blessed--the Christ of God.   The treasure then
is the things "hidden in Christ, " or the heavenly things, even
the Kingdom of Heaven.

The man who comes to the field, whether to the Scriptures or to Christ, finds the hidden treasure of wisdom.   Origen says that the Jews had first received the oracles of God,
but when the man buys the field or the Kingdom of God, then
it is taken away from the Jews and "given to a nation bringing
forth the fruits thereof" (Matt. 21:43).   Origen makes the
transition to this verse by saying that in another parable the
Kingdom of God is a vineyard, and in this verse the vineyard
will be given to a nation which will bring forth its fruits.
This is a frequent technique in Origen's exegetical method.
He introduces Scriptures from other contexts in order to make
his intended point.   But whether the treasure is the Scripture
or Christ, the application is the same.   The man sells all
that he has; for what was formerly his was a source of evil
to him.   Likewise, those who surrender their possessions
receive in their place a noble resolution and the field containing the treasure [ibid. , X, 4-5].

The second similitude is the Pearl of Great Price.
Origen begins his exposition by making an inquiry into the
nature of pearls.   He describes pearls found in various areas
and tells how they are formed and how they differ.   The

Indian pearl is superior because it has the marks of the best pearl--rounded off on the outer surface, very white in color, very translucent, and very large in size. British pearls are of a golden tinge but are somewhat cloudy and have a duller sparkle. Those found in the strait of Bosporus are darker than the British, but also livid, dim, soft, and small. The fourth class of pearls found in Acarnania are not very desirable because they are irregular in form and very dark and of poor color.

Jesus was well aware of the difference in pearls, and that accounts for his reference to "goodly pearls." The prophets can be likened to mussels which "conceive the dew of heaven, and become pregnant with the word of truth from heaven, the goodly pearls which the merchantman seeks." The leading pearl, however, is the very costly pearl--the Christ of God. He is the Word which is superior to the words and thoughts of the law and the prophets. If one is to speak further about the differences in pearls, "perhaps the muddy words and the heresies which are bound up with works of the flesh, are the darkened pearls, and those which are produced in the marshes, not goodly pearls."

Origen refers to the relationship between Christ, the pearl of great price, and the law and prophets, also goodly pearls, by quoting Ecclesiastes 3:1, "For everything there is a season, and a time for every matter under heaven." There is a time to gather goodly pearls, to become acquainted with the law and the prophets. For anyone who gains wisdom and truth must first be taught the rudiments and must receive the elementary instruction. He must appreciate it highly, but he dare not stop and dwell there. From the law and the prophets he must go on to find the one precious pearl which is Christ. As Origen puts it: "the perfect apprehension of the law and the prophets is an elementary discipline for the perfect apprehension of the Gospel, and all the meaning in the words and deeds of Christ" [ibid., X, 7-10].

Of the three similitudes, it is the Dragnet which most sharply reflects Origen's exegetical ingenuity. He observes that in the case of the similitudes relating to the Kingdom of Heaven the likeness does not extend to all the features of that to which the Kingdom is compared, but only to "those features which are required by the argument at hand." Consequently, Origen rejects the interpretation of those who say that those who come into the net represent the evil and the righteous.

Having refuted "false" interpretation, Origen suggests that "every kind" symbolizes the "varied character of the principles of action among men." Thus "every kind" includes both those worthy of praise and those worthy of vices. The variegated texture of the net refers to the Old and New Testaments which are woven from a great variety of concepts. As some fish are caught and held in various parts of the net, so it is with those who have come into the "net of the Scriptures." Some are caught in the "prophetic net"; others in the "net of the law"; others in the "Gospel net"; and some in the "apostolic net." This net has been cast into the sea--"the wave-tossed life of men in every part of the world," and "It swims in the bitter affairs of life." Before the coming of Christ the net was not wholly filled because the net of the law and the prophets had to be completed by him who says, "Think not that I came to destroy the law and the prophets, I came not to destroy but to fulfill" (Mat. 5:17). So "the texture of the net has been completed in the Gospels and in the words of Christ through the Apostles."

The expression "gathered from every kind" may also show the calling of the Gentiles from every race. Those in charge of the net are Jesus Christ, the "master of the net," and "the angels who came and ministered unto him" (Matt. 4:11). They do not take the net out of the sea, nor carry it to the shore, "to things beyond this life," unless it is full, i. e., unless the "fulness of the Gentiles" has come into it. After it is brought ashore a separation will be made between the righteous and the wicked, and the latter will be cast into the furnace of fire [ibid., X, 11-12].

In Matthew 13:52 Jesus says that every scribe who has been trained for the Kingdom of Heaven is like a householder who brings out of his treasure what is new and what is old. Origen suggests that the householder may be Jesus himself who brings out of his treasury things new, things spiritual, which are always being renewed by him; and things old written in the "stony hearts of the old man." But Jesus can enrich the scribe who is made a disciple of the Kingdom, and he can make him like himself.

But this parable may have a simpler interpretation. The things new which Jesus the householder brings from his treasury is the evangelistic teaching. The things old is the comparison of the sayings which are in the law and the prophets with similar examples in the Gospels. So Origen concludes: "and when the new and evangelical words came, living according to the Gospel we bring forth the old things of the letter from before the new, and he sets his tabernacle in us, fulfilling the promise which he spoke, 'I will dwell among them and walk in them'" (Lev. 26:12; 2 Cor. 6:16) [ibid., X, 15].

The parable of the Unmerciful Servant concerns forgiveness according to Origen. However, beyond this general conception there is a transcendental and mystical interpretation which could lead to the "right" understanding. This would require an examination of every detail in the parable and would be "beyond the power of man, requiring the Spirit of Christ." Nevertheless, in spite of this claim, Origen enters upon a lengthy exposition of the parable which is quite restrained insofar as mystical and allegorical considerations are concerned. In the course of his exegesis he makes reference to the parable of the Pounds. The nobleman who goes into a far country is Christ to receive the kingdoms of the world and the things in them. Those who receive ten talents are "those who have been entrusted with the dispensation of the Word which has been committed unto them." The nobleman's citizens who did not wish him to reign over them are perhaps Israel and also the Gentiles who disbelieved him. Moreover, his being a citizen in the world points to his incarnation [ibid., XIV, 6-13].

There is a choice example of Origen's allegorizing in his brief reference to the Asking Son. He comments: "God therefore will give the good gift, perfect purity in celibacy and chastity, to those who ask Him with the whole soul, and with faith, and in prayers without ceasing" [ibid., XIV, 25].

Bur Origen's "choicest" allegorizing is reserved for the parables of the Laborers in the Vineyard and the Good Samaritan. A. M. Hunter, in referring to these parables, remarks that Origen's "allegorical expertise almost takes our breath away."

In the former of the two parables Origen believes that the first shift of workers signifies the generations from creation to Noah; the second, those from Noah to Abraham; the third, those from Abraham to Moses; the fourth, those from Moses to Joshua; the fifth, those up to the time of Christ. The householder is God, while the penny represents salvation [A. M. Hunter quotes from Bugge, Die Hauptparabeln Jesu, p283].

Origen's explanation of the Good Samaritan is contained in homily **XXXIV** of his homilies on Luke [39 homilies on Luke translated into Latin by Jerome survive. In addition there are 91 fragments of these homilies in Greek. Fragment 71 contains Origen's allegorization of the Good Samaritan. For the texts of the homily and the fragment on the Good Samaritan, see Origenes, Homélies sur S. Luc (Paris: Cerf, 1962), pp400-11 (Latin and French texts) and pp520-21 (Greek and French texts). For an Italian text, see Origenes, Commento al Vangelo di Luca (Rome: Città Nuova Editrice, 1969), pp212-17 and 278]. Origen's exposition of the parable is as follows: the man going down from Jerusalem to Jericho represents Adam or the doctrine of man and the fall caused by his disobedience. Jerusalem signifies paradise or heaven; Jericho is the world. The robbers are the powerful adversaries or demons, or the false prophets who lived before Christ. The wounds are disobedience and sins. The man stripped of his garments represents man's loss of incorruptibility and immortality and of all his virtue. He is half dead because his human nature is dead but his soul is immortal. The priest is the law; the Levite is the prophets. The Samaritan is Christ; the beast of burden is the body of Christ. The wine is the word which instructs and corrects. The oil is the doctrine of charity, of pity or mercy. The inn represents the church, and the innkeeper the Apostles and their successors, bishops and officials of the church, or the angels assigned to guard the church. The two denarii are the two Testaments, or love toward God and the neighbor, or belief in the Father and the Son. The return of the Samaritan is the second coming of Christ.

In Origen the Alexandrian method of allegorizing Scripture found its most eminent spokesman. Working from the presupposition that Scripture contains hidden spiritual meanings, allegorization became the most predominant method of extracting these "treasures." But allegory was not confined to Alexandria; we confront it again with all its "breath-taking" force in the great bishop of Hippo, St. Augustine.

5   AUGUSTINE

The thought of Augustine is interwoven with biblical quotations and references to the Scriptures, and they form the foundation of his "system." As Albert Outler remarks: "The center of his 'system' is in the Holy Scriptures, as they ordered and moved his heart and mind. It was in Scripture that first and last, Augustine found the focus of his religious authority" [Confessions and Enchiridion: The Library of Christian Classics, vol VII (Philadelphia: Westminster, 1955), p13]. But it was not always so. In his Confessions (3. 5. 9; 3. 7. 12) he points out that his first contact with the Scriptures produced disdain because of their anthropomorphism. However, it was through the influence of Ambrose that Augustine gained an appreciation of the majesty and the authority of the Christian Scriptures. But it was also Ambrose's spiritual exegesis which caused Augustine to embrace the exegetical tradition of the Alexandrians. While he regarded the literal, historical meaning as fundamental, he did resort to spiritualizing and allegorizing if the literal sense appeared to be incoherent or obscure. Augustine, like the Alexandrians, believed that the Scriptures frequently used figures and symbolism which pointed to mysteries that needed to be uncovered. This is evident in his interpretation of some of the parables.

References to the parables occur frequently in Augustine's writings, especially in his sermons. They are seldom extended discussions on a parable or the methodology of interpreting parables, but consist rather of brief comments or a citing of certain phrases or verses from a given parable. As with his exegesis of Scripture in general, Augustine interweaves parabolic motifs into the fabric of his theological development.

The parable of the Barren Fig Tree forms the basis of one of Augustine's sermons (Sermon LX), and also affords us a good example of his allegorizing. Moreover, it is one of his lengthiest expositions of a parable. The fig tree is the human race. The three years during which the man came and did not find any fruit are three periods of time: one before the Law, the second under the Law, the third under grace. Augustine observes that there is nothing wrong with understanding the human race as the fig tree because when the first man sinned, he covered his nakedness with fig leaves. This tree represents the human race which because of sin would not bear fruit through the whole range of history. For this reason the axe was hanging over the unfruitful tree. However, the gardener intercedes for it; punishment is deferred so that help might be administered. And who is the gardener? He is "every saint who within the church prays for those who are without the church." The gardener prays that the tree might be spared this year also, i. e., that in this time of grace sinners, unbelievers, the barren and unfruitful might be saved. The decision is made to spare the tree and to dig around it and fertilize it, with this proviso, that if it bears no fruit next year, it will be cut down. The reference to cutting down the tree signifies the coming of Christ in judgment to judge the "quick and the dead." In the meantime the human race is spared. But what is the significance of the digging? "A ditch is low ground," and the digging has to do with the teaching of lowliness and repentance. The basket of manure is filthy, but it produces fruit. "The gardener's filth is the sinner's sorrow." Those who repent, repent in "filthy robes." Augustine concludes by saying that the call of Jesus is addressed to the tree (human race): Repent ye, for the Kingdom of Heaven is at hand" (Matt. 3:2).

Augustine makes further comments on the parable of the Fig Tree in Sermon XXII which is based on Matthew 12:33. He says that the Lord visited mankind several times (three years). If He did not visit mankind before the Law, Augustine asks, why then was He pleased to be called the Lord of Abel, Enoch, Noah, Abraham, Isaac, and Jacob? And if He did not visit mankind under the Law, He would not have given the Law itself. After the Law came the Master of the House in person (Christ). He caused the gospel to be preached throughout the world, but a certain tree continued to be unfruitful. A certain portion of mankind does not yet amend its ways. The husbandman intercedes so that the tree might not be uprooted. Again Augustine states that the digging represents the "lowliness of the penitent"; for "every ditch is low." He then resorts to moral suasion and admonishes each of his hearers to "be a good tree" and to "bear good fruit."

Sermon XXIII is given to an exposition of the parables of the Sower and the Tares and Jesus' explanation of them. Augustine says that the three places where the seed fell and did not grow are the same as the tares. At this point he makes brief observations about parabolic interpretation. The parallel between the three soils and the tares shows that they receive a different name in a different similitude. When similitudes are used and the literal meaning of a term is not evident, then "not a truth but a similitude of the truth is conveyed." From a literal standpoint visible things are "simply what they are." But in parables one thing may be called many names. Thus there is nothing inconsistent in referring to "bad Christians" as the "way side," "stony ground," "thorny places," and "tares," because "under a figure, things very different from one another may be called by one and the same name."

With this background, Augustine appeals to his audience in strong moral terms to repent and "be the good ground." The harvest will soon arrive. There are both wheat and tares among the laity as well as in the "high seats." The urgency of the situation demands that one must prepare for the harvest so that he will be gathered into the barn rather than destroyed as the tares. These same themes of judgment and moral preparation in reference to the parable of the Sower recur in Sermon XXXVIII. 3. In part 22 of this same sermon Augustine in speaking about the parable of the Tares emphasizes the universality of the church and the coming judgment. "That good Sower, the Son of Man, hath scattered the good seed not in Africa only, but everywhere.... Look then for the harvest throughout the whole world ... throughout the whole world bear with the tares even until the harvest."

Augustine's preference for a "spiritual" interpretation of the parables rather than a literal can be seen in two brief comments on the parables of the Pearl of Great Price. In his Fifth Homily on I John, Augustine is commenting on 3:15: "He that loveth not his brother." He believes that love or charity is the pearl which the merchantman in the Gospel went seeking and for which he sold all that he had. In a choice phrase Augustine observes: "Charity is that precious pearl, without which all that you have profits you nothing, and which suffices you if you have nothing else."

As for the parable of the Dragnet he notes that the nets were a figure of the church and that it should have good and evil fishes, even until they reach the shore which is the end of the world. Thus Christ spoke either openly or in parables to say that good and evil will be mingled together. Another evidence of this fact is Jesus' word about the wheat and the tares growing together until the harvest. But from this we cannot conclude that the discipline of the church was to be abrogated. Jesus said rather that it was to be used (Matt. 18:15-18). Augustine concludes that these parables show that there is a possibility of condoning evil persons in the church. But there is also a way of chastising and rebuking them, "of not admitting them to, or removing them from, the Communion."

Forgiveness is the theme of Sermon XXXIII, and Augustine uses Matthew 18:15ff. as the biblical basis. Jesus' word about forgiving "seventy times seven" becomes the "take off" for a grandiose description of the symbolism of "77." In the course of his exposition Augustine cites the parable of the

Unmerciful Servant which follows immediately after Peter's question to Jesus about forgiveness. This parable is also scrutinized as to the significance of the ten thousand talents which the unmerciful servant owed.

Before coming to the symbolism of the numbers, Augustine treats the parable in a fairly literal though provocative manner. He proclaims unqualifiedly that every person is God's debtor and has someone who is a debtor to him. The only person who would not be God's debtor would be one who is free from sin. Likewise, the person who would have no one as his debtor would be one against whom no one has sinned. Since no human being is in this position, Augustine concludes that "every man is a debtor, yet having himself his own debtors too."

Turning to Jesus' word about forgiving until seventy times seven, Augustine makes an analysis of the generations between Adam and Christ and finds that there were 77. Thus he says: "In the number seventy-seven is a mystery of the remission of sins. So many are the generations found to be from Christ to Adam."

Having "solved the problem of the meaning of seventy times seven," Augustine now directs his attention to the ten thousand talents in the parable. With another bit of "ingenious" reason Augustine first observes that righteousness consists in the observance of the Law of God. The Law is set forth in ten precepts. Thus the servant in the parable owed ten thousand talents. Furthermore, ten thousand talents "signifies all sins, with reference to the number of the Law." The other man in the parable owed a hundred denarii. One hundred is also derived from ten; "for a hundred times a hundred make ten thousand; and ten times ten make a hundred." Though one owed ten thousand talents and the other one hundred denarii (or ten times ten denarii), in either case there is no deviance from the "number of the Law," in both numbers you will find every kind of sin included."

At this point Augustine leaves the parable of the Unmerciful Servant except for a further brief reference. He says that at baptism every person has a new beginning and "goes out free." "The ten thousand talents are forgiven him." But when he goes out he will soon encounter someone who is indebted to him. There follows another extraordinary analysis of numbers--this time 11 and again 77. Augustine finds that just as ten denotes the Law, so eleven denotes sin because

"to get to eleven, there is the transgression of the ten. "
After further examples of the symbolism of these numbers,
Augustine concludes that Jesus was referring to all sins when
he said seventy times seven. And how does one reach this
conclusion? Multiply 11 seven times and the result is 77.
Therefore Jesus would have all sins forgiven because "he
marked them out by the number seventy-seven. " To this one
might only add that fascination with the symbolism of numbers
is not of recent origin.

The parable of the Laborers in the Vineyard has always
proved difficult when compared with conventional concepts of
prudence and justice. In Sermon **XXXVII** Augustine offers
some interesting observations about the parable. He notes
that each of the laborers received his denarius at the same
time even though they worked for varying lengths of time.
Augustine sees here a pattern for the community of faith. The
denarius which each receives is eternal life, and "in the life
eternal all will be equal. " All who are righteous will participate in the resurrection no matter whether they were called
at the "first" or the "ninth hour. " Abel and Noah were the
"first righteous men. " Though they were called at the "first
hour" they will receive with us the blessing of the resurrection. The Patriarchs were called at the "third hour"; Moses
and Aaron and their colleagues at the "sixth hour"; the Holy
Prophets at the "ninth hour. " All of these will participate
at the end of the world in the blessedness of the resurrection
together with all Christians who were called as it were at the
"eleventh hour" [the claim that the denarius signifies eternal
life is also discussed in Of Holy Virginity, **XXVII**].

Besides the above solution to the parable, Augustine
suggests that it may also afford insights into one's Christian
life in the present time. Those who were called at the first
hour are those who begin to be Christians "fresh from their
mother's womb"; boys are called at the third hour; young
men at the sixth; those approaching old age at the ninth hour;
while those who are altogether infirm are called at the eleventh hour. The truth remains that each of these will receive the one and the same denarius--eternal life. But this
demands a word of caution lest any delay their coming into
the vineyard since they are assured of receiving the denarius.
This injunction should not be put off, and one should come
when he is called because no one has any promise as to how
long he will live. Let us conclude Augustine's discussion of
the parable with his question which strikes a universal and
realistic note: "Why then dost thou put off him that calleth

thee, certain as thou art of the reward, but uncertain of the day?"

Augustine's treatment of the parable of the Wedding Feast and the Wedding Garment pays particular attention to the meaning of the wedding garment. He rejects the idea that it is any of the following: baptism, the altar or that received at the altar, fasting, miracles. What then is it? Referring to I Corinthians 13, Augustine says that charity is the wedding garment. He continues by expounding on the nature of charity and enjoining his hearers to nourish and perfect charity in their lives, to put on this wedding garment so that they can "sit down in security" and be clothed instead of being naked when the day of judgment comes [Sermon XL; Sermon XLV, 4-7].

The parable of the Ten Virgins affords us another insight into Augustine's fondness for number symbolism and allegorization. Augustine says that we should not think that "virgins" refers only to the religious. Rather the parable "relates to us all, that is, to the whole church together, not to the clergy only." Why are the virgins "five and five?" The number five denotes "every soul in the body" because "it makes use of five senses." Our only means of perception is through the five senses. Thus anyone who abstains from unlawful seeing, hearing, smelling, tasting, touching, "hath gotten the name of virgin." It is not enough, however, to be a virgin, but one must have a lamp which is the sign of good works. But both the wise and the foolish virgins have lamps. The difference between them relates to the oil which only the wise possessed. Augustine now resorts to a remarkable bit of exegesis regarding the meaning of the oil. Charity is signified by the oil because Paul in I Corinthians 13 spoke of charity as a "way above the rest." Does not oil "swim above all liquids"? One can pour water on oil or reverse the procedure, but in either case the oil will be on top. Just so, "Charity never falleth." Augustine continues with a fairly lengthy exposition of the differences between the wise and the foolish virgins, and then concludes with the plea to be ready for the judgment which will result in an eternal reward for those having the "inner oil of conscience" [Sermon XLIII].

Augustine's sermons on the parables follow a similar pattern. He first analyses the meaning of the parable and usually interprets it "spiritually" or allegorically. He concludes with warnings and moral exhortations. This pattern is

evident in Augstine's exposition of the parable of the Great
Supper in Sermon LXII.

The man who gave the great supper is none other than
"the mediator between God and men, the man Christ Jesus."
Those who were invited refers to those called by the prophets
who were sent before. The prophets invited the people of
Israel to Christ's supper, but they refused to come and instead killed Christ [see also Sermon XXXVII, 3]. But in so
doing they "prepared a supper for us"--the Lord's Supper to
which we are invited.

Those who were invited made excuses. Augustine
finds in these excuses some interesting insights. The buying
of a farm connotes the "spirit of domination" and the sin of
pride. So ensnared by pride and the will to power over
others, he would not come.

Another bought five pairs of oxen. "The five pairs of
oxen are the senses of this body." But there are five pairs.
It is evident that there are two eyes, two ears, two nostrils.
But what of taste and touch? Augustine observes that a certain "doubling" is to be discerned in the sense of taste because "nothing affects the taste, unless it is touched by the
tongue and the palate." While this "doubling" is less obvious
with relation to the touch, "there is both an outer and an
inner touch. And so it too is double." Through these senses
people seek earthly things and things of the flesh. But Augustine sees something more here. The man wanted to go and
prove the oxen. This points to the empirical spirit exemplified by Thomas who wanted proof beyond all doubt. Augustine
says: "He who wishes to prove, by the pairs of oxen, does
not wish to be in doubt, just as St. Thomas by these pairs
did not wish to be in doubt."

The third man refused the invitation to the supper because he had married a wife. This, says Augustine, is the
pleasure of the flesh, which is a "hindrance to many." The
parable then speaks of three conditions which exclude people
from the great supper: "the lust of the flesh, I have married a wife; the lust of the eyes (which denotes all five senses), I have bought five pairs of oxen; the ambition of life,
I have bought a farm."

Following the pattern described above, Augustine pleads
with his audience to avoid the excuses and the sins they represent and to accept the invitation to the great supper. Like

every master homileticist, Augustine preaches for a decision.
Could any contemporary evangelist improve on these words?
"Let us away then with vain and evil excuses, and come we
to the supper by which we may be made fat within. Let not
the puffing up of pride keep us back, let it not lift us up,
nor unlawful curiosity scare us, and turn us away from God;
let not the pleasure of the flesh hinder us from the pleasure
of the heart. Let us come, and be filled!"

One of Jesus' best-known parables--the Prodigal Son--
does not receive much attention in Augustine's writings. He
does, however, refer to the prodigal son theme at a number
of places in the Confessions (e. g. , IV, 30) to characterize
his own life before his conversion.

Before leaving Augustine let us turn to his exegesis of
the other familiar parable--the Good Samaritan [Quaestionum
Evangeliorum, II, 19]. Here the "allegorical art" reaches
one of the most "rarefied heights" in all parabolic exposition.
The man who went down from Jerusalem to Jericho represents
Adam who symbolizes the human race. Jerusalem is the ce-
lestial city from which he has fallen. Jericho signifies our
mortality. The thieves are the devil and his angels who deprive man of his immortality. The wounds which the thieves
inflict are sins to be forgiven. The man is left half alive,
half dead. This implies that that part of man which is spirit
or soul is alive, but the part of man corrupted by sin is
dead. The priest and the Levite stand for the Old Testament
whose people could not reach salvation. The Samaritan, which
means keeper or guardian, is the Lord Christ. His binding
up the man's wounds is doing away with sin. The oil is the
consolation of good hope while the wine is the exhortation to
action of a fervent spirit. The beast on which the man is
placed represents the flesh in which Christ saw fit to come to
us. To be seated upon the beast is to believe in the incarnation of Christ himself. In Sermon LXIX, 7, Augustine says
that the flesh of Christ may be called his beast; for on his
beast he raised him who had been wounded by robbers. The
inn is the church where travelers rest on their pilgrimage as
they return to their homeland. In Sermon LXXXI, 6, Augustine elaborates further upon the inn as the church. Man is
still in the process of being brought to the inn because "he is
still in the process of curing. " Augustine answers those who
say that baptism brought remission of sins by pointing out that
this is true but we are still "in the process of healing in the
inn. " Baptism is the "oil and wine which was poured in by
the way. " The man who fell among robbers was strengthened

by receiving oil and wine for his wounds. "His error was already pardoned, and yet his weakness is in the process of healing in the inn." Just so the church is for us the inn in the present time, but ultimately it will be a home from which we shall never remove. This will occur when "we shall have got in perfect health unto the Kingdom of Heaven." Returning to Augustine's exposition in Quaestionum Evangeliorum, he says that the "next day" when the Samaritan gave two denarii to the innkeeper, is after the resurrection of the Lord. The two denarii may be understood as either two precepts of charity which the apostles accepted from the Holy Spirit for the evangelization of others, or the promise of life present and future. In the Samaritan's promise to return, Augustine sees a relationship to Matthew 19:29: "And every one who has left houses or brothers or sisters or father or mother or children or lands for my name's sake, will receive a hundredfold, and inherit eternal life." Finally, the innkeeper is believed to be the Apostle Paul.

Augustine admitted that he enjoyed this method of biblical exegesis, and that as a preacher he found that it intrigued his hearers and gripped their attention. Who indeed would dispute his claim!

6   CHRYSOSTOM

As we have noticed, the Alexandrian exegetes, and those influenced by them, sought to discern the spiritual or mystical sense of Scripture. Consequently, allegorization became the natural and reasonable method of biblical exegesis, so much so that the results often bordered on incredulity.

However, there was another school, centered in Antioch, which minimized allegory and reflected a far more sober method of biblical exposition. Unlike the Alexandrians, the Antiochenes did not look for hidden meanings in the biblical text but sought to set forth the literal sense intended by the author. Their concern was more with the historical and grammatical than with the spiritual and mystical. The two foremost exponents of the school of Antioch were Theodore of Mopsuestia and John Chrysostom.

Chrysostom was one of the greatest preachers of antiquity, and he delivered a series of homilies on Genesis and on a number of New Testament books, including the Gospel of Matthew which affords us examples of his interpretation of the parables. Chrysostom says that because Jesus talked to his disciples in "dark sayings" he used parables which "makes the hearer more attentive" and "thoroughly rouses his mind. " Jesus did not use parables primarily to reprove his audience but in order to "make his discourse more vivid, and fix the memory of it in them more perfectly, and bring the things before their sight. In like manner do the prophets also" [The Gospel of Matthew, Homily XLIV, 3]. As for how parables should be interpreted, Chrysostom observes that they must not be explained throughout word for word because this can result in absurdities. This observation implies a rejection of allegorization and means that Chrysostom is interested in the central idea of a given parable. In fact he believes that this is the method which Jesus used in explaining the parable of the Tares. Chrysostom writes: "Thus he saith not at all who the servants are that came to him, but, implying that he brought them in, for the sake of some order, and to make up the picture, he omits that part, and interprets those that are most urgent and essential, and for the sake of which the parable was spoken; signifying himself to be judge and lord of all" [Homily XLVII, 1]. In Homily LXIV, 3, Chrysostom emphasizes the same point: "neither is it right to inquire curiously into all things in parables word by word, but when we have learned the object for which it was composed, to reap this, and not busy one's self about anything further. " So in distinction from the allegorical method, Chrysostom is advocating a more restrained, literal, and historical approach which does not seek hidden meanings in every part of the parable, but which attempts to find the central and essential point that Jesus intended to convey.

Chrysostom's analysis of the parable of the Two Builders, concluding the Sermon on the Mount, is in keeping with his exegetical principles outlined above. Those who obey Christ's teachings will receive blessings, not only in the future but also here and now. The blessing of the righteous is that he has strength which present adversities cannot destroy. "The truly marvelous thing being this, that not in fair weather, but when the storm is vehement, and the turmoil great, and the temptations continual, he cannot be shaken ever so little. " The "rain" and "floods" in Jesus' parable are metaphorical expressions for "all the ills in our life that anyone could mention. " The steadfastness of Christ's doctrine is the rock, "setting one above all the waves of human affairs" [Homily XXIV, 3]. Needless to say, there is a vitality and a directness about this type of exegesis which is a refreshing contrast to allegorization.

The parable of the Sower is a picture of Jesus and the spread of his doctrine. Chrysostom says that the seed means his doctrine, and the land signifies the souls of men. The sower of course is Jesus himself. As he sows he makes no distinction in the land but "indifferently casts his seed." Just so Jesus is no respecter of persons but seeks to discourse with all. Why was the greater part of the seed lost? "Not through the sower, but through the ground that received it; that is, the soul that did not hearken." As the parable suggests, there is not only one way to destruction, but many, as symbolized by the different soils. But the good ground gives hope for repentance and the possibility of turning away from the former conditions. "Hearing therefore these things, let us fortify ourselves on all sides, regarding his instructions, and striking our roots deep, and cleansing ourselves from all worldly things" [Homily XLIV, 4-7].

Comparing the parable of the Sower with the parable of the Tares, Chrysostom says that the former speaks about not receiving Christ while the latter refers to the "societies of the heretics." The devil's craft is characterized by trying to juxtapose truth and error so that he might cheat and deceive. With a somewhat freer spirit of interpretation than previously, Chrysostom suggests that the man's decision to allow the wheat and the tares to grow together signifies the hindering of wars with their blood and slaughter. He concludes that Jesus is not forbidding our "checking heretics and stopping their mouths, and taking away their freedom of speech, and breaking up their assemblies and confederacies, but our killing and slaying them." However, Chrysostom finds that there is a gentleness about Jesus portrayed in the parable because "he not only gives sentence and forbids, but sets down reasons" [Homily XLIV, 1].

The parable of the Mustard Seed follows that of the Tares and Chrysostom sees this as Jesus' attempt to allay the fears of those who should question the number of the saved in view of the damage described in the parable of the Tares. The Mustard Seed allays their fears because it leads them to belief and signifies that the gospel shall be spread abroad. Though the disciples were weak and "least of all," nevertheless, "because of the great power that was in them," the gospel has developed in every part of the world.

There is likewise encouragement in the next parable-- the Leaven; for as the leaven converts the large quantity of meal, "even so shall ye convert the whole world.... And as the leaven, though it be buried, yet is not destroyed, but by little and little transmutes all into its own condition; of like sort will the event be here also, with respect to the gospel. Fear ye not then, because I said there would be much injurious dealing: for even so shall ye shine forth, and get the better of all." Chrysostom adds a comment about both the parables of the Mustard Seed and the Leaven and implies that they were not given to convey hidden and esoteric meanings. He tells his listeners not to be surprised that Jesus made mention of a little seed and of leaven. He did this because he was talking with people who were "inexperienced and ignorant." Indeed they were "so simple" that "even after all this, they required a good deal of explanation" [Homily XLVI, 2].

Just as the Mustard Seed and the Leaven convey the same message--the power of the gospel and its certainty of prevailing over the world--so also do the parables of the Hid Treasure and the Costly Pearl. They tell us that we ought to value the gospel above all things. We ought to divest ourselves of everything and cling to the gospel. Moreover, this should be a joyful experience because we must know that "the transaction is gain and not loss" [Homily XLVII, 2].

Turning to the parable of the Dragnet, Chrysostom calls it an "awful parable." It is similar to the Tares, but there is one basic difference. The Tares refers to those who chose "wicked doctrines" and who ignored Christ's sayings. But in the Dragnet those who are cast away exhibit a "wickedness of life" and are therefore the "most wretched of all." They "attained to his knowledge and were 'caught,'" but they are not "capable of being saved." In a concluding statement and warning concerning the parables in Matthew 13, Chrysostom observes: "Seest thou how many are the ways of destruction? By the rock, by the thorns, by the wayside, by the tares, by the net. Not without reason therefore did he say, 'Broad is the way that leadeth to destruction, and many there are who enter by it'" [Homily XLVII, 3].

In the parable of the Unmerciful Servant Chrysostom emphasizes the contrast between sins against man and against God. The difference is "as great as between ten thousand talents, and a hundred pence, or rather even much more." With keen psychological insight, Chrysostom addresses the "covetous," the "merciless," and the "cruel," and reminds them that their cruelty and their revenge are finally directed against themselves rather than others. He warns: "Let us

not then thrust the sword into ourselves by being revenge-
ful.... So that we punish ourselves by hating others, even
as on the other hand we benefit ourselves by loving them. "
Chrysostom says that the parable requires two things of us:
"to condemn ourselves for our sins, and to forgive others. "
For him the parable of the Unmerciful Servant is clear and
straightforward; it is telling us to "cast away all anger, that
God may forgive us also all our trespasses by the grace and
love towards man of our Lord Jesus Christ" [Homily LXII].

The parable of the Laborers in the Vineyard lends itself quite readily to allegorization. Chrysostom appears to
move in this direction, but the overall thrust of his analysis
is restrained and the moral consideration remains central.
He suggests that the meaning of the vineyard is the injunctions
of God and His commandments. The time of laboring refers
to the present life. The laborers signify those who in different ways are called to the fulfillment of the injunctions.
The various hours when the laborers are hired represent those
"who at different ages have drawn near to God and approved
themselves. " The central object of the parable according to
Chrysostom is to produce more earnestness in those who are
converted so that they might become better persons in old
age and not suppose that they will receive a lesser portion.
The following summarizes his conclusion: "From everything
then it is manifest to us, that the parable is spoken with reference to them who from earliest youth, and those who in
old age and more tardily, lay hold on virtue; to the former,
that they may not be proud, neither reproach those called at
the eleventh hour; to the latter, that they may learn that it
is possible even in a short time to recover all" [Homily LXIV.
3-4].

Turning to the parable of the Marriage Feast and the
Wedding Garment, Chrysostom begins by comparing it with the
parable that immediately precedes--the Wicked Vinedressers.
These parables have an affinity with each other in that they
both portray God's long-suffering, His great providential care,
and the ingratitude of the Jews. But there are also differences
because the latter parable "proclaims beforehand both the
casting out of the Jews, and the calling of the Gentiles. " In
addition it tells about the strictness of life which is required
if one is to escape the great punishment reserved for the
careless. The wedding garment is "life and practice. "
Those who refused to come to the feast are the same as
those who come in with "filthy garments, " i. e. , a corrupt and
impure life. What we need is not costly and elaborate gar-

ments, but rather those that "adorn the inward parts." Since we are invited to "God's marriage," we ought to enter, "clad, and decked with fringes of gold." Where shall we look to see those who are so clad? In answer, Chrysostom singles out the hermits who "wear garments of hair" and dwell in deserts. "These above all are the wearers of the garments of that wedding...." No matter how many purple robes were given to them, they would refuse them. Chrysostom continues by further exalting those who have left "cities, and markets, and houses" to pursue the life of holiness. It appears here that he is emphasizing the superiority of the religious life over that of the average Christian [Homily LXIX, 1-3].

In his exposition of the parable of the Ten Virgins, Chrysostom moves closer to allegorization than he does with any of the other parables. Consequently, he seems to impose a number of presuppositions upon the parable which make it "say more" than Jesus intended. There appear to be over-tones of the religious life in his emphasis upon almsgiving, poverty, and virginity. Chrysostom believes that the central theme of the parable is "mercifulness in alms." This is evident when he raises the question as to why the parable is about "virgins" instead of about any person in general. His answer is that Jesus attempts to show that virginity, though it should reflect every virtue, if it is lacking in the "good things arising out of almsgiving," is "cast out with the har-lots." In one of his infrequent attempts at allegorization, Chrysostom says that the lamps are the gift of virginity it-self--the "purity of holiness." The oil signifies "humanity, almsgiving, succor to them that are in need." The fact that the virgins slept symbolizes death because "death is a sleep." The cry at midnight announcing the coming of the bridegroom may be a continuation of the parable, Chrysostom suggests, or Jesus may be showing that "the resurrection will be at night." The tragedy of the foolish virgins is that after all their labors and their struggle against natural appetite, they renounced everything and were disgraced because they lacked mercy. Chrysostom observes: "For nothing is more sullied than virginity not having mercy...." So the main point of the parable concerns "mercy in alms." The parable has a warning for everyone. Whereas we are ignorant concerning the time of our death, we should do acts of mercy and give alms now. Too many persons say that they will leave money to the poor at the time of their death, but some of them are suddenly taken before they had time to instruct their survi-vors about their intentions. Chrysostom joins the virtues of poverty and chastity when he suggests that the parable shows

us "how close Christ joined unto the virgins that strip themselves of their possessions; for this indeed is virginity" [Hom-
ily LXXVIII, 1-2].

The parable of the Talents follows that of the Ten Virgins, and Chrysostom gives a traditional interpretation without
any attempt at allegorizing. He notes the similarities and differences between it and the parable of the Pounds. Jesus'
word that to everyone who has more will be given, and from
him who has not, even what he has will be taken away, means
that anyone who does not use his gift will lose it. Likewise,
he who exercises diligence will gain this gift in more abundance. The talents in the parable are "each person's ability,
whether in the way of protection, or in money, or in teaching,
or in what thing soever of the kind." No one should imagine
that he cannot improve himself even with one talent. Our talents of whatever sort should be used for the neighbor's good.
"For nothing is so pleasing to God, as to live for the common
advantage." God gave us such faculties as speech, hands and
feet, strength of body and mind, and understanding, not only
for our own salvation, but also for the neighbor's advantage.
To use our talents to this end is to "imitate our Master"; to
use them otherwise is to imitate the devil [Homily LXXVIII,
2-3].

Let us finally turn to Chrysostom's treatment of the
parable of the Sheep and the Goats. The same restraint and
moral emphases are seen here as in almost all of his exegesis of the parables. Chrysostom notes a basic difference in
this parable in comparison with those preceding. There is
a universal dimension to this parable because Jesus is talking
about the "whole world" and not only about "two, three, or
five persons." Of course in the parables where Jesus, for
example, speaks of two persons, he is not referring to two
persons but to "two portions of mankind." Nevertheless, in
the present parable Chrysostom finds that Jesus is "handling
the word more fearfully and with fuller light." He is no
longer saying that the Kingdom is like thus and so, but now
he "openly shows himself" by referring to the coming of the
Son of man in his glory. In the scene of the final judgment
portrayed in the parable, Chrysostom discerns elements of
justice and grace. Those who did not minister to the needy
are punished justly. The others had done "ten thousand
things," but their reward is the result of the munificence of
grace; for "in return for services so small and cheap, such
a heaven, and a kingdom, and so great honor, should be
given them" [Homily LXXIX, 1-2].

7   THE MIDDLE AGES

Contrary to much popular opinion, the Middle Ages was not a period in which the Bible was neglected or ignored. Beryl Smalley in her fine work, The Study of the Bible in the Middle Ages [2d ed., Oxford, England: Basil Blackwell, 1952], states categorically that the Bible was the most studied book of the Middle Ages and that Bible study represented the highest branch of learning. Biblical commentaries and aids to study accounted for a good proportion of the monastic or cathedral libraries. Moreover, knowledge of the Bible was not confined to the specialist, but its language and content permeated medieval thought. Smalley observes that to make an accurate translation of a literary text in medieval Latin, one needs a concordance to the Vulgate [p xi]. The great bulk of the medieval commentaries on the Bible remain in manuscript form and have not been printed or translated. Consequently, much of this material is unavailable to modern scholarship. In addition to the biblical commentaries, the catena, consisting of patristic comments on the Scriptures, and the gloss were favorite medieval compositions.

George E. McCracken also underscores the centrality of the Bible in medieval thought. He points out that the writers drew their principal inspiration from two basic sources-- the Bible and the Fathers. They constantly cited biblical texts and supported their thought by reference to the sacred writings. McCracken maintains that in the medieval period the Bible was not a "closed book," and if the common people did not read it, this was because literacy was rather rare and not because the Scriptures were deemed dangerous and forbidden to them [Early Medieval Theology; The Library of Christian Classics (Philadelphia: Westminster Press, 1957), vol. IX, p16].

As for parabolic interpretation, it was the Alexandrian method which dominated over the Antiochene. Smalley observes that the soberest scholarship of the Middle Ages derived its permit and its direction ultimately from Alexandria. The Latin student preferred the Alexandrian method to the Antiochene because the former satisfied a paramount emotional need and corresponded to a world outlook while the latter struck him as cold and irrelevant [ibid., pp12, 19].

GREGORY THE GREAT

The beginning of the Middle Ages is often dated from

Gregory the Great (ca. 540-604) who was the fourth and last of the traditional Latin Doctors of the Church and the father of the medieval Papacy.

In his interpretation of Scripture Gregory propounded a threefold approach. To the traditional historical-allegorical sense, he added the moral. He did not, however, apply this method in a consistent or scientific manner. From his exegesis of the parables in homilies on the Gospels, it is apparent that he often neglected the historical meaning and concentrated on the allegorical and the moral. Moreover, these two often were fused together so that no clear delineation between the two could be discerned. [For a detailed analysis of Gregory's spiritual interpretation of the Scripture, see Dietram Hofmann, Die geistige Auslegung der Schrift bei Gregor dem Grossen (Münsterschwarzach: Vier-Türme Verlag, 1968), and also F. Homes Dudden, Gregory the Great: His Place in History and Thought (New York: Russell & Russell, 1967), vol. 2, pp 299-310.]

Gregory wrote a series of homilies--twenty-one on Ezekiel and forty on different passages from the Gospels-- Homiliae in Evanglia. At least ten of these are based on the parables. These have been translated into English by Nora Burke (Saint Gregory the Great: Parables of the Gospel [Chicago: Scepter, 1960]). Gregory's "spiritual" interpretation is quite evident in these homilies.

The parable of the Dragnet, Gregory believes, refers to "holy church." The church is "entrusted to fishermen" and "by means of her we are drawn out of the waves of this world and brought to the heavenly kingdom lest we be swallowed up in the abyss of everlasting death." She gathers together all classes of "fishes" because she offers pardon to every sort of person--wise and ignorant, free and slave, rich and poor, strong and weak. This net will finally enclose all of humanity. The sea represents time, while the shore signifies the end of time. At present all the "fish" mingle together, but at the end of time there will be a separation between the good and the bad [Homilia XI].

Gregory says that the parable of the Laborers in the Vineyard "calls for considerable explanation." The householder who hires the workers is our Creator who is the owner of the vineyard which is the universal church. From the time of Abel to the end of the world, she (the church) has and will produce saints, who can be likened to the vine's branches. The householder sending laborers into the vineyard shows us that God has not failed in sending teachers to instruct the faithful. The various hours at which the workers were hired can refer to different periods of biblical history. The morning of the world was from Adam to Noah; the third hour from Noah to Abraham; the sixth from Abraham to Moses; the ninth from Moses to the coming of Christ, and the eleventh from the coming of Christ to the end of the world. At the last hour he sent the apostles who though they labored only briefly, nevertheless received the full reward. Gregory continues by suggesting that the workers of the first, third, sixth, and ninth hours represent the Hebrew people who honored and revered God and "persevered in the cultivation of the vineyard from the beginning of the world." Those called at the eleventh hour were the Gentiles.

But the different hours may be taken to refer to the various stages in everyone's life. The morning is childhood; the third hour, adolescence, "because when the sun climbs high in the heavens the heat of age increases"; the sixth hour is youth, because like the sun reaching its zenith, so youth is the time when vigor comes to its full power; the ninth hour represents old age, and the eleventh, senility.

Gregory's homilies contain "spiritual" and allegorical interpretations, but the moral dimension is very prominent. The parables are not merely bearers of hidden and esoteric meanings, but they are meant to call us to repentance and to a quality of life which is becoming citizens of the Kingdom. Thus one hears Gregory calling for "stringent discipline" to correct the "untutored mind"; to think over one's conduct to see whether he is working in the vineyard of the Lord; to serve God with the zeal of charity and the desire to progress in virtue, etc. [Homilia XIX].

The theme of the good and the bad mingling together in the church recurs in the parable of the Marriage Feast. "Thus in the Catholic Church the good cannot be found without the wicked nor the wicked without the good." The church is the house where the marriage is taking place. The man who enters without a wedding garment is a member of the holy church by reason of his faith, but he lacks charity which is symbolized by the wedding garment. "All of you, then, who are members of the church and believe in God have indeed come to the marriage, but you are without a wedding garment if you discard the cloak of charity." This is the only garment that can give us beauty in God's sight [Homilia XXXVIII].

Gregory's exposition of the parables is reminiscent of Augustine since many of the same Augustinian motifs recur. Augustine's fascination with numbers is repeated in Gregory's exegesis of the parable of the Ten Virgins. This parable refers to the present church. Each person has five senses and five multiplied by two equals ten. The faithful consist of persons of both sexes; thus "the church is said to be like ten virgins." The oil in the vessels of the wise virgins represents the "brightness of glory, while the vessels are our hearts "in which we carry all our thoughts." So the prudent virgins had oil in their lamps because "they kept hidden in their consciences the luster of this inward glory." The foolish virgins did not take oil with them because "they did not hide their glory within, but sought it from their neighbors' lips." For Gregory the real thrust of this parable is a warning to be prepared for the eventuality of the judgment which will come unexpectedly and with suddeness [Homilia XII].

Gregory's analysis of the parable of the Barren Fig Tree is most imaginative. The owner came three times looking for fruit. The first time refers to God's coming "before the written law when he gave man, by the light of natural reason, the capacity to judge how he should act toward his neighbor." His second coming was at the time of the written law when he taught men his commandments. Finally, after the written law he came through grace and showed his mercy to the human family. But even yet he complains because many have neither been corrected by the inspired law nor instructed by his commandments. Gregory says that the vinedresser must represent those who rule the church. The first man to care for the vineyard was Peter. However, every time we labor in God's vineyard, even though unworthily, we follow Peter in that ministry. Gregory asks about the meaning of the digging and the dung and says that the former means the rebuking of "those souls which fail to give fruit," while the latter refers to the "remembrance of our sins." Thus "the tree is fertilized back to fruitfulness, as the soul recovers new life through the consideration of its sins." But many refuse to do penance in view of their sins. Consequently, "they stand green upon the earth, fruitless before God" [Homilia XXXI].

Let us finally examine Gregory's treatment of the parable of the Rich Man and Lazarus. He begins by giving some guidelines for biblical interpretation. Assuming that there is allegory, Gregory says that it is necessary first to expound the historical truth, and then to discern the spiritual meaning

of the allegory. The allegorical "fruit" is more easily grasped if the narrative is interpreted within its historical framework. Allegory has the potential of strengthening one's faith,
while the historical aspect is related to morals. Gregory
decides to reverse the order for this parable and to first
treat briefly its allegorical meaning before turning to its
moral significance.

The rich man who was elaborately clothed and who
feasted sumptuously every day represents the Jews who "made
a cult of exterior things, using the delights of the law which
they had received, for vain motives and not for true profit."
Lazarus, covered with sores, signifies the Gentiles. They
were not ashamed to confess their sins, i. e., "they had many
wounds and open sores." Lazarus wanted merely to eat the
crumbs that fell from the rich man's table, and no one would
give him any. "Those proud people disdained to admit the
Gentiles to the knowledge of their law." In the Bible "dog"
sometimes refers to a preacher. When dogs lick wounds,
they cure them. "Thus when the holy doctors intrust us in
the confession of our sins, we may say that they touch the
ulcer of our mind with their tongue." To put it another way,
when the holy doctors receive the confession of the Gentiles,
"they cure the wounds of their soul."

"At death Lazarus goes to eternal repose, but the rich
man goes to hell. He is in torment and craves even a drop
of water to cool his tongue. The unfaithful people had upon
their lips the words of that law which they chose not to fulfill. So that member will burn the more, which would not
put its knowledge into effect."

Gregory makes the transition from the allegorical
to the moral in these words: "Now that we have considered,
dearly beloved, the hidden significance of the allegory, it
remains to understand in a broader fashion, the moral it
contains." He proceeds with a lengthy "moral" interpretation
of the parable in which he cautions against ostentation and
exalts the virtue of poverty. Furthermore, he admonishes
his hearers to lose no opportunity for doing works of mercy.
Gregory's closing paragraph is worthy of note; for it is truly
a homiletical gem.

> Learn, brethren, to despise all the things of earth;
> scorn all transient honors and seek the glory which
> endures. Respect all the poor you meet, and when
> you see them ignored by the world, treat them as

friends of God. Share your riches with them so
that they, in their turn, may share theirs with
you. Remember what has been said by the apostle
of the Gentiles: 'In this present time let your
abundance supply their want, that their abundance
also may supply your want.' Remember also
Christ's words: 'As long as you did it to one of
these my least brethren, you did it to me.' Why,
then, are you slow to give, when everything you
give to the poor man on earth, you give to him
who is in heaven? But may Almighty God, who
speaks to you through me, impress these truths
upon your minds, God who lives and reigns with
the Father, in the unity of the Holy Ghost, world
without end. Amen [Homilia XL].

BEDE

The Venerable Bede of Jarrow (673-735) is perhaps
best known for his Historia Ecclesiastica Gentis Anglorum
(completed in 731), which is a primary source for early English history. His most numerous writings, however, are
theological, and consist of commentaries on various books of
the Bible, homilies, and treatises on separate portions of
Scripture.

Bede's work was influenced by Augustine, Jerome,
Ambrose, and Gregory, and in his comments on the parables
the allegorical methodology is very evident. The following
expositions of the parables by Bede are taken from Christian
A. Bugge, Die Haupt-Parabeln Jesus [Giessen: J. Ricker'
sche Verlagsbuchhandlung (Alfred Töplemann), 1903].

Concerning the parable of the Sower, Bede says that
the seeds which did not germinate and bear fruit symbolize
one who hears a sermon, but because his thoughts are evil,
the evil spirits remove the message from his memory.

As for the parable of the Hidden Treasure, the treasure is the longing for heaven, and the field is heaven where
the treasure of every human kindness is hidden and preserved
from unclean spirits.

The drawing of the net ashore in the parable of the
Dragnet refers to the end of the world.

The parable of the Unmerciful Servant refers to the

Jews, Bede believes. The unmerciful servant represents the Jews, who though they were subject to the Decalogue, nevertheless, were guilty of many transgressions. They were ungrateful to the Savior who could have freed them from the law. Moreover, they submitted to a new sin, that of despising their fellow-servants, the Gentiles.

The householder in the parable of the Laborers in the Vineyard is God; the vineyard is the church; those hired are the saints of all ages; the denarius is the divinity of Christ. The various hours refer to different periods of biblical history, and Bede's understanding of them is the same as Origen's [see Origen, p17].

In the parable of the Marriage Feast, Bede finds that the byways are the teaching and errors of the heathen. The one without a wedding garment represents all the assembly of the wicked. The wedding garment itself is every fulfilled precept and that which belongs to the new life.

The five wise virgins in the parable of the Ten Virgins refer to resistance to temptation which presents itself in a five-fold manner--the lust of the eyes, the ears, smell, taste, touch. The oil symbolizes joy.

The five talents in the parable of the Talents are the five senses, while the one talent which was buried in the ground symbolizes the reception of spiritual gifts by one who is entangled in wordly affairs.

Concerning the parable of the Friend at Midnight, Bede thinks that it teaches that man is not to be reprimanded if he makes use of the fruits of the earth, but for putting his entire trust in money.

As for the Lost Sheep and the Lost Coin, the shepherd and the woman signify God and the wisdom of God.

On the parable of the Unjust Steward Bede observes that the wise of this world must learn how foolish their wisdom is, and must seek after the wisdom that comes from God. Furthermore, those who give the meal of the spirit will become more certain of the reward which awaits them.

Finally, in the parable of the Pharisee and the Publican, Bede says that the Pharisee is the Jews while the publican is the Gentiles. This parable seeks to show us that one should not flatter himself by vain experiences and understanding because Jesus demands genuine deeds of faith instead of mere words.

* *

Proceeding to a later period of the Middle Ages, we have a good example of how contemporary theology influenced the interpretation of the parables in Peter Lombard's (ca1100-1160) comments on the parable of the Good Samaritan. "The Samaritan, approaching the wounded man, used the bands of the sacraments to heal him, since God instituted the remedies of sacraments against the wounds of original and actual sin" [The Four Books of Sentences, Book IV, Distinction I, chap. 1].

A further example of medieval allegorization is to be seen in a sermon preached by a friar in an English country church about 1150. It is the twelfth Sunday after Pentecost, and the New Testament lesson for the day is the parable of the Good Samaritan. In the course of his sermon the friar shows that it was man who went down to Jericho when Adam sinned and fell among demons. The priest passed down the same way, when the order of patriarchs followed the path of mortality. The priest left him wounded because he had no power to aid the human race since he himself was sore wounded with sins. The Levite went this way because the order of prophets also had to tread the path of death. The Lord was the good Samaritan, and he went down this way when he came into this world from heaven. The allegorization continues when the preacher observes that the two pence are given to the innkeeper when the doctors are raised on high by scriptural knowledge and temporal honor [Clifford W. Dugmore, The Interpretation of the Bible (London: Society for Promoting Christian Knowledge, 1944), pp26-28].

THOMAS AQUINAS

The most influential theological figure of the medieval period was Thomas Aquinas (ca. 1225-1274). For him the interpretation of Scripture was especially important because it was the primary source of revelation. Aquinas emphasized the literal sense of Scripture, and minimized the allegorical, so that with him allegorization neared its end as a viable and meaningful method of biblical exegesis. This is not to say that he rejected allegory completely, nor that his contemporaries and subsequent biblical exegetes no longer allegorized; but with the advent of the Renaissance and the Reformation and the rise of higher biblical criticism, allegorizing could no longer hold "center stage" as it did in the patristic and early medieval periods. In the Summa Theologica Aquinas sets forth his views on literal interpretation most fully. He categorically declares theology's independence from allegorization as follows: "nothing necessary to faith is contained under the spiritual sense which is not elsewhere put forward by the Scripture in its literal sense" [quoted from Robert M. Grant, A Short History of the Interpretation of the Bible, rev. ed. (New York: Macmillan, 1963), p125: this is an authoritative and readable study of biblical interpretation from the New Testament period to the early 1960s]. In a 1971 scholarly monograph, Maximino Arias Reyero characterizes Aquinas' exegesis under three categories: Exact literalness, Metaphorical literalness, and Spiritual sense. There are principles of interpretation underlying each of these categories. Exact literalness implies that there is a source of divine revelation which can be expressed in words and deeds. The metaphorical literal assumes that there can be a human method of communication and knowledge of revelation, but that while man can know truth, his knowledge of the unique revelation is always partial. The spiritual sense of biblical interpretation implies that it issues from a concrete history-- the history of Jesus Christ--which is the norm for an historical community--the church [see Maximino Arias Reyero, Thomas von Aquin als Exeget (Einsiedeln: Johannes Verlag, 1971), pp153ff].

Turning to Aquinas' interpretation of the parables, one can discern elements of the above typology. The following expositions of the parables by Aquinas are taken from Christian A. Bugge, Die Haupt-Parabeln Jesus [Giessen: J. Ricker'sche Verlagsbuchhandlung (Alfred Töplemann), 1903].

The parable of the Sower is a picture of the spiritual life and represents a threefold perfection. The seed which yielded thirtyfold is the usual or average attainment. The sixtyfold yield refers to one who has gone beyond the usual and has attained somewhat more. The hundredfold increase symbolizes one who has progressed so far in his spiritual growth that he has experienced a foretaste of ultimate salvation.

Aquinas is reminded of three types of evil persons by the parable of the Tares: bad Catholics, schismatics, heretics. The good can exist without the bad but not vice versa.

Through the parables of the Hidden Treasure, the Costly Pearl, and the Dragnet, the gospel is presented in three respects: as abundance (Treasure), as beauty (Pearl), as community (Net).

The parable of the Unmerciful Servant refers first to the mercy of God. Then it demonstrates the quality or nature of ingratitude. Finally, it portrays the judgment which awaits the ungrateful.

In the Laborers in the Vineyard Aquinas moves away from the literal sense toward the metaphorical. He says that the vine is justice and as the vine has many branches, so there are many virtues. The denarius signifies eternal life since each denarius is worth as much as ten others.

Aquinas continues the metaphorical exposition in the parable of the Wicked Vinedresser. This parable can be understood in a double sense. First, the vineyard is the Jewish people and the tower is an offering or the altar. Secondly, the vineyard is God's righteousness hidden in the Scriptures and the tower is the wine of love which is pressed out through the depths or profundity of the Scriptures.

In the parable of the Marriage Feast Aquinas says that the byways represent the teaching and errors of the heathen. The wedding garment is Christ. The binding of the feet of the one without the wedding garment has to do with evil motives.

The relationship between the Ten Virgins and the parable of the Talents is that the former concerns inner needs and shortcomings while the latter describes the indifference about shutting out the outward affairs of life. The lamps are those who are illuminated through faith which is received at baptism. The bridegroom symbolizes reward while the bride is human nature. The oil is good works or mercy or joy or sacred teaching. The five talents represent five spiritual abilities; the two are the senses and the understanding, while the one talent is understanding alone.

In Aquinas' interpretation of the parables there are elements of both the literal and the metaphorical; and while he emphasized the importance of literal interpretation, it remained for subsequent exegetes to practice this methodology more completely and consistently.

8   MARTIN LUTHER

In his methodology of scriptural exegesis, Luther was a staunch advocate of the historical or literal approach in contrast to the allegorical or spiritual of the patristic and medieval periods. While he was well conversant with Origen's commentaries and had many words of appreciation for him, nevertheless, he regarded Origen as the "chief culprit" of allegorization. Luther acknowledges that in his earlier life he resorted to allegories. "When I was a monk I was a master in the use of allegories. I allegorized everything" [Martin Luther, Works, Jeroslav Pelikan, et al., eds. (St. Louis: Concordia Pub. House; Philadelphia: Muhlenberg Press; Fortress Press, 1955-76), vol. 54, p47]. "When I was young I dealt with allegories, tropologies, and analogies and did nothing but clever tricks with them. If somebody had them today they'd be looked upon as rare relics. I know they're nothing but rubbish" [ibid., p406]. After working through the Epistle to the Romans Luther says that he came to some knowledge of Christ and consequently recognized that allegories are nothing because "it's not what Christ signifies but what Christ is that counts."

Luther can seldom be charged with understatement, and his castigation of the allegorizers is no exception. Though Origen was a great teacher, nevertheless, he "played the fool" and led St. Jerome and many others astray with him through his allegorization. However, he reserves some of his choicest descriptions for Karlstadt. Luther criticizes him especially for his allegorical and spiritual interpretations of Paul's Epistles. Karlstadt's method is "pure jugglery." It is "devoid of foundation or truth; it is the product of his own fancy, and forced upon the text." He continues: "If such spiritual juggling were to prevail, I would like to put Dr. Karlstadt and all his prophets to school for another three years." If this method were accepted, Luther says that the "spiritual jugglers would not leave a single letter in Scripture" [op. cit., vol. 40, pp187-90].

The alternative to allegorization, which Luther chose and advocated, was to interpret the Scriptures in their "plain sense." "The literal sense does it--in it there's life, comfort, power, instruction, and skill. The other is tomfoolery, however brilliant the impression it makes" [op. cit., vol. 54, p406]. In his criticism of Karlstadt Luther says that he was thoroughly "drilled in this method when I first began to study the Bible ten years ago, before I discovered the true method."

He describes the "true method" thus: "The natural meaning
of the words is queen, transcending all subtle, acute sophi-
stical fancy. From it we may not deviate, unless we are
compelled by a clear article of faith" [op. cit., vol. 40,
p190]. One other quote must suffice to underscore Luther's
penchant for the literal or historical method of biblical exposition. "Who has so weak a mind as not to be able to launch
into allegories? I would not have a theologian devote himself
to allegories until he has exhausted the legitimate and simple
meaning of the Scripture, otherwise his theology will bring
him into danger, as Origen discovered" [op. cit., vol. 35,
p110].

In light of the above, one might characterize Luther's
approach to Scripture as historical-Christological. One must
begin with the plain and literal sense and pursue it as far as
possible before considering any hidden or symbolic meanings.
But there is a reference point and a center of meaning which
must provide the context for all biblical interpretation, and
that is Jesus Christ. Everything must be understood and
evaluated in relation to him. As Luther put it: "It is not
what Christ signifies but what Christ is that counts."

Let us now turn to the parables and see how closely
Luther adheres to the exegetical guidelines outlined above.
Some of the parables are used by Luther to set forth an ethical challenge or a moral imperative. In a sermon on sabbath observance he refers to the parable of the Good Samaritan. This parable teaches us to get our priorities straight.
When one sees his neighbor in need and in dire danger, he
should not pass by like the priest and the Levite did and let
him lie there to perish. Under the pretense of keeping the
sabbath pure, one can become a murderer of his brother.
Rather, like the Samaritan, one should help him, bind up his
wounds, set him on his beast, and bring him to an inn [op.
cit., vol. 51, p344].

The Rich Man and Lazarus appears to be one of Luther's favorites. The rich man was not damned because he
robbed and did evil with his wealth, but because he neglected
to do good to his neighbor, namely, Lazarus. "This parable
adequately teaches us that it is not sufficient merely not to
do evil and not to do harm, but rather that one must be helpful and do good. It is not enough to 'depart from evil;' one
must also 'do good'" (Psa. 37:27) [ibid., p8].

Luther makes an interesting comment about the parable of the Mustard Seed. Referring to Jesus' words in John 14:12: "Greater works than these will you do," he says that Christ is the grain of mustard seed, but we are the bushes. Thus "the authority of Christ when he taught wasn't so great as ours is today" [op. cit., vol. 54, p88].

Luther uses the parable of the Pharisee and the Publican to make some observations on pride in contrast to humility. The nature of pride as exemplified by the Pharisee is threefold. One who is proud asks nothing of God; he praises himself; he derides and accuses the one who is praying and accusing himself [op. cit., vol. 51, pp14-17].

Returning to the Rich Man and Lazarus, Luther's comments assure us that the problems posed by parapsychology for the Christian faith are not of recent origin. This parable, he believes, clearly shows us that "God does not desire to have the dead teach us, but that we should cling to the Scriptures." Furthermore, we hear from this parable that "in the eyes of God it is an abominable and pagan thing to consult the spirits and practice necromancy; it is strictly forbidden" [op. cit., vol. 52, pp179-80].

In Luther's hands the parables also become channels for apologetic against the Catholic Church. They breathe the spontaneity and fervor of the newly-born Reformation. Thus Abraham's word to the rich man in Luke 16:19 represents Christ's underscoring the authority of the Scriptures. But in opposition to this "true and godly teaching" certain "learned scholars" have devised all kinds of ways to learn the truth. Among these are "innumerable laws, statutes, articles, and doctrines, invented by men, as for example canon law and similar rules for religious orders." In addition to this, they point to the lives and example of the saints "in order to prove their human doctrines." Moreover, the saints' exposition of Scripture is presented as a light and as authority [op. cit., vol. 52, pp172ff].

Another instance of this polemical stance concerns the parable of the Great Supper, especially Luke 14:7-9 where Jesus cautions against taking the place of honor lest a more eminent person arrives and takes that place. This will result in shame and embarrassment because the person will be demoted from the place of honor to the lowest place. In a choice bit of exegesis, Luther applies this incident to the canon of the mass. The canon of the mass was invited to the marriage feast and sat down in a place of honor. But "it should now get up with shame and give place to Christ, its master, and sit in the lowest place, as it should properly have done in the beginning" [op. cit., vol. 36, p185].

We have noted that the vortex of Luther's hermeneutic is Christ. The central category of his Christology and soteriology is sola fide, and this is reflected in his interpretation of the parables. It often appears strained and as a presupposition superimposed upon a given parable. Here perhaps Luther does some "spiritual jugglery" of his own, and reflects (albeit from a different perspective) a methodology which he found so distasteful in the allegorizers. The note of grace and faith appears in a number of parables according to Luther, and some of his expositions reflect a rudimentary form of allegorization.

The foolish virgins in the parable of the Ten Virgins were rejected, Luther suggests, not because they had not served but because "they had served without oil." He infers that "oil" is grace because, he continues: "They had done good on their own resources and not by virtue of grace. They sought their own glory, and it is impossible for man to be without this fault" [Luther: Early Theological Works, vol. XVI of Library of Christian Classics (Philadelphia: Westminster Press, 1962), pp302-03].

In a discussion concerning law and grace and sin and grace Luther states that the parable of the Good Samaritan pertains to these themes "through and through." The priest and the Levite who were "ministers of the law" saw the man but did not help him. The Samaritan, however, picked him up and cared for him, thus making provision for his healing. He observes: "To revert to what I said, the law makes sin known, but Christ heals through faith and restores man to the grace of God" [ibid., p352]. In one of his sermons Luther emphasizes the same themes but comes closer to outright allegorization of the parable. He notes that it was Adam who fell among the robbers and thereby implanted sin in all of us. Except for the coming of Christ, the Samaritan, we should all have had to die. It is Christ who binds our wounds, carries us into the church and is now healing us. Consequently, we are now "under the Physician's care" [Luther, Works (Pelikan, ed.), vol. 51, p373].

Luther sees the concept of faith in at least two other parables. The parable of the Leaven symbolizes faith because "faith is the gift and the inner good which is opposed to sin and which purges it; it is that leaven of the gospels thoroughly hidden in three measures of meal" [vol. XVI, Library of Christian Classics, p349]. Luther finds another reference to faith in "Abraham's bosom" (Luke 16:22) in the parable of the Rich Man and Lazarus. "'Abraham's bosom' is doubtless that faith which is promised in the gospel" [ibid., p214]. At two other places, however, he says that "Abraham's bosom" is the promise or the covenant which God made with Abraham [Luther, Works (Pelikan, ed.), vol. 35, p83; vol. 36, p39].

While Luther is not entirely free from the "spiritual jugglery" which he found in others, nevertheless, his interpretation of the parables exhibits a historical and literal sense which is far removed from much of the exegesis which preceded him. Moreover, there is a pronounced Christocentricity and a moral earnestness which ground the parables in a precise and meaningful theological and ethical framework.

9   JOHN CALVIN

In Calvin's theological system the Bible was the primary and indisputable source and authority. He had a thorough knowledge of its contents, and he wrote commentaries on most of the biblical books. His acquaintance with the Old Testament was remarkable, and while he emphasized the advance beyond the Old Testament in the New Testament, nevertheless, his principle of interpretation reflects a firm view of the unity and continuity of Scripture.

As for Calvin's parabolic interpretation, there is an absence of allegorizing and a lucidity which seeks to go immediately to the central point of the parable. This procedure is quite evident in his reference to the parable of the Good Samaritan. Like an arrow heading straight for its mark, Calvin declares, "the chief aim is to show that neighborliness which obliges us to do our duty by each other is not restricted to friends and relations, but open to the whole human race." He continues by castigating those who have allegorized the parable: "An allegorical interpretation devised by proponents of free-will is really too futile to deserve an answer." Calvin describes three ways in which the parable has been allegorized, and then levels a further charge against this methodology: "None of these strikes me as plausible: we should have more reverence for Scripture than to allow ourselves to transfigure its sense so freely. Anyone may see that these speculations have been cooked up by meddlers, quite divorced from the mind of Christ" [Calvin's Commentaries: A Harmony of the Gospels Matthew, and Luke, vol. 3, A. W. Morrison, trans., David W. Torrance, Thomas F. Torrance, eds (Edinburgh: Saint Andrew Press, 1972), pp37-39].

The same penchant for getting to the central theme of the parable can be discerned in Calvin's comments on the parable of the Ten Virgins. The intention of the parable, he believes, is to teach the faithful that they will need perseverance and endurance and preparation for the long spiritual journey ahead. "Christ says now that the faithful need constant replenishment of power to foster the light kindled in their hearts: otherwise their speed will give out on them halfway up the course." Calvin cautions against speculation over minor details. The object is to understand the main point, and therefore there is no reason to labor over minute details which are "quite beside Christ's intention." The closing scene of the parable when the foolish virgins are unprepared and the door is shut against them shows that those who make no provision for the long term will be condemned. Returning to the central themes of preparation and perseverance, Calvin concludes his exposition of the parable: "It follows at last that the door of the heavenly Kingdom will be shut on all who have made poor provision, for failing in mid-course. We must not here seek the details, how Christ says that the foolish virgins set out to buy, for it simply means that all must be excluded from entry to heaven who at the precise moment are not prepared" [ibid., pp109-11].

The parable of the Unjust Steward, which Calvin acknowledges "seems hard and far-fetched," is telling us that "we must treat our neighbors humanely and kindly, so that when we come before God's judgment seat, we may receive the fruit of our liberality." This was "Christ's intention" and "those who investigate minutely every single part of a parable are poor theologians." The parable is speaking about responsible stewardship and is a warning that judgment awaits those who misuse the good things of God and neglect beneficence. Concerning Luke 16:8, Calvin says that here also it would be foolish to insist on details. Jesus is not comparing the "wisdom of the Spirit and of the flesh;" rather he is arousing believers to consider more carefully the future life and not to lose sight of the light of the gospel when "they perceive the blind better sighted in their darkness." They should be challenged all the more when they see how much foresight the children of the world have for the sake of this transitory life which passes in a moment. How much more diligent

should the sons of light be for their eternal well-being [ibid.,
vol. 2, pp111-12].

In his exposition of the parable of the Tares, Calvin
again emphasizes a literal and direct interpretation. It is
necessary to grasp "Christ's intention." After refuting several possible interpretations, he states that the intention of
the parable is simple. "So long as the church is on pilgrimage in this world, the good and the sincere will be mixed
in it with the bad and the hypocrites. So the children of
God must arm themselves with patience and maintain an un-
broken constancy of faith among all the offences which can
trouble them." Calvin acknowledges that some have investi-
gated every detail of the parable, but his preference is "to
be sparing in philosophising and to be satisfied with the simple and genuine sense" [ibid., pp77-78].

The object of the parable of the Master and the Servants is that all the duty that we try to do in no way puts
God under obligation to us. God already claims for Himself
all that is ours, and He possesses us as His bond servants.
We are obliged and bound to God in our service, and there
is no way by which He can be obliged to us. Here we have
another example of Calvin's tendency to go directly to what
he regards as Jesus' central intention in giving the parable
[ibid., pp122-24].

The parable of the Rich Man and Lazarus shows us the
final state of those who neglect the poor and revel in pleasures
and indulge themselves, all the while destroying those with
"cruel hunger" whom they ought to assist as opportunity affords. Calvin observes that "the rich man is like a bright
mirror in which we can see that temporal felicity is not to
be sought for if it ends in eternal destruction." Calvin notes
that many interpreters have philosophized about "Abraham's
bosom." He rejects their views and regards it as a metaphor
which points to the fact that God's children are strangers and
pilgrims in the world, but as they follow the faith of their
father Abraham, so when they die they will inherit that blessed rest where he awaits them. In hell the rich man "lifted
up his eyes." Calvin says that Jesus is using figurative
language here because souls are not endowed with such faculties as fingers and eyes. "The Lord is painting a picture
which represents the condition of the future life in a way that
we can understand" [ibid., pp116-22].

Calvin gives a straightforward interpretation to the

parable of the Sower. "The sum of it all is that the preaching of the gospel is like seed broadcast and is not fruitful everywhere, for it does not always fall on fertile and well tilled soil." Naming various types of soil does not imply that Jesus was predetermining the number or percentage in each category, nor was he dividing those of whom he spoke into equal parts. He was simply saying that where the Word is sown the harvest of faith is not always the same; sometimes it is poor, other times, more abundant. Moreover, Jesus is also warning that the seed dies in many because of various faults by which it is immediately corrupted, or dried up, or slowly impaired [ibid., pp70-73].

Calvin's analysis of the "parables of the Kingdom" in Matthew 13 reflects the same methodology as that employed in the parables discussed above. As for the parable of the Mustard Seed, it serves as an encouragement to those who would shrink back in offence at the lowly beginnings of the gospel. Irreligious persons may scoff at the gospel because it is proclaimed by obscure and unknown ministers and because it is not received with universal applause, but has only a few insignificant followers. It is easy to despair when one measures the outcome by the beginnings. But Calvin feels that the Lord deliberately inaugurated His Kingdom from weak and lowly beginnings so that the eventual progress might all the more glorify His power. The parable of the Leaven conveys something of the same message. "From this we learn that although Christ's Kingdom appears contemptible to the eyes of the flesh, it raises our minds to the infinite and inestimable power of God, which once created all things out of nothing and now daily, transcending men's thoughts, raises up the things that are not" [ibid., pp79-80].

The aim of the parables of the Hid Treasure and the Costly Pearl was "to teach believers to put the Kingdom of Heaven before the whole world and to renounce themselves and all carnal desires, so that nothing might prevent them from enjoying this great blessing." To put it another way, both parables tell us that only those are capable of receiving the grace of the gospel who renounce all other desires and devote themselves and their studies completely to making it their own [ibid., pp82-83].

The parable of the Dragnet adds nothing new but confirms the parable of the Tares that the church is an admixture of good and bad, and it is never free from dirt and stains. Calvin says that Jesus cleverly compared the preaching of the

Gospel with a "net sunk under the water" to illustrate the
present confused state of the church. But the end result
will be quite otherwise; God will consummate His Kingdom
at the last day, and the church will finally be free from all
imperfections [ibid., pp83-84].

In the parable of the Seed Growing Silently, Calvin
finds a parallel with the parable of the Sower and the Mustard Seed. However, he believes that here Jesus is referring particularly to ministers of the Word. They should be
diligent and enthusiastic in their office even though no fruit
appears immediately. With this parable Calvin seems to depart somewhat from his strict, literal course, especially
when he writes: "Therefore he tells them to be like farmers
who sow seed in the hope of harvesting it and are not wor-
ried and anxious but go to bed and get up--in other words,
they get on with their daily work and are refreshed by a
good night's sleep--until at last in its own time the corn
is ripe. Therefore although the seed of the Word lies
choked for a while, Christ bids all godly teachers to be of
good cheer and not to let distrust diminish their zeal" [ibid.,
p80].

The Laborers in the Vineyard has been a favorite of
the allegorizers. Calvin again rejects this method and observes that to want to examine the details of this parable
precisely would be "empty curiosity." Some have found the
Jews and Gentiles in this parable, but Calvin says that
"cleverness like this is out of place." He makes no attempt
to find hidden symbolism in the denarius or in the various
hours when the workers were hired. One should look for
"nothing more than Christ intended to tell us." Calvin thinks
that Christ's "one aim" in this parable was "continually to
incite his people to keep going." Lack of perseverence can
be the result of over-confidence, and that is why many sit
down in the middle of the race as if they had already attained the goal. But the parable also points to the sovereignty of God. God is under obligation to no one, and He
calls whomever He wills. Furthermore, "He pays those
whom He has called the reward which seems good to Him"
[ibid., pp264-67].

The parables of the Lost Sheep, the Lost Coin, and
the Prodigal Son in Luke 15 confirm the same truth, viz.
that God rejoices over the repentance of each sinner. The
intention of the parable of the Prodigal Son is twofold. The
first part shows how ready and willing God is to pardon our

sins, while the second part pictures the maliciousness and perversity of those who disparage His mercy. In this parable Jesus describes the situation of every sinner who becomes disgusted with his condition and returns to the grace of God. God is like the father who not only forgives the prodigal but runs to meet him. For Calvin the central point of the parable is found in verse 20. God does not wait for a long prayer of repentance, but as soon as the sinner sets out to confess his fault, He meets him willingly and accepts him. In verse 22 the father asks for the best robe. Calvin reiterates his contention that it is foolish to apply all the details in parables. Nevertheless, he feels that it is not distorting the literal meaning to say that God not only pardons our sins and blots them from his memory, but He also restores the gifts of which we were stripped. Just so He takes them from us to punish our ingratitude and "forces us to shame at the reproach and immodesty of our nakedness." The second part of the parable tells us that if we want to be the children of God, we must be willing to forgive others their faults which God pardons in a fatherly way. In a word, our pattern must always be the father of the prodigal and never his elder brother [ibid., pp221-25].

In the parable of the Marriage Feast in Matthew 22, Calvin believes that Jesus is referring to the Jews. The sending out of the servants to call them that were bidden points to the twofold grace of God--that He preferred the Jews before all other races, and that He revealed His adoption of them through the prophets. The Jews were chosen by God before all others, and He called them by the prophets to share in the promised redemption which was to be celebrated in the marriage feast. However, "their ingratitude and malice deprived them of it. For from the beginning that people had an ungodly contempt of God's invitation." Jesus concluded the parable by saying: "For many are called, but few are chosen." Calvin thinks that this shows the intention of the parable. Although more have been gathered into the church by the word of the gospel than by the law, yet only a small portion of them prove their faith by newness of life. "Therefore, do not let us flatter ourselves with an empty title of faith but let each one examine himself seriously so that in the final choosing he may be reckoned among the genuine guests" [ibid., pp105-10].

Calvin's exegesis of the parable of the Pharisee and the Publican reflects some basic motifs of Calvinistic theology, viz. God's sovereignty and grace and human depravity.

This parable tells us that believers should approach God without pretensions; for there is no more deadly sin than pride. Jesus is condemning two faults here: "a depraved self-trust, and pride in despising our fellow-men." Moreover, the one springs from the other. Whoever deceives himself with his own goodness will inevitably exalt himself above others. The Pharisee's attitude is a denial of God's grace, and he is placing his trust in the merit of his works. "Therefore let us realize that although a man may ascribe the praise for good works to God, yet if he imagines that the righteousness of those works is the cause of his salvation, or trusts in it, he is condemned for perverted pride." The Pharisee sinned in two ways: he falsely claimed righteousness for himself and so left nothing for God's mercy, and he despised everyone else. The publican was also a sinner, but he looked to God for mercy and pardon. In order to receive favor he confesses that he is not worthy of it. If we want God to accept our prayers, we must start with confession since it is only by the forgiveness of sins that God is reconciled to us. This means that righteousness is not related to our goodness or our works, but it consists in the forgiveness of sins. Calvin summarizes the matter as follows: "I reply that however much a man may advance in the worship of God and in true holiness, yet if he considers how far short he falls, he will be unable to pray in any other way than by beginning with confession of guilt.... Wherefore Christ is without doubt laying down a law for all, as if He said that God is appeased only when we cease to trust in our works and pray to be reconciled freely" [ibid., pp127-30].

Another example of pride and self-sufficiency is in the parable of the Rich Fool. Calvin refers to this parable as "like a mirror to show us a living image of the truth that men do not live from their abundance." Everyone needs to guard against covetousness and the fallacy that they are blessed because they are rich. The parable demonstrates the brevity and transciency of life and shows that riches cannot lengthen one's life. But there is a further truth implied though not expressly stated: "The best remedy for believers is to ask their daily bread from the Lord and rest quietly on His providence, whether they are rich or poor." The rich man harbored the illusion that his life was in his own hand, when in reality it lay in the power of another. Calvin states the purpose of the parable thus: "The plans will fail, the efforts will be ridiculous, for those who trust in the abundance of their riches and do not rest on God alone, who are not satisfied with the measure He gives nor prepared for ill or good. At the last they will receive the punishment of their futility" [ibid., pp92-94].

Calvin considers the parable of the Talents and the parable of the Pounds together, and while he recognizes the differences, he believes that both convey the same message. Jesus' intention in both parables was to refute the disciples' belief that his kingdom was already established and that he was going to Jerusalem to set up a prosperous state. These parables undercut their hope of a present kingdom and encourage them to wait with hope and patience for the futuıe Kingdom. Jesus teaches them that they must face troubles and hardships for a long time before they finally inherit the Kingdom. Calvin interprets "into a far country" as Jesus' reference to his long absence from the time of his death to his second advent. He can be understood to be absent from his people until he shall come again, adored with a new kingship. "Therefore when the apostles foolishly grasped at the shadow of a kingdom, the Lord declared that he must seek his Kingdom afar, so that they may learn to bear delay." Calvin finds no significance in the number of servants or in the sums of money they were given. He believes that both Matthew and Luke are in agreement that Christ would be absent from his people until the final day of resurrection. However, it would be wrong for them to be idle during this interim; for to each person is entrusted "a certain office in which he may engage." Moreover, there is nothing worse than keeping God's graces buried and not using them because "their force consists in their fruit." The real message of the parable has an urgent moral dimension, for as Calvin says: "This should make the good more eager, since they know that their work is not at all wasted; and on the other hand it should greatly frighten the lazy and idle. We therefore learn that we should daily spur ourselves on, before the Lord come and enter into a reckoning with us" [ibid., pp285-89].

Let us conclude with Calvin's exposition of the parable of the Wicked Vinedressers. Here perhaps more than with any of the parables he departs from a strictly literal interpretation. The parable refers to the Jews and particularly to their priests and shows that there is nothing new in the priests' "wild and wicked effort to rob God of His rights." They had mistreated the prophets and now they were prepared to kill the Son, but God will defend His right and in the end they will be punished. Calvin believes that the object of the

parable is twofold: "to reproach the priests for their base
and criminal ingratitude, and to remove the offence which
was coming in the approaching death of Christ." The
phrase "planted a vineyard" means that though God appointed pastors for his church, he did not relinquish His rights
to them, but acts as a proprietor who expects them to
"cultivate and annually deliver the proceeds." The "wine-
press" and "tower" signify the "aids that were added to
strengthen the faith of the people in the teaching of the Law,
such as sacrifices and other rites. God like a provident
and careful head of the house spares no effort to arm His
church with every means of defense." This parable can
strengthen our faith in at least two respects. First, we
should not be troubled by men's wicked efforts to obstruct
Christ's Kingdom because in this parable God has warned
us before such events occur. Secondly, no matter what
men contrive, God has testified to the victory of His power
in establishing the Kingdom of Christ. To put it otherwise,
the parable teaches us to yield ourselves to Christ's command with a mild, flexible disposition, and then to be
strong and courageous in the face of evil because a dreadful
end awaits those who perpetuate it [ibid. vol. 3, pp16-23].

10   JOHN MALDONATUS

Maldonatus (1534-1583) was a Spanish exegete and
theologian. After studying at Salamanca and Rome he became a Jesuit and was ordained in 1563. He was professor
of theology at Paris for nine years and enjoyed enormous
popularity until his teaching was interrupted in 1574 because
the Sorbonne professors accused him of denying the doctrine
of the Immaculate Conception. He withdrew to Bourges
where he composed his commentaries on the four Gospels
which have been highly regarded until modern times. From
these commentaries we discern that Maldonatus had a distrust for allegorizing, and insofar as the parables are concerned, he ignored the peripheral and focused on the central
intent and message.

Maldonatus says that a parable is a kind of sermon
in which one thing is said and another meant, and it is
wrapped in obscure comparisons [John Maldonatus, A Commentary on the Holy Gospels; S. Matthew's Gospel, Chapters
I to XIV, George J. Davie, trans. and ed. (London: John
Hodges, 1888), p422].

Maldonatus treats the parable of the Sower in a conventional fashion. It refers to one's response or lack of response to the Word of God. He cites various attempts by some of the "Ancients" to allegorize the parable. However, he himself does not subscribe to any of these. In Matthew 13:23 he finds a refutation of the views of Luther and Calvin concerning works righteousness. Contrary to them, Maldonatus maintains with Augustine that each one of us can attain or lose merit by making himself a good or bad soil. Furthermore, this verse contradicts Luther and Calvin in their contention that the reward of all the blessed will be equal [ibid., pp430-35].

In the parable of the Tares Jesus sought to teach three things especially: (1) In the church there is both good seed (good persons) and bad seed (bad persons). (2) Christ is not the author of the bad seed, but of the good. The bad was sowed by the devil. (3) Christ would endure the bad seed sowed by the devil with patience even to the harvest. It should not be rooted out before [ibid., p436].

The third "parable of the Kingdom" in Matthew 13 likens the Kingdom of Heaven to a mustard seed. Maldonatus implies that the Kingdom of Heaven can be understood as the church, or the gospel, or faith, or evangelical doctrine, of the Word of God. "They all arrive at the same end." The gospel had a small beginning and has sprung to "admirable size." Just so, the church had a small and obscure beginning in Jerusalem but increased until it filled the whole world. The reference to the birds dwelling in the branches, Maldonatus believes, may apply to kings and princes and those in high places. It may signify those who are sustained by the gospel and the church. Referring to Daniel 4:10-12, Maldonatus concludes: "The church was formerly in the state. The state is now in the church [ibid., pp438-39].

The parable of the Leaven has the same intention as the Mustard Seed, viz. that from small beginnings the gospel and the church have greatly increased.

Turning to the final three parables in Matthew 13, Maldonatus says that while the former parables described two pecularities of the Kingdom of Heaven--how it takes a different effect upon different persons, and how from a small beginning it gains a great increase--Jesus now puts forth its value, to show how great is its worth, and with what diligence men should seek it.

The Hid Treasure teaches us that he who finds the Kingdom of Heaven or the gospel ought to be careful not to allow it to slip from his grasp and should take all measures to secure it. Hiding the treasure does not imply that another may not find it, but that he himself may not lose it. One does not lose the Kingdom when another finds it, for it can be equally found and equally possessed by all.

The parable of the Costly Pearl has the same meaning as the Hid Treasure. "We ought to resemble the merchant, and when we have found the Kingdom of Heaven, we ought to spare no pains, no expense, nothing whatever, that we may possess it."

The Dragnet has similarities to the Tares and has the same meaning although the order of events differs. The Kingdom of Heaven may signify either the gospel or the church. In either case, we have a strong argument against "modern heretics." If we say that Jesus is referring to the gospel, then we must see that not all who receive it, i. e., the faith, will be saved, but only the good fishes, i. e., those who have both faith and good works.

If we apply the parable to the church, then Augustine should serve as our guide. Maldonatus observes that Augustine refuted the Donatists frequently and effectively by comparing the church to a net let down into the sea, and filled with every kind of fish coming into it. At this point Maldonatus reflects the heat of the Reformation controversy when he suggests that Augustine wrote not so much against the Donatists as "against the followers of Luther and Calvin long after." He continues: "This is so great a matter, that whoever reads them may substitute for the word Donatists those of the followers of Luther and Calvin" [ibid., p446].

The meaning of the parable of the Unforgiving Servant is evident and is expressed in Matthew 18:35. God will not forgive us unless we forgive another since it is more right that we should forgive him than that God should forgive us. Other persons are like us, but God is unlike us. Our sins against God are numberless and infinitely grievous. In contrast, the sins of another against us are both few and for the most part trivial. Maldonatus makes a comment about this parable and about all parables, and thus reflects his preference for a literal methodology of parabolic interpretation. He writes: "There are in this parable as in all the others, some things necessary and properly parts of it; others which are emblems, embellishments, and additions to complete the whole" [A Commentary...; S. Matthew's Gospel, Chapters XX to the End, pp113-15].

Maldonatus believes that in the parable of the Laborers in the Vineyard Christ teaches that the glory of each laborer would not be equal because it is not bestowed freely but according to merits. That which is given according to merits is not given equally to all, but more is given to some and less to others, according to the merits of each. So Maldonatus observes, it is with those who labor in the church of God. As the laborers in the vineyard merited their day's penny, so those who work in the church merit eternal life. "The end of the parable is that the reward of eternal life answers not to the time each has labored, but to his labor and work performed." This is the object of the parable to which the different parts tend. As with each parable, there are "proper and necessary parts" and others which are adjuncts for the "explanation or ornamentation of the whole." Maldonatus finds eight necessary parts in the parable, and he proceeds to analyse each one by referring to the interpretations of various patristic writers and then developing his own position. The eight necessary parts are (1) the householder, (2) the day during which the laborers were hired and worked, (3) the vineyard, (4) each of the hours, (5) the market-place, (6) the penny, (7) the evening when the penny was paid, and (8) the householder's command that those who came last should be paid first. In comparison with many of his predecessors, Maldonatus leans toward a restrained and non-allegorical analysis of the parable. He cautions against speculation about irrelevant details because such a procedure may be following what is "void of truth." He concludes: "For whoever seeks for that which does not exist, sometimes imagines what he is looking for, and will believe what is false rather than nothing. The human mind must be held in check or it will be led astray by its own subtelty, beyond all reason, and on matters of no consequence" [ibid., pp162-73].

The parable of the Two Sons in Matthew 21 was often understood by those of the patristic period to refer to the Gentiles and the Jews. Maldonatus believes that the parable probably refers to two types of Jews. He says that the father of the two sons was undoubtedly God. The one son probably represents the people and publicans, har-

lots, and sinners who were commanded by God to labor in
his vineyard, i.e., to observe the law. Their answer was
not in words but in deeds, and they refused to do so. Af-
terward, however, moved by the example and preaching of
John the Baptist, they repented and not only observed the
ancient law but also accepted the gospel. The second son
is the priests and Pharisees who consented to work in the
vineyard, i.e., they professed obedience to the law. But
in fact they did not go because they did not keep the law
nor did they believe in John of whom Christ said the prophets had spoken. Finally Maldonatus allows the possibility
that Christ might have been referring to the Jews and the
Gentiles because the publicans and harlots could be an image
of the Gentiles and the priests, Scribes, and Pharisees of
the Jews.

After comparing the parables of the Guests Who
Made Excuses in Luke 14 and the Marriage Feast in Matthew 22, Maldonatus concludes that though the details differ,
they give the same meaning. Jesus seems to have intended
to teach two things by these parables. First, many are
called to the Kingdom of Heaven, i.e., the church, but few
come. Secondly, not all who come to the church when they
are called will be saved. The parable is directed against
the Jews who refused to come when they were invited, and
who have now been replaced by the Gentiles. Following
his usual methodology, Maldonatus proceeds to analyse the
details after giving the overall intent and teaching of the
parable. Referring to the wedding garment he notes that
many different opinions have been offered as to its meaning.
For example, "the followers of Calvin say that it is faith--
for everything is faith with them when they themselves have
no faith...." Reflecting one of the basic cleavages between
the theology of the medieval church and that of the Reformers, Maldonatus says that the wedding garment is not faith.
He writes: "Let these men pardon us, then, if we show
from this passage that faith alone is not sufficient for salvation; for the guest at this feast had faith, but because he
had no marriage garment--that is, good works--he was
cast into outer darkness. So Maldonatus finds in the parable not only a polemic against the Jews, but also against
the Reformation doctrine of sola fide. On the Day of Judgment God will cast out those who have faith without its
good works. However, "if to their faith they had added
good works, they would have been transferred to heaven"
[ibid., pp222-30].

The intent of the parable of the Ten Virgins is to

caution us that we should always be ready because the Lord
will come at a time unknown to us. Consequently, we
ought "always to prepare by good works for His presence."
Maldonatus finds no significance in the number of virgins.
The number ten was probably chosen to show a great number of persons, and to express the concept of universality.
The oil refers to good works and teaches us to prepare for
Christ's future coming with a "treasure of good works."
Maldonatus injects a further bit of Catholic theology when
he refers to the foolish virgins asking the wise for some of
their oil. "It is clear that the meaning is that men who
have no good works of their own, when it is too late, and
they are called to judgment, will implore the help of the
saints ... as if they wished to cover themselves under the
good works of others."

Maldonatus thinks that the parable of the Talents in
Matthew 25 is not to be equated with the Pounds in Luke 19.
The departure of the man into a far country in Matthew "no
one can doubt to be Christ." The servants probably refer
to all Christians rather than to the Doctors of the Church.
The talents are "all the gifts of God to us." Maldonatus
sees no mystical or mysterious meaning in the numbers of
talents. The intent of the parable is to show that "the
good use of grace received, merits additions of the same."
This is in keeping with the teaching of the Catholic Church
and with Christ's words in Matthew 25:28-29.

In the final parable in Matthew concerning the Sheep
and the Goats, Maldonatus finds additional evidence for the
place of reward and merit in the scheme of salvation. Calvin held that Matthew 25:34 destroyed all idea of merit.
The Calvinists say that heirship is not reward, and that it
is not given because of labor or merit, but by birth. We
are sons of God and thus heirs (Rom. 8:17). They say we
are sons by faith, "but with them heresy is faith...."
Referring to various New Testament passages, Maldonatus
says that the Calvinists cannot deny that eternal life is
called a reward in Scripture. But they hold that it is given
like a reward after labor and not because of labor. Maldonatus, however, is uncompromising in his conclusion. "If
there were no other passage but this, it would be clear
that eternal life is given not only post opera, but propter
opera, and is therefore truly and properly a reward....
For that it is properly a reward the heretics themselves
are forced to confess, and given not only post but propter
laborem. That it is so given we know from the fact that

to the greater labor is given the greater reward, and to the less labor the less reward" [ibid., pp318-28].

11 RICHARD C. TRENCH

For many years the standard English work on the parables was Archbishop Trench's Notes on the Parables of Our Lord, which was published in 1841 and appeared in many subsequent editions. Even a cursory examination of this work reveals that Trench was a man of immense learning who was familiar with Greek and Latin and with the writings of the Church Fathers, as well as with what had been written about the parables up to his time. The scope and erudition of Trench's work led A. M. Hunter to speak of it as "a marvelous mine of learning." Referring to the footnotes, the publisher of a recent edition said that they are "eloquent witness of the breadth and depth of the mind and spirit of its author," and that "they give the work the value of an encyclopedia."

Trench begins by defining a parable in the sense of distinguishing it from the fable, the mythus, the proverb, and the allegory. Comparing the parable and the fable, he notes that the intention of the former is to set forth a spiritual and heavenly truth while the latter is essentially of the earth and never rises above it. The fable has no higher aim than to inculcate maxims. The parable differs from the mythus in that a mythic narrative and the truth become indistinguishable. There is an unconscious blending of the deeper meaning with the outward symbol. In the parable, however, the two remain separate and separable. There is a distinction between form and essence, shell and kernel, the precious vessel and yet more precious wine which it contains. The difference between the parable and the proverb is not so evident because the terms are used interchangeably in the New Testament. A proverb is often a concentrated parable, and in general a parable might be understood as an extended proverb. As for parable and allegory, they differ in form rather than essence. An allegory compares one thing with another, but transfers the properties and qualities and relations of one to the other. In a parable, however, the two areas of comparison are kept separate and distinct and are placed side by side [Richard C. Trench, Notes on the Parables of Our Lord (Westwood, N. J.: Revell, 1953), pp1-10].

In his teaching Jesus gave no doctrine in an abstract

form or "skeletons of truth." Instead what he said was
"all clothed, as it were, with flesh and blood." His intention was to make intelligible the new by the help of the old:
by the aid of the familiar he introduced that which was
strange; from the known he passed more easily to the unknown.

In comparing the various gospels in their presentation
of the parables, Trench singles out Matthew and Luke. John
has only allegories, and Mark's parables present no distinctive features. Matthew's are more theocratic; Luke's, more
ethical. Matthew's are more parables of judgment; Luke's,
of mercy. The former are statelier; the latter, tenderer.
Matthew's parables are frequently introduced as containing
mysteries of the Kingdom of God, while such language is
absent from Luke. In Matthew the note of God as King and
Judge is prominent, while in Luke the concept of mercy is
more pronounced. This contrast is especially evident if we
compare the Marriage of the King's Son in Matthew 22:1-10)
and the Great Supper in Luke 14:15-24), which Trench believes to be two different versions of the same parable. In
Matthew a king is the chief personage, and a marriage festival is made for his son. "All is here theocracy; all seems
to grow directly out of an Old Testament root." Add to
this the double doom of the open foe and the false friend.
In Luke it is simply a man who makes a supper. The acts
of judgment fall into the background, and the grace, the
mercy, and the compassion of the giver of the feast pre-
dominate. He is eager to "gather in the meanest, the
most despised, the most outcast, to his table." Trench
suggests that these are but slight hints on a matter which
each student of the parables might profitably follow out for
himself [ibid., pp24-30].

Turning to the problem of interpreting the parables,
Trench sets forth a number of principles or guidelines.
The most important and fundamental question the interpreter
faces is, how much of the parables is to be taken as significant? He notes the differing positions running the gamut
between those who would trace only the most general correspondence between the sign and the thing signified, and
those who extend the interpretation to the minutest detail.
Trench admits that no absolute rule can be laid down beforehand to guide the expositor as to how far he shall proceed.
He quotes Tholuck with approval as giving "the nearest
approach, perhaps, to a canon of interpretation": 'It must
be allowed that a similitude is perfect in proportion as it

is on all sides rich in applications; and hence, in treating
the parables of Christ, the expositor must proceed on the
presumption that there is import in every single point, and
only desist from seeking it when either it does not result
without forcing, or when we can clearly show that this or
that circumstance was merely added for the sake of giving
intuitiveness to the narrative. We should not assume anything to be non-essential, except when by holding it fast as
essential, the unity of the whole is marred and troubled. "
Trench says that it will be most helpful in determining
what is essential and what is not, if before attempting to
explain a parable, we obtain a firm grasp of the central
truth which the parable would set forth, and then distinguish
it in the mind as sharply and accurately as we can from
all cognate truths which border upon it. Only as one sees
it from this point will the different parts appear in their
true light.

Another rule which is so obvious that it is often neglected is that one must pay careful attention to the introduction and the application of a parable. To ignore these
often results in untenable explanations. As an example
Trench refers to the parable of the Laborers in the Vineyard. Many of the elaborate interpretations of this parable
would never have been so much as once proposed if heed
had been given to the context, or the necessity been acknowledged of bringing the interpretation into harmony with the
saying which introduces and concludes the parable. A proper interpretation must be in accordance with the parable's
context but never by forcing it into such agreement. Trench
calls for a methodology of interpretation which is "easy, "
perhaps not always easy to discover, yet capable of being
easily discovered. Such an approach has a wholeness and
a unity reminiscent of the laws of nature. It provides a
framework which gives meaning to all the phenomena, and
not merely some. A false interpretation will "invariably
paralyse" or distort some important part of the whole. If
we have "the right key in our hands" there will be no need
for "grating or over-much forcing" and the resulting interpretation will scarcely need to be defended and made plausible by means of erudite learning and scholarship.

A final principle of interpretation is that the parables
dare not be made into primary sources and bases of doctrine. Doctrines already established may be illustrated or
further confirmed by the parables, but it is not allowable
to use them to constitute doctrine. The order of Scripture

interpretaion "has ever been recognized" as moving from the literal to the figurative, from the clearer to the more obscure. But Trench observes that this rule has often been forgotten, and "controversialists" have invented arguments in order to sustain some weak position. Trench proceeds to cite instances from the time of the Church Fathers to his own wherein the parables were misused in order to promulgate doctrine [ibid., pp29-48].

In his exegesis of the individual parables, Trench follows the order in which they appear in the Gospels, beginning with the Sower in Matthew 13 and concluding with the Pounds in Luke 19. It is evident that Trench keeps looking back to the Fathers for his views, and is reticent to employ the new critical methods which were developing in his time. He objected to those who superimposed their own spiritual or theological presuppositions upon the parables, and he rejected extravagant allegorization. Nevertheless, the method of allegory is most congenial to him, and on the whole it was this understanding of the parables which he favored. A. M. Hunter said that when one opens Trench's book today, one cannot help feeling that Trench is still in the Middle Ages and has learned nothing from Calvin. Several examples tend to bear out Hunter's observation. In his interpretation of the parable of the Good Samaritan, Trench notes that the Samaritan reminds one of Christ. "Neither is it far-fetched to regard the 'inn' as the figure of the church, the place of spiritual reflection, in which the healing of souls is ever going forward ... whither the merciful Son of man brings all whom he has rescued from the hand of Satan, where he cares for them until they shall have been restored to a perfect health...." Trench says that it would be entering into "curious minutiae" to identify the "two pence" with the two Sacraments, or the two Testaments, or the Word and the Sacraments, or unreservedly to accede to any of the ingenious explanations which have been offered for them. He nevertheless suggests that it is better to say that the two pence "include all gifts and graces, sacraments, powers of healing, of remission of sins, or other powers which the Lord has left with his church, that it may keep house for him till his return."

Turning to the parable of the Prodigal Son, Trench refers to the father's giving a robe to the Prodigal which could signify the imputation of the righteousness of Christ, or the restoration of sanctity to the soul. "If we see in it his rehabilitation in his baptismal privileges, then both will be included. " Referring to Zechariah 3:4, "Behold, I have caused thine iniquity to pass from thee, " Trench says that if this passage is brought to bear upon the parable, it is most probable that the robe signified that act of God which, considered on its negative side, is a release from condemnation, a causing of the sinner's iniquity to pass from him. On its positive side, it signifies an imputation to him of the merits and righteousness of Christ. The elder brother in his refusal to go into the house and join the celebration leaves one with an "ominous presentiment. " "The parable was fearfully fulfilled, and on the largest scale, when the Jews in the apostolic age would take no part in the great festival of reconciliation with which the Gentile world's reception into the Kingdom of Heaven was being celebrated; nay rather, with all their might set themselves against it" [ibid., pp411-12, 422]. So the parable contains both allegorical and prophetic mysteries; and while Trench holds that the main point of the parable is to describe God's relationship to persons and their relationships with each other, nevertheless he is quite amenable to finding "truths" which go well beyond the main point.

A final example of Trench's inclination toward allegorization must suffice. The oil in the parable of the Ten Virgins reminds Trench of the different ways that the "Romanists" and the "Reformers" use the word faith. The former regard faith as the "outward profession of the truth" while the latter understand it as "the root and living principle of Christian life. " The foolish virgins remind one of "those going through a round of external duties, without life, without love, without any striving after inward conformity to the law of God, whose religion is all husk and no kernel"; or of those who confess Christ with their lips, but who neglect good works. Trench states that it is clear that whatever is merely outward in the Christian profession is the lamp and that whatever is inward and spiritual is the oil reserved in the vessels. Thus, following the book of James, the faith is the lamp, the works the oil in the vessels. But if we turn to St. Paul, then the works are the lamp, and faith the oil which must feed it. Trench carries the "Romish-Reformed" dichotomy to greater lengths in his reference to the wise virgins' refusal to give oil to the foolish, "Lest there be not enough for us and you. " "There lies an argument against works of supererogation, however the Romish expositors may resist the drawing of any such conclusion from the words.... The wise do not fancy that they have anything over, which, as not needing for them-

selves, they may transfer to others; happy if their own
lamps have been maintained in such brightness as that they
may be themselves allowed to make part of the bridal festal
chamber" [ibid., pp253-54, 263].

Thus while Trench cautions against extreme allegorization, and while he maintains that one should not regard
the parables as primary sources of doctrine, one must
question how far he departs from these premises when he
turns to an analysis of the individual parables. One can
appreciate A. M. Hunter's observation that while Trench
rightly says that the details in a parable are ancillary to
the making of the main point, yet in practice he tries to
squeeze some spiritual meaning out of most of them.

12   ALEXANDER BALMAIN BRUCE

Writing in 1882, A. B. Bruce noted that books of a
devotional or homiletical character on some or all of the
parables abound, but that there is a scarcity of works in
English of a more elaborate and critical nature. Consequently, he felt no need for apology for publishing a new
work on the parables--The Parabolic Teaching of Christ;
A Systematic and Critical Study of the Parables of Our Lord.

Bruce's intention was to make a "fresh attempt to
unfold in a scholarly yet genial manner the didactic significance of these beautiful sayings of our Lord." Furthermore,
he meant to adhere strictly to the historical method of exegesis in contrast to the allegorizing method of the Fathers,
and "largely favored by the chief English writer on the subject" (Archbishop Trench). Bruce "sought help from the
moderns more than from the ancients." A. M. Hunter referred to Bruce's work as the first major book in English
to harvest the fruits of the new criticism. His adoption of
the new principles of biblical criticism caused the General
Assembly of the Free Church of Scotland to criticize him,
although no formal censure was passed.

In his interpretation of the parables, Bruce desires
"to get at the kernel of spiritual truth enclosed within the
parabolic shell: to get at it for ourselves, and to communicate it at the same time to others." The primary
question is that of methodology. Shall the parables be considered one by one as they occur in the gospels, beginning
with Matthew and proceeding to Mark and Luke? or shall

one classify them according to a given principle? and if so,
on what principle is the classification to be made? Bruce
believes that it is possible to group the parables because
they manifest real and important resemblances, and he proceeds to describe the principle of distribution he plans to
follow.

Bruce observes that Jesus' teaching ministry "falls
naturally into three divisions": Christ was a master or
rabbi with disciples whom he taught; he was an evangelist
who went about doing good among the common people and
preaching the gospel of the Kingdom to the poor; and he
was a prophet, not chiefly in the predictive sense, but especially in the sense that he proclaimed to his contemporaries the great truth of the moral government of God over
the world at large, and over Israel in particular, and the
sure doom of the impenitent. The parables may be "con-
veniently and usefully" distributed into three groups corresponding to these three aspects of Jesus' ministry: master,
evangelist, prophet. Under the first head comes all that
relates to the training of the twelve; the second represents
Jesus' miscellaneous activity as a teacher and healer among
the general population, as the Good Shepherd seeking to
save the lost sheep of the house of Israel; the third concerns his conflict with the unbelieving political and religious
leaders of Jewish society.

First, then, there is a class of parables which may
be termed theoretic because they contain the general truth
about the divine Kingdom. Secondly, there is a large group
of parables which may be called the evangelic because their
emphasis is upon the grace, the mercy, and the love of
God as the source of salvation and the law of the Christian
life. Thirdly, there is a group which may be characterized
as the prophetic, not so much in the predictive as in the
ethical sense. These parables convey the idea that in them
Jesus, as the messenger of God, spoke works of rebuke
and warning to an evil time. They proclaim the righteousness of God as the Supreme Ruler who rewards people according to their works.

Bruce does not claim any originality for the above
typology. However, he notes that there is an "increasing
consensus of opinion" in favor of this classification. Moreover, another fact has attracted much attention, viz. that
Matthew and Luke stand in distinct relation to the several
groups of parables. Most of Matthew's parables belong to

the first and third groups while most of Luke's belong to
the second. Bruce excludes Mark since he has very few
parables in his gospel. After describing and defending his
classification of the parables, Bruce proceeds to distribute
them under the above three headings.

Under the theoretic or didactic parables Bruce includes the seven in Matthew 13: the Sower, the Tares, the
Dragnet, the Hid Treasure, the Costly Pearl, the Mustard
Seed, the Leaven. These seven together with the parable
of the Seed Growing Secretly in Mark 4:26-29 all relate to
the nature of the Kingdom of God. Besides these the Friend
at Midnight and the Unjust Judge concern the delays of Providence in fulfilling spiritual desires, or to perseverance in
prayer. Other parables in this group include: the Farmer
and His Man (Luke 17:7-10), the Laborers in the Vineyard,
the Talents, the Pounds. This is a total of 14.

The evangelic parables comprise four in Luke: the
Two Debtors, the Lost Sheep, the Lost Coin, the Prodigal
Son. The parable of the Wedding Guests in Mark 2:19f.
(and parallels) is an apology for the joy of the children of
the Kingdom. The parables of the Places at Table (Luke
14:7-11) and the Pharisee and the Publican teach that the
Kingdom of God is for the humble. The Great Supper
teaches that the Kingdom is for the hungry. Other parables
included here are: the Good Samaritan, the Unjust Steward,
the Rich Man and Lazarus, the Unmerciful Servant. The
last two together reveal which are the unpardonable sins.
The total in this category is 12.

The following parables are included among the prophetic or judicial: Playing Children, containing Jesus' moral
estimate of the generation in which he lived; the Barren
Fig Tree, the Two Sons, the Marriage Feast "exhibit more
or less clearly the action of divine judgment upon the nation of Israel"; the Servant in Authority (Luke 12:42f.; Matt.
24:45f.) and the Ten Virgins exhibit similar judicial action
within the Kingdom of God. In this category there are
seven parables.

Bruce observes that the foregoing groups do not include all the parabolic sayings of Jesus recorded in the
gospels. Those omitted are the Two Builders which concludes the Sermon on the Mount, the Tower Builder and
the Warring King (Luke 14:28-35), and the Rich Fool. These
are excluded not because they do not fit into Bruce's typo-

logy but because "they are of no independent didactic importance. " The parables he proposes to consider all embody
truths that are deep, unfamiliar, or unwelcome--"mysteries
of the Kingdom. " Such a parable like the Rich Fool conveys "nothing new or abstruse, " but "simply teaches in concrete lively form a moral commonplace. " Bruce feels that
such parables were not distinctive of Christ as a teacher but
were shared in common with the Jewish rabbis. He spoke
these parables as a Jewish moralist. But the parables
which Bruce examines were uttered by Jesus as the "Herald
of the Kingdom of Heaven" [Alexander Balmain Bruce, The
Parabolic Teaching of Christ; A Systematic and Critical
Study of the Parables of Our Lord (New York: A. C. Armstrong and Son, 1908), pp v-vi, 1-9].

Proceeding according to the above scheme, Bruce
enters into a detailed analysis of the individual parables
which are grouped according to his three categories.

As already noted, Bruce was perhaps the first interpreter of the parables who attempted to deal with them
along the lines of higher criticism. Geraint Vaughan Jones
says that within the limits of hermeneutical possibilities
before Jülicher, Bruce's study of the parables was the most
ambitious of its kind. Jones notes further that his work
was, as the subtitle indicates, a "systematic and critical
study" which, taking into account the condition of New Testament criticism at the time, has not been surpassed in English [Geraint Vaughan Jones, The Art and Truth of the
Parables (London: S. P. C. K. , 1964), pp8-9].

A second feature of Bruce's interpretation was his
repudiation of allegory. A typical example of his attitude
can be seen in his comments on the parable of the Lost
Coin. The central teaching of the parable is that repentance,
even of the meanest or degraded calls forth a sympathetic
thrill in the heart of God. "It teaches us that all souls and
their moral history are precious in God's sight, that every
human being has value in the esteem of heaven, is endowed
with reason and free will, and subject to moral possibilities. " This is all that needs to be said about the parable.
Some, however, "indulge in spiritualising interpretation, "
telling us that the house is the church; the woman, the in-
dwelling Spirit; the drachma, man with the image of God
stamped upon him, but lying in the dust of sin and corrup-
tion; the candle, the Word of God held forth by the church;
and the sweeping, the disturbance caused by the action of

the Spirit in the individual and in society, making dust rise and fly about, and turning the world upside down. For Bruce this style of interpretation "savors of frigidity" and "Pharisaism." It looks as if these interpreters could discover no real interest in the story, taken as a natural illustration of the joy of finding things which were lost. Instead they found it necessary "to fly to the spiritual sense to get something to say." Their attitude is that the parable as a scene from ordinary life is of no account, and that it must be transformed into theological equivalents before it is worthy of attention. "How much better to try first of all to feel the human pathos of the parable as a story of real life, and then to make that pathos the one link of connection between the natural and the spiritual" [ibid., pp278-79].

Theologically Bruce reflected the prevailing liberalism of his time. The Jesus who emerges from his interpretation of the parables has a romantic quality reminiscent of Renan. He has "rare qualities of mind and heart, ready wit, kindly humor, gaity of spirit, profound yet homely originality of thought, clear insight, confidence, resolute determination, patience, tolerance." His conduct was "in accordance with right reason"; his behavior was characterized by a "sweet reasonableness, " and therefore it was easy to find parallels thereto in ordinary life, the naturalness of which would be recognized by everyone [ibid., pp308, 328].

Jülicher praised Bruce's work on the parables especially for his knowledge of works in German, English, Greek, and Latin which was as extensive as that of Trench. Jülicher also credited Bruce with breaking with the allegorical method of interpretation and for his adopting the linguistic approach to the parables. However, Jülicher felt that Bruce dissipated his interest and his strength by his attempt to categorize the parables in a three-storey scheme of classification. This prevented him from propounding a theory of the nature of parables or of defining what a parable is and is not [Adolf Jülicher, Die Gleichnisreden Jesu I (Darmstadt: Wissenschaftliche Buchgesellschaft, 1963), p300]. Perhaps the most far-reaching and significant evaluation of Bruce's work was that of his student, James Denny, who said, "He let me see Jesus."

13 ADOLF JÜLICHER

The name of Adolf Jülicher looms like a colossus in

the history of interpretation of Jesus' parables. Geraint V.
Jones suggests that the history of parable interpretation can
be characterized "before and after Jülicher" [this is the
heading of his first chapter in The Art and Truth of the
Parables (London: S.P.C.K., 1964)]. After six years as a
pastor, Jülicher became a professor of church history and
New Testament at Marburg--a position he occuped from
1888 until his retirement in 1923. In 1886, while still a
pastor, Jülicher published Die Gleichnisreden Jesu which
dealt with the general meaning and purpose of the parables.
This was followed in 1888 and 1899 with two further editions
which were in two volumes. Jülicher apparently hoped to
rework the 1899 edition, but illness and other duties prevented him. Consequently, in 1910 he published a second
unaltered edition of the 1899 work. The first of the two
volumes deals with the authenticity, nature, purpose and
worth of the parables. This volume concludes with a lengthy
exposition of the history of interpretation of the parables.
The second volume which is longer consists of a detailed
exegesis of the individual parables.

The central lines of Jülicher's parable theory is contained in his chapter on the essence or nature of Jesus'
parables in Die Gleichnisreden Jesu. This chapter consists
of an extensive analysis of the categories into which he
divides the parabolic speech of Jesus. He suggests that the
two basic units in parabolic speech are the "simile" (Ver-
gleichung) and "metaphor," a distinction which Aristotle had
made long ago. In order to understand a metaphor, one
must replace it by another word. As an example Jülicher
gives the incomprehensible statement, "A lion rushed on."
Only by replacing the word "lion" with "Achilles" can the
reader comprehend the real intention of this statement. But
with the simile the situation is quite different so that the
reader knows at once how the one thing is meant to illustrate the other. Thus, "Achilles rushed on like a lion" is
a simile.

Jülicher is insistent that there is a basic difference
between the nature of the metaphor and that of the simile.
Their only common characteristic is that both regard one
thing as being "like" another. Except for this, Jülicher
regards the distinction between metaphor and simile as absolute. He accentuates the difference by characterizing
the metaphor as a non-literal or indirect form of speech
(uneigentliche Rede), while the simile is a literal or direct
form (eigentliche Rede). This implies that the metaphor

says one thing but means something else; it needs to be interpreted and remains incomprehensible apart from its context; it is meant to be interesting but puzzling and to lead
the mind from a lower to a higher level of inquisitiveness
so that one asks, "What is this?" The simile, on the
other hand, needs no interpretation; it is clear and self-
explanatory; its purpose is to teach, and therefore there is
no need for questions regarding its meaning and intention
[Adolf Jülicher, Die Gleichnisreden Jesu (Darmstadt: Wissenschaftliche Buchgesellschaft, 1963), pp52-58].

Next Jülicher discusses the nature of, and the relationship between, the "similitude" (Gleichnis) and the
"allegory." The allegory is a succession of metaphors
taken from the same sphere and arranged to form a coherent
narrative. The similitude is an expanded simile which compares two thoughts or sentences, each of which contains a
relationship. Since Jülicher derives his basic categories
from the similitude, he enters into an extended discussion
of it just as he did with the simile. He suggests that two
relationships make up the similitude--the picture (Bild) and
the object (Sache). Moreover, these two relationships are
always joined by a comparative particle whose function is
to challenge the hearer to find the point of coincidence.
This structure discloses the purpose of the similitude: as
that of confronting the hearer with the necessity of deciding
or forming a judgment. Its intention is to prove [ibid.,
pp58-80].

The next form of comparison, which Jülicher considers to be the most famous, is the "fable" (Fabel). The
fable is not to be confused with an animal story, and so
Jülicher refers to it as a parable (Parabel) in the narrow
sense. A fable has all the attributes of a similitude, but
it is an imaginary story related to past time, and from it
one may draw a general truth [ibid., pp92-111].

The final category Jülicher discusses is the "example
story" (Beispielerzahlung). It differs from the similitude
and the fable in that its purpose is not only to divulge a
truth. Rather, the example story is in itself an illustration
of the truth it is meant to demonstrate. It has an existential dimension and is like a mirror in which the reader or
hearer can see a reflection of his own situation. Its intent
is to have the reader compare himself with the characters
who confront him and to thereby find guidelines for his own
behavior. Jülicher cites as illustrations of the example

story the parables of the Good Samaritan, the Rich Fool, the Rich Man and Lazarus, and the Pharisee and the Publican [ibid. , pp112-15].

One of the most difficult and mystifying passages concerning the parables is Mark 4:10-12, 33-34 where Jesus suggests that he spoke in parables so that those outside the circle of the disciples might not understand the "secrets of the Kingdom of God. " Taken literally these verses imply that Jesus wanted to keep the public "in the dark" concerning the Kingdom, and therefore he resorted to parables. These verses have encouraged allegorization because Jesus had embedded secrets and esoteric meanings in the parables which needed to be unraveled and made clear. But this tendency was diametrically opposite from Jülicher's understanding of the parables. For him the parables were clear, and each one was intended to convey one point or moral which was to be interpreted in as general terms as possible. Jülicher rejected unequivocally the view that the parables were allegories intended to confound and confuse the public. Such a view runs counter to Jesus' telling his disciples about preaching from the housetops what they had heard in secret. The gospels are full of indications that Jesus' intention was not to confine his teaching to a small limited group.

Jülicher points out that the authenticity of the parables cannot simply be assumed. Jesus did not utter them as we now read them. They have been translated, transposed, and inwardly transformed. This can be noted by the fact that the reports that two or three evangelists give of the same parable never fully agree. Not only does the expression vary, but also the viewpoint, the arrangement, the occasion, the interpretation. Thus Jülicher says that one can speak of a Lucan accent in the parables in contrast to the Matthaean. The evangelists' accounts of the parables must be critically examined, and without careful testing one can never identify the voice of Jesus with the voices of the evangelists. This approach, however, should not lead to a hopeless scepticism about recovering Jesus in the parables. On the contrary, we must ascribe a relative authenticity to them because almost without exception they have a genuine nucleus that goes back to Jesus himself [ibid. , p11].

What has happened unfortunately is that the evangelists and their sources before them have confused the "pictorial speech" of Hellenistic literature as seen for example in Sirach, with the parable of Scripture. The former is the twin sister of the "puzzle" while the latter is characterized by breadth and naturalness. In a word, the evangelists understand by "parable" not simply speech that is intended to make something clear by means of comparison, but on the contrary speech that is obscure, that requires interpretation. We must conclude, Jülicher maintains, that the meaning and understanding of the parables that the evangelists present represent a misunderstanding of the essence of Jesus' parables. The evangelists regarded the "parables" as allegories which to some extent required translation. The fact is, however, that before the parables came into the hands of "zealous redactors," they were something very different: parables, fables, example paradigmatic stories, but always literal discourse [ibid., pp42, 49].

Jülicher is insistent that the parables are not allegories. In spite of the many centuries of allegorical interpretation, and in spite of the greater authority of the evangelists, Jülicher refuses to regard the parables as allegories. Everything speaks against allegorization. The synoptists regard the parables as discourses which mean something other than the words imply. Moreover, the disciples had to ask Christ to solve the riddles that they did not understand. Jülicher observes that with two exceptions (the parables of the Sower and the Tares) the evangelists have left no "solutions of riddles." Does this mean that except for the two parables which Jesus "decoded," all the rest must be unintelligible for us? Or are we more clever than the disciples? No one will assent to this question. Consequently, we are left with only the choice: either the parables are allegories requiring a "solution," and since none has been provided for us, they must remain sealed to us; or we can understand them without any transmitted interpretation, and thus an interpretation was never absolutely necessary and the parables are not allegories [ibid., p81]. There is no shadow of doubt that for Jülicher the second alternative is the only true one. The issue is clear, and one is confronted with an either/or choice--either the evangelists or Jesus. Both cannot be right. His concluding plea for this decision reflects high emotion. He speaks about the necessity of placing Jesus in high respect and not depriving him of the diamonds in his eternal crown of honor. If we are not to deprive Jesus of his honor, we must begin breaking down the wall of tradition which imprisons him and his words. In so doing we will acknowledge that the purpose of the parabolic speech is much simpler and more direct than the evangelists would allow [ibid., p148].

Jülicher's rejection of allegorization was nearly total; there was one case where he was willing to grant an exception. The parable of the Sower (Mark 4:3-9) and the allegorical interpretation which follows (verses 14-20) belong closely together. However, since this is the singular exception to the non-allegorical character of the parables, one must favor the view that it is not a genuine parable of Jesus, but an allegory of the early church. The parable of the Wicked Husbandmen (Mark 12:1-9) is an allegory, but again it is not from Jesus, but is an allegory of the early church [ibid., pp535, 386, 405ff].

To summarize Jülicher's views, though the parabolic speech of Jesus may vary in form, the basic unit is always the simile. The parables are characterized by literal speech and are self-explanatory. They are related to real life and their intention is to convey one point or moral. Their purpose is to compel the reader to form a judgment. Thus the parable of the Talents points to faithfulness in every trust. The parable of the Unjust Steward shows that the prudent use of the present opportunity is the best preparation for a happy future. The ultimate consequences of a life of wealth and pleasure are set forth in the parable of the Rich Man and Lazarus, etc. Toward the end of the first part of Die Gleichnisreden Jesu [p317], Jülicher offers this summary of his position:

> So far as I see, once we have broken with Origen and his theory of the deeper meaning of parables, we cannot stop half way...; either the parables are wholly figurative speech or wholly literal--a mixture of both could be found in individual instances, but in this case would be a sign of clumsiness. The desire in the first place to have details interpreted can never have the occasion for parabolic discourse; either everything in them ought to be allegorized, or we ought to take everything in them as it stands and learn something from it, or let it clarify something, in order to utilize it for a higher order. For, though the similarities between the half that illustrates and the half that is illustrated be numerous or limited to a single point: the parable is there only to illuminate that one point, a rule, an idea, an experience that is valid on the spiritual as on the secular level.

The view of Jesus which emerges from Jülicher's

exposition of the parables is in agreement with 19th-century liberal theology and biblical criticism. Jülicher suggests that any biographer of Jesus cannot overdo immersing himself in and familiarizing himself with the parables. Here, as scarcely anywhere else, he gains insight into the extensive, interrelated, coherent lines of thought of Jesus. Moreover, from these simplest of all discourses he is overwhelmed by an overpowering feeling for the exalted nature of this "child of God." Jesus is wholly unpretentious and so exalted in his simple, hearty truth. No matter what Jesus' mood, he is involved in the parables with his whole heart and soul. He never thinks of himself, but only of his work, his aim, his people. To misunderstand either the essence or the purpose of the parables, is to misunderstand him. Jülicher writes: "Let us sum up the results of this investigation. In his parables Jesus has left us 'masterpieces of popular eloquence.' Here also, in terms of art, he demonstrates himself as Master; so far as we know, nothing higher and more perfect has ever been accomplished in this area" [ibid., p182]. Jülicher attests further to Jesus' creative genius when he says: "I venture to describe the parables of Jesus as not merely good but as beautiful, for they are the free creations of an outstanding noble imaginative power ..." [ibid., p156]. So the Jesus who gave us the parables is an unsophisticated, straightforward person whose sayings are clear and readily understood, yet characterized by creative ingenuity and eloquence.

As could be expected, Jülicher was not without opponents. But his work is of such impressive proportions that any treatment of the parables which does not reckon with him will be grossly inadequate. Jülicher definitely imparted a new direction to parabolic interpretation, for he broke decisively with the allegorical exegesis which, with few exceptions, had predominated since the patristic period.

14   RABBINIC SCHOLARSHIP

CHRISTIAN A. BUGGE

Four years after the publication of Jülicher's book, there appeared a work entitled Die Haupt-Parabeln Jesu by the Norwegian scholar, Christian A. Bugge. Bugge acknowledged the monumental importance of Jülicher's work and asserted that if it had not been for his stimulus, Bugge's own work would never have been brought to fruition. However, Bugge took issue with Jülicher's contention that the parables of Jesus are clear and that there is no room for allegorization. It does not follow that because some parables are self-evident, all must be so. Not all of Jesus' sayings are clear, and Bugge cites 16 examples of paradox where the point of the saying is hidden by its form [Christian A. Bugge, Die Haupt-Parabeln Jesu (Giessen: J. Ricker'sche Verlagsbuchhandlung, 1903), pp15-16].

One of Bugge's basic criticisms of Jülicher's methodology was that he was too closely tied to the Aristotelian and Greek view of parables, and that he ignored the rabbinical roots of the parables. Bugge affirms that in his work he is going to give attention to the Jewish background [ibid., pp19-20]. Consequently, Bugge gives detailed attention to the nature of the Hebrew concept of mashal which in the Septuagint is rendered parabolē. He observes that as far as he knows no complete classification of Jewish mashal forms had been undertaken. However, according to Jewish rhetoric an allegory is a mashal and a parable is a mashal; the boundaries are indeterminate and mixed parables are not unique. He points out that there is Old Testament precedent for the use of allegory as for example in Ezekiel 31:6, 17:22; Daniel 4:12. Therefore there is no reason that in the parable of the Mustard Seed, which illustrates a great truth about the Kingdom of God, the birds should not stand for the nations [ibid., pp34-35].

Bugge accuses Jülicher of not merely "taking a small stone out of the wall of traditional parabolic interpretation" but of destroying the parable element in the Synoptic Gospels. Bugge maintains that he proceeds according to simple historical principles and not abstract principles and presuppositions which, as he believes, affect the authenticity of three-fourths of the parables. He wants to explore the principles of Jewish rhetoric and the characteristics of the mashal rather than follow the way of Jülicher which was governed by Aristotelianism and dogmatic assumptions, and which obscured a historical approach to the parables.

Again, contrary to Jülicher's contention, there were good reasons that Jesus employed "secret parables" as represented in Mark 4:11ff. Bugge lists four reasons why Jesus spoke obscurely by means of parables. (1) He did not want to reveal his unusual conception of his messiahship and of the Kingdom of God. (2) The masses were obtuse and lacking in understanding and insight. (3) He needed to consider the Disciples. (4) It was unnecessary for him to reveal too much because of the slow development of his messianic pretensions [ibid., pp38-55].

Bugge draws up a register or classification of the parables which numbers 71. Thirty-six of these are very short sayings which he calls Parabelembleme (following Delitzsch). He proceeds to divide the parables into two major groupings, argumentative and illustrative. The latter border on allegory and it is oftentimes difficult to distinguish them from allegories. The difference between the two categories is that the "argumentative parable" seeks to make a moral point by reference to an analogy taken from actual life or from nature, while the "illustrative parable" attempts to convey moral truth with the aid of an illustration from a different area. An example of the former would be Mark 2:21: "No one sews a piece of unshrunk cloth on an old garment...." This is "argumentative" in that it uses an instance from daily life to refer to the coming of Jesus and his relationship to the pharisaical system. "You are the salt of the earth," and "You are the light of the world," are "illustrative" because they use an analogy from another domain or dimension to describe the nature of discipleship.

There are two other terms which appear in Bugge's classification of the parables--paradox and didactic. Some of the parables such as the Laborers in the Vineyard have a paradoxical-didactic quality. Through these parables we learn something new which we did not formerly understand. The Laborers in the Vineyard illustrates a paradoxical characteristic of the Kingdom of grace, viz. that the last can be first and the first can be last. Therefore this is a "didactic parable" because a dimension of God's Kingdom is unveiled which formerly was not known [ibid., pp59-66].

In spite of his many differences with Jülicher, Bugge agrees that the major parables are concerned with one idea and lead to one conclusion, but one which is at the same time illuminated by the individual details. Moreover, there is no reason for rejecting the concluding aphorism of a parable as inauthentic because it is a natural ending which completes the parable and gives focus to its meaning [ibid., pp67-68].

Following the discussion of his methodology of parabolic interpretation, Bugge proceeds to give a detailed exegesis of individual parables which exhibits a broad acquaint-

ance with parabolic scholarship in various languages. He
treats these parables in three sections: the secret parables
and the Kingdom of God concept, the later Kingdom parables in Matthew, and the individual parables of Luke. After
his exegesis of each parable, Bugge gives brief quotations
from various writers, particularly of the patristic and medieval periods, concerning the parable under discussion. This
amounts to a history of interpretation of each of the parables which Bugge discusses.

Perhaps Bugge's most significant contribution to the
history of interpretation of the parables was his study of
the relationship between Jewish parables and those of Jesus.
This area was studied in much more detail by Paul Fiebig
to whom we now turn.

PAUL FIEBIG

Fiebig's first study on the relationship between Jew-
ish parables and the parables of Jesus was Altjüdische
Gleichnisse und die Gleichnisse Jesu which appeared in 1904.
Like Bugge's work, it is a response and reaction to Jülicher.
Fiebig looked with favor on what Bugge had done but be-
lieved that a more thorough study needed to be made because
Bugge had relied largely on familiar and secondary sources.

In the first section of his book Fiebig says that his
interest is not in making an etymological analysis of mashal
nor in discussing the meaning of such terms as allegory,
fable, parable, similitude, riddle, etc. Rather he wishes
to examine parabolic or allegorical sayings or stories from
the Mekilta, which is a midrashic commentary on part of
Exodus. Fiebig sets forth 53 of these, some of which are
by known authors while others are from unknown authors
[Paul Fiebig, Altjüdische Gleichnisse und die Gleichnisse
Jesu, (Tubingen, Leipzig: J. C. B. Mohr, 1904), pp14-73].

After presenting this "hitherto unknown material,"
Fiebig turns to a comparison between it and the Synoptic
parables. There is a similarity between the method Jesus
employed and that of the rabbis. In both cases the background and the occasion are provided. There are also
similarities in the use of an opening formula such as "What
is the matter like?" in the case of the rabbinic parables.
Following these introductory materials the story is told and
comments and explanation are given. In several instances
the material in the parables of Jesus and those of the rabbis

have slight resemblances. Moreover, while the rabbinic parables are not pure allegories they do contain allegorical material. Thus Fiebig cannot subscribe to Jülicher's bold rejection of allegorization because he believes that Jesus' method was rooted in the rabbinic tradition.

While acknowledging certain similarities between the parables of Jesus and those of the rabbis, Fiebig affirms unmistakably the superior quality of the parables of Jesus. They reflect a lifelikeness and a creativity that is absent from the rabbinic parables. Jesus' parables concern such great themes as sin and grace, prayer, mercy, and love. The Kingdom of God is the object of most of them, but Fiebig asserts that in the whole of Jewish literature he did not find a single parable concerned with the Kingdom.

The question of the originality of Jesus' parables is closely related to the problem of chronology, that is, was Jesus influenced by the rabbinic parables if in fact they antedated him? Fiebig points out that the parabolic form was not new in the time of Jesus, and he concludes that the parables of the Mekilta date from a period around A. D. 90 at the latest. The originality of Jesus' parables does not reside in their form but in their content. Compared with the parables of the Mekilta they reflect a charming freshness and distinctness. Moreover, they deal with the real general human condition and are free from triviliaty (Kleinigkeit) and the exegetical spirit of Judaism. Jesus' parables are so superior to the parables of the Mekilta and demonstrate a quality in themselves that one must conclude that no one except Jesus alone could have given them [ibid., pp107-63].

In 1912 Fiebig published a second work on the parables [Die Gleichnisreden Jesu im Lichte der rabbinischen Gleichnisse des neutestamentlichen Zeitalters (Tubingen: J. C. B. Mohr, 1912)] in which he continued his criticism of Jülicher's interpretation of the parables. His intention was to find a middle way between exegetes like Jülicher who disregarded rabbinic material and such sceptics like Arthur Drews who held that the rabbinic writings helped confirm that the Christ of the Synoptic Gospels was a mythical figure invented from contemporary traditions.

Fiebig begins by citing 36 parables selected from the Babylonian and Jerusalem Talmuds, the Mishnah, Tosefta, and the Midrash. He notes that the resemblances between

these parables and those of the Gospels are striking. Therefore an examination and study of the rabbinic parables is
significant for the understanding of Jesus' parabolic method
[Die Gleichnisreden Jesu ..., pp6-118].

Turning to Jülicher's parabolic methodology, Fiebig
notes that Jülicher has no acquaintance with rabbinic literature. For him the Talmud is a terra incognita, and the
Mishna, Tosephta, etc. are empty names. The major
problem with Jülicher's exegesis is that he derived his
theory from Greek throught, particularly that of Aristotle.
Instead he should have turned to rabbinic writings because
they represent the closest approximation to Jesus' parables.
Jesus was no philosopher who thought academically, sche-
matically, systematically, or philosophically. Rather he
was a Jew and an Oriental, and as such he thought concretely
and intuitively instead of abstractly. His thought was popular and closely related to specific life situations. Jülicher
failed to take this into account, and consequently he had a
distorted view of the parables. If he had been familiar
with Jewish thought, he would not have dismissed allegorization to the extent that he did because the parables of Jesus
are not always free from allegorical elements. Jesus was
oriental and a Jew, but Jülicher made him into a German
professor, a philosopher or educated man of the 19th century who lived in Germany and who was, furthermore, instructed more in the learning of the Greeks than in the
teaching of his Jewish contemporaries. Fiebig agreed with
Jülicher, however, that Jesus' parables had all the marks
of having originated with a single, creative individual. They
were by no means a mere imitation of contemporary materials. On the one hand, they possess an ethical seriousness which is lacking in Jewish apocalyptic; on the other
hand, in contrast to rabbinic parables, they are marked by
a strong eschatological interest, yet lack the "exegetical-
trifles" of rabbinic examples. Thus Fiebig confirmed at
greater length the claim of his earlier work that the originality of Jesus' parables lay, not in their form, but in
their content [ibid., pp119-32, 222-78].

In light of Fiebig's criticims of Jülicher, he proceeds
to examine each of the 53 parables which Jülicher dealt
with in his work and to indicate where he feels that Jülicher
was mistaken in his interpretation. Jülicher had erred in
regarding the parables as editorial recensions of existing
documents. Fiebig anticipated form criticism by pointing
out that the evangelists resorted to oral traditions, and this

fact accounted for the differences between parallel versions of the same parable more adequately than the contention that they had made these changes themselves for doctrinal or other reasons [ibid., pp132-220].

Fiebig's contribution to parabolic interpretation has been evaluated both positively and negatively by subsequent critics. Though he emphasized the oral as against the written tradition as the main factor in the transmission of the parables and thus was in keeping with later form criticism, Rudolf Bultmann has some harsh words for him. Bultmann disagrees with Fiebig's claim that the rabbinic parables contain allegorical features. What Fiebig calls allegories are nothing of the kind but are rather examples of quite customary metaphors for God (as king) for man (as slave), etc. Or it may simply be that the correspondence between the image and the reality has been expressed in the primitive form of an identification. Bultmann states that he has not found any instance in Fiebig of allegory in Jewish similitudes, corresponding to the frequent features in the Synoptic similitudes. Bultmann believes that methodologically speaking Jülicher is entirely right over against Fiebig. Whether Jülicher is always right in particular instances when he detects allegorical features is another question [Rudolf Bultmann, The History of the Synoptic Tradition, rev. ed., John Marsh, trans. (New York: Harper & Row, 1968), p198].

Perhaps the most significant feature of Fiebig's work was his emphasis upon the Jewish background, which throws light on certain features of the parables of Jesus. Jack Dean Kingsbury, in evaluating Fiebig's contribution, concludes:

> The contributions of Fiebig to parable exegesis consist in his demonstrating that the closest analogies to the Gospel parables at our disposal are the Rabbinic meshalim, and that the simile and metaphor, because they are more similar than dissimilar, can naturally be combined in a unit to produce mixed-forms, i.e. allegorical parables and parabolic allegories. While these insights certainly do not negate the validity and usefulness of Jülicher's categories, they none the less invest them with a degree of latitude Jülicher himself did not envisage [Jack Dean Kingsbury, The Parables of Jesus in Matthew 13 (Richmond, Va.: John Knox Press, 1969), p7].

15   PROTESTANT LIBERALISM

The terms "Protestant liberalism" or "liberal Protestantism" characterize a theological movement, or perhaps
better, theological temper or mood, which originated in the
19th century and which reached its zenith in the United
States in the decades preceding World War II. Among its
motifs was a minimizing of dogma and an emphasis upon the
experiential and ethical elements of the Christian faith. The
"fathers" of liberalism are generally regarded to be Friedrich Schleiermacher (1768-1834) and Albrecht Ritschl (1822-
1889). To generalize broadly, Schleiermacher emphasized
the experiential, while Ritschl emphasized the ethical dimensions of the Christian faith.

For Schleiermacher religion must be seen as an
affection or intuition and is discerned in one's awareness of
absolute dependence upon God. The task of theology is to
explicate the nature and content of this distinctive consciousness. Schleiermacher understood Christianity as essentially
a redemptive religion which was grounded in "the constant
potency of Christ's God-consciousness" [Friedrich Schleiermacher, The Christian Faith, H. R. Mackintosh and J. S.
Stewart, eds. (Edinburgh: T. & T. Clark, 1928), p385].
Christ's work of redemption is to induce in us an approach
to his perfect God-consciousness. This occurs as he calls
persons into fellowship and association with him in the
church or the Kingdom of God. For Schleiermacher the
Kingdom of God is the corporate human God-consciousness
which is the existence of God in human nature and which
comes into being as a result of Christ's God-consciousness
[ibid., p723].

Johannes Weiss observed that it was Ritschl who
brought the concept of the Kingdom of God to the center of
contemporary theological thought. Indeed, the Kingdom is
the outstanding feature of his doctrine. He described Christianity as an ellipse with two foci--redemption and the Kingdom of God. The latter is to be understood essentially in
moral terms. It is the moral organization of humanity
through action inspired by love. Moreover, it has a specifically teleological aspect and is the common end of God
and of Christians as a community. The Kingdom of God is
the goal to which the believer directs his spiritual and
ethical activity [Albrecht Ritschl, The Christian Doctrine of
Justification and Reconciliation, vol. 3, H. R. Mackintosh
and A. B. Macaulay, eds. (Edinburgh: T. & T. Clark,
1902), pp11-13].

The thological heritage of Ritschl was carried on and extended, especially by three members of the "Ritschlian School"--Wilhelm Herrmann, Julius Kaftan, and Adolf von Harnack.

Wilhelm Herrmann was a renowned teacher at Marburg, and his influence was felt not only in Germany but also in Great Britain and the United States. In his interpretation of the Kingdom of God Herrmann speaks of both its present and future reality. The Synoptic Gospels depict Jesus as one who was convinced that the Kingdom of God was coming through his own life and work. Its advent was bound up with his appearance in history. Jesus shared two opinions about the Kingdom which were current in Judaism: the Kingdom of God will bring blessing to men, and the Kingdom is something that is to come. It cannot develop out of the present order or be realized through human activity. It comes as a miraculous act of God from another world. Thus, it is God's gift rather than the result of human achievement. While Herrmann acknowledges the futuristic side of the Kingdom of God, nevertheless, he prefers to emphasize its present reality and its relationship to person's lives in the here and now. Referring to Matthew 6:33, Herrmann says that Jesus identifies striving after righteousness with striving after the Kingdom. According to the messianic hope the Kingdom would come from the other world, but "that which was regarded as the content of the Kingdom of God was of this world; for it was the product of the earthly desires of men. " However, human longing cannot be equated with the Kingdom of God. Jesus rejected all attempts to present the Kingdom as a supreme good or to confuse it with political hopes. Entering the Kingdom presupposes an inward freedom from longing and ambition. Moreover, we cannot understand it by ourselves, but only as it is given to us. If we are to understand the Kingdom aright we must turn to the inner life of Jesus. In all probability Jesus thought first about God's sovereignty when he referred to the Kingdom of God. But the essence of the Kingdom is to be discerned in his perfect surrender to God. The longing for the Kingdom in Jesus' life implied love of God with all the heart and soul. Therefore, Jesus understood the Kingdom of God in terms of the experience of the complete sovereignty of God. But each of us is far from this ideal because of our darkness and our sin. Therefore the complete sovereignty of God in our lives remains a future goal of our hope and desire. But in Jesus we see that God comes near us, and that can bring us blessing. Consequently it is the redeeming power of Jesus that enables us to look with eager hope toward the future. To put it another way, through Jesus' impact upon us the Kingdom becomes a reality in our lives. He is the one who brings to us the Kingdom of God.

Herrmann observes that Jesus never described the Kingdom of God. Neither do his parables give a picture of it because they have another purpose. In his preaching Jesus sought to make clear something quite different. "He tries continually to make clear what real righteousness is, and he tries to stimulate men to put their trust in the goodness of God." The intention of the parables was to express the real meaning of moral good which is the "Will to Fellowship" and which issues in inner freedom won in and through fellowship. But Jesus appears also to be the first one who equated the moral good with the command to love God. In correlating love to neighbor and to God Jesus expressed the very essence of both morality and religion. In his parables and teachings which speak of righteousness and of putting one's trust in the goodness of God, Jesus sought to introduce his hearers to the Kingdom of God. Thus Herrmann feels that what Jesus understood by the Kingdom now becomes clear. "He must have meant that the beginning of the Kingdom of God is given to men in the stirrings of such righteousness and such trust or religion in their hearts. So Herrmann finally puts the emphasis upon the immanent reality of the Kingdom. Man cannot realize the Kingdom; it is God's gift. But Jesus understood it as the rule of God which man may see and experience--"above all, therefore, the rule of God in man's own heart." The parables and the sayings of Jesus are intended to make man desire the rule of God in his heart as his supreme good. To experience the presence of the Kingdom of God is to place one's absolute trust in God and to practice the good we know. The blessedness of the Kingdom is only evident to us when God transforms our inward life so that we are fully submissive to Him. Only when such a transformation occurs in our lives does the future reality and blessedness of the Kingdom of God open before us [Wilhelm Herrmann, The Communion of the Christian with God, Robert T. Voelkel, ed. (Philadelphia: Fortress Press, 1971), pp94-97; Wilhelm Herrmann, Systematic Theology, Nathaniel Micklem and Kenneth A. Saunders, trans. (New York: Macmillan, 1927), pp43-49].

Another leading exponent of the "Ritschlian School"

was Adolf von Harnack. In his understanding of the nature
of Jesus' teaching and of the meaning of the Kingdom of
God, Harnack stands close to Herrmann. In his well known
lectures Das Wesen des Christentums, (What Is Christianity?) Harnack describes the quality and the essence of Jesus'
teachings. Jesus' whole being was suffused with religion--
with his relation to God. However, he was no fanatic who
shut himself off from the world. Harnack pictures Jesus
as a kind of romanticist who "looked at the world with a
fresh and clear eye for the life, great and small, that
surrounded him. " His discourses were generally in the
form of parables and sayings, and they reflect various linguistic techniques and the whole range of human emotions.
He uses words of reproof and judgment, and yet he is
characterized by a quiet and resolute demeanor. Harnack
observes that Jesus never employs ecstatic language, and
stirring prophecy is rare. Everything about him was directed to one goal--to bring persons into relation with God.
Consequently, his eye and ear were open to every impression
of the life around him. The parables enlivened his discourse, and yet they were clear even to those of childlike
mentality. He spoke about children's play, leaving home,
gathering and scattering, marriage, wealth and poverty,
the sower and the reaper in the field, the lord of the vin-
tage among his vines, the idle workman in the marketplace,
the shepherd searching for the sheep, the dealer in pearls,
the woman anxious about the barrel of meal and the leaven,
the lost piece of money, the widow's complaint to the surly
official, and so on. These examples tell us more than that
Jesus spoke in picture and parable; they exhibit an inner
sense of freedom and a cheerfulness of soul in the midst of
strain such as no prophet ever before possessed. The
parable is Jesus' most familiar form of speech, and though
he strikes notes of judgment and confronts men with ultimate
decisions, parable and sympathy pass into each other. Like
one who has rest and peace of soul, he is able to give life
and peace to others. With him the strongest emotion seems
to come naturally; "he clothes it in the language in which a
mother speaks to her child. "

Harnack suggested that the message of Jesus can be
summarized under three headings: the Kingdom of God and
its coming; God the Father and the infinite value of the
human soul; and the higher righteousness and the commandment of love.

Jesus' message about the Kingdom of God has both a

future and immanent dimension. There is ambiguity here
because the one pole represents the Kingdom as a future
event and the external rule of God, while the other pole
pictures it as something inward and already present. Harnack rejects the view that the Kingdom of God is to be
understood essentially in futuristic terms. The notion of
two kingdoms, one of God and the other of the devil, which
are in conflict until God will defeat the devil at some future
time, was an idea which Jesus shared with his contemporaries. It was not original with him, but he retained it from
the Jewish tradition in which he grew up. What was his
own, however, was the view that the Kingdom of God was
already here. If one wants to know what the Kingdom of
God and its coming meant in Jesus' message, he must read
and study the parables. Harnack says that the Kingdom
comes by coming to the individual and entering into his soul
and laying hold of it. The Kingdom of God is the rule of
God, but "it is the rule of the holy God in the hearts of
individuals." This is what the parables are about--the parable of the Sower, of the Costly Pearl, of the Hid Treasure.
They point to the word of God, to God Himself--the Kingdom of God. The essence of Jesus' message is not found
in his apocalyptic imagery, but in his description of God
and the soul, the soul and God.

But the conception of the Kingdom of God as the
power that works inwardly can also be seen in Jesus' healing of others and above all by his forgiving sin. Now for
the first time everything external and future is abandoned,
and it is the redeemed individual who finds in the Kingdom
of God his strength and the goal at which he aims. This
is what the parable of the Hid Treasure and the Costly Pearl
are teaching. A person will sell all that he has to gain the
Kingdom, but thereby he is converted and made God's child
and witness.

The Kingdom of God is also like a seed which grows
steadily and silently and bears fruit. It is like a spiritual
force or power which goes within a person and can be understood only from within. And although it is in heaven and
will come with the day of judgment, it is likewise within.

Harnack summarizes the essential elements in Jesus'
teaching about the Kingdom of God in three statements: it
is something supernatural, a gift from above, not a product
of ordinary life; it is a purely religious blessing, the inner
link with the living God; and it is the most important experi-

ence that a man can have, that on which everything else depends--it permeates and dominates his whole existence, because sin is forgiven and misery banished.

So the Kingdom of God brings joy and newness of life, and it is the clue to the meaning and aim of existence. It is the Eternal entering time and is like a light which makes the world look new. This is Jesus' message of the Kingdom, and is the focus of all his teaching so that his whole "doctrine" can be understood as a message of the Kingdom [Adolf von Harnack, What Is Christianity? Thomas B. Saunders, trans. (New York: Harper & Row, 1957), pp34-37, 51-62].

16   THE ESCHATOLOGICAL REACTION

The prevailing liberal theology of the latter part of the 19th century, as represented by Herrmann and Harnack, tended to understand Jesus' teaching about the Kingdom of God as being primarily concerned with religious experience --as the rule of God in men's hearts. Ritschl and the Social Gospel movement construed the Kingdom to mean the exercise of the moral life in society and its fuller realization through the gradual development of an ideal society on earth.

JOHANNES WEISS

In 1892 a short work of about 67 pages, Die Predigt Jesu vom Reiche Gottes by Johannes Weiss, appeared. It proved to be the most important criticism of the Ritschlian and liberal Protestant interpretation of the Kingdom of God. Weiss began by welcoming liberalism's "serious attention to and emphasis upon the concept 'Kingdom of God.'" However, he believed that it was now necessary "to submit the historical foundations of this concept to a thorough investigation." There is always the danger of bypassing the original historical character of biblical concepts and reinterpreting or converting them to new purposes in accordance with new viewpoints. Consequently, Weiss concluded: "In this regard, it might not be superfluous if we attempt once more to identify the original historical meaning which Jesus connected with the words 'Kingdom of God,' and if we do it with special care lest we import modern, or at any rate alien, ideas into Jesus' thought-world" [Johannes Weiss, Jesus' Proclamation of the Kingdom of God, trans., ed.,

and with Introduction by Richard Hyde Hiers and David
Larrimore Holland (Philadelphia: Fortress Press, 1971),
pp57-60].

Weiss' proposal sounds obvious and innocuous enough,
but his consequent findings produced a major upheaval in
biblical and theological interpretation. The Kingdom of God
which Weiss found in Jesus' teaching had very different
characteristics from that of Ritschl and the Ritschlians.
The essence of his research was that Jesus viewed the Kingdom in purely eschatological terms. It was to be realized
in the near future through God's action alone. Moreover,
the coming of the Kingdom would be a cataclysmic event
marked by judgment and the destruction of the old world
and the creation of a new one. [For a summary of the
principal results of Weiss' study, see his Jesus' Proclamation..., pp129-31.]

The ensuing controversy attending Weiss' study led
him to write two other works in which he defended and
elaborated his ideas. The first was Die Idee des Reiches
Gottes in der Theologie (1900) which was a critical study
of the use of the concept of the Kingdom of God in systematic theology. He next wrote a second edition of Die Predigt Jesu vom Reiche Gottes (1900) which grew to 214 pages.
It included a thorough study and criticism of the views of
his contemporaries, and especially those of Ritschl. [For
a discussion of the second edition of Die Predigt Jesu, see
Norman Perrin, The Kingdom of God in the Teaching of
Jesus (Philadelphia: Westminster Press, 1963), pp17-23.]

The teaching of Jesus was primarily concerned with
the hope of the coming of the Kingdom of God. He was
convinced that the Kingdom was truly coming; the time of
waiting was past and the fulfillment of the Kingdom was at
hand. The crisis was inevitable, and the day of salvation
was no longer a dream, but an indubitable reality [Johannes
Weiss, Die Predigt Jesu vom Reiche Gottes, 2. Aufl. (Göttingen: Vandenhoeck & Ruprecht, 1900), p69].

The view that Jesus understood the Kingdom of God
as a gradual process of development which would be carried
out in the world is often substantiated by reference to the
parables of the Mustard Seed and the Leaven. These parables are supposed to show that Jesus regarded the consummation of the Kingdom as a slow, secret, evolutionary
process. But Weiss maintains that this is not what these

parables imply. They are not parables of growth, but of contrast of the small cause and the great effect, the inconspicuous beginning and the overpowering great result. Just as in nature the small and insignificant can have the greatest of effects, so also the at-first scarcely visible effects of Jesus will in the future excel all expectations [ibid., pp 82-83]. Weiss believes that the Evangelists used the parables of the Mustard Seed and the Leaven to interpret the "visible Kingdom of God," viz. the church. The mustard tree signified the church; the birds, the people who stream to it; the meal and leaven, the disciples who are like light, salt, and leaven in the world. Mark notes that the birds make nests under the shade of the mustard tree. Weiss says that the birds in Mark are naturally a reference to the heathen. The parables of the Mustard Seed and of the Sower in Mark are also to be understood as parables of contrast in the sense outlined above [ibid., pp48-49].

The parable of the Seed Growing Secretly (Mark 4:26-29) shows that man cannot realize the Kingdom of God through his own efforts. Rather it will come according to God's will and in His time. It reminds us to wait patiently and warns against arbitrary interference. The parable is not answering the theological questions as to how the Kingdom of God comes, but the burning discontentment regarding the time of the Kingdom's coming. Can't one do something to hasten its coming? Weiss observes that the parable is not referring to an immanent development of the Kingdom in the sense of an ethical perception about which one must do much, but about a transcendent restoration of God's dominion according to His will and His time [ibid., pp84-85].

Weiss deals with certain critical questions concerning the parables. One is the use of the formula "the Kingdom of Heaven (or God) is like" which appears nine times in Matthew and far less frequently in Mark and Luke [ibid., pp45-48]. In a lengthy article ["Die Parabelrede bei Marcus," Studien und Kritiken (1891), 289-321] Weiss analyzes the sources of the parables in Mark, especially with reference to the parable of the Sower. He discusses the place of "Ur-Mark" in the construction of the parables. He believes that Jesus originally told the parable of the Sower as an allegory and that its meaning has been incorrectly reproduced in the Marcan interpretation.

ALBERT SCHWEITZER

The eschatological interpretation of Jesus' teachings

begun by Johannes Weiss was popularized and broadened by Albert Schweitzer. Schweitzer acknowledged his thanks and indebtedness to Weiss, but believed that he had not gone far enough. Not only Jesus' teachings, but his whole life and outlook were influenced by his certain belief that the Kingdom of God was coming in the immediate future. In comparing Weiss and Schweitzer, Norman Perrin writes:

> As an interpretation of the Kingdom of God in the teaching of Jesus it [Schweitzer's] is inferior to the work of Johannes Weiss, to which it owes so much.... It has had an impact far greater than that of Johannes Weiss, who restricts himself with true academic sobriety to the teaching of Jesus and to the implications of his interpretation of this for systematic theology. Not so Schweitzer! He plunges into the whole life of Christ and thus strikes a note of tremendous interest and impact to all Christians whether they be academically interested in New Testament theology or not [Norman Perrin, The Kingdom of God in the Teaching of Jesus (Philadelphia: Westminster Press, 1963), p34; for a good summary of Schweitzer's views, see Perrin, pp28-36].

In keeping with his "consistent eschatology," Schweitzer offers an intriguing analysis of the "parables of the secret of the Kingdom of God" in Mark 4. These include the parables of the Sower, of the Seed Growing Secretly, of the Mustard Seed, plus the parable of the Leaven. Schweitzer notes that these parables are generally used as an illustration of a constant and gradual unfolding through which the meager initial stage of a development is connected with the glorious final stage. The seed already contains the harvest which develops according to natural law. So the analogy is made to the Kingdom of God. Like the seed, the Kingdom develops to magnificent proportions from small and obscure beginnings.

However attractive the evolutionary interpretation of these parables is, it nevertheless takes from them the "character of secrets." It is not the idea of development which is foremost in these parables, but the apparent absence of causation. The notion of a steady development or unfolding through the processes of nature is no secret. By interpreting the parables according to our scientific knowledge we unite different stages by the conception of development. However, such an understanding has no prominence in the parables. They aim at suggesting, rather, how and by what power incomparably great and glorious results can be infallibly produced by an insignificant fact without human aid. For the unschooled person of ancient times nature still had secrets to offer. One was the certain and inexplicable connection between two utterly distinct conditions such as the seed and the harvest. How can the final stage proceed from the initial stage?

Schweitzer proceeds to interpret these parables beginning with the Sower. A man sowed seed, and even though a great part of it was lost because of diverse circumstances, yet the produce of the seed which fell in good ground was so great that it increased thirty, sixty, even a hundred times. Schweitzer believes that the detailed interpretation of the description of the loss and the application to particular classes of persons as we now have it in Mark 4:13-20 is the result of a later view which no longer perceived the secret in the parable. Originally the single parts of the description were not independent, but the intent was to present a unified contrast between the seed that was lost for one reason or another and the seed which fell upon good ground. The way in which the seed was destroyed has no importance for the parable. The focus of attention must be upon the secret, viz. that the sowing was so small, considering all that was lost, yet the harvest was so great. How did that come about?

A man sowed seed and did not bother any further about it, but slept and went about his affairs. But before he realized it a glorious harvest appeared even though he did nothing to help it. How did it happen that after the seed was scattered the ground of itself brought forth the blade, the ear, and the full corn? By what power was that effected? That is the secret.

An extremely minute mustard seed was sown, and from it there grew a great bush with branches under which the birds of the heaven could take refuge. The bush could not have been contained in the tiny seed. How did this happen? That is the secret.

Or a woman added a little leaven to a large amount of dough. Afterwards the whole lump was infused with leaven. How can a little leaven leaven a large mass of dough? That is the secret.

Schweitzer says that these parables are not at all devised to be interpreted and understood. Rather their intent is to make Jesus' hearers cognizant of the fact that in the affairs of the Kingdom of God there is a mystery or a secret like that which they observe in nature. They are signals. Just as harvest follows the seed-sowing, without anyone's being able to explain the process, so also will the Kingdom of God come with power as the sequel to Jesus' preaching. The moral renewal which results from Jesus' preaching stands in a necessary but inexplicable connection with the dawning of the Kingdom of God. The same God who through his mysterious power in nature brings the harvest will also bring to pass the Kingdom of God.

The initial fact of these parables is the sowing. Thus the Kingdom of God must follow as certainly as harvest follows seed-sowing. A man believes in the harvest without being able to explain it simply because the seed has been sown. So with the same assurance he may believe in the Kingdom of God. What does the sowing symbolize? Jesus is referring to something already existing--the movement of repentance initiated by John and now intensified by his own preaching. The growing grain and the resulting harvest point to the heavenly harvest, the revelation of the Kingdom of God.

But, for Schweitzer, the Kingdom of God is related to the harvest not only symbolically or analogically, but literally and temporally. At the moment when Jesus gave the parables, the time of sowing was past and the seed was "slumbering in the ground." Thus he is telling his Galilean audience not only to watch for the harvest but to watch for the Kingdom of God. The harvest which was ripening when Jesus spoke was the last! With the harvest would also come the Kingdom which would bring in a new age. When the reapers go into the fields, the Lord of Heaven will cause His harvest to be reaped by the holy angels. Schweitzer writes: "If the three parables of Mark 4 contain the mystery of the Kingdom of God, and are therefore capable of being summed up in a single formula, this can be nothing else than the joyful exhortation: 'Ye who have eyes to see, read, in the harvest which is ripening upon earth, what is being prepared in heaven!' The eager eschatological hope was to regard the natural process as the last of its kind, and to see in it a special significance in view of the event of which it was to give the signal" [Albert Schweitzer, The Quest of the Historical Jesus,

William Montgomery, trans. (London: A. & C. Black, 1931), p355].

The analogical and temporal parallelism between the harvest and the Kingdom of God becomes complete, Schweitzer feels, if we assume that the movement begun by John the Baptist began in the spring. It is significant that according to Matthew 9:37-38, before sending out the disciples to proclaim the nearness of the Kingdom, Jesus spoke about the rich harvest. This seems like a final expression of the thought contained in the parables about the seed and its promise, and finds its most natural explanation in the supposition that the harvest was actually at hand. But whatever one thinks about this attempt to probe historically the secret of the Kingdom of God, there is one factor that cannot be avoided, viz. that the initial fact to which Jesus points, under the figure of the sowing, is somehow or other connected with the eschatological preaching of repentance, which had been inaugurated by the Baptist.

The eschatological insight of Johannes Weiss ended the modern view that Jesus founded the Kingdom. Weiss did away with all activity exercised upon the Kingdom of God, and made Jesus' role purely a waiting one. According to Schweitzer, the activity now comes back into the preaching of the Kingdom, but this time it is eschatologically conditioned. The secret of the Kingdom of God which Jesus reveals in the parables about confident expectation in Mark 4 and which he declares in so many words in his eulogy on the Baptist (Matt. 11), amounts to the fact that in the movement to which the Baptist gave the first impetus and which still continued, there was to be discerned the coming of the Kingdom in a way which was miraculous and unintelligible, but unfailingly certain, because it lay in the power and purpose of God.

In the parables and at the sending out of the Twelve, Jesus uses the formula: "He that hath ears to hear, let him hear" (Mark 4:23; Matt. 11:15). This word signifies that the plans of God are concealed and that they are intelligible only to the chosen few. For all others they remain veiled. If this historical interpretation of the mystery of the Kingdom of God is correct, as Schweitzer assumes, then Jesus must have expected the Kingdom to come at harvest time. "And that is just what he did expect." This is the reason that he sends out the disciples to make known to Israel the urgency of the situation. Jesus was motivated by a dogmatic idea. This is evident because according to Mark the mission of the Twelve followed immediately his rejection at Nazareth. Their unreceptiveness made no impression upon him, but he <u>was</u> astonished at their unbelief (Mark 4:6). What asto<u>n</u>ished him was that in his native town of Nazareth there were so few believers, i.e., the elect who knew as he did that the Kingdom of God might appear at any moment. Thus the dogmatic motif of eschatology permeated not only Jesus' teaching but his entire outlook. "His life at this period was dominated by a 'dogmatic idea' which rendered him indifferent to all else ..." [The Quest of the Historical Jesus, pp353-56; Albert Schweitzer, The Mystery of the Kingdom of God, Walter Lowrie, trans. (New York: Dodd, Mead, 1914), pp106-10].

In another of his works Schweitzer raises the question as to whether certain of the parables do not support a spiritualized view of the Kingdom of God. The "life of Jesus" research assumed that both the ethics of Jesus and his view of the Kingdom of God were to be understood in a spiritual way. This scholarship maintained that Jesus rejected contemporary Jewish expectations concerning the Kingdom as too materialistic and that he taught a more spiritual doctrine. Neither did Jesus accept the generally-held view of messiahship. He rejected the conception of the Messiah endowed with supernatural form and might, and instead regarded the Messiah as one uniquely endowed with the power of the Spirit of God. He inaugurated the ethical Kingdom of God with his preaching and summoned others to join in its extension and realization.

Schweitzer observes that as long as the four Gospels were regarded as equally authentic sources for our knowledge of Jesus, this view was to some extent tenable. The Fourth Gospel presents Jesus as giving teachings which are more spiritual than those of Judaism. However, in time it was recognized that this spiritual teaching was not primarily related to Jesus' inward ethics, but to the Greek view of the Logos. It was intended to make Christianity acceptable to the Greeks as the true religious knowledge which had been incomprehensible to the Jews.

This spiritualized view of the Kingdom was further substantiated by reference to certain parables which relate to the Kingdom's establishment and growth. Among these parables are: the Sower, the Tares, the Mustard Seed, the Leaven. Appealing to the findings of New Testament critical scholarship, Schweitzer says that the two oldest Gospels (Mark and Matthew) do not present a doctrine of the Kingdom of God and Jesus' messiahship. This silence of Jesus appeared to justify the acceptance of a spiritual view of the Kingdom corresponding to his ethics. But this was an error. "If Jesus had wished to replace the view of the Kingdom and the Messiah current among his hearers with a different one, he would have had to give clear expression to his views, and in doing so would have provided the scribes and Pharisees with plenty of material for controversy" [Albert Schweitzer, The Kingdom of God and Primitive Christianity, L. A. Garrand, Trans. (New York: Seabury Press, 1968), pp89-90].

The eschatological emphasis which Weiss and Schweitzer brought to the fore, was applied more explicitly to the parables at a later period by C. H. Dodd and Joachim Jeremias. Rudolf Bultmann also recognized the eschatological dimension and made it one of the criteria for judging the genuineness of Jesus' similitudes. The upshot of the eschatological analysis of the parables was to divorce them from a moralistic understanding of their nature and purpose. Thus the movement begun by Weiss and Schweitzer moved parabolic interpretation farther away from Jülicher's moralistic approach, and Dodd and Jeremias made a concerted effort to arrive at the original meaning of the parables in the ministry of Jesus by recognizing their eschatological milieu.

17 THE SOCIAL GOSPEL

The Social Gospel is the name given to a movement which developed in American Protestantism during the last decades of the 19th century and the first three decades of the 20th century. The "father" of the Social Gospel in the United States was Washington Gladden (1836-1918) who was a Congregational pastor. Its best-known spokesman and ablest theologian, however, was Walter Rauschenbusch who was a Baptist pastor and later professor of church history at Rochester Theological Seminary.

As the name implies, the Social Gospel maintained that human existence is basically social, and a relevant Christianity must call men to repentance because of their collective sins. Thus the movement concentrated on such

areas as the unequal distribution of wealth, the rise of the
labor movement, the development of vast cities with their
teeming slums. It leveled sharp criticisms against the prevailing social injustices, particularly economic, and advocated more revolutionary social action on the part of the churches.

The Social Gospel was closely identified with Protestant liberalism, and the Kingdom of God was one of its
central motifs. The Kingdom of God was not to be viewed
as essentially an other-worldly goal; rather it was related
to the development of a more just social order on earth.
The Kingdom of God is a goal toward which God is working
in the world, and it will be characterized by the progres-
sive reign of love in human affairs.

This optimistic note of spiritual and social development and progress could be seen especially in the "parables
of the Kingdom" in Matthew 13. In a sermon, "Things New
and Old, " Washington Gladden referred to the Kingdom of
Heaven as "an organism steadily developing under the divine
hand. " "The parable of the Sower, the parable of the
Wheat and the Tares, the parable of the Seed Growing Secretly, the parable of the Mustard Seed, the parable of the
Leaven, all involve this thought of an orderly development
of the Kingdom of righteousness in the hearts of men, and
in the life of society" [Washington Gladden, "Things New
and Old" in Discourses of Christian Truth and Life (Columb-
us, Ohio: A. H. Smythe, 1883), pp3-4]. In another
work, Gladden referred to the Kingdom of God as one of the
"ruling ideas of the present age. " The reality of the Kingdom is here now, but its completion is yet to come. Like
the leaven in Jesus' parable it is at work everywhere. "It
is as silent as light, as subtle as life, and mightier than
either. "

The futuristic concept of the Kingdom of God has
been derived from a too literalistic reading of the apocalyptic texts. Gladden suggests that there may be future forward social movement which could be described as the
coming of Christ to the world with power and great glory.
As an example of such a situation he cites the possibility
of love as the law of all life being applied to industrial
society. "None of the apocalyptic symbolism would over-
state its dramatic significance. " He continues: "The point
to be noted is that the Kingdom is here, a Kingdom still
increasing; and that the coming which we pray for can be

nothing more than the fuller development and manifestation of the blessed life which now, in so many places, and by so many heavenly ministries, is making the earth beautiful and glad. " So the Kingdom is related to progress and social evolution. It is the same Kingdom of Heaven which Jesus proclaimed, "into which is gathered the harvest of the centuries, and by which the kingdoms of this world are being subdued to righteousness" [Washington Gladden, Ruling Ideas of the Present Age (Boston: Houghton, Mifflin, 1895), pp289-99].

For Walter Rauschenbusch the Kingdom of God was the central doctrine of the Social Gospel, and all other doctrines must be revised so that they will "articulate organically with it. " The doctrine of the Kingdom of God is itself the Social Gospel. [For Rauschenbusch's discussion of the Kingdom of God as the theological basis of the Social Gospel, see his A Theology for the Social Gospel (New York: Macmillan, 1917), pp131-66].

The popular concept of the Kingdom of God in Jesus' day and shared by Jewish apocalypticism was that it would come in the future by means of divine intervention. Moreover, its coming would be sudden and catastrophic. Rauschenbusch suggests that Jesus was moving away from the popular messianism of his time, and that in many of his parables a radically different view of the Kingdom could be discerned. If we take his real humanity seriously, we must view him as a growing personality and as one whose ideas were in the making. A person's ideas are developed by bringing them into dialogue with those of others. This is the case with Jesus' eschatological views. His "parables of the Kingdom" are all polemical in character. He chose the parabolic form of teaching because he wanted to veil and yet reveal his polemical departure from current messianic ideas. Using illustrations from organic life, he expressed the idea of the gradual growth of the Kingdom. Like germinating seeds the Kingdom of God was growing continuously and quietly until it would eventually be culminated by God. Thus Jesus was working his way toward evolutionary conceptions of the Kingdom. And because this view was so new to his followers, he used parables to avoid antagonism. Since the Kingdom of God was already at work ar.d already present, it was possible to aid in its growth and development. Rauschenbusch summarizes the above as follows:

Jesus had the scientific insight which comes to most men only by training, but to the elect few by divine gift. He grasped the substance of that law of organic development in nature and history which our own day at last has begun to elaborate systematically. His parables of the Sower, the Tares, the Net, the Mustard Seed, and the Leaven are all polemical in character. He was seeking to displace the crude and misleading catastrophic conceptions by a saner theory about the coming of the Kingdom. This conception of growth demanded not only a finer insight, but a higher faith. It takes more faith to see God in the little beginnings than in the completed results; more faith to say that God is now working than to say that he will some day work.

Because Jesus believed in the organic growth of the new society, he patiently fostered its growth, cell by cell. Every human life brought under control of the new spirit which he himself embodied and revealed was an advance of the Kingdom of God. Every time the new thought of the Father and of the right life among men gained firmer hold of a human mind and brought it to the point of action, it meant progress ... [Walter Rauschenbusch, Christianity and the Social Crisis (New York: Macmillan, 1907), pp59-60; see also A Gospel for the Social Awakening: Selections from the Writings of Walter Rauschenbusch (New York: Association Press, 1950), pp51-52; and his A Theology for the Social Gospel, pp219-20].

We have noted that the Social Gospel was concerned especially with economic injustices. A central facet of this area related to the aquisitive instinct and the question of wealth. Commenting on the parable of the Rich Fool, Rauschenbusch noted that most people would find no fault with this man because he was only practicing what most people in the modern world are trying to do. "Having made a pile, he proposed to make a bigger pile. Meanwhile he slapped his soul on the back and smacked his lips in anticipation." But Jesus regarded the "fat farmer" as a tragic comedy because there was no higher purpose in his life to redeem his acquisitiveness. Rauschenbusch says that if wealth is saved to raise and educate children, or achieve some social good, it deserves moral respect or admiration.

However, if the acquisitive instinct is without social feeling or vision, and centered on the self, it gets no commendation, at least from Jesus. Wealth has a way of growing stronger than the one who owns it so that it comes to own him and causes him to lose his moral and spiritual freedom [A Gospel for the Social Awakening, pp73-74; Christianity and the Social Crisis, pp74ff].

Rauschenbusch makes further observations about wealth in reference to the parable of the Rich Man and Lazarus. The rich man is not accused of any crimes or vices, and yet he is sent to hell. Rauschenbusch notes that Jesus must have regarded as deeply immoral and sinful a life given to sumptuous living and indifferent to the want and misery of a fellow human at his doorstep. Jesus used his energies to bring people close together in love, but wealth divides because it creates semi-human relations between social classes. It regards a small dole as the full discharge of obligations toward the poor. The real sting of this parable is in the reference to the five brothers who were still living as Dives had lived, and whom he was vainly trying to contact [A Gospel for the Social Awakening, p75].

Another aspect of the moral difficulties attending wealth can be seen in the parable of the Unjust Steward. Rauschenbusch observes that there are something like 36 different interpretations on record, and the parable has been so widely allegorized that there is doubt whether the lord of the steward is God or the devil. Rauschenbusch believes that the parable is simple if we "handle it as Jesus did." Jesus' application of the parable is that the men who had the dishonest money of the present era should use it in their brief term of power before the coming of the Messianic era. They should exercise kindness to the children of the Kingdom so that they themselves might get "some sort of borrowed shelter" when the tables are turned and they will be at the mercy of the pious poor.

Rauschenbusch notes that this parable shows a very keen insight into contemporary methods of grafting and into the state of mind of the grafter. Moreover, no one could have told this story who had not thought incisively about social conditions. There is no need to defend Jesus because he appears to hold up an immoral transaction for admiration and imitation. Jesus was so far above financial trickery that he could use such illustrations just as a confirmed

socialist might illustrate the strengths of socialism by referring to the watering of stock or to some other under-
handed economic practices. This parable has been distorted
by allegorization, but it applies to the rich, and Rauschenbusch says that Jesus' contemporary hearers saw the point.
Jesus' intention was to warn the rich that they must show
generosity now before it is too late and before they are
cast into hell as Dives was.

Of the evangelists, Luke is the most socially aware
and has the strongest sense of economic justice. He alone
reports the parables of the Rich Fool, the Unjust Steward,
and Dives and Lazarus. But Luke is also the one who
alone gives the parables of the Good Samaritan, the Prodigal Son, and the Pharisee and the Publican. Thus Rauschenbusch writes about Luke: "The socialist among the evangelists was also the one who has given us the richest expressions of the free grace of God to sinful men, without which
our evangel would be immeasurably poorer" [Christianity
and the Social Crisis, pp78-82].

18   FORM CRITICISM

The "history of forms" (Formgeschichte) which is
commonly known as "form criticism" is a method of analysis and interpretation of preliterary or oral traditions. The
form critical methodology was applied to the Bible and represented an attempt to trace the history of the biblical
material before it was written down. The pioneering work
was done in the Old Testament and later in the New Testament, especially the Synoptic Gospels, where it received
its widest recognition. Form criticism is based on the
assumption that the traditions of a community are determined and shaped by its life and needs. Thus various
settings and purposes give rise to specific forms. The
form critic attempts to discern the Sitz im Leben for the
forms studied. Rudolf Bultmann notes that every literary
category has its Sitz im Leben ("life situation"), whether
it be worship in its different forms, or work, or hunting,
or war. Applying form criticism to the Synoptics, Bultmann "sets out to give an account of the history of the
individual units of the tradition, and how the tradition passed from a fluid state to the fixed form in which it meets us
in the Synoptics...." Bultmann states that "The aim of
form criticism is to determine the original form of a piece
of narrative, a dominical saying, or a parable. In the

process we learn to distinguish secondary additions and forms, and these in turn lead to important results for the history of the tradition" [Rudolf Bultmann, The History of the Synoptic Tradition, rev. ed., John Marsh, trans. (New York: Harper & Row, 1968), pp3, 4, 6]. Martin Dibelius in From Tradition to Gospel [Bertram Lee Woolf, trans. (London: James Clarke, 1971), p6] states the objective of this volume as "the right to read the Gospels from the standpoint of the development of their form."

One of the first scholars to relate the form critical method to the Bible was Hermann Gunkel whose work was primarily in the Old Testament. It was, however, with criticism of the Gospels that form criticism became most widely identified. The pioneers here were Karl Ludwig Schmidt, Martin Dibelius, Rudolf Butlmann, and Martin Albertz. In reference to the parables, Dibelius and Bultmann discuss them in some detail, while Schmidt and Albertz make only brief and passing references to them. [For comments on Schmidt's and Albertz's references to the parables, see Geraint Vaughan Jones, The Art and Truth of the Parables (London: S. P. C. K., 1964), p48].

MARTIN DIBELIUS

One of Dibelius' basic contentions regarding the sayings of Jesus is that the early church perceived them in paranetic or moral-hortatory terms. The sayings were originally brought together not to deal with the life of Jesus or for the sake of their christological interest, but that they may be followed and in order that they may instruct. "The sayings of Jesus were originally gathered together for a hortatory end, to give the churches advice, help, and commandment by means of the Master's words" [Dibelius, From Tradition to Gospel, pp245, 246]. This hortatory character of many of Jesus' words was emphasized and strengthened by tradition and can be seen in certain parabolic narratives.

The parable of the Unjust Steward contains an example of decision and translated into eschatological terms it offers doctrine and warning in the face of great change. Yet in Luke 16:9 there is an exhortation which forms a conclusion to the parable: "Make friends for yourselves by means of unrighteous mammon." The parable of the Marriage Feast (Matt. 22:1-10) has been filled out by the parable of the Wedding Garment (Matt. 22:11-14). Dibelius

observes that the hortatory significance of the latter is clear.
Whoever is invited to the Kingdom must have a wedding garment, i. e., something which identifies him as a subject of
the Kingdom. The effort, however, to provide the churches
with as many exhortations as possible sometimes occasioned
complete misunderstandings of parables. The exhortation
to choose the lowest place at the wedding was originally
meant as a parable cautioning against false-righteous pretensions before God. Dibelius concludes, by reference to Luke
14:7-11, that the exhortation to exhibit humility at a feast
to which one is invited shows that a rule for conduct at
table has grown out of an eschatological warning [ibid.,
p248].

Dibelius distinguishes between four types of parabolic material: (1) what is commonplace, as the parable of
the Leaven; (2) what is typical, as in the parable of the
Playing Children (Matt. 11:16f; Luke 7:3f.) and the Sower;
(3) what is extraordinary; and (4) imaginary cases. The
distinction between the first two types is that in the narrative of the commonplace events, what is said is unimportant in itself, because it is always happening, while in the
second type it is brought out because it is frequent, and it
is noteworthy, but not remarkable, in the common sense of
the word. The last two types concern remarkable matters.
The third group deals with isolated events in real life; the
fourth with improbable or impossible happenings which have
been imagined in order to serve a didactic purpose. Dibelius says that in general the great parables of Luke belong
to the third group, and that it is difficult to classify some
other parables because we cannot answer the question of
the possibility of the events concerned.

Concerning the differences in the application of the
parabolic material, Dibelius believes that three methods of
application may be observed. First, the story of the parable sometimes contains a didactic thought in its application
as in the Good Samaritan and the Pharisee and the Publican.
In the latter parable there is a paranetic tendency to add
an ethical meaning even when it is evident. Secondly, the
story "really clothes the leading thought." Thus the action
takes place not by its own right, but as dictated by a didactic conception. One can explain the parable of the Tares
in this way because the "enemy" is presented as if he were
a known personality, but is rather arch-"enemy," the devil.
Consequently, we have an allegory even though the servants
are not "explained." Dibelius observes that the clearest

mark of allegorical purpose is the fictitious character of the narrative which cannot be altogether understood from itself alone. The third type of application is the story which exists by its own poetic right. However, an element of the action is concerned with the idea of teaching although this belongs to quite another sphere than the action of the comparison. This is the nature of parable in the special sense of the word [ibid., pp253-54].

The question as to whether a parable is concerned with only one point is difficult to answer because those who made use of the parables often extended and edited them. Any certainty of judgment is impossible because as a rule we do not know to what situation a given parable was originally directed. "We must reckon with the fact that we do not know the original references of numerous parables" [ibid., pp254-55].

Another problem related to the parabolic tradition is rooted in the fact that certain metaphors were already customary in Jewish exhortation and the hearer was prone to understand the words in the usual sense even when the parabolic narrative gives no occasion to do so. Dibelius notes that the mention of a king referred to God; a vineyard, to the people; a field, to the world; a harvest, to the Last Judgment; a marriage, to the commencement of the Messianic era. In this way half-allegorical forms might have arisen, for in retelling the parables those metaphors might have been unwittingly employed. Also, the recognized metaphorical words, perhaps occurring in the text of the parable without special significance, were allegorically transmuted. The introduction of such metaphors into a parable may have resulted occasionally in a kind of allegory of which the narrator was scarcely conscious. What happens, however, is that the style of the pure parable is considerably altered by such allegorization, and the result is a type of narrative which can neither be called pure parable-form nor allegory. Dibelius concludes that it is difficult to say to what extent such half-allegorical forms go back to Jesus.

What can be said, however, is that the tendency of the churches to derive as much exhortation as possible from the words of Jesus must have affected the transmission of the parables. This development toward exhortation can be illustrated by the parable of the Sower. One may consider the parable as a short didactic narrative with a typical but not ordinary "story" containing nothing which

is invented for the benefit of the explanation. If the parable existed originally without application its meaning is certain: it was intended to convey consolation in the face of
misfortune and failures--just as the parables of the Mustard
Seed and the Leaven give comfort in regard to small beginning which may have referred to the movement which Jesus
initiated. But the paranetic influence comes into play, and
more was desired from the narrative than consolation. There
needed to be a teaching or warning against misfortune, and
so the different types of bad ground which yielded no fruit
were explained. Originally the parable offered comfort,
noting that misfortunes are unavoidable, for even the sower
does not escape them. But in the explanation the warning
is given that one should not be like those among whom the
word does not find good soil. But this paranetic transformation is so close to the growth of tradition that we can
scarcely conceive the parable in tradition apart from its
explanation. Consequently, Dibelius says that we owe the
preservation of the words of Jesus in this parable to the
desire for exhortation. As Dibelius noted earlier, the parables of the Unjust Steward and of the Pharisee and the Publican received a hortatory conclusion. This is likewise the
case with the parable of the Rich Fool [ibid., pp255-58].
Thus, in keeping with the form-critical methodology, Dibelius maintains that one of the major factors influencing the
development and transmission of the parabolic narratives,
as well as their interpretation, was the paranetic or hortatory tendency or requirement of the early Christian community.

RUDOLF BULTMANN

One of the most significant and detailed contributions
to form criticism was Bultmann's Die Geschichte der synoptischen Tradition (1921) (The History of the Synoptic Tradition). In this work Bultmann devotes a section to the
characteristics and development of the parabolic material.
He uses a number of categories to describe this material.
There are Bildworte (word-pictures, figures), and in the
Synoptic Gospels there are a whole series of them, e.g. the
city on the hill, the fruitful and unfruitful trees, the physician and the sick, fasting at the wedding feast, physician
heal thyself, etc. Moreover, they often consist of parallels, as for example, figs, grapes; disciples, teacher; new
garments and old; new wine and old.

A second form is metaphors which are related to

Bildworte, being shortened comparisons lacking the comparative word. Examples are the Mote and the Beam, the Narrow Way and the Narrow Gate, Good and Bad Treasure in
the Heart, the Laborers and the Harvest, Putting One's
Hand to the Plow.

Next are the Gleichnisse (similitudes) which are distinguished from Bildworte and metaphors only by the detail
in which the picture is painted, and a similitude can be
formed from the latter two indifferently. In this category
Bultmann includes: the Tower and the War, the Lost Sheep
and the Lost Coin, the Faithful Servant, Children at Play,
Mustard Seed, Leaven, Hid Treasure, Pearl of Great Price,
Dragnet, Two Builders, etc. Bultmann analyzes each of
these briefly as to their development and application.

Fourthly, there is the parable which does not bring
two sorts of facts together, but transposes the facts which
serve for a similitude into a story which does not picture
a typical condition or a typical, recurrent event, but some
particular situation. Bultmann lists 15 parables: the
Friend at Midnight, the Importunate Widow, the Sower, the
Barren Fig Tree, the Great Supper, the Prodigal Son, the
Unjust Steward, the Talents, the Ten Virgins, the Tares,
the Unmerciful Servant, the Laborers in the Vineyard, the
Wicked Vinedressers, the Two Debtors, the Two Sons.

Bultmann's fifth category is Beispielerzählungen
(exemplary stories or tales) which have a close formal relationship to parables. Here Bultmann classes the Good
Samaritan, the Rich Fool, Dives and Lazarus (which has
two points), the Pharisee and the Publican, and the Places
for Seats at the Feast [Rudolf Bultmann, The History of the
Synoptic Tradition, John Marsh, trans. (New York: Harper
& Row, 1968), pp. 166-79].

In a section on the form and history of the parabolic
material, Bultmann notes that just as the figurative sayings
begin without any special introduction so does the similitude
which is a development of it. However, it would be wrong
to conclude that in every case this primitive form was the
original of the similitude. The similitudes which have grown
out of a metaphor may begin with or without an introductory
question. Bultmann discusses the variations to be found
in the construction, the form of statement, and the ending
of similitudes. He attempts to trace the development of the
tradition and to discern the primary and secondary elements.

In order to "complete the analysis of style," Bultmann digresses from the history of the tradition to deal with the "technique of telling a similitude." He discusses 12 techniques or characteristics:

(1) Conciseness and economy characterize the narrative. Only the necessary persons appear. In the story of the Prodigal Son, for example, there is no mother; in the parable of the Importunate Friend there is no wife of the disturbed sleeper. There are never more than three chief characters, and for the most part only two as in the Unjust Judge and the Pharisee and the Publican. Groups of people are treated as a single person as in the Wicked Vinedressers and are only differentiated in so far as it is necessary. Only two speakers or actors appear at one time. If others are present, they remain in the background. If more than two have to speak or act, they have to do it in separate successive scenes, e. g. the steward deals with his master's debtors one by one; the father asks his sons one at a time to go into his vineyard; the servants come with their talents one after another to their master, and he does not receive a report from all three before he distributes rewards and punishment.

(2) There is a single perspective so that one is not asked to watch two different series of events happening at the same time. In the parable of the Prodigal Son the whole story is told from the point of view of the Prodigal. The same is true of the Unforgiving Servant. Bultmann notes that the only exception to this pattern is in Luke's version of the parable of the Talents, but this is due to "secondary editing." In Matthew the story proceeds from a single perspective.

(3) Only seldom are the characters portrayed by some attribute. For the most part people are characterized by what they say or do, or how they behave.

(4) Feelings and motives are mentioned only when they are essential for the action or the point. Generally feelings are only portrayed indirectly or left to the hearer's own imagination.

(5) Secondary participants are only described when necessary. In the Good Samaritan there is no description of either the man who went down to Jericho or the innkeeper. The Importunate Widow is only characterized by her persistency.

(6) One of the major characteristics of the parables is the complete lack of motivation because it is irrelevant to the point of the parable. Thus the Prodigal's request for his share of the inheritance and his journey into a far country are unmotivated. Similarly we are not told why the employer needed so many laborers for his vineyard as to go out every three hours to employ more. The reason for the travelers' journey in the parable of the Good Samaritan is not disclosed. Likewise the reason for the different answers and the different behavior in the parable of the Two Sons is not included in the story.

(7) A conclusion is absent if it is self-evident or irrelevant. We are not told whether the Rich Fool died the same night, or what success the Unjust Steward's deceit brought. Did the barren fig tree bear fruit that year? or what happened to it? Did the man whom the Good Samaritan helped recover quickly? or did he have to spend more money on him? It is irrelevant or unnecessary for us to know the answers to these questions.

(8) There is an economy governing the description of events and actions so that anything unnecessary is omitted. We are not told how the widow implored the judge, but are given just a very brief indication that she did. However, whatever is described is done so in very concrete terms, e. g. the Prodigal Son becomes a swineherd; when he returns home his father clothes him with the best robe, adorns him with a ring, and kills the fatted calf. The luxury of the Rich Man and the deplorable condition of poor Lazarus are vividly portrayed.

(9) There is the use of direct speech and soliloquy. Examples of the latter are to be found in the parables of the Prodigal Son, the Unjust Steward, the Unjust Judge, the Rich Fool, the Unfaithful Servant, the Wicked Vinedressers, the Pharisee and the Publican.

(10) The law of repetition is exemplified in the repeating of the phrase, "Have patience with me, and I will pay you," in the parable of the Unmerciful Servant. The Prodigal Son confesses twice. A threefold repetition is in the parable of the Great Supper. Three types of guests make their excuses. Three sorts of servants are entrusted with money. Priest, Levite, and Samaritan go down the road to Jericho. The owner of the fig tree has already looked for fruit on it in vain for three years.

(11) The most important thing is left to the end. In the parable of the Sower the fruitful seed is mentioned last. The Rich Man is portrayed before Lazarus because the story is intended to tell the poor to be contented with their lot. The Publican is introduced after the Pharisee. The Servant who did not use the money entrusted to him is presented last in keeping with the hortatory nature of the story.

(12) The hearer's judgment is precipitated although the moral quality of the characters is not always the subject of judgment, e. g. it is evident that the Steward and the Judge are unscrupulous. But they should not be judged on this account, and we should realize that it is possible to learn something even from such rascals as these. In other cases we are required to pass a moral verdict on some action as in the parables of the Prodigal Son, the Talents, the Unforgiving Servant, the Two Sons, where the point of the parable is directed to such a verdict. Such a purpose is also often served by the antithesis of two types: the Two Debtors, the Two Sons, the Wise and Foolish Virgins, the Two Servants, the Rich Man and Lazarus, the Pharisee and the Publican, the Priest and Levite and the Samaritan.

Concerning the development of the parabolic narratives Bultmann notes several further characteristics. The parables have been set in a particular context which may take the form of an introduction which does not strictly belong to the parable as such, e. g. Luke has used the question about the greatest commandment as an introduction to the parable of the Good Samaritan. Matthew attached the parable of the Unforgiving Servant to the saying about forgiveness. The parable of the Lost Sheep in Matthew 18:12-14 has been given a new meaning by its introduction. Thus Bultmann says that we must always raise the question whether the evangelists have given the parables their proper setting.

Another method by which the parabolic material has undergone even more radical expansions and transformations in the history of the tradition can be seen in the so-called double similitudes. Examples are the Building of the Tower and Going to War; Divided Kingdom and Divided House; Mustard Seed and Leaven; the Treasure and the Pearl: the Lost Sheep and the Lost Coin. In these instances a new similitude is put alongside another which is quite complete and independent in itself, thus providing a parallel structure in which the same idea is clothed in new material. As to whether the doubling is original or whether the second portion is a secondary accretion, Bultmann feels that the former alternative is the more likely since "such doubling is a very old and widespread instrument of the story teller's art."

There are further expansions and combinations in the tradition. One instance is in Luke 12:45-48 where a narrower meaning is given to the parable of the Servant in Authority by combining it with the figurative saying in verses 47ff. Similarly the parable of the Great Supper in Matthew 22:1-10 is enlarged by an allegorical appendix in verses 11-14 which Bultmann feels is secondary when compared with the Lucan parallel. A comparison with Matthew 25:14-30 shows that Luke 19:12-27 is a secondary combination of the parable of the Talents with an allegory of the departure and return of Jesus. Given the tendency toward expansion and combination, Bultmann questions whether the second part of the parable of the Prodigal Son, Luke 15:25-32, is not a secondary expansion of the first part, Luke 15:11-24, and whether originally the first part was told more briefly. He likewise challenges the authenticity of the second part of the parable of the Rich Man and Lazarus and suggests that a Jewish story lies behind Luke 16:19-31. Other passages which Bultmann believes to be secondary are Mark 13:33-37 and Luke 12:35-38.

Another special class of transformation is the allegorical expansion. To this class belong Matthew 22:11-14 and Luke's addition in 19:12-27. Bultmann replies to Jülicher's critics who maintain that his method of dismissing everything allegorical does violence to the material in the interest of abstract theory. What Fiebig, for example, adduces as allegorical features in rabbinic parables are not that at all, but metaphors.

In summary, Bultmann emphasizes that the original meaning of many similitudes has become irrecoverable in the course of the tradition. There is no doubt that the parables of the Fig Tree and the Faithful Steward are rightly interpreted as parables of the Parousia. In other instances the general meaning is clear enough, but not the special point, because the occasion which prompted the parable is not known.

In comparing the Synoptic and Jewish traditions,

Bultmann says that it is possible to suppose or to maintain
that Jewish material has been introduced into the Synoptic
tradition. Therefore one must ask whether some of the
Synoptic parables have not been taken from the Jewish tradition by the church and put into Jesus' mouth. One example of very great probability, according to Bultmann, is
Luke 16:19-31. Other elements of community formulations
can be discerned in the parables of the Wicked Vinedressers
and the Ten Virgins. The same applies to the "secondary
composition," Mark 13:33-37 and Luke 12: 35-38, and for
the parables of the Lost Coin and of the Leaven, if they are
viewed as analogous formulations to those of the Lost Sheep
and the Mustard Seed. Moreover, Bultmann contends that
for the rest, the possibility remains even when no proof
can be provided in particular cases. In conclusion, Bultmann proposes a criterion for judging whether a given parable is a genuine parable of Jesus or not. It is genuine if
it expresses a contrast between Jewish morality and piety
and the distinctive eschatological temper which characterized the preaching of Jesus; and if it contains no specifically Christian features [ibid., pp179-205].

The contribution of form criticism to our understanding of the parables does not lie in the interpretation
or the application of them but in an attempt to ascertain the
"history" of the Synoptic tradition and of the forms or types
in which that tradition has come down to us. The form
critics are primarily concerned with the transition from the
oral tradition to the written word. Dibelius' and Bultmann's
work is helpful and illuminating because it aids us in understanding the community's probable motivation and intention
in the transmission of the parabolic narratives; and it assists
us in recognizing the various forms and characteristics of
this material. But beyond that the form critics cannot go,
and one must ask whether some of their conclusions (especially Bultmann's) are not more ambitious than the available
evidence warrants. Let us conclude with Geraint Jones'
observations regarding form criticism and the parables:

> Although it throws some light on the traditional
> character of Jesus' method of teaching, it throws
> none on the question of its application. Form
> criticism, too, is the study of a process, not of
> the idea, though it may help to elucidate the
> final form in which the idea appears. It is dif-
> ficult to see how form criticism can go further
> than this.... What is reasonably certain is that

the parables share in the same process of transmission as the other words of Jesus in the Synoptic Gospels. How far those which have no parallel versions by which they can be checked are to
be regarded as the ipsissima verba cannot be as-
certained ... [Jones, Art and Truth of the Parables, p51].

19   A. T. CADOUX

Writing more than 30 years after Jülicher's epochal
work, Cadoux observed that while Jülicher showed that the
parables of Jesus were not allegories, nevertheless, no one
had made "thorough use of the methods which must thus
supersede those of the hitherto usual allegorical interpretation." Cadoux hoped to rectify this situation even though
his conclusions might be called "far-fetched" [A. T. Cadoux,
The Parables of Jesus: Their Art and Use, (London:
James Clarke, 1930), p7]. Jülicher's notion that a parable
dealt with one point was widely accepted. The view, however, that it grows out of and is a response to a given
historical situation, was not adequately examined until after
the advent of form criticism. Cadoux consequently sup-
plemented Jülicher's work by applying his method as well
as that of form criticism. Subsequent parabolic scholarship
reveals that Cadoux was a notable precursor of the significant work of Dodd and Jeremias. He also reflected existentialist motifs which were to play a vital role in certain
20th-century interpreters of the parables.

Cadoux's intention is to illuminate the parables' Sitz
im Leben. While the parables of Jesus are works of art,
they are not art in its highest form. They are rather "art
harnessed for service and conflict." Cadoux's major contention is that the parables had a polemical and apologetic
intent. He believes that almost all the parables of Jesus,
of whose occasion we are fairly sure, were spoken in attack or defence. "The parable is thus both more and less
than a work of art.... In its most characteristic use the
parable is a weapon of controversy, not shaped like a son-
net in undisturbed concentration, but improvised in conflict
to meet an unpremeditated situation [ibid., pp11-13].

In reference to the question of the parable and the
early church, Cadoux finds in both Matthew 13 and Mark 4
evidence that when the gospels took their present form,

there was confusion of thought with regard to the parables and their intelligibility. Cadoux questions whether Jesus ever interpreted his parables. If he had made this a regular practice, the interpretations would have been preserved as faithfully as the parables themselves. What happened was that the church, later finding the parables unintelligible, added interpretations some of which came to be attributed to Jesus. When the material passed from oral tradition to written document, it must often have been very difficult for the writer to distinguish between the words of Jesus and the comments of the apostles and others. What happened was that the endeavor or controversy which the parables were rooted in and dealt with was forgotten and ignored, and therefore "its concrete and vital movements must grow unintelligible." Cadoux concludes that it should be expected and should not surprise us that the early church, putting its own interpretation upon history, and living in conditions that differed from those of its birth, lost the meaning of many of the parables. But one must also conclude that the causes that made them unintelligible would contribute to the positive understanding of some of them. An examination of many of the parables leads Cadoux to the observation that where the interpretations have been appended to the parables or implied by the arrangement of material, they give evidence of coming from someone other than the author of the parable. Cadoux adds further that this conclusion has very few exceptions. In contrast to this, where the parable and the circumstances of its origin are preserved for us, the point of the parable at once finds its incidence in the circumstances of its origin [ibid., pp15-42].

As long as the evangelists held that the parables could not be understood without interpretation, they regarded them as allegories instead of parables, and as allegories they interpreted them. Cadoux credits Jülicher for insisting upon the difference between parable and allegory as vital to an understanding of the parables. However, Jülicher and his followers suffer from a serious defect which was also common to the allegorizers whom they dethroned. In his insistence that a parable was intended to enforce one single general principle, Jülicher ignores the point of the parable's application. What one must look for, according to Cadoux, is an answer to the problem of the parable's concrete circumstance. Whenever there is reliable indication of the parable's occasion, Cadoux states that we have to ask three questions: What is the natural point of the picture or story? What is the outstanding interest of the occasion? What does the point of the story persuade us to think about the outstanding interest of the occasion? It is reasonable to assume that Jesus would not use parables when plain speech would serve as well. Consequently, Cadoux believes that they belong to occasions of controversy and difficulty and that we should therefore expect to find their application in the concrete conditions of Jesus' work. To this another important consideration must be added, viz. that the parable elicits a judgment in one sphere in order to transfer it to another [ibid., pp43-49].

One of Cadoux's major claims is that the parables must be understood within the context of Jesus' relationship to the Jews. His aim was to win Israel as a nation for the service of the Kingdom of God. However, Israel rejected and killed him, but his followers tended to forget this and regarded all his hope and intent as having been fulfilled in the church. Hence there was a tendency to regard certain of his utterances as having been spoken to his followers, when the utterances themselves indicate that they were spoken to Jews as Jews. In a lengthy chapter "Parables of Israel and the Nations," Cadoux interprets a number of Jesus' parables and sayings in order to substantiate his thesis [ibid., pp80-115].

As we have noted, Cadoux holds that the parable is characteristically a weapon of controversy. In some of the parables this element is especially prominent, and he believes that these happen to be those of whose exact occasion we are best informed. A case in point is the parable of the Two Sons in Matthew 21:28-32 in which Jesus sets before the authorities these two sons and asks their opinion. Jesus answered them by saying that in giving their preference to the hypocritical son they have made their own condemnation complete.

Another example is Jesus' "most beautiful parable"-- the Prodigal Son. Cadoux observes that it is vitally related to its occasion, apart from which we should not understand why the story did not end with the prodigal's return. All three parts of the story, though the last chapter has the "fighting point," call from us a judgment which becomes our answer to the criticism of scribe and Pharisee.

Cadoux believes that the parable of the Rich Man and Lazarus reflects another challenge of the Pharisees. In Mark 8:11-12 the Pharisees seek from Jesus a "sign from

heaven." The Pharisees and the Sadducees were sharpely
divided on the question of future life. The Sadducees refused to believe in it on the ground that it went beyond
what was in the Law. Cadoux notes:

> In the story of the Rich Man and Lazarus, Jesus
> hints that here, where the Pharisees were going
> beyond the Law, a sign from heaven would seem
> at first sight exactly what they needed to warrant
> their belief, and that its absence could be ac-
> counted for only on the assumption that heaven
> knew that a sign from heaven was useless in mat-
> ters of belief. But if that was so in the Phari-
> sees' case, why not in his? [He then adds,] We
> see in this story the art by which parable serves
> better than naked argument.

Another "parable of conflict" is the Unjust Steward.
The main point of the parable, according to Cadoux, concerns the way in which the steward tried to secure his own
safety and comfort at the expense of his trust. The original application of this point was to the high priests. Like
the steward they had neglected that which had been entrusted
to them, and in order to secure their position they succeeded in gaining favorable treatment with those who were willing for a time to maintain them in a position of ease and
dignity. Jesus' severe indictment in this parable "follows
fitly upon the half-pitying, half-contemptuous picture which
the parable gives of the political astuteness of the high
priestly party." Cadoux further concludes: "This parable
follows immediately upon that of the prodigal. There the
elder brother gives us the spirit of scribe and Pharisee:
here the fraudulent steward stands for Jesus' judgment upon
the high priests. And these were the two classes that com-
bined to kill him" [ibid., pp116-37].

In addition to the foregoing parabolic categories,
Cadoux sets forth several others. Certain of Jesus' parables are "parables of vindication" which were given to
vindicate his conduct when critics challenged it, or when it
needed explanation or justification to his disciples or the
multitude. Among these are: the Wineskins, the Patch,
the Hid Treasure, the Pearl of Great Price, the Ten Virgins, the Sower, the Tares. Though Cadoux's interpretation of these parables may appear strained, nevertheless,
he finds that each one has its Sitz im Leben in Jesus' attempt to vindicate himself [ibid., pp138-59].

Other types of parables which Cadoux describes are:
"parables of crisis and opportunity, " e. g. the Two Builders;
"parables of the future, " e. g. the Budding Fig Tree, the
Unjust Judge; "parables of duty and personality, " e. g. the
Good Samaritan; and "parables of God and man, " e. g. the
Talents, the Pharisee and the Publican, the Prodigal Son,
the Lost Sheep [ibid. , pp160-242].

20   C. H. DODD

In the spring of 1935 C. H. Dodd delivered the Shaf-
fer Lectures at the Divinity School of Yale University which
were subsequently published as The Parables of the Kingdom.   This work proved to be a significant milestone in the
history of the interpretation of the parables.   His purpose
was two-fold: to explore the eschatological dimensions of
the parables, and to determine the original intention of a
given parable in its historical setting.

Dodd noted that the parables are perhaps the most
characteristic element in the teaching of Jesus as recorded
in the Gospels, and that there is certainly no part of the
Gospel record which has for the reader a clearer ring of
authenticity.   Their interpretation, however, is another
matter.   In the traditional teaching of the church for centuries they were treated as allegories, and this approach
prevailed down to the time of Archbishop Trench.   It was
the great merit of Jülicher that he applied a thoroughgoing
criticism to allegorization and showed that the parables in
general do not admit of this method at all.   But he and his
followers tended to make the process of interpretation end
with a generalization.   Dodd had followed Jülicher in rejecting the allegorical method of interpretation, but he found
that he was unable to follow him much farther.   Dodd was
not convinced that all the wealth of observation and imagination in the parables was intended by Jesus to simply
teach the great enduring commonplaces of morals and religion.

One reason that Dodd could not accept Jülicher's conclusions was his concern about the problem of eschatology
in the Gospels, particularly as it bears upon the idea of the
Kingdom of God.   Johannes Weiss and Albert Schweitzer
maintained that Jesus' understanding of the Kingdom of God
was apocalyptic and otherwordly and that its advent was
imminent.   Dodd believed that after Schweitzer's Quest of

the Historical Jesus "it was no longer possible to dispose of difficult eschatological passages by declaring them unauthentic or treating them as marginal and unimportant." However, Dodd was unconvinced by Schweitzer's formula of consequente Eschatologie. One needed still to seek, and Dodd believed that in order to arrive at a clearer view of the problem it was necessary to take special account of the Gospel parables, particularly those which deal with the theme of the Kingdom of God.

The eschatological nature of the parables confronts the interpreter with the task of finding out, if he can, the setting of a parable in the situation contemplated by the Gospels, and hence the application which would suggest itself to one who stood in that situation. The teaching of Jesus is not the leisurely and patient exposition of a system by the founder of a school. Rather it is related to a brief and tremendous crisis in which he is the principal figure and which indeed his appearance brought about. Thus we should expect the parables to bear upon the actual and critical situation in which Jesus and his hearers stood, and in seeking their application we must look, not to the area of general principles, but to the particular setting in which they were delivered. As noted previously, and as Dodd acknowledges, this was the great merit of A. T. Cadoux's work. In a summary statement, Dodd writes:

> I have tried to show that while Jülicher laid the foundation for a right understanding of them, his method needs to be supplemented by a serious attempt to relate the parables to their particular setting in the crisis which the ministry of Jesus created. That setting, so far as we can discover it, must determine the original meaning and application of any parable, even though it may be both legitimate and useful to look for the general in the particular, and so find a secondary application to ourselves [C. H. Dodd, "The Gospel Parables," Bulletin of the John Rylands Library 16 (July 1932), 405-06, 412].

In his book, The Parables of the Kingdom, Dodd devotes a lengthy section to the "Kingdom of God" and the "Day of the Son of Man" in which he sets forth his position of "realized eschatology."

The eschaton has moved from the future to the

present, from the sphere of expectation into that
of realized experience.... Here then is the fixed
point from which our interpretation of the teaching
regarding the Kingdom of God must start. It represents the ministry of Jesus as 'realized eschatology,' that is to say, as the impact upon this
world of the 'powers of the world to come' in a
series of events, unprecedented and unrepeatable,
now in actual process [C. H. Dodd, The Parables
of the Kingdom, rev. ed. (New York: Scribner's,
1961), pp34-35].

It is within this context--this Sitz im Leben--that Dodd analyzes 32 of the parables and brings them within the framework of the announcement of the Kingdom as the arrival of
the great decisive moment.

Among the parables explicitly referring to the Kingdom of God, two of the shortest and simplest are the Hid
Treasure and the Costly Pearl. Dodd believes that these
parables are not intended to illustrate any general maxim,
but to enforce an appeal which Jesus was making for a
specific course of action then and there. If one agrees that
the Kingdom of God was in some way identified with the
cause of Jesus, then the argument may be stated thus:
You agree that the Kingdom of God is the highest good: it
is within your power to possess it here and now, if, like
the treasure-finder and the pearl-merchant, you will throw
caution to the winds: "Follow me!" Two other parables
that reflect the same situation are the Tower-Builder and
the King Going to War (Luke 14:28-33). These are associated by the evangelist with the call of Jesus to take great
risks with open eyes. The two parables of the Patched
Garment and the Wineskins show that it is folly to accom-
modate the old and the new. The ministry of Jesus is
something entirely new and must not be understood as an attempt to reform Judaism. In other words, "The Law and
the prophets were until John; from his time the Kingdom of
God is proclaimed" [ibid., pp85-87, 90].

Dodd observes that the most difficult of the parables
referring to the existing situation is that of the Wicked
Husbandmen. He disagrees with Jülicher and his followers
who view it as an allegory constructed by the early church
with the death of Jesus in retrospect. Dodd thinks that it
may have been somewhat expanded, but that the story in its
main lines is natural and realistic in every way. The para-

ble stands on its own feet as a dramatic story which invites judgment from the hearers. There is no need for allegorizing because the application of the judgment is clear enough. Nevertheless, the climax of iniquity in the story suggests a similar climax in the situation to which it is applied. We know that Jesus did regard his own ministry as the culmination of God's dealings with His people, and that he declared that the guilt of all righteous blood from Abel to Zechariah would fall upon that generation. Consequently, the parable would suggest, by a kind of tragic irony, the impending climax of the rebellion of Israel in a murderous assault upon the successor of the prophets. Taken in this way, the parable of the Wicked Husbandmen helps to illuminate those sayings of Jesus in which he foretells his own death and the disasters to fall upon the Jews. Thus, Dodd concludes, that although it is only in the secondary comment in Matthew that there is any allusion to the Kingdom of God, yet this parable is a true "parable of the Kingdom, " since it points to the final crisis in the dealings of God with His people [ibid. , pp96-102].

In the parables discussed thus far there is no difficulty in seeing that they had a contemporary reference which has been generally recognized in the exegetical tradition. Dodd suggests that many other parables originally had a similar reference, but this reference has been more or less obscured in our Gospels through the influence of readily recognizable motives arising out of the changed situation after the death of Jesus. The standpoint of the church changed, and this had an effect on the interpretation of the parables.

Dodd believes that the church which preserved the teaching of Jesus kept vivid for a long time the sense of living in a new age which is implied in Jesus' declaration, "The Kingdom of God has come upon you. " Beginning with the apostolic preaching in the book of Acts, through the Epistles of Paul, Hebrews, and the Fourth Gospel, the testimony of the church is unanimous, that it is living in the age of fulfillment. However, the situation of the church was different from the situation in which Jesus taught. The church originally expected that the whole meaning of the crisis would reveal itself before all eyes in the shortest possible time. But as the months and years passed by, the sense of crisis faded. Those who took Jesus' words literally now built up a new Christian eschatology along the lines of Jewish apocalyptic literature. This is evident in the apocalyptic section of Mark 13, in Matthew, and completed in the book of Revelation. The assumption is that at a date in the future the interrupted eschatological process will be resumed.

The result of this development was that the original unity and continuity of the eschatological process was broken up. Thus there is a profound and significant difference between the outlook of the sayings of Jesus and that of the formed tradition of his teaching as it entered into our written Gospels. The sayings were uttered in and for a brief period of intense crisis: the tradition was formed in a period of stable and growing corporate life, conceived as the interval between two crises, one past, the other yet to come. Dodd suggests that this condition would lead the church to reapply and reinterpret Jesus' teaching according to the needs of the new situation. This would happen in two ways. One, the church would tend to give a general and permanent application to sayings originally directed towards an immediate and particular situation; and two, it would tend to give to sayings which were originally associated with the historical crisis of the past, an application to the expected crisis of the future [ibid., pp102-05].

There is a group of parables designated by Dodd as "Parables of Crisis," which are intended to refer to the expected second advent of Christ. They consist of the parables of the Faithful and Unfaithful Servants, the Waiting Servants, the Thief, and the Ten Virgins. They are set in the context of exhortations to be ready, alert, wide-awake.

The most elaborate of these parables is the Ten Virgins. It is introduced as a parable of the Kingdom, and it is clear that for the evangelist the parable is a warning to be prepared for the advent of the Son of Man, and this is for the evangelist the coming of the Kingdom of God. The moment of crisis is represented by the return of the bridegroom and this is paralleled with the return of the master in the parables of the master in the parables of the Waiting Servants and of the Faithful and Unfaithful Servants. Dodd says that all the vivid dramatic detail is intended only to emphasize the folly of unpreparedness and the wisdom of preparedness. However, the preparedness is not for some distant, future event, but for the developments actually in process in the ministry of Jesus. Dodd concludes:

It seems possible, therefore, to give to all these

'eschatological' parables an application within the
context of the ministry of Jesus. They were intended to enforce his appeal to men to recognize
that the Kingdom of God was present in all its
momentous consequences, and that by their conduct
in the presence of this tremendous crisis they
would judge themselves as faithful or unfaithful,
wise or foolish. When the crisis had passed, they
were adapted by the church to enforce its appeal
to men to prepare for the second and final world-
crisis which it believed to be approaching [ibid.,
pp122-39].

There is a further group of parables--"parables of
growth"--which on the surface appear difficult to fit into
Dodd's framework of realized eschatology. These are the
Sower, the Tares, the Seed Growing Secretly, and the Mustard Seed. To these must be added the parables of the
Leaven and of the Dragnet, which are closely connected in
the Gospels with those of the Mustard Seed and the Tares
respectively.

Dodd notes that the predominant interpretation of
these parables makes them refer to the future history of
the Kingdom of God in the world. These parables indicate
that the Kingdom is present only in germ, and that there is
an indefinite period of growth and development before the
consummation. This was the view of consequente Eschatologie, and Schweitzer believed that the stages of sowing,
growth, and harvest were intended to correspond literally
with the actual lapse of time between the beginning of the
ministry of Jesus and the date at which he expected the
catastrophic irruption of the Kingdom of God.

Dodd rejects the consistent eschatological interpretation of these parables as "strained and artificial." For him
the key to their understanding centers in the idea of harvest.
The harvest was an old and familiar symbol for the eschatological event, the Day of the Lord, the Day of Judgment.
The Kingdom of God is like the harvest; it is the fulfillment
of the process. Jesus regarded his work as the fulfillment
of the work of the prophets, and he saw in the success of
John the Baptist a sign that the power of God was at work.
Consequently, the figure of the harvest suggests that the
crisis which has now arrived is the climax of a long process
which prepared the way for it. Dodd believes that these
parables can be given a consistent and pointed application

to the historical situation which does justice to the processes of growth, and yet does not contemplate a long period of
development after the death of Jesus. The parables of the
Sower, the Tares, and the Seed Growing Secretly all illustrate in various ways the coming of the Kingdom of God in
the ministry of Jesus, under the figure of harvest. Applying the same motifs to the parable of the Mustard Seed,
Dodd assumes the stance of the allegorist. He notes that
we must suppose that in this parable Jesus is asserting that
the time has come when the blessings of the Reign of God
are available for all men. That the outcast and neglected
of Israel and perhaps even the Gentiles are hearing the call,
is a sign that the process of obscure development is at an
end. "The Kingdom of God is here: the birds are flocking
to find shelter in the shade of the tree."

    The parables of growth, then, can be so interpreted
as to make them into a commentary on the actual situation
during the ministry of Jesus during which the Kingdom of
God came into history. They should not be understood as
implying a long process of development introduced by the
ministry of Jesus and to be consummated by his second advent, although the church later understood them in that way.
The eschaton has come, not by any human effort, but by
act of God. Moreover, it came not by an arbitrary, catastrophic intervention, but it is the harvest following upon a
long process of growth. It is this perspective which the
parables introduce. The coming of the Kingdom of God is
indeed a crisis brought by divine intervention. However, it
is not an unprepared crisis unrelated to the previous course
of history. The teaching of Jesus attests to the fact that
an obscure process of growth has gone before it, and the
fresh act of God which calls the crisis into being is an answer to the work of God in history which has gone before.
Jesus did not strip history of its value, for he declared
that the eternal order was present in the actual situation,
and that this situation was the "harvest" of history that had
gone before [ibid., pp140-56].

    Dodd seeks to answer the objections of those who
would claim that his approach to the parables rules out their
general application and reduces their value as instruments
of religious teaching. Does his insistence upon the parables' particularity as comments upon an historical situation
leave us with little more than their historical interest? No,
says Dodd, because the parables are works of art and as
such have significance beyond their original occasion. Their

teaching may be applied to all sorts of new situations which were never contemplated at the time when they were spoken. However, if we are to interpret them and to apply them to our own new situations along "right lines," we should have an understanding of their original import in relation to a particular situation in the past. Dodd has no doubt that the "particular situation" is best understood in terms of realized eschatology. For the parables represent the interpretation which Jesus offered of his own ministry. While he employed the traditional symbolism of apocalypse to indicate the "other wordly" absolute character of the Kingdom of God, he used parables to enforce and illustrate the idea that the Kingdom of God had come upon men there and then. The inconceivable had happened: history had become the vehicle of the eternal; the absolute was clothed with flesh and blood.

Dodd's analysis of the parables leads to a "theology of history" which is characterized by crisis rather than evolution. History's primary religious significance is not to be understood in terms of teleology but of crisis. Every crisis is a thing by itself, unique and nonrecurrent. Consequently, we need not try to reduce all events, great and small, to the same scale, as elements in a uniform process, governed by general laws, and deriving its significance from the remote goal to which it tends. Thus we are at liberty to recognize in one particular series of events a crisis of supreme significance, and to interpret other events and situations with reference to it. The Christian faith finds this supreme crisis in the ministry and death of Jesus Christ with the immediate sequel. The supreme significance of this "crisis" lies in the fact that here history became the field within which God confronted men in a decisive way, and placed before them a moral challenge that could not be evaded [ibid., pp157-69].

Needless to say, Dodd has had his detractors, and one could fault him for superimposing upon the parables a schemata into which they do not "easily fit." However, following Weiss and Schweitzer, Dodd has taken the eschatological character of Jesus' teachings seriously, and he has forced us to confront the "actual situation" in which the parables were given. The primary intention of the parables is not to make a moral point. Rather, they interpret life to us, by initiating us into a situation in which, as Christians believe, the eternal was uniquely manifested in time, a situation which is both historical and modern in the deepest possible sense. Just as Jülicher represented a turning point in parabolic interpretation, so also does Dodd; and his suggestions that the parables must be understood within their historical context and that they have a distinct existential quality are motifs that have had significant influence upon subsequent exegetes.

21 B. T. D. SMITH

One of the significant English studies of the parables is B. T. D. Smith's The Parables of the Synoptic Gospels (1937). Before analyzing the individual parables, Smith has a lengthy Introduction which is noteworthy for its discussion of the nature of parabolic literature in the Synoptic Gospels and its background in the pre-Christian era.

Smith begins by noting that the Greek word parabolē was the term commonly chosen by the Septuagint translators to represent the Hebrew, mashal, which meant "to be like." He then proceeds to describe the characteristics of mashal and to give examples from the Old Testament and from rabbinical literature. A comparison of the rabbinic parables with those of the Gospels reveals the latter as "supremely beautiful examples of an established art" [B. T. D. Smith, The Parables of the Synoptic Gospels: A Critical Study (Cambridge, England: Cambridge University Press, 1937), pp3-15].

In the Synoptic Gospels there are several varieties of figurative speech. The simplest forms are the simile and metaphor. In both one thing is compared with another. In the simile this comparison is formally expressed while in a metaphor it is effected by transferring to the one the designation of the other. Using examples from Aristotle: "He sprang on them like a lion," is a simile. "The lion sprang on them," is a metaphor. The employment of simile or metaphor postulates the existence of some point of likeness between the things compared, which in all other respects may be entirely different. Smith prefers the term similitude, not simile, when the illustration depicts familiar scenes and relationships and is given in some detail. Metaphor is used in "Hear, O thou Shepherd of Israel"; simile, in "All we like sheep have gone astray." But when the shepherd seeks for his lost sheep and rejoices over its recovery, we have a similitude.

The term parable when contrasted to similitude

is used to denote those illustrations which are in narrative form. Smith acknowledges that the use of these two terms is confusing and it would be desirable if another term could be found for narrative parables. However, such is not the case since "fable" is unsatisfactory. A further distinction is that the similitude is a picture of familiar happenings; the parable depicts something as having once happened. The similitude opens characteristically with the words, "What man of you...?"--the parable, with "A certain man...." But the distinction between similitude and parable is not easily made, and Smith says that we must recognize that parable and similitude are essentially akin and that they serve the same ends and shade off into one another.

Four of the Gospel parables, all of which are found in Luke, must be put in a class by themselves. The parables of the Pharisee and the Publican, of Dives and Lazarus, of the Rich Fool, and of the Good Samaritan are what Jülicher called Beispielerzahlungen (example-stories). They furnish examples of character and conduct to be imitated or avoided and, in contrast to the parable, they teach directly instead of by analogy. Consequently, strictly speaking they do not belong to "figurative" speech.

Another form of figurative speech found in the Gospels is what Smith calls "brief proverbs and figurative sayings," in which a general rule is stated in the form of a particular instance of the rule. Examples are: "If the blind guide the blind, both shall fall into a pit"; "Wheresoever the carcass is, there will the vultures be gathered together"; and "Physician, heal thyself."

The characteristic of figurative speech is to arrest attention and excite interest, but it also serves other purposes. One is description. A writer's task is to present his thought in a manner which makes it real to the reader so that the reader's imagination can grasp it vividly and bring it home to himself. It is to imagery that one naturally turns when he wishes to express and to arouse emotion and to convey his description in a form that will attract or repel.

A second quality is illustration. A proverb gives a concrete example of a truth of general application. By means of simile and similitude the unfamiliar and difficult can be explained in terms of the known and recognized, as when Jesus uses the illustration of parental love to make comprehensible his concept of the all-forgiving love of God.

Figurative speech can also be employed for argument. This characteristic of the parable manifests itself in the question with which many begin or end. In the argument from analogy a thesis is supported by showing that in similar circumstances to those under discussion this proposition obviously holds good. An example is the parable of the Laborers in the Vineyard which sets forth the proposition that heavenly reward is not necessarily in proportion to length of service is supported by the analogous case of the employer and the hired men.

A final type of figurative speech which Smith discusses is the allegory which differs from similitude and parable in that it does not set one thing by the side of another. One marked distinction between allegory and similitude and parable is that the allegory must be interpreted point by point in order to understand it. As far as possible everything in the allegory must represent something else. It is a description in code or esoteric symbolism. Parable and similitude must be lifelike or they fail in their purpose. Allegories, however, need not conform to any laws of probability or possibility. In similitude and parable the figures are always precisely what they profess to be, while in allegory they point to or are symbolic of something else. Smith observes that there are only two clear examples of allegory in the Synoptic Gospels--the Marcan "parable" of the Wicked Husbandmen and Matthew's version of the parable of the Unwilling Guests. He feels that the originality of the one is highly suspect and that the secondary character of the other is beyond question. The following observation by Smith concerning the nature of allegory and its relation to the Gospel tradition is noteworthy:

> The creation of allegories is one thing, the allegorical interpretation of something already in existence is another. Allegorical interpretation affords a means whereby the venerated traditions of the past may be brought into line with the ideas and beliefs of the present. It enabled the Stoic to discover pantheism in the Greek mythology, the Hellenist Jew to discover Greek philosophy in the books of Moses, the Rabbi to discover edification even in the place-names of the Old Testament,

and the Christian to discover the Gospel in the
Law. Some of the parables of Christ robbed of
their contexts, offered a very obvious field for the
application of the same method. By its aid they
could be regarded as prophetic oracles, commu-
nicating 'things hidden from the foundation of the
world.' Since the allegorical interpretation of the
parables began very early and at a time when the
Christian tradition was still fluid, it has left its
mark upon that tradition.... [ibid., pp16-29].

Employing methodology characteristic of form criticism, Smith makes a detailed analysis of "the form and
history of the Synoptic parables." Among his conclusions
are that most of the figurative sayings at one time existed
apart from the contexts in which they are now embedded.
With one doubtful exception (the Two Debtors), the original
setting of none of the parables and similitudes appears to
have been preserved in the Christian tradition. We cannot
tell whether collections consisting entirely of parables existed and were drawn upon by the evangelists. However,
the fact that the two later of the Synoptic evangelists had
available so many parables apparently unconnected with other
material makes this probable.

The history of the transmission of the parables from
the time when they lived only in the memory of those who
were eyewitnesses to the time when they were incorporated
into the Synoptic Gospels must be understood within the context of the life and needs of the early Christian community.
Certain parables were probably put into circulation as soon
as believers began to be added to the Lord. These could
be used to illustrate the lessons of the need for repentance,
watchfulness, preparedness, faithfulness, and patience in
view of the approaching Parousia of the Lord Jesus. Or
persecution would bring to mind those sayings which spoke
of the price that had to be paid to gain a great prize, or
which warned would-be-disciples to count the cost. Smith
intimates that the large number of parables relating to the
mission of Jesus to the outcasts may reflect the controversy
between Jew and Gentile in the early church.

Thus the circumstances and history of the Christian
community were responsible for bringing into circulation
among its members a number of parables. Converts, especially those from among the Gentiles, were in need of
instruction in the Christian way. Consequently, Christian

teachers accumulated a store of sayings and parables of
Jesus to be used for such catechetical purposes. Smith
likewise suggests that the parables were employed in homi-
letics. Some were used to convey general maxims for the
instruction and admonition of the faithful. Evidence for this
is afforded by the applications appended to some of the parables.

The process of parabolic transmission leads to the
possibility that certain parables may represent creations of
the Christian teachers or borrowings from rabbinic sources.
Smith concludes, however, that we have good reasons for
believing that the great majority of the parables of the Synoptic Gospels represent authentic parables of Jesus. Like
the authenticity of paintings attributed to an artist, so Jesus'
parables represent subjects which he has made peculiarly
his own and which exhibit his particular technique. Moreover, many of them are marked by special characteristics.
The presentation is realistic; the characters are living persons and not dummies; the element of unexpectedness is
present. "Of all the Christian tradition, it is perhaps the
parables, with their kindly, intimate presentation of human
character, their humor and their irony, which reveal to us
most clearly Jesus of Nazareth" [ibid., pp30-60].

Smith observes that the parables afford us a picture
of life in Palestine as it was known to the pious poor of
Galilee. We see a society that is predominantly agricul-
tural and pastoral. Little knowledge is shown of the life
of the rich and powerful. It is life in the "little house"
rather than the "big" which is brought most vividly before
us. Thus the shadow of poverty and debt is never far distant.

Smith discusses the background of the parables and
examines their possible relationship to popular tales and
rabbinic parallels. One piece of popular literature which
may have influenced the parables of the Servant in Authority and the Barren Fig Tree and perhaps a few details in
the Prodigal Son is the Story of Ahibar. It is likewise
possible that a popular tale lies behind the parable of Dives
and Lazarus. There are a few similarities in Indian tales
to the parables. One is a Buddhist parable which has similarities to the Prodigal Son. Another is the Buddhist parable of the Sower. There is also a Jaina parable with some
semblance to the parable of the Talents. Smith concludes
that these Indian parallels are far too remote to suggest

dependence. In the Thousand and One Nights there is a
story reminiscent of the parable of the Rich Fool. Here
too, Smith, agreeing with Bousset who first called attention
to the parallel, says that they are independent of each other.

Turning to rabbinic parallels in the Talmud and Midrash, Smith notes that there are parables of sowing and
harvesting, sheep farming and house building, of stewards
and farmhands, and landlords and tenants, as well as many
others drawn from a different environment and unrepresent-
ed in the Gospels. But as with the other parallels, Smith
feels that only rarely is the resemblance between the rabbinic parables and those of the Gospels so close as to suggest any direct relationship, and it is probable that behind
both lies a common background of popular tales and illustrations and Scripture exposition [ibid., pp61-73].

Before discussing the individual parables, Smith
writes about the "Gospel of the Parables. " The rule of
God or the Kingdom of God in the teaching of Jesus is
strikingly different from the conception presented in the
apocalyptic and rabbinic writings. His view was marked by
a single-minded concentration upon the religious and a complete elimination of the purely national aspect of the Jewish
hope. The notion that the rule of God means the supremacy
of Israel and the downfall of the Gentiles disappears. Jesus'
views about the Kingdom are reflected in the parables. One
must wait upon God for its full manifestation as the farmer
waits upon God for the harvest, confident that it will come,
though he knows not how. Man must prepare for the Kingdom's advent, but he cannot bring it about. Moreover, its
coming will be sudden and will result in judgment. But
only a faithless servant need dread the coming of his lord;
only an unprofitable servant need fear the day of reckoning;
only late-comers to a wedding feast find the door shut.
However, the note of warning is mingled with that of joy.
It is to the welcome sign of the budding fig tree that Jesus
compares the signs of the coming rule of God.

A fundamental part of Jesus' eschatological gospel
was his teaching on poverty and wealth. In the parable of
the Rich Man and Lazarus there is the assumption that
poverty and piety, wealth and ungodliness, are to be equated.
The measure of a person's fitness to enter the Kingdom is
his readiness to do without the things of this world. The
parables of the Costly Pearl and the Hid Treasure show that
when one is faced with the prospect of great gain, he must

be ready to surrender all else for the Kingdom's sake. The parables afford us a good entree into Jesus' understanding of the Kingdom of God, and the early church, for whom the gospel of the Kingdom had become the gospel of Jesus Christ the Son of God, found its Lord mirrored in the central figure of more than one parable. However, as Smith points out, none of the parables (excluding the allegory of the Wicked Husbandmen) throws light upon his conception of his own relation to the Kingdom, and only the Fourth Gospel illustrates the significance of his death in parable form [ibid., pp74-86].

The actual number of Jesus' parables varies from one interpreter to another and depends on how many of Jesus' short figurative sayings are included in the reckoning. Smith finds 62 parables which he groups under the following headings: Parables of the Times; Parables of Growth; Parables for Rich and Poor; Parables for the Hierarchy and the Scribes; Parables for Pharisee and Sinner; Various Parables. His commentary on the individual parables together with his introduction make Smith's work one of the best studies in English. It reflects an extensive knowledge of both biblical and extra-biblical sources as well as a wide acquaintance with past and contemporary scholarship on the parables. These factors in addition to his employment of form critical methodology make Smith's book, as his title suggests, a noteworthy and significant "critical study."

22   JOACHIM JEREMIAS

One of the most important and widely-read studies on the parables is Joachim Jeremias' Die Gleichnisse Jesu, which was first published in 1947. Since then it has been rewritten, revised, and expanded through many editions, the eighth German edition having been published in 1970. The last major revision was the sixth German edition of 1962, which took account of the parables in the newly discovered Gospel of Thomas. There was an English translation, The Parables of Jesus, of the third German edition in 1954. A revised English edition with the same title was published by Scribner's in 1963, and a third revised edition by SCM Press in 1972. An abridged edition, Rediscovering the Parables, which omitted the book's "purely technical and linguistic content," was published by Scribner's in 1966.

Jeremias acknowledges his dependence upon the work

of Dodd and Jülicher. He notes that Dodd's book The Parables of the Kingdom opened a new era in the study of the
parables, and although he differs with Dodd in some details,
"Yet it is unthinkable that there should ever be any retreat
from the essential lines laid down by Dodd for the interpretation of the parables of Jesus. " It was Dodd who a-
chieved a breakthough in the direction first indicated by
Cadoux, viz. that the parables must be placed in the setting of the life of Jesus. "In this extraordinarily significant book [of Dodd's] for the first time a really successful
attempt was made to place the parables in the setting of the
life of Jesus, thereby introducing a new era in the interpretation of the parables. " The one drawback of Dodd's work,
according to Jeremias, is that he limited his attention to
the parables of the Kingdom of Heaven, and the "one-sided
nature" of his realized eschatology resulted in a contraction
of the eschatology which has continued to exercise an influence upon his otherwise "masterly interpretation" [Joachim
Jeremias, The Parables of Jesus, rev. ed. , S. H. Hooke,
trans. (New York: Scribner's, 1963), pp9, 21].

As for Jülicher, we owe to him the final discarding
of the allegorical method of interpretation. He not only
proved incontestably by hundreds of cases that allegorizing
leads to error, but also maintained that it is utterly alien
to the parables of Jesus. Although his emphasis may have
been too one-sided, nevertheless his work remains fundamental. Jeremias says, however, that Jülicher left the
work half done. His anti-allegorizing position suffers from
a fatal error. He regarded the parables as a piece of real
life and drew from them a single idea of the widest possible
generality. Herein lay the error that the broadest application was believed to be the true one. Jülicher held that the
parables announce a genuine religious humanity, thereby
stripping them of their eschatological import. Imperceptibly
Jesus is transferred into an "apostle of progress, " a teacher
of wisdom who inculcates moral precepts and a simplified
theology by means of striking metaphors and stories. Jeremias maintains that such a view of Jesus is nothing like him
at all. Jülicher "has rid the parables of the thick layer of
dust with which the allegorical interpretation had covered
them, " but he failed to proceed beyond this point. The
main task still remains to be done, and this is to recover
the original meaning of the parables [ibid. , pp18-19].

Jeremias is confident that the parabolic tradition
which has been transmitted to us in the Synoptic Gospels

stands upon a firm historical foundation. When the Gospel parables are compared with contemporary literature of the same type, such as Pauline similitudes or rabbinical parables, they reveal a definite personal character, a unique clarity and simplicity, a matchless mastery of construction. Consequently, one must conclude that the parables represent a particularly trustworthy tradition and that they bring us into immediate relation with Jesus. Nevertheless, the parables confront us with the difficult task of recovering their original meaning.

The problem as Jeremias sees it is essentially simple but involves far-reaching consequences. It is that the parables of Jesus are not primarily literary productions, nor is their object to lay down general maxims, but each of them was uttered in an actual situation of the life of Jesus, at a particular and often unforeseen point. Moreover, they were preponderantly apologetic in nature. They correct, reprove, attack, and are for the greater part weapons of conflict. They have an existential dimension in that everyone of them calls for immediate response. The task then is to recover the definite historical setting of each of the parables. What did Jesus intend to say at this or that particular moment? What must have been the effect of his word upon his hearers? For Jeremias these are the questions we must ask if we are to recover the original meaning of the parables of Jesus and if we are to hear again his "authentic voice" [ibid., pp11-12, 21-22].

Our return to Jesus via his parables must of necessity be from the primitive church. This means that the parables as they have come down to us have a double historical setting. There is the original historical setting in some specific situation in the activity of Jesus. Many of the parables are so vividly told that it is natural to assume that they arise out of some actual occurrence. The other historical setting of the parables is grounded in the primitive church. Before they assumed a written form they "lived" in the early Christian community which employed the words of Jesus for purposes of preaching and teaching. The church collected and arranged Jesus' sayings in accordance with her special needs. In the process they were expanded here and allegorized there, always in relation to the church's own situation between the Cross and the Parousia. Thus in studying the parables it is important to be aware of the difference between the situation of Jesus and that of the primitive church. Moreover, this process of editing, reinterpreting, changing, and adapting the texts of the parables was not a random, haphazard process. Jeremias maintains that as soon as we attempt to ascertain the original historical setting of the parables, we meet with certain "definite principles of transformation" which can be grouped under ten headings:

(1) The Translation of the Parables into Greek. Jesus spoke Galilean Aramaic. The translation of his sayings into Greek necessarily involved innumerable changes of meaning. Consequently, the retranslation of the parables of Jesus into his mother-tongue is perhaps the most important aid to the recovery of their original meaning.

(2) Representational Changes. In the process of translation into Greek, not only the vocabulary of Jesus' sayings was changed, but also the Palestinian background was "translated" into terms of the Hellenistic environment. For example, in the Lucan parables we find phrases that presuppose Hellenistic building technique, Roman law-court procedure, and non-Palestinian horticulture and landscapes. In Luke 13:19 a man sows a mustard seed "in the garden." In the Hellenistic world mustard is included among the garden herbs, but in Palestine the cultivation of mustard in garden beds was forbidden. In Mark we have the Roman division of the night into four watches instead of the Palestinian division into three. Jeremias points out that one must go cautiously in this area, however, because Jesus repeatedly and intentionally uses Levantine methods of punishment by way of illustration. He concludes that non-Palestinian conditions do not always indicate editorial revision or lack of authenticity and that we can reach a fairly reliable judgment only in those cases where the tradition is divided.

(3) Embellishment. A comparison between the parables of the Talents and the Pounds, which Jeremias regards as one, and the Great Supper in Luke 14 and Matthew 22, show evidence of expansion and embellishment. Other cases of embellishment include the use of stylistic expedients that are supposed to enliven the narrative. An example is the insertion of the words "They said to him" in Matthew 21:41, which are not found in Mark 12:9 or Luke 20:16. A characteristic of Jesus' use of parables is that they are drawn from life, but they show numerous unusual features, intended to arouse the attention of the hearers and carrying for the most part special emphasis. Such elements as exaggeration and unexpectedness are still used in Oriental story

telling, and their frequent occurrence in the parables shows that Jesus intentionally adopted this style. Jeremias concludes that a comparison of the parallel forms in which the parables have been transmitted to us show that in many cases they have been elaborated, and that the simpler version is probably the original one.

(4) Influence of the Old Testament and of Folk-Story Themes. In some of the parables there are references to the Old Testament (Mark 4:29, 32; 12:1, 9a, 10-11; Matt. 25:31, 46, cf. Luke 13:27. 29). The number of such references is "remarkably small" and Jeremias says they are reduced by the fact that those in Matthew and Luke are secondary. After examining the parables in the Gospel of Thomas, Jeremias observes that there is a tendency to illustrate by or to add Scripture references. There is the possibility that Jesus occasionally referred to Scripture in a parable. This is very probable at the end of the parable of the Mustard Seed and at the end of the parable of the Seed Growing Secretly.

Closely related to references to Scripture are occasional folk-story themes which found their way into the parables. Two cases which Jeremias considers to be secondary are in the parables of the Hid Treasure and the Marriage Feast. In the latter parable the description of a punitive expedition is inserted.

(5) The Change of Audience. The parable of the Laborers in the Vineyard is a good example of how the tradition underwent a change or restriction of the audience. Jeremias believes that this parable was originally addressed to the Pharisees but that the primitive church related it to Jesus' disciples, and so applied it to the Christian community. A similar case is the parable of the Lost Sheep which Jesus originally used to defend the gospel against his opponents. Matthew, however, put it into the setting of the disciplinary order of the community as an exhortation to its leaders to be faithful in their pastoral duties. Thus there are many parables which were originally addressed to a different audience, namely the Pharisees, the scribes, or the crowd, and were subsequently connected with Jesus' disciples by the primitive church.

(6) The Hortatory Use of the Parables by the Church. Jeremias discerns a shift from the eschatological emphasis to the hortatory. As time went on the early church saw

itself midway between two crises, one past, the other future. Standing between the cross and Christ's return, the church looked to Jesus' teachings for guidance. Thus their changed situation caused the primitive church to interpret the "parables of crisis," which were intended to rouse people to a sense of urgency, as directions for the conduct of the Christian community. In a word, the stress moved from the eschatological to the hortatory. Of the many examples of this change of emphasis, the parable of the Unjust Steward is typical. The church did not completely eliminate the eschatological element from the parable, but it shifted the emphasis because of the change of audience.

(7) The Influence of the Church's Situation. That the early church related the parables to its own concrete situation can be seen in the five Parousia parables--Burglar, Ten Virgins, Watchman, Servant in Authority, Talents. These parables were originally a group of crisis-parables intended to rouse people to a realization of the terrible gravity of the moment. But the primitive church gave them a christological meaning, and regarded them as a warning addressed to the community not to become slack because of the delay in Christ's return. Two other needs of the early church which affected the parables were missionary activity and regulations for the church's leadership.

(8) Allegorizing. One of the major means of reinterpretation was allegorizing whereby an allegorical interpretation could be added to a parable. The Sower is a good example where verses 14-20 of Mark 4 have been added as the parable was transmitted in the early Christian communities. Christological allegorizing was quite evident so that the characters in many of the parables were taken to represent Christ. Also where the themes of reward and punishment were in question, there was a readiness to allegorize. The number of secondary interpretations is much greater in that each of the Synoptists agrees in finding in the parables obscure sayings which are unintelligible to outsiders. Jeremias concludes that most of the allegorical traits that figure so prominently in the parables' present form are not original. Therefore we must discard these secondary interpretations and features if we are to understand what Jesus' parables originally meant.

(9) Collection and Fusion of Parables. In the Synoptic Gospels there are many paired parables and similes where the same ideas are expressed in different symbols,

e. g. patches and wineskins, a divided kingdom and a divided family, salt and light, birds and flowers, dogs and swine, stone and serpent, grapes and figs, foxes and birds, mustard seed and leaven, tower-builder and king, lost sheep and lost coin, etc. Jeremias believes that most of the double parables and double metaphors were either transmitted alone without the other member of the pair, or separated from it by other material. It appears that Jesus himself favored the duplication of similes as a means of illustrating, choosing his pairs of related ideas preferably from nature, especially from the animal world. However familiar the twin parables may be to us, each case must be examined individually, and we must reckon with the possibility that the double parables were spoken independently on different occasions, and not joined till later.

The church began early to make collections of parables. The most evident example is the seven parables in Matthew 13. But in trying to discover the parables' meaning we should not necessarily rely on the meaning of the adjacent parables. This is substantiated by the fact that all seven of the parables in Matthew 13, except the last, recur in the Gospel of Thomas where they are independent and spread over the whole book.

Another tendency of the tradition to form collections of parables occasionally led to the fusion of two parables into one, as in the Matthaean form of the parable of the Great Supper. Sometimes parables are fused in such a way that only one or more features are transferred from one to another, while in one case (Luke 13:24-30), a new parable has arisen from the fusion of the end of a parable with certain similes. Jeremias holds that if we are to get to the parables' original meaning, we must discard all these "secondary connections."

(10) The Setting. The form-critical view that the gospel narrative's framework is largely secondary is also true of the parables. Jeremias observes that a comparison of the Synoptic Gospels shows that the symbolic element has been transmitted with greater fidelity than the introduction, interpretation, and context, and that this is of great importance for a right understanding of the parables. The most important result of Jeremias' study of the setting of the parables is that there was a strong tendency to add to the parables conclusions in the form of generalizing sayings. Where such generalizations are found, they are predominantly

secondary in their present place in the context. This is
supported by the fact that they are entirely missing from
the Gospel of Thomas. The intention of the conclusions
was to give the parables the widest possible application.
Through the addition of such generalizations, the parables
have acquired a moralizing sense which obscures the original situation and blunts the sense of conflict, the sharp edge
of the eschatological warning, the sternness of the threat.
Moreover, these generalizing conclusions enable us to hear
the voice of the Christian preacher, or teacher, whose
intent is to interpret Jesus' message. They show us how
early the tendency arose to make the parables serviceable
in this way for the Christian community by giving them a
general instructional or hortatory meaning. This tendency
finally transformed Jesus into a teacher of wisdom--a theme
which came to its greatest triumph in Jülicher's exposition
of the parables. So, if one is to recover the parables'
original meaning, he must be aware of this tendency and
make allowance for it [ibid., pp23-114].

As we have noted, for Jeremias the main purpose of
the scholarly exposition of the parables is to enable us to
"hear the voice of Jesus" as his contemporaries heard it.
Our task is to rediscover "here and there behind the veil
the features of the Son of Man." As outlined above, Jeremias set forth ten "principles of transformation" designed
to aid us in our return to Jesus through the "veil" with
which the primitive church surrounded him.

With the aid of the "laws of transformation" Jeremias
believes that the total impression of the parables has been
immensely simplified. We find that many parables express
one and the same idea by means of varying symbols. Moreover, differences which are commonplaces to us, are now
understood to be secondary. Thus it becomes clear that a
few simple ideas stand out with increased importance. We
also realize that Jesus never tired of expressing the central
ideas of his message in constantly changing images. Jeremias suggests that the parables and similes fall naturally
into groups, and he proposes ten which "present a comprehensive conception of the message of Jesus." The major
reference of these ten themes is eschatological and they
focus on the secret of the Kingdom or the dawning of the
messianic age. They are as follows: (1) Now Is the Day
of Salvation, (2) God's Mercy for Sinners, (3) the Great
Assurance, (4) the Imminence of Catastrophe, (5) It May
Be Too Late, (6) the Challenge of the Hour, (7) Realized

Discipleship, (8) the Via Dolorosa and Exaltation of the Son of Man, (9) the Consummation, and (10) Parabolic Actions [Jeremias' discussion of the parables and their relationship to the above themes may be found, ibid., pp115-229].

In the conclusion to his book, Jeremias accents existential and eschatological motifs. One thing becomes clear in an attempt to recover the original significance of the parables of Jesus, and that is that all of them compel his hearers to come to a decision about his person and mission. In this context Jeremias refers approvingly to Ernst Fuchs' suggestion that the parables imply a christological self-attestation. Jeremias also finds in C. H. Dodd's realized eschatology a meaningful category for understanding the parables. They are full of "the secret of the Kingdom of God"--the recognition of "an eschatology that is in process of realization" (sich realisierende Eschatologie) [Jeremias says that this term was communicated to him in a letter by Ernst Haenchen, and that to his joy, Dodd agreed with it]. The urgent note sounding through all the parables is that the hour of fulfillment is come.

> The strong man is disarmed, the forces of evil are in retreat, the physician has come to the sick, the lepers are cleansed, the heavy burden of guilt is removed, the lost sheep has been brought home, the door of the Father's House stands open, the poor and the beggars are summoned to the banquet, a master whose grace is undeserved pays his wages in full, a great joy fills all hearts. God's acceptable year has come. For he has been manifested whose veiled kingliness shines through every word and through every parable--the Savior [ibid., p230].

Jeremias' exposition of the parables is a prodigious achievement, and like Jülicher before him, he has become the object of both positive and negative criticism. It is generally agreed that Jeremias has rendered a significant service in stressing the need of recovering the force and the point of the original parables, and that his work represents the most dedicated concern that we hear again the voice of Jesus in the parables. [For critical analyses of Jeremias' work, see David M. Granskou, Preaching on the Parables (Philadelphia: Fortress Press, 1972), pp29-35; Geraint V. Jones, The Art and Truth of the Parables (London: S.P.C.K., 1964), pp32-36; and Norman Perrin, Jesus

and the Language of the Kingdom (Philadelphia: Fortress
Press, 1976), pp91-107.]

23   T. W. MANSON

In his work The Teaching of Jesus (Cambridge, England: Cambridge University Press, 1951), T. W. Manson
devotes a section to the nature of the parable as a fundamental feature of Jesus' teaching [see pp56-81]. He is concerned chiefly with two issues: (1) What is a parable, and
which among the utterances of Jesus belong to this class?
(2) On what principle or principles did he make use of this
form of teaching?.

Manson observes that there is a common, albeit
faulty, notion that the parables of Jesus are akin to the
"illustrations" used in sermons. The predominantly Western
notion stems from the classical writers on rhetoric, particularly Aristotle. But if the object of the parables was
simply to illustrate or to illuminate the obscure, then every
parable should itself be clear and understandable. To a
certain point this view of the parables is adequate as for
example the parables of the Good Samaritan and the Lost
Sheep. However, it soon becomes evident that this idea of
parabolic interpretation will not cover all the parables, nor
will it be in keeping with some of the things said about
them.

Turning to a discussion of the mashal in the Hebrew
tradition, Manson notes that in the vast majority of the Old
Testament examples there is nothing corresponding at all
closely to what we generally refer to as a parable. There
are, however, in the Old Testament a few cases which are
quite similar to the parables found in the Gospels. The
story of the Ewe Lamb which Nathan tells to David is such
a case, and shows that every real parable is significant in
two ways. It has its own meaning as a story, but also a
further meaning in that it applies to persons or events or
both together. One can follow and appreciate the former
without having the slightest inkling of the latter. Thus in
the parable of the Ewe Lamb David understands every detail of the story, but it is only Nathan's "Thou art the man,"
which confronts him with its application. Such other illustrations as Ezekiel 21:5-10 show that a parable may be
quite intelligible although its application is hidden from the
hearers.

With this background from both the Old Testament
and the Gospels, Manson offers the following conception of
a parable: "A parable is a literary creation in narrative
form designed either to portray a type of character for
warning or example or to embody a principle of God's gov-
ernance of the world and men. It might partake of both
natures. In logical terminology it might almost be called
a concrete universal" [ibid., p65]. Thus a parable cannot
be regarded as a mere sermon illustration designed to
state some abstract ethical or theological proposition in
simple pictorial form for the simple and unlearned. Rather,
the aim of a parable is to stimulate the conscience and/or
awaken religious insight in the hearers. Its intent is to
confront persons with the word of God so that they may be
moved to repentance and faith. One must have "eyes to
see and ears to hear" if the parable is to perform its intended function.

Manson proceeds to group the parables and says that
there are a total of 65, allowing for doublets. Moreover,
they can be divided into two main groups according to a
principle which is equally applicable to the Old Testament
parables. That is, the parables present either a type of
human conduct or a principle of God's government of the
world. In the former case the primary appeal is to the
conscience, while in the latter it is to the religious insight
and faith of the hearers. Even though both features may
be present in a given parable, one side generally predominates.

Manson regards the following parables as example of
the ethical type: Workers in the Vineyard, Wise and Foolish Builders, Faithful and Unfaithful Stewards, Pounds
(Talents), Two Sons, Ten Virgins, Two Debtors, Good Samaritan, Rich Fool, Pharisee and Publican, plus a good
many more. The main feature of this type of parable is
that a certain kind of conduct is sketched in a most vivid
manner and held up before the audience so that they might
apply it to themselves either as an example or a warning.
Usually two types are contrasted in these parables, in
sharp either-or terms. There is no room for compromise
or vacillation, but one is called upon to make a clear and
urgent decision. There is no place for haggling or bar-
gaining; one must "Go and do likewise."

In several cases the direct appeal to conscience is
underscored by questions appended to the parable or by

questions prefixed to it. Thus, "What will the lord of the vineyard do?" "Which of the two did the will of his father?" "Who is the faithful and prudent steward?" These parables have an existential quality. They hold before the hearer a mirror in which he can discern the reality of his situation and make the fitting response. They are not simply entertaining stories, but disturbers of the peace and of the conscience so that I know unequivocally that "Thou art the one," and "Go and do likewise."

The second feature of the parable, according to Manson, is that they exhibit some aspect of God's rule. Among these parables are: the Seed Growing Secretly, the Mustard Seed, the Fig Tree, the Bread and Stone, the Leaven, the Tares, the Hid Treasure, the Pearl of Great Price, the Laborers in the Vineyard, the Prodigal Son. In these cases some natural phenomenon or human relation is used to suggest or symbolize a religious truth. The appeal is to the faith and insight of the hearers. Moreover, these teachings of Jesus are not to be viewed as apologetics. God is not an article of faith but its subject and object. The parables are not meant to demonstrate the existence of God but to make known the nature of the God whose existence is the common ground for Jesus and his audience. Manson cautions against a common Western notion that the parables are easy substitutes for philosophical or theological reflection. They are not devices which lead less-sophisticated persons to the same conclusions which could otherwise be reached as the result of elaborate processes of reasoning. The true parable is not an illustration to "bail one out" of a theological discussion, but is rather a mode of religious experience. "It is not a crutch for limping intellects, but a spur to religious insight: its object is not to provide simple theological instruction, but to produce living religious faith" [ibid., p73].

Still another type of parable is that which combines the characteristics of the ethical type and a principle of the divine government. This class includes the Vineyard, the Pounds (Talents), the Unmerciful Servant, the Unfruitful Fig Tree, the Great Feast, the Prodigal Son. In these parables some aspect of God's activity is compared or contrasted with typical human conduct. In the parable of the Prodigal Son the divine attitude to the repentant sinner is contrasted with the human in the figures of the father and the elder brother respectively. Manson says that in these instances the parabolic art attains its highest expression because the parable speaks to both the moral and religious side of human nature, and brings into one vivid picture the deepest needs and highest hopes of persons, and their complete satisfaction in God.

In a succinct conclusion to his section on the parables, Manson writes:

> A parable is a picture in words of some piece of human experience, actual or imagined. As such it is a work of art. Further, this picture portrays either an ethical type for our admiration or reprobation, or some principle of the rule of God in the world, or it does both things at once. That is to say it embodies the moral insight and the religious experience of its creator. Its object is to awaken these things in those to whom it is addressed, to pierce through the husk of self-satisfaction and worldly cares and interests to the essential man, to arouse the slumbering conscience, to turn the affections from things that change and pass to things that have the quality of eternity, to induce repentance and faith. In actual working, then, every true parable is a call to a better life and a deeper trust in God, which things are but the Godward and manward sides of true religion, the obverse and reverse of the one medal. For its effectiveness the parable requires a certain responsiveness on the part of those who hear it: and this response, in practice, separates those who may go farther from the others who make no advance. The parable becomes a kind of test which determines who shall be disciples [ibid., pp80-81].

[For a critical commentary by Manson on the individual parables in Matthew and Luke, see T. W. Manson, The Sayings of Jesus (London: SCM Press, 1949), reprinted in 1950 and 1954 and first published as Part II of The Mission and Message of Jesus, 1937, by Henry D. A. Major].

24 ARCHIBALD M. HUNTER

In his customary lucid style, A. M. Hunter has written two books on the parables--Interpreting the Parables (1960) and The Parables Then and Now (1971). The format

of both books is fairly similar and in each Hunter devotes
a section to the history of parabolic interpretation. He expresses the purpose of Interpreting the Parables as attempting to show the ordinary reader how modern scholars understand the parables. Furthermore, he wants to sketch the
history of interpretation and to suggest how parables, originally addressed to a specific historical situation in Palestine
1900 years ago, can still speak to Christians in the 20th
century. In order to accomplish the second objective he
will deal with the question of whether all allegorizing of the
parables is forbidden and how far we can go in moralizing
them. He views his second volume, The Parables Then and
Now, as a sequel to the earlier work. In the former volume the accent fell on the "Then" while "in this one the
stress is on the 'Now'; and it seeks to make the parables
speak to our predicament today, and that in an existential
rather than a merely moralizing way."

Hunter acknowledges his indebtedness to the work of
Dodd and Jeremias, and one might regard his volumes as
popular and readable explications of their positions. This
is not to suggest, however, that Hunter is only an echo of
these "mighty voices"; he diverges from them at points and
he establishes himself in his own right as a competent exegete of the parables. However, his methodology and his
overall analysis stand clearly within the Dodd-Jeremias
orbit. In an article in The Expository Times, Hunter re-
calls the significant impression that Dodd's Parables of the
Kingdom made upon him. He writes: "I can still remember
the thrill with which I read that book. Dodd, if I may
adapt Lowell's words, cut the cables and gave me a glimpse
of blue waters" ["The Interpretation of the Parables," The
Expository Times 69 (Jan. 1958), p101].

A basic question for Hunter concerns the situation or
the contemporary background from which the parables e-
merged. Jülicher with his insistence that a parable makes
one point which is designed to teach "moral commonplaces"
had left the task of interpretation "half done," according to
Hunter. The Jesus who emerged from Jülicher's research
was a 19th-century Liberal Jesus who went about the Galilean countryside teaching moral truths through a skillful use
of parables. But this is not the real Jesus; for who would
have bothered to crucify one "who told pleasant stories to
enforce prudential platitudes." To get a true glimpse of
Jesus and the Sitz im Leben of his parables, one must reckon with the issue of eschatology. Indeed this is precisely

what Jülicher did not do and what Dodd and Jeremias did do.
"They put the parables back into their true setting, which
is the ministry of Jesus seen as the great eschatological
act of God in which He visited and redeemed His people. "
With this perspective it becomes possible to restore the
parables to their original settings and see them against their
proper historical background. What terminology can we use
to describe this background? Dodd provides the answer:
"it is what we have learned to call 'realized eschatology.'"
This is undoubtedly the true background, Hunter observes,
against which the parables of Jesus become meaningful.
They are "weapons of war in the campaign of the Kingdom
of God against the Kingdom of the Devil. " This approach
to the parables enables one to arrange them in groups, "so
that the Kingdom themes which Jesus meant them to illustrate stand out, and the essential notes of the Galilean gospel ring out vividly and memorably" [ibid. , pp101-02].

Whereas Jeremias proposed an eight-fold grouping of
the parables, Hunter uses four. These groupings are found
in both his books on the parables and in the article in The
Expository Times, but under slightly different captions.
The parables within these groups also vary in the three
sources. The four groups in Interpreting the Parables are:
the Coming of the Kingdom, the Grace of the Kingdom, the
Men of the Kingdom, and the Crisis of the Kingdom.

The first group of parables tell of the Kingdom's
coming, growth, victorious progress, and joy. They include
the Patch and the Wineskins, the Mustard Seed, the Leaven,
the Seed Growing Silently, the Tares, the Dragnet, the
Sower, the Divided Realm, the Strong Man Bound, the Empty House, the Wedding Guests. In his later work, The
Parables Then and Now, Hunter reduces the number of
parables in the first category to five. These are the Sower,
the Seed Growing Secretly, the Mustard Seed, the Leaven,
and a new one, the Grain of Wheat (John 12:24). While
these parables relate to the nature and growth of the Kingdom, the authentic note of the Gospel--God's mercy to sin-
ners--is absent. It is the second group of parables which
makes up for this lack.

The dominant note of the next group of parables is
the grace of God. Under the theme of "The Grace of the
Kingdom, " Hunter includes the following parables: the
Laborers in the Vineyard, the Two Sons, the Two Debtors,
the Great Supper, the Places at Table, the parables of the

Lost Coin and Lost Sheep in Luke 15, the Pharisee and the Publican.

Three things can be noted about these parables. First, behind them lies Jesus' own "ministry of reconciliation" so that this ministry is the text on which they provide the commentary.

Second, in these parables Jesus makes no open christological claim, and could not because "he kept his Messiahship a secret. However, he acts as God's Representative, as the Divine Grace incarnate. In effect he is saying: 'It is because God is like this that I act as I do.'"

Third, Hunter believes that most of these parables were originally answers to criticisms of Jesus' ministry made by scribes and Pharisees. But these "answers" were always tempered by the grace of God so that in the mouth of Jesus "the wrath of man is turned to God's praise, and human hard-heartedness made to proclaim divine grace."

In the third grouping ("The Men of the Kingdom"), Hunter lists eight parables in The Parables Then and Now and "a dozen or more" in Interpreting the Parables. Included are the Tower Builder and the Warring King, the Hid Treasure and the Precious Pearl, the Disobliging Neighbor and the Callous Judge, the Farmer and His Man, the Two Builders, the Unjust Steward, the Asking Son, the Friend at Midnight, the Unmerciful Servant, the Good Samaritan. These parables, Hunter feels, describe the qualities necessary for those who would enter the Kingdom. Such persons must be ready to "count the cost and to sacrifice everything for God's cause." They are summoned to a victorious faith and to obedient service. But of paramount importance is their willingness not only to hear Jesus' teaching but to practice it.

The fourth category of parables which Hunter discusses relate to "The Crisis of the Kingdom." Now the apocalyptic note predominates. Jesus understood his ministry as moving inexorably toward a supreme climax in God's dealing with His people. This crisis would bring judgment and destruction to Israel. Moreover, it would mean death for the Messiah followed by victory and the rise of a new Israel. Against this background of "darkening skies and mounting tension," Hunter suggests that the parables in this group become pregnant with meaning. The parables to be considered are the Way to Court, the Great Supper, the Talents, the Unjust Steward, the Ten Bridesmaids, the Owner's Son or Wicked Vinedressers, the Weather Signs, the Playing Children, the Rich Fool, the Savorless Salt, the Lamp and the Bushel, the Servant in Authority, the Barren Fig Tree, the Defendant (Luke 12:57-59; Matt. 5:25-26), Dives and Lazarus, the Waiting Servants (Luke 12:35-38), the Burglar (Matt. 24: 43; Luke 12:39), the Sheep and the Goats. Through these parables Jesus is urging his hearers to "discern the signs of the times," and hopefully to repent before it is forever too late. He warns them about the grave perils which await those who refuse God's invitation into his Kingdom. They must remain alert and act with resolution lest they be caught unprepared. So the "atmosphere is charged with both peril and possibility." The "zero hour" has arrived and the "crisis of the Kingdom" is at hand. These "parables of crisis" are Jesus' Weckruf to his contemporaries, urging them to turn toward the light of the Kingdom before the darkness of the present world engulfs them [Archibald M. Hunter, Interpreting the Parables (Philadelphia: Westminster Press, 1960), pp42-91; Hunter, The Parables Then and Now (Westminster Press, 1971), pp36-107].

To the above four classifications of the parables Hunter adds an additional category in The Parables Then and Now--"Eternal Issues." Four parables which are "not easily fitted into the four main categories" are included. These parables deal with "eternal issues"--salvation, final judgment, and eternal life. They are: the Good Samaritan, given in answer to the lawyer's question about eternal life; Dives and Lazarus, which was probably directed at the Sadducees who did not believe in a future life; the Last Judgment, which answers the question concerning the criterion by which the heathen will be judged; the Narrow Door, which is Jesus' reply to a man who had asked him, "Are only a few to be saved?" Following a brief introduction to this grouping, Hunter proceeds to give his interpretation of these four parables. This is also his procedure with each of his four main classifications [The Parables Then and Now, pp 108-21].

In his work on the parables, Hunter is especially interested in how they can be understood today and how they can be used in preaching. The modern study of the parables, particularly that of Dodd and Jeremias, leads to at least two conclusions. First, there dare be no more "arbitrary allegorizing" of the parables. Second, the parables should

not be used "simply as pegs for moralizing sermons."
Preaching based on the parables ought always to begin with
the primary meaning of the parable, i.e., the meaning it
had when Jesus gave it. The task of the preacher is to try
to discover the parable's original setting in the ministry of
Jesus. To whom did Jesus speak the parable and why did
he speak it? "Our first concern should be the original
'thrust' of the parable." After this task is completed, the
minister is free to translate the parable into contemporary
terms or to moralize, warn, instruct, or exhort. Only
after the first task is completed, will the second have a
firm "dominical basis."

As for Hunter's principle regarding allegorizing, he
cannot agree with Jülicher that all allegorizing must be excluded. For the most part the parables are similitudes,
not allegories. However, some of these similitudes have
allegorical elements, and Hunter believes that one of the
parables--the Wicked Vinedressers--is indeed an allegory.

Are there any guidelines that one can follow as to
where allegorizing should begin and end? Hunter observes
that "some of the wisest things ever said on this score"
were said by James Denny. He summarizes Denny's view
as follows: "The golden rule is this: Don't try in the interests of an arbitrary theory to eliminate everything allegorical and so trim the texts into pure parables. On the
other hand, don't allegorize to the point which marks the
one lesson which every parable was meant to teach." To
this Hunter adds a further "touchstone" for detecting allegorical elements in the parables. "Elements in a parable
which, either in the Old Testament or in current Jewish
theology, bore a familiar symbolical meaning, and were
therefore likely to be so taken by Jesus' audience, should
be so interpreted."

After Jülicher, one of the chief temptations in preaching the parables was to moralize them. In view of the interpretation of Dodd and Jeremias, moralizing becomes an
untenable methodology. Does this mean that we should re-
frain completely from moralizing the parables? Hunter says
that this would be a state of perfection and that what we
ought to strive for is "temperance" rather than "total absti-
nence." Certain of the parables such as the Two Builders,
the Two Sons, the Pharisee and the Publican, and the Good
Samaritan have a distinct ethical emphasis and moralizing is
unavoidable. Moreover, even the "parables of crisis" are

"ethical" because they call for repentance which has clear
and strong moral implications. Moralizing is not "to be
avoided like the plague, " but what is to be avoided is indis-
criminate moralizing. Hunter feels that a minister has no
right to go to the parables for guidance on politics, economics, eugenics, pacifism, capital punishment, etc. However,
a "temperate moralizing" is permissible so long as "we know
what we are doing" and are sure that our moralizing of the
parables is "in accordance with the revealed mind of Christ. "

In his most recent work on the parables (The Parables Then and Now), Hunter discusses another method of
interpretation which can make them speak meaningfully today. This is to expound them existentially. Existential
thinking involves response, commitment, and obedience; and
Hunter says that "the parables of Jesus almost cry out for
such exposition. " The parables are invitations to decision
and spurs to perception and action. But there are different
"brands" of existentialism, and its language is often turgid
and opaque. Hunter understandably exclaims: "God help
the humble hearer in the pew if before he can understand
a parable of Jesus he must first be indoctrinated in Heidegger's philosophy of being and then in Bultmann's theology!"
After commenting on Geraint V. Jones' Art and Truth of
the Parables as a helpful approach to interpreting the parables existentially, Hunter finally singles out Helmut Thielicke's The Waiting Father as the most practical and effect-
ive existential exegesis of the parables.

Let us conclude our discussion of Hunter's analysis
of the parables with this summary statement:

> The long and short of it is this, that, in expound-
> ing the parables, we should try to combine scholar-
> ly integrity with New Testament truth and existen-
> tial concern. In other words, if we must always
> begin by trying to discover what Jesus meant to
> say in his parable to those who heard it, our task
> will not be completed till we have made it say,
> 'Tua res agitur. It concerns you, and me, and
> all of us' [The Parables Then and Now, pp23-31;
> Interpreting the Parables, pp92-109; 'The Inter-
> pretation of the Parables, ' 103-04].

25   AMOS N. WILDER

Even though Amos Wilder has never devoted an entire

book to the parables, he has had a significant influence upon recent American parabolic interpretation. He brings to his work a dual expertise in that he is a major New Testament scholar as well as a poet and an authority on general literary criticism. Among those who acknowledge their indebtedness to Wilder and whose work reflects his insights, are Norman Perrin, Robert Funk, Dan Via, and Dominic Crossan. One can almost speak of an "American school" of parable interpretation and say that Wilder is one of its seminal figures. Norman Perrin, who was one of Wilder's staunchest admirers, writes:

> As a New Testament scholar he fully appreciated
> the discussion among New Testament scholars; as
> a literary critic he was in a position to begin to
> remedy the deficiency in that discussion at the
> level of literary criticism; while as a poet
> he was able to appreciate both the creative
> force of poetry as primordial language, and the
> dynamics of the relationship between the poet's
> own vision and that which comes to expression
> in his words [Jesus and the Language of the
> Kingdom (Philadelphia: Fortress Press, 1976),
> pp127-28].

The work most often referred to in reference to Wilder's analysis of the parables is his book, Early Christian Rhetoric: The Language of the Gospel, which was published in a second edition in 1971. It contains a new Introduction in which Wilder states as his purpose: "to locate more particularly the aim and method of the work, to discuss the significance of this approach in current biblical interpretation, and to take account of some of the most recent developments in the specifically 'literary' and rhetorical aspects of New Testament study" [Amos N. Wilder, Early Christian Rhetoric: The Language of the Gospel, 2d ed. (Cambridge, Mass.: Harvard University Press, 1971), p xi].

In reviewing the relationship between literature and theology, and particularly the literary study of the Bible, Wilder notes that the earlier tendency was to separate the literary aspects from the dogmatic. This methodology often resulted in a dualistic view of reality so that the "spiritual" was seen as a higher order than the "natural." The Kingdom of God was the domain of spiritual sensibility, of Beauty, Truth, and Goodness. The understanding of the parables often tended toward a "cloudy spirituality" so that the elements in the natural world pointed to great corresponding truths in the spiritual world. Today, however, the sittuation is changing in that there is a new appreciation for the unity and the inseparable relation of form and content in all texts. In a word, the wide gulf that existed between the literary and the religious approach is in the process of being closed, and this fact has widespread implications for New Testament studies. It is precisely here that Wilder is able to make a unique contribution because of his ability to combine the techniques of New Testament scholarship and literary criticism.

Wilder notes that in contemporary literary criticism attention is being directed to the given work as a self-sufficient aesthetic whole which should be allowed to make its own impact apart from extraneous considerations having to do with the author and his circumstances or intentions or with distinctions between matter and form. The particular "Word" of a given text is to be encountered at the level of its own coherent and interrelated pattern of imagery and design. A corresponding development can be observed in New Testament studies during the past few decades. The tendency is to move away from the analysis of the formal elements appropriated by the evangelists to a recognition of the total structure of each gospel [ibid. , pp xxi-xxv].

One of the objections to the above approach is that the emphasis on unity and coherence may go so far as to isolate a particular work from its wider context of meaning. If one focuses too exclusively on the self-sufficient aesthetic pattern of a text, it can be divorced from its potential as a bearer of existential disclosure. Existential criticism, as reflected in the so-called "new hermeneutic," insists that "meaning" is not primarily related to a literary work as object, but to Being which discloses itself in the work--the work being only the vehicle of the "language event." The language event transcends the subject-object relation so that what is said stands disclosed in a way that unites text and reader, past and present.

Wilder is prepared to accept this view of language in his analysis of the language of the Gospel, but "only with reservations." He acknowledges the "claustrophobic error" of viewing a text as an independent aesthetic object. Meaning does emerge in our reciprocal encounter with the work. However, there is a danger of vagueness and of using too easy a formula for the characterization of Being and of meaning. In theological hermeneutics, Wilder says, there is a leap through the various particular "language events," or the sacred texts, to the Word of God in its immediacy. But this process can shortchange the rich and varied structures of religious experience, or it can often take the form of a quest for Being in its purity or some immaculate Word.

The methodology which Wilder adopts takes cognizance of both the particularity of different authors as well as the revelatory possibilities when a text becomes a "language event." In a summary statement he writes:

> In the following chapters we recognize the novelty of each Christian discourse and language forms, as well as the trans-historical impulse which prompts such novelty and power, and which continues to operate whenever these texts come to speech in new times. But we are constrained to observe and safeguard the particularity and concreteness of each such text. What is crucial here is that all such manifold particularity in the language and the language events--in the various genres, voices, and images--requires a corresponding rich structure in Reality itself, in Being itself. This aspect of the ultimate mystery-- whether the approach be in aesthetic, philosophical, or theological terms--does not always come into its rights in existential criticism and interpretation [ibid., pp xxvii-xxx].

In his discussion of the parables themselves, Wilder weaves the various strands--literary, existential, eschatological--into a pattern of interpretation that places him in the forefront of contemporary parabolic exposition.

One should never assume that Jesus' prime motive in telling parables was to hold the attention of his hearers by means of good pedagogical strategy. What we must see is that the parables reflect certain basic assumptions about existence and a world view which regarded the historical process as moving toward a denouement. There is a revelatory quality about the parables which Wilder wants to stress. Like the teachings of the prophets and the apocalyptists, they unveil mysteries, but above all they mediate reality and life.

Of special interest to Wilder is the fact that the parables "are so human and realistic." There is a "secularity" about them because the persons, scenes, and action in them are not usually "religious." It is true that there is a large element of quasi-allegorical religious reference to Old Testament themes. However, allegorization in the parables must often be attributed to the hand of later editors. There is a realism about the parables because they are about human life and-or nature and they are characterized by action and happenings which have an authentic tie to things as they are in real life. There is a naturalness and a secularity about them which leads Wilder to observe that in them "we recognize Jesus the layman."

But there is another side of this picture, for Jesus gives the parables applications which are moral and religious. Jesus is pointing beyond the actual stories to their meaning and application. He is not merely clarifying difficult ideas, but is leading men to make a judgment and come to a decision. There is a dynamic quality about the parables which has the capacity to arouse dormant awareness and conscience. Wilder begins his section on the parables with a quote from Gerhard Ebeling which succinctly describes this dynamic and existential dimension of the parables: "The art of the parable ... is none other than that of bringing the hearer face to face with what it is to be human and thereby to make clear what it means for God to draw near" [Zeitschrift fur Theologie und Kirche 58 (1961), 135; quoted by Wilder, op. cit., p71].

The uniqueness of Jesus' parables does not lie in their vivid and concrete presentation of human life. Wilder notes that vividness of portrayal can be found in numerous authors and in various forms of literature, both ancient and modern. The difference between these and the parables has to do with the depth or superficiality with which man is presented. Jesus' parables represent a unique fusion of theological and moral mystery with ordinariness, naturalness, and secularity.

In terms of form, the parables of Jesus can be compared with those of the rabbis. Wilder quotes Jeremias with approval that the parables "reveal a definite personal character, a unique clarity and simplicity, a matchless mastery of construction." The rabbis used the parable to illustrate a wide variety of topics and there was more tendency toward allegory. What is remarkable about Jesus'

parables is their sobriety of style and their sharpness of
focus in view of Jesus' intense eschatological consciousness.
They are marked by an incomparable human and naturalistic
and artistic portrayal of human life in spite of the acute
eschatological crisis from which they emerged. There is
"no stridency and no fanaticism, " and while there are "high-
pitched aspects and accents, " the parables never took the
"form of shrillness, of the esoteric or the angelic. " Wilder
observes that Jesus' eschatological challenge is sometimes
clothed in hyperbole, but only in such a way as to suggest
the element of surprise or contrast in a situation [Wilder,
op. cit., pp71-77].

In Jesus' mode of speech, and especially in his parables, we discern another clue to the mystery of his being.
In the history of human culture there have been kairotic
moments when some great genius brought to fulfillment the
initiatives of his predecessors and thus made available fresh
insights for subsequent thought and action. Jesus represents
such a synthesis, and in him many ancient tributaries merged.
He unites in himself many roles, among them prophet, law-
giver, and wise man. The most obvious synthesis in Jesus'
teachings is that of the wise man and the prophet. He is
at home with both the wisdom tradition and the prophetic
oracle. But Jesus is neither sage nor apocalyptist, though
he draws upon both traditions. Wilder notes that Jesus
transforms and reconciles these different rhetorics. He
united both proverbial wisdom and eschatological imagery
and brought them into direct relation with the realities of his
time.

The rhetorical perfection and dispassionate quality of
Jesus' parables could readily lead one to assume that he was
essentially a teacher or an artist. We do not usually as-
sociate concern for form with eschatological fervor and passion. Wilder, however, maintains with Ernst Käsemann
that felicity and sophistication of form is perfectly compatible
with prophetic, and, indeed, extempore utterance. The
genius of Jesus is that he transcends all these paradoxes and
dichotomies. Wilder concludes that the artistic form of the
parables does not make them in any way incompatible with
Jesus' eschatological sayings. Nor should we think of them
as artistically premeditated in contrast with other sayings
seen as ejaculations or outbursts. In the parables, just as
in all of Jesus' sayings, we are confronted with his immediacy and presence [ibid., pp78-82].

In the final section of his discussion of the parables, Wilder singles out the so-called parables of the Kingdom in Mark 4 and Matthew 13. Here, he believes, we can be confident of having reached "bedrock" so that we can "hear Jesus of Nazareth speaking." Even though these parables were adapted and generalized in the process of transmission, "Jesus' creative speech was so fresh and significant that it could, as it were, breed speech true to itself."

When we seek to identify the authentic words of Jesus, there are certain guidelines which can aid us. One criterion is that of form. Wilder suggests that the characteristic design and the "tight form" of the parables guarantee them against change and supplementation. They have an organic unity and coherence which makes them resistant to change. However, is it not possible that followers of Jesus could have created some of the parables? Wilder admits that there are critical reasons for suspecting the genuineness of the parable of the Tares. But the crucial test concerns the question of "focus and depth." In the parables "there is no blurring or incongruity." Neither are they discursive. Rather, they are characterized by a "depth of concern and intensity of vision."

It is with the parables of the Kingdom, Wilder maintains, that we can have maximum confidence that we are hearing Jesus' authentic words. They are closely knit and clearly shaped by a single vision and are therefore less subject to modification.

Another consideration bearing on the authenticity of Jesus' parables concerns the role of image and metaphor. Wilder makes an observation, reminiscent of Paul Tillich, that a true metaphor or symbol is always more than a sign; it is a bearer of the reality to which it refers. The hearer is not a passive bystander, but a participant in that reality. Jesus' speech possessed this quality because it was fraught with "compelling imagination, spell, mythical shock, and transformation."

Returning to the parables of the Kingdom, Wilder says that they are prophetic in character rather than discursive or argumentative. Moreover, they are not to be understood primarily in moralistic or allegorical, but in christological and existential terms. If we see them in Jesus' own situation, then their real authority and power emerge. Jesus' own certain faith and the intensity of his

own vision is reflected in the image of the great harvest.
The disciples are encouraged not by homiletical illustrations
drawn from nature but by Jesus' impartation to them of his
own vision by the power of metaphor. Wilder adds: "For
us, too, to find the meaning of the parable we must identify
ourselves with that inner secret of Jesus' faith and faithfulness." Wilder recognizes that this sort of christological
interpretation of the parables is subject to the charge that
he is reading a dogmatic view of Christ into them. But
this is not his intention at all. What he is saying is that
the parables "should be understood in relation to the speaker and the occasion; not in connection with his titles but in
relation to his way and his goal."

Wilder suggests that we get a better view of the
historical Jesus if we see him as using two media to proclaim the Kingdom. On the one hand he used the eschatological imagery and categories which were the current theological symbol of his time and place. But on the other
hand he said the same things in his parables by means of
common speech or "layman's language." Thus Jesus translated theology into common parlance and brought it down
into daily life and into the immediate everyday situation
[ibid., pp82-88].

One can readily understand why Wilder has had such
prominence, especially in recent American interpretation
of the parables. His literary, critical, and theological
analysis of the parables serves as a foundation for further
constructive work. His insights, though brief in compass,
are highly suggestive for fresh directions in parabolic research. Though he is intent on applying the methods of
contemporary literary criticism to the parables, nevertheless, his basic concern is christological. Thus he views
the parables as bearers of Jesus' vision of reality. Wilder
is concerned to establish the relationship between the one
who spoke the parables and the text so that we who seek to
interpret them in a subsequent and quite different situation
might confront and hear anew the one who is indeed our
eternal contemporary.

26   GERAINT V. JONES

In 1964 Geraint V. Jones published a book on the
parables which was not intended as an exhaustive survey,
but as a study concentrating on their art and literary form

and their existential significance. He noted that after the
work of such scholars as Bultmann and Jeremias the criti-
cal-analytical method had reached its pinnacle and a new
approach to the parables was necessary. The method which
Jones proposes is existential in that he sees the parables
as not only moral exhortations, or christological formulas,
or even evangelical proclamations, but also as disclosures,
in particular images, of the general human condition.

The interpreters who followed the lead of Dodd and
Jeremias were concerned with the Sitz im Leben of the parables and with Jesus' intention in giving them. For Jones
this approach is too restrictive, and he is interested in
widening their relevance. This is possible because the parables are essentially art forms, and therefore they can be
lifted out of their first-century milieu and can be transposed
into images of our perennial human experience. Before
this can be done, however, the parables must be examined
as a literary genre and form of art. Jones maintains that
this is a prerequisite for possibilities of further creative
interpretation, i. e. , existential interpretation [Geraint V.
Jones, The Art and Truth of the Parables: A Study in Their
Literary Form and Modern Interpretation (London: S. P. C. K. ,
1964), pp ix-xii].

Before beginning his discussion of the parables as a
literary form, Jones surveys the history of interpretation of
the parables during the modern period, i. e. , from Jülicher
to the form critics. A noteworthy feature of this history is
Jones' treatment of some of the lesser-known interpreters of
the parables such as Edward Gresswell, C. E. van Koestveld, Siegfried Goebel, J. F. McFadyen, J. A. Findlay, A.
M. Brouwer, and others.

Turning to a literary analysis of the parables, Jones
begins by comparing Jesus' parables with the Hebrew tradition. He notes that there is a uniqueness about them as a
literary genre. Insofar as the Scriptures are concerned,
the Gospel parables are virtually a new and highly original
form, as regards both purpose and content. There is nothing like them elsewhere in the New Testament, and little in
the Old. We should not, however, imagine that the parables appear in full bloom without any antecedents. In the
Old Testament, especially in the Wisdom Literature, there
are various forms of comparisons, proverbs, maxims, etc.
which have resemblances to the parables. But apart from
Nathan's parable of the Ewe Lamb, there is little that can

be recognized as being of equal status with the Synoptic parables. Jones observes that in comparison with the fully-developed parable of the New Testament, what the Old Testament offers is not much more than the germ. If we wish to assess more accurately the character of the Jewish background to the parables, we must look at the rabbinic writings because they resemble the parables far more closely than do the biblical writings [ibid., pp59-64].

Jones acknowledges that it was largely through the work of Paul Fiebig that the comparison between rabbinic parables and those of Jesus can be pursued along profitable lines. After citing a number of parables from the Talmud, Jones observes that there is a similarity between them and some of the Gospel parables. There is the introductory formula, often in question form: "What is the matter like?" There is also the pithy narrative which leads up to a point which, however, must be elucidated as it is not self-evident. Jones concludes that the rabbinic parables do not show the variety and creativeness of the Gospel parables. But the chief difference is found in their content. The purpose of the rabbinic parables is usually to illuminate or comment on biblical passages. They are also concerned with ethical instruction and are tinged with humor. Short anecdotes and brief argumentative discourses are also typical of rabbinic parables. But human situations occur less frequently than in the Gospels. Though the Synoptic parables share these various formal characteristics, Jones maintains that their content differs conspicuously from those of the rabbis. While Jesus' parables deal with religious and ethical ideas, they are often markedly apocalyptic and focus, as the rabbinic parables do not, upon the person and work of Jesus. Moreover, they are less answers to questions than challenges to pronounce judgments on a situation or attitude. "The main difference between the parables of Jesus and those of the rabbis is that the former are the work of one with a superbly creative imagination providing profound insights without parallel" [ibid., pp64-79].

In an analysis of the figures of speech in the Gospels, Jones retraces the terrain that many of his predecessors had taken. Thus he discusses the nature of metaphor, similitude, parable, and allegory. On the problem whether or not there are allegorical elements in the parables, Jones makes some noteworthy observations. He feels that much of the past argument was misdirected and unnecessary because those who engaged in it were not men of letters or

philosophers of art. If they had been, they would have distinguished between symbolism and allegory. Jones points
out that symbols may be allegorical, but a symbolic tale is
not necessarily an allegory, and the recurrence of certain
symbols in some parables and of their single occurrence in
others does not turn them into allegories. For example,
the Pearl is a symbol of the Kingdom, but the parable is
not an allegory. The parable of the Wicked Husbandmen,
which comes closer to allegory than any of the parables,
should nevertheless be understood as a complex symbol of
the line of prophets and of the Messiah.

Jones says that there is no reason why Jesus should
not have told allegorical tales, and contentions to the contrary are not demonstrable. Since the parable is a work of
art, it should be judged as such. Dogmatic assertions as
to what Jesus did or did not do, whether or not he spoke in
symbol or allegory as well as in pure parable, whether or
not his parables had one or more points, whether or not he
"applied" his parables--all such procedure is difficult to defend, unless one comes to the parables with fixed presuppositions [ibid., pp80-109].

While the parables in the main consist of short or
extended similes and narratives, they reflect a variety of
teaching methods and of content. Each is appropriate to its
Sitz im Leben so that some of the parables are told in response to controversial questions relating to Jesus. Others
consist of judgments on national, religious, or personal
situations. Still others involve the self-criticism of the
listener as in the parable of the Unforgiving and Forgiving
Creditors. There are, moreover, different kinds of parables covering differences of content, method of narration,
length, and application. While the parable is not a completely new literary form, Jones insists that it is so superior to the mashal or similitudes of the rabbinic tradition
that "they may be regarded as virtually the invention of a
powerful and vivid intellect with a remarkable gift for ex-
temporization." It is human life, shaped by Jesus' creative imagination, which provides the "raw material" for
the parables. One should not forget that Jesus was not only
a religious teacher but also a creative artist of unusual
skill and penetration. Jones observes that the christological
significance of Jesus' activity as an outstanding creative
artist has not been fully explored, possibly because "the de-
humanized christology of the church in the classical period
of its theology has not been an encouragement to think of
him as a great story-teller."

As art the parables have the potential of doing what metaphysical or theological abstractions cannot. They describe the existential truth about man who encounters the empirical world instead of the bloodless world of thought of the theological or philosophical speculator. This means further that the parables, like a work of art, have the quality of time-and place-transcendence so that they are never obsolete but belong to any age. Moreover, they continue to stimulate new responses and to agitate the mind into fresh creative thinking. To use Bultmann's categories, they are geschichtlich, historisch, because their disclosure of God's being and activity and of man's existential situation is not altered by the passage of time or changing environment.

Jones raises an interesting question concerning the anonymity of the characters in Jesus' parables. For example, in the parable of the Prodigal Son the characters are anonymous, as they are in all the parables with the exception of the Rich Man and Lazarus. Yet these characters have attained an existence and an immortality of their own. Jones notes: "Nowhere else in the world's literature has such immortality been conferred on anonymity." Jesus had the sheer genius of being able to impart the quality of time-and-place-transcendence to the characters in his parables. What is it that gives them this quality of self-transcendence?

In seeking an answer to this question Jones refers to an essay by Jakob Wassermann, written in 1922, in which he notes that as soon as an event or a person has entered the transforming stream of myth, it takes on a living form, transcends the ages and outlasts them. Wasserman's observation is true concerning the famous biblical personages and the characters in the parables. "Time, tradition, and usage have transformed them into living personalities with a kind of independent existence of their own, even when they are legendary (though not unhistorical)." Jones suggests that a strictly non-theological approach to the biblical literature can be of assistance in enforcing its value as revelation. An intriguing paradox attends certain biblical stories, such as the Temptation and Fall in the early chapters of Genesis, as well as the parables. We discover that what is not "true" historically or anthropologically, is true existentially. Adam and Eve and the Prodigal Son are representative and symbolical of truths about human existence, even though we admit their factual "untruth." Myth and art have the potentiality of exposing facets of experience which otherwise might remain hidden from us. They possess the quality of inspiration, imaginativeness, insight, illumination, the ability to transform experience so that it assumes a universal quality and thereby makes a particular moment, incident, or experience available to all through imaginative participation.

> There is a reality which is not identical with that of the empirical world. It has its own laws and constitution. This reality is the creation of the author's vision; it is given form and symbol by the imagination. Its medium and instrument is art, which is the world of illusion made real, and of reality transformed into symbol [ibid., pp110-32].

In developing his existentialist interpretation of the parables, or as he also calls it, a "wider interpretation," Jones notes that the modern study of the parables has shown that the application of some is limited by various factors, such as their immediate historical context and perspective or their didactic character. The "historical" and christological parables have a particular and limited significance in that they can be interpreted but cannot easily be applied to other situations.

Since the parables are characterized by a wide diversity of form and content, Jones rejects any attempt to limit them to one type of discourse or to apply indiscriminately the same principle of interpretation without regard to their special differences. The notion that a parable shall have only one point, or that it shall be understood only as a whole, and not in relation to its parts--that is "pure dogmatism." Jones is interested not primarily in a thematic classification of the parables, but in one which focuses on the manner of their applicability and to the type of parable to which they belong. He says that there are about fifty parables and major parabolic sayings, and he proposes to classify these into three groups.

First, there are those parables which have little or no meaning apart from their context and setting-in-life. This group numbers 19. Among them are: the Great Supper, the Rich Man and Lazarus, the Laborers in the Vineyard, the Ten Virgins, the Unjust Steward, and the Wicked Husbandmen.

The second group, of 21, include those capable of only one interpretation because they illustrate some particular teaching or injunction and are mainly didactic. Among these are the parables of the Kingdom which cannot be legitimately applied to anything else, yet which are not evoked by any particular or momentary situation. Other examples are the Importunate Widow, the Lost Sheep and the Lost Coin, the Pharisee and the Tax Collector, the Rich Fool, the Unmerciful Servant, the Two Builders, the Last Judgment.

The third and smallest group consist of those parables which can be given a "wider or existential interpretation." Their contextual or historical interpretation is usually clear and they arise from the situation in which they occur. Yet they are capable of a wider or more generalized application to situations which may not necessarily be similar to those originally provoking them. In this group Jones lists the following parables: the Empty House, the Good Samaritan, the Prodigal Son, the King at War, the Tower Builder, the Talents, the Pounds, the Hand to the Plow.

Jones maintains that all three of the above groups have one thing in common--the impact made by the summons to a decision. This is especially true of the parables in the third group.

It is in the writings of Bultmann that Jones finds a trenchant basis for his existentialist analysis of the parables. According to Bultmann, Jesus had no intention of proclaiming any general or ethical truth in his parables. Rather, they illumine man's understanding of the meaning and character of his existence, that is, as the being whom God has placed in the position of having to make an existential decision directed towards the future.

The interpretation of the parables, or for that matter, any text, must take account of the fact that each interpreter brings to his task a particular "life setting"--a mental or theological approach which influences what he sees [Bultmann uses the term Vorverständnis, or "pre-understanding" to characterize this phenomenon]. Jones suggests that this notion of Vorverständnis should apply to our approach to the parables in two ways. The primary presupposition is christological. The parables mediate revelatory truth and are authoritative for Christians because of the person who spoke them. His status as the Christ places the parables in a context which sets them apart from the wisdom literature, tales, and aphorisms in the rabbinic tradition.

The second form of pre-understanding is the recognition that the parables are art forms, and as such they offer "expanding possibilities of impact on the mind and imagination with a recreative and seminal potency." Jones maintains that because the parables are a form of art, they are the medium of a truth which is both revelatory and existential, and that in this approach lies the potentiality for widening the field of their interpretation and application.

But if we are to extend the interpretation of the parables and to remove them from their particular situation in the past, the element of allegory must be introduced. Such parables as the Wicked Husbandmen, the Sower, and the Tares are not readily understandable apart from their being representational stories or allegories. As Jones sees it, there is nothing improbable in believing that some of the parables were allegorically conceived by Jesus himself. On the whole, however, allegorization is not necessary, and a wider interpretation is possible without it because the parable indicates a pattern of human behavior, a paradigm of existence, or a picturesque account of God's relation with man. For Jones the most comprehensive example of this type of parable is the Prodigal Son.

In an existential understanding of a parable the Sitz im Leben is not of prime importance. Over-insistence on the original context (which is often no more than conjecture) can become a mere academic exercise so that the wider implications of the parable are lost sight of. Unless the existential dimensions of a parable are discerned, all our painstaking historical research may miss the mark. Having laid the ground work for a "wider interpretation" of the parables, Jones turns his attention to an existential exposition of "the greatest and most artistically satisfying of all the parables: the Prodigal Son" [ibid., pp135-66].

The parable of the Prodigal Son is an ideal example of the existential possibilities inherent in the parables. As great art it appeals to the imagination. We can readily identify with its characters because they are created out of the same pool of existence as our own experience. Its artistic qualities enable it to speak with an eloquence that is not possible for propositional and doctrinal statements and discursive language. Moreover, the parable is infused

with a transforming vision which moves us and causes us
to pass judgment on life and people. It tells its story,
largely free from didactic comments, and leaves it to the
listener of that time and this to frame his own judgment
and reach his own conclusion.

Jones discerns in the parable a number of motifs
which have become well-known in existentialist thought.
Without reading into it more than it can bear, he perceives
such themes as freedom and responsibility, estrangement,
the personalness of life, longing and return, grace, anguish,
reconciliation. In an obvious allusion to much recent parabolic interpretation, Jones remarks that if we were to exclude the above perceptions in the interest of obedience to
a principle of interpretation limited to the immediate setting, we would rob the parable of most of its richness and
impoverish it beyond measure. The greatness of the parable of the Prodigal Son must be seen in its potentiality for
recreation and reproduction and its ability to open before
us broad vistas of thought and experience. As Jones writes:

> It is not the context alone which confers immortality
> on the parable of the Prodigal Son (or the Lost Boy)
> but the form, the pressure of its style, the vigor of
> its imaginative conception, its delineation of charac-
> ter, and its exposure of motives and attitudes. It is
> a piece of life transfigured and given meaning by
> vision, and has become an archetypal pattern of hu-
> man existence [ibid. , pp167-205].

In Jones' The Art and Truth of the Parables we have
a thorough and perceptive work on the parables of Jesus
from an existentialist point of view. His work represents
a departure from a number of emphases which have predominated in the modern period of parable research. With
his insistence that whenever possible the parables should be
approached existentially, Jones challenges the contention
that they are primarily theological or soteriological statements. He observes that in the parables Jesus begins, not
with statements about salvation, but with a picture of existence. The parables concern salvation, not as doctrine, but
as a dynamic power which encompasses the totality of man's
historical and spiritual existence.

Just so, Jülicher's contention that a parable is not
an allegory and contains one point only and should be interpreted as a whole and not in detail, represented a significant

advance in parabolic interpretation. While this was a useful corrective, nevertheless, it was too restrictive. As noted above, Jones allows for some kind and degree of allegorization because a number of the parables cannot be understood apart from the allegorical factor.

Another approach about which Jones is skeptical is the eschatological which was so central to Dodd. As Jones sees it, if one understands the parables in terms of an undefined "crisis" or with the expected end of the world-order or even with Christ's second advent, they cannot be given much more than this very particular application, and thus there is little that they have to offer the Christian of today.

Following Dodd, and especially Jeremias, much attention has been given to the recovery of the original situation in which the parables were spoken. However, in many instances the context has been irretrievably lost, while in others its recovery is a matter of conjecture. Jones contends that the relevance of a saying or parable to the contemporary situation does not depend upon its being anchored in the original circumstances of its delivery, though knowledge of it may be helpful to its exposition [ibid., pp206-22].

Enough has been said to indicate that Jones is interested in "freeing" the parables from any historical, hermeneutical, or theological schemata which might hinder their potential for disclosing the permanent and universal dimensions of human existence. Whether he has succeeded in this endeavor, or has instead bound the parables with a "new dogma," remains a relevant question.

27   NORMAN PERRIN

Among present-day American New Testament scholars and interpreters of Jesus' parables, Norman Perrin, the Chicago New Testament professor, occupied until his untimely death in 1976* a prominent place. One of his chief areas of concentration was the teachings of Jesus, and therefore much of his writing has centered upon the Kingdom of God and the parables. But within this framework Perrin

*On November 25, just short of his 56th birthday; he had just completed proofreading of his final work, The Resurrection According to Matthew, Mark, and Luke.

gave special attention to the problem of hermeneutics--that is, what is involved in the act or process of interpreting a given text?

As one examines Perrin's works, one soon discovers that his thought has been in the process of developing, and that in the current discussion on the parables he was both contributing and receiving. Among those whose influence he has readily acknowledged are Jeremias (his one-time teacher), Bultmann, Fuchs, Wilder (for whom he had the highest regard), Paul Ricoeur, Funk, and Via. Perrin's writing is characterized by a clarity which sacrifices nothing to the dimensions of breadth and depth. He dealt with the modern history of interpretation of the parables in an essay in Interpretation and in an admirable section of his recent book Jesus and the Language of the Kingdom. [See Norman Perrin, "The Modern Interpretation of the Parables of Jesus and the Problem of Hermeneutics," Interpretation 25 (1971), 131-48; Perrin, Jesus and the Language of the Kingdom (Philadelphia: Fortress Press, 1976), pp89-205.] The latter is particularly significant because of its treatment of contemporary American interpretation of the parables--an account which Perrin himself has had no small part in shaping.

Our purpose is not to deal with Perrin's analysis of the individual parables, but to attempt to describe the hermeneutical methodology which he regarded as essential to our understanding of them. [For Perrin's interpretation of the individual parables, see his Rediscovering the Teaching of Jesus (New York: Harper & Row, 1967), pp87-130, 155-59.] Perrin's methodology draws from various movements, while his basic concern was to bring to the forefront of contemporary discussion the hermeneutical interaction between author, text, and reader.

Perrin's approach to the nature of the gospel tradition stands squarely within the context of form criticism, or more exactly, redaction criticism (Redaktionsgeschichte), which is an outgrowth of form criticism. He has written a book on redaction criticism and was one of its leading American exponents and interpreters. [For his discussion of redaction criticism, see Norman Perrin, What Is Redaction Criticism? (Philadelphia: Fortress Press, 1969).]

A prerequisite for studying the synoptic tradition is a historical analysis of that tradition which seeks to reconstruct its earliest form and reach its primary stratum. The question must be raised as to whether a given saying should be attributed to the early church or to the historical Jesus, or perhaps to ancient Judaism. If and when the original form is reached, then a criterion which can test its authenticity must be devised. Perrin suggests three criteria by which one can judge the authenticity of the synoptic tradition.

First, there is the "criterion of dissimilarity." A saying can be regarded as authentic if it can be shown to be distinctive of Jesus, i. e., if it is dissimilar to known tendencies in Judaism before him or in the early Church after him. This will be particularly the case where Christian tradition oriented towards Judaism can be shown to have modified the saying away from its original emphasis. Perrin notes that this criterion was not reached on the basis of theoretical considerations but in the course of practical work in the synoptic tradition. Moreover, it was first used by Bultmann in his discussion of the parables.

A second criterion, suggested by Harvey K. McArthur, is the "criterion of multiple attestation." Material may be accepted which is found in a multiplicity of sources or forms of the tradition--but only if this multiple attestation is not due to the influence of some widespread church practice such as the Eucharist. Perrin acknowledges that this criterion is somewhat restricted and that he has some reservations about it.

Thirdly, by means of the "criterion of coherence" one can accept material which coheres or is consistent with the emphases found in the tradition and with material established as authentic by other means.

Perrin contends that future synoptic and life-of-Jesus research must proceed according to this methodology because form and redaction criticism has made this kind of stringency possible. Insofar as the parables are concerned, wherever these criteria are applicable "they are always the starting-point for our discussion" [Rediscovering the Teaching of Jesus, pp38-48; What Is Redaction Criticism? pp70-71].

In examining the form of the parables, Perrin believes that there are a limited number of instances where the parable in very much its original form made a point of significance to the early church, even if that was different

from the point originally intended by the historical Jesus.
The Good Samaritan and the Prodigal Son represent such
cases, and they may approximate their original form. But
these are exceptions which underscore the findings of form
criticism. The reason that they are presented in more or
less their original form is that they served the purpose of
the church, or the evangelist, and not because there was
any historical interest in the original form as such. Unlike
the cases just cited, most of the parables have been modified in the tradition; some have been transformed into allegories; new conclusions have been supplied; and most have
been interpreted and reinterpreted. But the basic reason
for such modification has always been the need of the church
in a changing situation. Perrin concludes: "Certainly, every
single parable in the tradition has to be approached with the
basic assumption that, as it now stands, it represents the
teaching of the early church: that the voice is the voice of
the risen Lord to the evangelist, and of the evangelist to
the church, not that of the historical Jesus to a group gathered by the Sea of Galilee." But compared with other elements in the tradition, Perrin maintains that the parables
are characterized by an individuality and an originality, and
that they are stamped with the personality of their author
[Rediscovering the Teaching of Jesus, pp21-22].

Modern interpretation, particularly following Dodd,
has held that the Sitz im Leben of the parables is eschatological. They are focused upon the Kingdom. Perrin is
much impressed by Wilder's statement that a true metaphor
or symbol is more than a sign; it is a bearer of the reality
to which it refers. Therefore Jesus' parables must be
understood as bearers of his own vision by the powers of
metaphor. Thus the parables have the capacity of impart-
ing to their hearers something of Jesus' vision of the power
of God at work in the experience of the men confronted by
the reality of his proclamation. Perrin takes note of an
observation by Eberhard Jüngel that there are only a very
limited number of parables concerned with proclaiming the
Kingdom of God per se. The vast majority of parables are
concerned with the experience and/or subsequent activity of
men confronted by the reality of God at work. Perrin proceeds to group the parables under seven headings, and he
notes that in only two of the seven groups is there a concern with proclaiming the Kingdom in the same sense that
the eschatological similes proclaim it [ibid., pp82-83].
While the parables may be grouped into categories which
describe the activity of God, they should never be under-

stood as being propositional statements. They must be allowed to speak for themselves because their linguistic form
is marked by a dynamic quality which resists translation
into other modes of discourse.

In a later work Perrin suggests that Jesus' speech
tends to revolve around two distinct poles or foci of concern
--"proclamation" and "parenesis." The parables do not set
forth propositional statements about the Kingdom; rather they
proclaim that the Kingdom is present and that the incursion
of the divine can be discerned in the experiences of everyday. In a word, the parables proclaim the reality of the
Kingdom's presence. But at the same time, there is a
second focus of concern which Perrin calls "parenesis"--
the element of response to the reality being proclaimed. In
the history of parable interpretation this aspect was not
developed because the emphasis was upon the problems of
the interpretation of the parables in general. Now, however,
with the current emphasis upon the linguistic character of
the parables, new possibilities are present for exploring
their parenetic quality [Jesus and the Language of the Kingdom, pp194-95].

One method by which a parable can be interpreted,
according to Perrin, rests upon the contention that it deals
with two parallel, analogous situations. Therefore the secret of interpretation is to find the analogous situation and
thus come to understand the point of the comparison.
Jesus' parabolic method is to tell a story which relates to
a point which has its parallel, or analogy, within the experience of some of those to whom it is addressed. The
parable becomes clear and meaningful only after one discerns both the central point and the parallel or analogy in
the situation of the ministry of Jesus or that of his hearers confronted by that ministry. "The primary task of the
exegete of the parables, then, is to set the parable in its
original context in the ministry of Jesus so that, by an
effort of historical imagination, he may grasp the crucial
point of the parable itself and then find the parallel or
analogy to which it is directed."

This raises the question of the relationship between
parable and allegory and of whether allegorization is a
permissible method of parabolic interpretation. Perrin
points out that one of the most striking things about the
parables is that they were almost immediately and totally
misunderstood, that they were treated as allegories and

not as parables. Jesus' intention in telling parables was
to draw vivid pictures from daily life and then by comparison to extract lessons from them with respect to God's
activity in the world. Perrin holds that the explanations of
the parables and the allegorical elements in the tradition
"are certainly not from Jesus." Jesus' normal practice
was probably to end the parable without supplying any application. Thus the hearers could grasp the point and find
the parallel or analogy for themselves. But if this were
the case, then we must conclude that the point of a parable must have been comparatively obvious and simple to
grasp. Consequently, there was no need on the part of
Jesus to explain or allegorize the parables because they
were understandable when he gave them.

But there is something more fundamental involved in
the distinction between parable and allegory. To allegorize
a parable is to lose the original point that Jesus intended,
but more than that, it is to misunderstand the essential
nature of the parable as a parable. For Perrin it is the
combination of these things that matters. It is only to be
expected that subsequent generations would draw meanings
from Jesus' parables which he in fact did not intend. But
the crucial factor is the translation of one literary form
into another, in this case, parable to allegory. A text
which has an ongoing life has also a distinctive form which
the literary critic can recognize. Moreover, that form
functions in one way and not in another. Perrin insists
that allegorization of the parables is never a valid method
of interpretation, not because it reads from the text meanings which Jesus did not intend, but because it does violence to the form and function of the text as a text. To
put it another way, it is eisegesis and not exegesis. This
for Perrin is extremely important, indeed crucial. His
uncompromising position is evident when he writes:

> The parables of Jesus are open-ended and may
> indeed be interpreted in ever-new ways in ever-
> new situations, but the moment the interpreter
> crosses the line from parable to allegory, the
> interpretation has become invalid, not because
> it does violence to the intent of Jesus but be-
> cause it does violence to the integrity of the text
> as a text" [Norman Perrin, "Historical Criticism,
> Literary Criticism, and Hermeneutics: The
> Interpretation of the Parables of Jesus and the
> Gospel of Mark Today," Journal of Religion 52

(1972), 367; Rediscovering the Teaching of Jesus, pp83-87].

Let us discuss further Perrin's view of what is involved in the act of interpreting a given text, and try to understand its relevance for interpreting the parables. The act of interpretation includes three distinct but interrelated aspects. These are: "historical criticism, " "literary criticism, " and "hermeneutics. " The fact that a text was spoken or written in a distinct historical situation and for a definite purpose, and that it was intended to have a particular meaning and to be understood in a particular kind of way, concerns historical criticism. In the case of the parables, the task of historical criticism is to recover this information and place the parable in its original setting. This method of necessity, however, has its limitations because a work of art, such as the parables, which was given in one situation for one purpose, can take on a life and vitality of its own as it moves into other situations. Thus a text can be interpreted and reinterpreted in any number of new and different situations, and therefore can take on different meanings and be understood in new and different ways.

Literary criticism focuses upon the form and language of a text. A text has a given form, and this form functions in one way and not another. Moreover, it is written in a certain kind of language, and this language has a certain force and not another. Our understanding and interpretation of a text are in no small way determined by its form and language.

Finally, a text is read and interpreted by an individual, and a dynamic relationship ensues between the text and the individual. This is what Perrin calls "hermeneutics, " and it is here that we come to the epitome of the hermeneutical enterprise.

It is in the areas of literary criticism and hermeneutics, and their relationship to each other, that Perrin believes the most creative and significant parabolic interpretation is taking place. It is this "frontier" that he and his American colleagues are exploring. As noted above, Perrin is drawing on various streams of recent parable analysis. He is impressed with Wilder's suggestion that a metaphor is more than a sign or symbol because it participates in the reality it describes. The "linguistuality of human existence, " the nature of metaphor and its ability to involve the hearer as participant--these are themes developed by Fuchs, Via, and Funk which Perrin regards as extremely important.

For Perrin the central issue for hermeneutics and for our understanding of the parables concerns the dynamic interaction between text and interpreter. This is the heart of the hermeneutical enterprise and is worth every effort to understand. It is here that everything else must focus and come into play. Questions of historical intent and purpose, of the author's vision, of the literary and linguistic form of the text--all must serve to enable us to approach a parable with the kind of openness which the parable itself demands and which will aid us in hearing the "answers" to the questions the parable poses. All the effort which has been expended and the skills which have to be developed must be directed toward the end of allowing the texts to speak for themselves.

This "hermeneutical moment, " as Perrin calls it, has distinct christological implications insofar as the parables are concerned. They are highly personal texts which through metaphor and metaphor extended in narrative express Jesus' vision of reality. Like certain other examples of great art, one cannot contemplate the parables except in dialogue with their creator. Perrin notes: "There are some artistic creations that are so intensely personal that they cannot be separated from the vision of reality which gave them birth. " One cannot read, for example, the parable of the Prodigal Son without perceiving that its author believed that the prodigal's extravagant welcome is indicative of a reality that can be experienced in this world. Just so, the parable of the Good Samaritan brings to our remembrance its author's death for the things he was trying to express. In our interpretation of the parables we should make use of all the tools available to us, be they historical, textual, or linguistic. However, what ultimately matters is the author's vision of reality and the challenge of that vision of reality to ourselves. To realize such a hermeneutical moment must be the end toward which all our resources are directed. But it is also obvious that this is much easier said than done [Jesus and the Language of the Kingdom, pp199-204; "Historical Criticism, Literary Criticism, and Hermeneutics..., " 361-75; "The Modern Interpretation of the Parables of Jesus and the Problem of Hermeneutics, " 145-48].

Such in broad outline was Perrin's methodology for

biblical and particularly parable interpretation. Well acquainted with the history of this interpretation, he was in
the forefront of those who are charting new courses. In
looking back, Perrin saw Jülicher as the one who rescued
the parables from the allegorizers, but lost sight of the
fact that they were parables of Jesus. The historical exegetes are doing justice to them as parables of Jesus but are
in danger of locating them in the past with no bearing upon
the present. Those who treat them as metaphors or as
aesthetic objects both illumine them historically and in some
respects bring them into the present, but at the cost of doing
perhaps less than justice to them both as parables and as
parables of Jesus [Norman Perrin, "The Parables of Jesus
as Parables, as Metaphors, and as Aesthetic Objects: A
Review Article," Journal of Religion 47 (1967), 346].

As Perrin saw it, the outlines of a viable hermeneutical method to be used in connection with the parables is
beginning to emerge. It must take cognizance of historical
criticism and its results. But it must also pay attention to
Ernst Fuch's hermeneutical endeavor. While taking historical criticism for granted, Fuchs suggests that there are
three facets of the hermeneutical task. These are the necessary involvement of the author in the text he has created,
the power of the text itself as a text, and the role of the
hearer or reader confronted by the text. These themes
Wilder, Funk, and Via have developed in reference to the
parables. It is the further working out of this methodology,
which Perrin calls the hermeneutical interaction of author,
text, and reader, that shows great promise for the future
of parable interpretation.

28   THE NEW HERMENEUTIC

Within the past two decades a movement has developed which has had a widespread influence upon biblical and
theological thought and interpretation. In this country it is
called "the new hermeneutic," while in Germany it is referred to simply as Hermeneutik. Unlike many past theological developments which originated in Germany, the new
hermeneutic has developed through dialogue between theologians in Germany and the United States. The discussion on
the new hermeneutic focuses primarily on the writings of
two German theologians, Ernst Fuchs and Gerhard Ebeling.
Fuchs, who recently retired, was Bultmann's successor at
Marburg, and both he and Ebeling were students of Bultmann

and acknowledge their indebtedness to him. Just after World War II they were together at Tübingen, and there developed a close friendship and a unity of position so that the new hermeneutic can be regarded as a single school of thought with a shared leadership.

The new hermeneutic began with the publication of Fuchs' Hermeneutik in 1954. However, like other movements, it developed from prior philosophical and theological antecedents. Among these the most immediate and direct were the works of Martin Heidegger and Rudolf Bultmann. They raised the problems and formulated the methodology which occupied the new hermeneutic. [Two English works on the new hermeneutic are noteworthy: The New Hermeneutic, Vol. II of New Frontiers in Theology, James M. Robinson and John B. Cobb, Jr., eds. (New York: Harper & Row, 1964)--significant because it includes essays by Fuchs and Ebeling as well as those of American scholars; and Paul J. Achtemeier, An Introduction to the New Hermeneutic (Philadelphia: Westminster Press, 1969).]

From 1923 to 1928 Heidegger was a professor in the department of philosophy at the University of Marburg where he and Bultmann were colleagues, since the latter held a chair in theology (New Testament). It was this relationship which later led Bultmann to adopt the basic tenets of Heidegger's philosophy for his own analysis of the New Testament, particularly in reference to the concept of demythologization.

Heidegger's works are certainly among the most abstruse in the history of philosophy. Paul Achtemeier observes that attempting to follow his thought is rather like trying to follow a path that gradually disappears as it leads one into the densest part of the forest. Interpreters of Heidegger commonly refer to the "earlier Heidegger" and the "later Heidegger." His most influential work Sein und Zeit (Being and Time), which is an existential analysis of Being and of man's response to Being, was published in 1926. It represents the earlier Heidegger, and it was this work's analysis of human existence which so profoundly influenced Bultmann.

It is the later Heidegger who has had a significant influence upon the exponents of the new hermeneutic. In more recent times Heidegger has increasingly turned his attention to the question of the meaning and function of language. The earlier view of language regarded it as basically "ex-pression," the putting into words or the outward expression of one's own subjectivity, of the understanding of one's existence (Bultmann). Heidegger regards this view as inadequate, for language has a primordial function and it has a power of its own because it owes its existence not to man but to Being. Language is called forth by Being and is therefore a response to Being. Such language has the power to disclose Being and becomes the most concrete manifestation of Being or world. It is this phenomenon of bringing Being or world into language which Fuchs calls "language-event" (Sprachereignis) and which Ebeling calls "word-event" (Wortgeschehen).

Besides Heidegger, Rudolf Bultmann has occupied a position of central importance in the development of the new hermeneutic. This is true because he has been the mentor of both Fuchs and Ebeling, and they have formulated the new hermeneutic against a Bultmannian background and in reaction to it. There is no doubt that Bultmann has been the dominant figure in 20th-century New Testament scholarship. As noted before, he has been one of the chief interpreters of form criticism. But he has also provoked intense discussion and dispute, especially with his suggestion that the New Testament must be demythologized if it is to become intelligible to our contemporaries. In the discussion which follows we will concentrate on two aspects of his thought--demythologization and his understanding of the relationship between the kerygma and the historical Jesus. These issues have a crucial bearing upon the new hermeneutic and upon its understanding of Jesus' parables.

While Bultmann has written extensively on a great variety of subjects, he is best known today for his claim that the New Testament must be demythologized. This notion was first set forth in 1941 in an essay entitled "Neues Testament und Mythologie: Das Problem der Entmythologisierung der neutestamentlichen Verkündigung." It was not until the close of World War II that this work came to the attention of theologians in countries outside Germany.

Bultmann's essay came out of a deep concern for the domain of the practical. The real problem for the contemporary church is how to communicate the Christian message to modern persons so that they will be challenged to a genuine decision. If the kerygma is to be meaningfully proclaimed, we must take seriously the discrepancy between the cosmology of the first century and the contemporary world-view of modern science. The New Testament kerygma is set in the context of a mythological view of the universe. Moreover, the earth is the scene of supernatural activity on the part of God and the angels on the one hand, and of Satan and the demons on the other. Miracles are quite frequent in this scheme and history is viewed as hastening to its end. The event of redemption is clothed in mythological language. It is this mythical picture of the world together with the mythological language of the redemptive event which poses the fundamental problem for Bultmann. He believes that for modern persons the mythical view of the world is obsolete and therefore the kerygma also becomes incredible for them. But does the New Testament embody a truth which is quite independent of its mythical setting? If so, then theology must undertake the task of stripping the kerygma from its mythical framework, of "demythologizing" it [Hans Werner Bartsch, ed., Kerygma and Myth: A Theological Debate, trans. Reginald H. Fuller (New York: Macmillan, 1955), Vol. I, pp1-5; Rudolf Bultmann, Jesus Christ and Mythology (New York: Scribner's, 1958), pp14-15].

For Bultmann, and (Bultmann believes) for the New Testament writers as well, the real purpose of myth is not to present an objective picture of the world as it is, but to express man's understanding of himself in the world in which he lives. "Myth should be interpreted not cosmologically, but anthropologically, or better still, existentially." The important point is that the essence of myth is not in its imagery but in the understanding of human existence which is expressed through the imagery. Bultmann defines this procedure as follows:

> This method of interpretation of the New Testament which tries to recover the deeper meaning behind the mythological conceptions I call demythologizing--an unsatisfactory word, to be sure. Its aim is not to eliminate the mythological statements but to interpret them. It is a method of hermeneutics. To demythologize is to reject not the Scripture or the Christian message as a whole, but the world-view of Scripture, which is the world-view of a past epoch, which all too often is retained in Christian dogmatics in the preaching of the church. To demythologize is to deny that the message of Scripture and of the church is

bound to an ancient world-view which is obsolete
[Jesus Christ and Mythology, pp18, 35-36].

Bultmann's claim that the existentialist understanding
of existence is the best way to understand and interpret the
New Testament mythology reflects his dependence upon Hei-
deggerian philosophy. He maintains that all exegesis is in-
escapably dependent, either consciously or unconsciously,
upon some philosophy or other. For him it is Heidegger's
philosophy which offers the most adequate perspective and
conceptions for understanding human existence. It is the
philosophy of Heidegger's Sein und Zeit which for Bultmann
offers the best aid to exegesis. This is evident when he
writes: "Above all, Heideggers' existentialist analysis of
the ontological structures of being would seem to be no
more than a secularized, philosophical version of the New
Testament view of human life" [Kerygma and Myth, Vol. I,
p24].

A second area which has been a central concern of
the new hermeneutic relates to the relationship between the
kerygma that now addresses us and the historical events
out of which the kerygma arose. In what sense is the historical Jesus meaningful for faith and how is he to be known?
The "new quest of the historical Jesus" was inaugurated by
the "Bultmänner" because they discerned in their mentor
too wide a discontinuity between the historical Jesus and the
kerygma.

Bultmann's understanding of history has been influenced especially by Dilthey, Heidegger, and R. G. Colling-
wood. Each of them espouses an "existentialist" approach
to history and sees a definite relationship between history
and the historical existence of the historian himself. Bultmann rejects the possibility of an "objective" view of history which may collect facts out of history but which does
not learn anything genuinely new about history and man.
Just so he rejects the method of psychologically penetrating
into the meaning of the past--a method which was used so
extensively by the lives-of-Jesus movement. Bultmann expresses his "view-point" regarding history which underlies
his work on Jesus succinctly: "Thus I would lead the reader not to any view of history, but to a highly personal encounter with history" [Rudolf Bultmann, Jesus and the Word,
trans. Louise Pettibone Smith and Erminie Huntress Lantero
(New York: Scribner's, 1958), p6].

For Bultmann the note of decision is a key category
in his understanding of history. "The historicity of the
human being is completely understood when the human being
is understood as living in responsibility over against the
future and therefore in decision" [Rudolf Bultmann, History
and Eschatology (Edinburgh: University Press, 1957), p136].
The character of every historical situation is that the problem and the meaning of past and present are enclosed and
are waiting to be unveiled by human decisions. Every moment is the now of responsibility, of decision, and it is
from this that the unity of history is to be understood [ibid.,
pp141-43]. It is this view of history which makes the
Christian faith meaningful for Bultmann. He speaks of
Jesus Christ as the eschatological event which becomes
present in the act of preaching. "It becomes an event repeatedly in preaching and faith. Jesus Christ is the eschatological event not as an established fact of past time
but as repeatedly present, as addressing you and me now
in preaching" [ibid., pp151-52]. Preaching is an address
to me, and as such it demands an answer, or decision.
In this decision of faith I am given a new understanding of
myself as free from myself by the grace of God.

Bultmann's view of Jesus is influenced primarily by
two aspects of his theological construction--form criticism
and the existentialist interpretation of history. Form criticism leads him to the position that the New Testament
writers had little interest in the personality of Jesus, but
that they were primarily interested in the work of Jesus.
The existentialist interpretation of history leads him to
speak of Jesus as the eschatological event which calls men
to decision now. So Bultmann's primary interest is not in
the historical Jesus or the Jesus who can be known through
historical research, but with the ever-present eschatological
event.

Though Bultmann emphasizes the teaching or the
message of Jesus, it is the kerygma of the Christian community which seems to loom larger and larger. He speaks
of the message of Jesus as a presupposition for the theology
of the New Testament rather than a part of that theology itself. That the kerygma rather than the historical Jesus and
his message is decisive for Christian theology is implied
when Bultmann writes:

But Christian faith did not exist until there was
a Christian kerygma: i.e., a kerygma proclaim-

ing Jesus Christ--specifically Jesus Christ the Crucified and Risen One--to be God's eschatological act of salvation. He was first so proclaimed in the kerygma of the earliest church, not in the message of the historical Jesus, even though that church frequently introduced into its account of Jesus' message, motifs of its own proclamation. Thus, theological thinking--the theology of the New Testament--begins with the kerygma of the earliest church and not before. But the fact that Jesus had appeared and the message which he had proclaimed were, of course, among its historical presuppositions; and for this reason Jesus' message cannot be omitted from the delineation of New Testament theology [Theology of the New Testament, trans. Kendrick Grobel, (New York: Scribner's, 1970), Vol. I, p3].

At the center of the kerygma is the cross of Christ which is an historical event. However, the meaning of the cross is not dependent upon a mere event in the past. Rather it acquires cosmic dimensions; it is an ever-present reality--the eschatological event in and beyond time. But how do the cross and resurrection become meaningful for us? Bultmann's answer is that in the preaching of the cross we are confronted with the decision to be crucified with Christ. Christ as the Crucified and Risen One meets us in the word of preaching which confronts us as the word of God. In accepting the eschatological event we are given a new understanding of our existence. In and through the word of preaching the door to authentic existence is opened before us. It is through the word of preaching that the saving event is made contemporary--made into the eschatological "now."

With this all too brief survey of the precursors of the new hermeneutic, let us turn our attention particularly to Ernst Fuchs who, while deeply indebted to Bultmann, goes beyond him at crucial points. [Bultmann has responded to the arguments raised by the "new quest" in a lecture entitled "Das Verhältnis der urchristlichen Christusbotschaft zum historischen Jesus." It has been translated into English and appears as "The Primitive Christian Kerygma and the Historical Jesus," in The Historical Jesus and the Kerygmatic Christ: Essays on the New Quest of the Historical Jesus, trans. & ed. Carl E. Braaten and Roy A. Harrisville (New York: Abingdon Press, 1964), pp15-42. Bult-

mann's thought is discussed in considerable detail in Warren
S. Kissinger, "The Problem of the 'historical Jesus' from
Schweitzer to Bultmann," unpublished master's thesis, Lu-
theran Theological Seminary, Gettysburg, Pa., 1964.]

ERNST FUCHS

Of the two German exponents of the new hermeneutic
we will be concerned with Ernst Fuchs because his special-
ization is in New Testament, and thus he gives more attention to the parables of Jesus than does Ebeling. Since
1954 Ebeling has taught in the field of systematic theology,
and while the new hermeneutic has implications for systematic theology, our interest in this study is not primarily in
that area.

Fuch's interpretation of the parables is not concentrated in any single work. Instead his discussion is dis-
seminated throughout three volumes of collected essays and
two volumes on the topic of hermeneutics [Zum hermeneuti-
schen Problem in der Theologie (Tübingen: J. C. B. Mohr,
1959)--a number of these essays have been translated by
Andrew Scobie and appear in Studies of the Historical Jesus
(London: SCM Press, 1964 Naperville, Ill.: A. R. Allenson, 1964; Glaube und Erfahrung (Tübingen: J. C. B.
Mohr, 1965); Hermeneutik, 2d ed. (Bad Cannstatt: R.
Müllerschön Verlag, 1958); and Marburger Hermeneutik
(Tübingen: J. C. B. Mohr, 1968)].

Of those who influenced his thinking, Fuchs singles
out Bultmann as the one who made the greatest impression
upon him. But while Fuchs is one of the eminent "Bultmann
Schüler," he must also be considered a "post-Bultmannian."
He goes beyond his mentor in at least two respects--in his
understanding of the relationship between the kerygma and
the historical Jesus and in his conception of hermeneutics.
Together with Ernst Käsemann, Fuchs has been a leading
proponent of the "new quest of the historical Jesus." And
in the development of his "new hermeneutic" he stands
closer to the later Heidegger than to Bultmann. Both the
"new quest" and the "new hermeneutic" are integrally related to Fuchs' interpretation of the parables.

As for the historical Jesus, Fuchs acknowledges that
Christian faith is centered in Jesus Christ as Lord and is
therefore faith in Jesus Christ. However, when all the
findings of form criticism are considered, there remains

a fundamental question: How does it happen that the Gospels want to narrate words and deeds of the historical Jesus, as Matthew, Mark, and Luke have clearly done? The issue is not whether these words are authentic or not; what is decisive is that they are narrated at all. Why didn't the gospel writers content themselves with a proclamation of the kerygma, the proclamation of the crucified and resurrected Lord, as Paul did? What does this interest of the evangelists in the historical Jesus mean? Fuchs maintains that the evangelists are interested in the historical Jesus--that man who before his crucifixion had lived and had been loved by his followers. They are saying that the Christian faith applies to him. Thus Fuchs believes that the Gospels serve as a corrective to the primitive Christian kerygma as expressed in the Pauline epistles. With Bultmann clearly in mind, Fuchs writes:

> Or have we understood this kerygma inaccurately? We would do well to think in terms of the latter possibility. In any case, we cannot deny that the Gospels intended to include the historical Jesus in the kerygma and that for this purpose they appealed to what he said and did. This is true in principle, as well as in detail, of both the Gospel of John and the other three. Could our conception of the historical be in need of correction? This is indeed my opinion ["The New Testament and the Hermeneutical Problem, " in The New Hermeneutic, Vol. II of New Frontiers in Theology, James M. Robinson and John B. Cobb, Jr. , eds. (New York: Harper & Row, 1964), pp113-15, 136].

In still another work Fuchs says: "I am convinced that the question of the immediate meaning of Jesus for us cannot be answered apart from the question of the 'historical' Jesus. We are not interested in exchanging this Jesus for some idea about Jesus. The New Testament--particularly in the Gospels--claims to talk of Jesus himself. We must therefore attempt to examine, and indeed to fulfill this assertion on the part of the New Testament" [Studies of the Historical Jesus (Naperville, Ill. : A. R. Allenson, 1964), p7].

Fuchs has no interest in establishing "facts" concerning the person or ministry of Jesus. Instead he speaks about Jesus' understanding of his own existence and of his own situation. The best though not exclusive sources for this undertaking are the parables of Jesus. While they are not to be regarded as the authentic words of Jesus, nevertheless they represent the content of what Jesus must have talked about. Moreover, they are what Fuchs calls "language-events" (Sprachereignisse). In them Jesus brings to speech his understanding of his situation in the world and before God, and they can create the possibility of the hearer's sharing that situation. [Cf. Zur Frage nach dem historischen Jesus, 2d ed. (Tubingen: J. C. B. Mohr, 1965), pp136-42, 267, 329, 379, 411, 415, 424-30; Glaube und Erfahrung, pp216-30, 239f, 244f; "The New Testament and the Hermeneutical Problem, " pp124-30.]

Fuchs clearly goes farther than Bultmann in his views on the historical Jesus and the parables as reflections of Jesus' understanding of his situation. Bultmann would have viewed the parables as relating to the question of human existence and as calling the hearer to decision. However, the idea that the parables give us an insight into Jesus' understanding of his existence or his faith, Bultmann would have dismissed as unwarranted psychologizing about Jesus. Recourse to Jesus' own faith signifies for Bultmann a "relapse into the historical-psychological interpretation. " The "absurd result" of psychologizing can be seen in Fuchs' suggestion that in the parable of the Prodigal Son Jesus defended his own attitude. Bultmann says that if this is true, it merely establishes a psychic motive and says nothing of the parable's intention or of the understanding of existence which underlies it [Rudolf Bultmann, "The Primitive Christian Kerygma and the Historical Jesus, " in The Historical Jesus and the Kerygmatic Christ, C. E. Braaten and R. A. Harrisville, eds. (New York: Abingdon Press, 1964), pp23, 32-33].

In discussing the nature of language in the New Testament, Fuchs accepts the typology first developed by Jülicher and subsequently adopted by Bultmann in his work on form criticism. Thus he distinguishes between simile and metaphor though they are not mutually exclusive because they both live from the power of analogy. Allegory, however, is fundamentally different from simile and metaphor, and Fuchs maintains that Jesus refrained from using allegory.

The parables are understood in terms of comparison, of setting two things side by side. Another designation for this is analogy, which Fuchs views as the most unique type of speech in the New Testament. Analogy embodies the very "language-power of existence" (Sprachkraft der Existenz).

In this context the purpose of analogy is not to impart factual or descriptive information about the subject matter which the words suggest. Rather the language of analogy is indirect speech; it talks about one thing while another is actually meant. Its purpose is existential in that it attempts to influence the hearer's stance and attitude toward the subject matter or character. The pictorial language of parable brings to expression the reality to which it points. It has the potential for changing the hearer's existence and his relationship to reality, e. g. Jesus, God, the Kingdom of God. Thus there inheres in analogy the "language power of existence." Or as Fuchs also observes, parabolic speech can become a "language-event" (Sprachereignis) [Hermeneutik, pp212-19; Zur Frage nach dem historischen Jesus, pp 379, 424-30; Glaube und Erfahrung, pp239ff.].

Fuchs states that the clearest expression of analogy is the parable. With Jülicher he regards a parable as a story which relates a typical past situation, but which captures the hearer's interest by portraying some aspect of the world in which he lives. As for the stylistic framework of a parable, it has a "picture-half" (Bildhälfte) and a "reality-half" (Sachhälfte). The latter is not mentioned in the picture-half but nevertheless comes to expression in it. The point of contact between these two "halves" Fuchs calls the tertium comparationis. It is this point of comparison between them through which the message of the parable is disclosed. In the case of the Sower the tertium comparationis is the note of future harvest or the final reckoning. In the parable of the Mustard Seed the point of comparison would be the equation, "small stake equals vast yield." The function of the point of comparison is to bring the hearer to decision. Moreover, this shows that at the beginning the narrator and the hearer may not be in agreement about the parable's meaning. One of two possibilities follow: the decision which the hearer makes will be the one intended by the narrator, and agreement will result; or it will be contrary to the narrator's intention, and opposition will occur. Thus Jesus' parables either created a common view of existence and fellowship followed; or they produced opposition and alienation resulted. But in any case, the parables produced a "language-event" so that the "language power of existence" impinged upon the hearer [Hermeneutik, pp219-29; Zur Frage nach dem historischen Jesus, pp291-92].

Fuchs speaks of the time of Jesus as a new time in contrast to the time of old. Likewise through Jesus a new word is announced. Moreover, the most significant expression of this new word appears in the parables. Since the power of analogy is inherent in the parables and since the existentialist interpretation is the proper method of analyzing them, they therefore constitute language-events [Zur Frage nach dem historischen Jesus, pp328-29]. What is a language-event and how does the new word of Jesus become language-event in the parables?

Fuchs' basic category for interpreting Jesus' proclamation, of which the parables are a central part, is "language-event." Jesus did not create new concepts, but particularly in the parables, Jesus' understanding of his situation "enters language" in a special way. Moreover, this implies that through the parables we can identify with Jesus' situation. Thus we are in a new context before God like that of the prodigal son and his father or like the laborers who came too late to the generous lord of the vineyard. Jesus' intention was to "bring God into language" so that now one can enter into a like relationship with God as he did. A language-event, however, has a communal or social dimension in that it creates unity. In language, unlike in thinking, I do not remain self-contained because I expose my conceptions to the agreement or contradiction of others. Language is the bearer of being and it discloses our situation. Therefore Fuchs states that situation is the essence of the language-event.

In the parables then, Jesus reveals his understanding of his being and his self-understanding. They express his obedience to God and his understanding that he was the witness of a new situation--the authentic witness for the exposition of the future of the rule of God. Jesus brought God into language. The parables as language-events confront us with the necessity for decision--a decision which will enable us to come to a new self-understanding before God. In other words, the parables verbalize Jesus' understanding of his situation and afford us an opportunity of sharing that situation [Studies of the Historical Jesus, pp219-28].

Let us turn to a number of Jesus' parables to describe further how they become language-events. In the parable of the Hid Treasure and the Costly Pearl a situation is described which makes use of a typical proceeding. This does not mean that Jesus' hearers were pearl merchants, but they lived in a society where such scenes were not uncommon. Thus the hearers were addressed in their own sphere. These parables exemplify a particular action which for a perceptive hearer would be appropriate in the given circumstance. Jesus draws the hearer to his side by means of the artistic medium so that the hearer may think together with Jesus. The hearer is given an invitation to participate in Jesus' situation.

These parables proclaim that the Kingdom is coming for the sake of Jesus' hearers and that they can joyfully recognize that something great is underway. Just as the man had to first acquire the field before he could share the reward, so they had to accept the gift of Jesus and thus be sure of the Kingdom. The central theme of the parables is their certainty about God's call to them. A great investment can be sure of a great gain, and the beginning can be certain of its outcome. Through these parables Jesus has mediated a sense of certainty and of joy in God. But what is more, they reveal the secret of the rule of God, of the love that is grounded in Jesus' own experience. Thus these parables can become a language-event for those who perceive that God is their ultimate security and that He has acted to draw them to His side. Such an event truly places the existence of the recipient in a new perspective [Zur Frage nach dem historischen Jesus, pp291ff, 329-36].

A second parable which is a language-event is that of the Mustard Seed. The decisive point is the contrast between the meager beginning and the end which towers above everything. Fuchs believes that this parable is not so much an explanation of the Kingdom as it is of Jesus' own situation. He is thinking about his situation and that of his hearers when he proclaims the Kingdom to them. Jesus is somehow accommodating to his audience in that he is saying that God in his coming accommodates Himself to our circumstances. We are the seed from which the Kingdom will arise in a marvelous way. The parable has an existential dimension and becomes a language-event. Fuchs says that it is no longer a pious address, but "has the effect of a sudden flash of lightning that illumines the night." The intention of a parable is that we must be able inwardly to adhere to it and to participate in it. In the case of the Mustard Seed the hearer must relate everything to himself, and this implies the significant difference between beginning and end, present and future. In the parable the person is unconditionally intended and addressed. Jesus is issuing a summons for the Kingdom. Moreover, his proclamation "creates an 'existentiell' state which transfers those who are called to God's side" [ibid., pp287-91, 342-48].

A final parable which brings Jesus' word and situation to expression is the Laborers in the Vineyard. The fact that the householder agreed to pay each worker the same wage is unusual enough, but the climactic moment in the parable is when the last to be employed are paid first. Since the parables speak of God, Fuchs believes that the central theme of the parable is the kindness (Güte) of God-- not kindness necessarily as a divine attribute, but kindness as an act of God. Furthermore, the parable has a definite christological character. Jesus intends his hearers to make a decision about himself. The parable equates Jesus' conduct with God's, and those who discern its meaning will ally themselves with the truth of Jesus' claim. But it will depend upon our own hearing or faith whether we today gain the opportunity of trusting along with Jesus in God's kindness for us. However, the parable does not simply ask us to believe in God's kindness. Rather it contains a concrete pledge of Jesus that there will be no disappointment for those who found their hope on an act of God's kindess which Jesus brought to speech and which continues and demands our faith and summons us to decision. The intention of the parable is that we should come to know God as a result of His superior acts of kindness.

The parable of the Laborers in the Vineyard emphasizes the event of kindness (or kindness as an event). Jesus brings God's kindness to speech and this is cause for rejoicing. This is "the miracle of kindness," as Fuchs entitles a sermon based on the parable. Through the parable Jesus enables his hearers to participate in his understanding of God's kindness. He brings God to speech and thereby calls us to decision--to relate ourselves to God as Jesus did. Fuchs says that the intention of the entirety of Jesus' message is that everyone who is called to the Kingdom is meant to have God on his side, with the result that he is drawn over to God's side and learns to see everything with His eyes [ibid., pp139f, 219-26, 361-64; Glaube und Erfahrung, pp219f, 471-79].

It is difficult to summarize Fuchs' interpretation of the parables because he is very difficult to follow and understand. His style lacks the precision and coherence of some of the other exegetes. Therefore there is the real possibility that one has both misunderstood and oversimplified him.

Jack Dean Kingsbury gives the following summary of Fuchs' views:

> Fuchs understands Jesus to have utilized parables to proclaim his new word to men and so to give insight into his own situation. The substance of this new word was God's 'Yes' to men, and through parable it became event in his hearers' lives as it mediated to them faith, hope, love, joy, and willingness to suffer. Consequently, through the parables of Jesus, God's 'Yes' shaped the existence of men even as it had previously shaped Jesus' own existence, making of him for all time to come the norm of conduct and of understanding of existence ["Ernst Fuchs' Existentialist Interpretation of the Parables," Lutheran Quarterly 22 (1970), 391-92].

It is too early at this point to evaluate Fuchs' contribution to the history of parabolic interpretation. However, he has had a prominent influence upon the contemporary scene both in Europe and in this country. Among those especially indebted to him are his students, Eta Linnemann and Eberhard Jüngel, and Robert Funk and Dan Otto Via. [For a further discussion and evaluation of Fuch's interpretation of the parables, see Norman Perrin, Jesus and the Language of the Kingdom (Philadelphia: Fortress Press, 1976), pp120-27, and Jack Dean Kingsbury, op. cit., 392-95.]

ETA LINNEMANN

The insights of Fuchs' new hermeneutic in reference to the parables of Jesus have been developed and applied by two of his students, Eta Linnemann and Eberhard Jüngel. Linnemann has written a book on the parables entitled Gleichnisse Jesu; Einführung und Auslegung, 3d ed. (1964; 1st ed., 1961), which has been translated into English as Jesus of the Parables (1966). A basic purpose of the book was to aid the teacher of religious education, and so its style is not nearly so heavy as that of Fuchs. In the introduction Fuchs observes that "the whole is written in a completely intelligible manner." One wishes that the same could be said about his works! Linnemann does not add anything essentially new to Fuchs' basic patterns. Her chief contribution is that she makes available to a wider, non-scholarly audience the main themes of the new hermeneutic's analysis of the parables of Jesus.

In categories which have become familiar since Jülicher, Linnemann describes four types of figurative speech,
a knowledge of which is indispensable for the interpretation
of the parables. These are the similitude, the parable proper, the illustration, and the allegory.

The similitude describes a typical situation which is
closely related to reality and is formulated as briefly as
possible. Jesus' seed and harvest similitudes are good examples of this type. The similitude relates two aspects--
event and reality, and it is the tertium comparationis which
clarifies this relationship. Usually the point of comparison
comes at the end of the similitude so that the climax and
the conclusion coincide.

While the similitude describes a typical or universal
situation, the parable is narrower in that it deals with that
which happened only once. Moreover, the parable has the
form of a freely composed story. The parables of the Marriage Feast and the Prodigal Son are examples of the parable type. Like the similitude, the parable is so arranged
that the point of comparison comes out clearly [Eta Linnemann, Jesus of the Parables: Introduction and Exposition,
John Sturdy, trans. (New York: Harper & Row, 1966), pp
3-12].

Using the term in its wider sense, the parable is
basically a form of communication in which the speaker intends not merely to make something known intellectually,
but to influence the hearer's judgment, to force him to decision, to convince him or prevail upon him. The most
significant role of the parable is to meet and overcome the
opposition of the hearer by inducing him to make a decision
which is in keeping with the mind of the narrator, and
thereby bringing him to a new understanding of the situation.
Although the parable has its origin in a dialectical situation,
it can only be adequately understood within the context of
its original situation. Linnemann states that it is not enough
to consider what ideas the narrator has connected with the
parable; it must also be observed what ideas, images, and
evaluations were at work in the hearers of the parable, in
what the opposition between the narrator and his listeners
consisted, and how accordingly his words must have acted
on them. In a word, we can only grasp what a parable is
saying when we know what it conveyed to its original listeners in that concrete situation [ibid., pp18-23].

Linnemann understands the parables to be forms of argument, and for this reason they have only one point of comparison. As soon as one derives from the parable more than one significant point, one can be sure that he is missing the meaning that the narrator intended. The tertium comparationis brings together the "picture part" and the "reality part" of a parable. The distinction between the "picture part" and the "reality part" is that the former is what the narrative portrays while the latter portrays what it means. But these categories can be misleading if the context of the parable is neglected. The original listeners did not need an interpretation of the narrative because they understood the parable immediately from the situation. But for later readers and commentators the situation is otherwise. This is especially true for the parables which are intended to overcome an opposition between the narrator and the listeners. Such parables open up the possibility of coming into agreement with the narrator. The original listeners participated immediately in this free gift of the speaker. The later interpreter, however, only gets access to it by reckoning with the point of view which the compiler or commentator puts at his service [ibid., pp 23-30].

The view that the parables are set in the context of the opposition between narrator and hearer is a central one for Linnemann; and it is evident in her analysis of the parables as language-event. A parable is an event that decisively alters the situation. It creates a new possibility which did not exist before--a possibility that the opposition between narrator and hearer can be bridged. Such a possibility is dependent upon the narrator bringing into language in a new way the matter which is in dispute between them. Thus the possibility of a new understanding is initiated.

A parable is an event in a two-fold sense. It creates a new possibility in the situation, and it compels the hearer to a decision. Even if understanding is not attained through the parable, one is forced into the stance of explicit opposition. Moreover, the deeper the cleavage between speaker and hearer, the more significant is the decision which the parable compels him to make. Such oppositions penetrate the depths of existence, and Linnemann holds that most of Jesus' parables are addressed to the kind of situation in which the opposition is very pronounced.

As language-events the parables offer the possibility of changing one's existence, of achieving a "new life."

Something decisive happens, and the sharper the opposition, the more so is this the case. It is when the opposition touches the depths of existence that the parable teller "is thrown back on the power of language." Following Heidegger and Fuchs, Linnemann says that it is only when man succeeds in following the basic features of language that his word has force.

But language is subject to historical change, and this factor is crucial for our understanding of language-event. Language is related to its cultural and historical context and words can acquire a "different ring" so that they no longer communicate to us. However, the essential nature of human existence remains the same in all cultural and historical settings. Moreover, it must "come into language" in ever new forms. While the parables have been passed down to us, the language-event which they effected cannot be transmitted to us. They do not become a language-event simply by our reading or listening to them because we no longer stand in the situation of the original hearers. Even though the opposition may be the same, it confronts us in a different context. Add to this the fact that our language has changed, and we see that the parables no longer reach us the same way they did the original listeners.

How is this problem to be resolved since the language-event of the parables cannot be transmitted to us? Linnemann suggests that while the event cannot be passed on, it can be made intelligible and that this is the task of the expositor. As with Bultmann and Fuchs, Linnemann says that it is in preaching that the language-event can be repeated. Through preaching the event which happened to those who heard Jesus' parables can again occur. Linnemann intimates that this process is an act of grace which reorients one's existence and helps one to move from unbelief to faith. There is a dynamic dimension to Christian preaching which not only receives instruction from the parables as to how it should be done, but which "is grounded in what Jesus did when he risked his word" [ibid., pp30-33].

The event effected by the parables is grounded in an historical context, and it cannot be divorced from its origin so that one might discern an "eternal truth." The parables must be interpreted in their connection with their original historical situation, for this is how they reveal their meaning, though it reaches far beyond that situation. Linnemann notes that every attempt to master the parables directly, without this return to the historical situation, only yields a theological utterance or a moral demand. Moreover, this is something very much less and quite different from the parable's original meaning. If, as far as this is possible for us, we want to "hear the parables of Jesus as their hearers did," we must take into account two factors of far-reaching significance: the only thing that could give weight to the words of Jesus was the words themselves; the words of Jesus had to bridge over a deep opposition which existed between him and his hearers.

As for the first point, Linnemann states that to see the historical situation correctly we must see Jesus as a true man and not as the God-man which he became in later theological thought. We cannot presuppose that the original listeners to Jesus' parables regarded him as the Christ. His words were heard as a word of man, not as an appointed revealer of God's secrets. Linnemann holds that Jesus' words were not supported by the authority of an office. He was not a theologian or a qualified teacher by profession. Nor did he appeal to the Scriptures like an expositor does, or like a prophet to a special revelation from God. "The only thing that could give weight to the words of Jesus was the words themselves, and who Jesus is for his listeners depends entirely on what he becomes for them through his words."

In the second proposition Linnemann resorts again to the theme of Jesus' opposition. The opposition between Jesus and his hearers must be understood against the background of his proclamation regarding the Kingdom of God. Jesus' opponents had rather fixed ideas about the Kingdom-- ideas which were influenced by Jewish nationalism and the apocalyptic thinking of late Judaism. Consequently, when Jesus announced the arrival of the Kingdom, they could not reconcile this with their understanding. Their view of the Kingdom was externally and objectively oriented, and they "saw" little or nothing that convinced them that the Kingdom had come. It was not so much a dispute about ideas as it was about whether the decisive time of salvation had already come. Linnemann observes that Jesus' paradoxical time-announcement confronted his hearers with a "subjective" decision of faith or unbelief. This ran counter to their "objective" understanding of the Kingdom, and thus a tension or opposition ensued between Jesus and those who heard his parables. It was basically a question about existence. Shall one base his existence upon some visible, worldly order, or on what one hears, on the word that demands belief and makes it possible?

Linnemann says that this note of opposition must be kept in mind if we are to expound the parables properly because Jesus' intention in giving the parables was to strive for the agreement of those who heard him. But this way is fraught with great risk because the outcome of his opponents' decisions is not in his hands. Thus Linnemann suggests that a direct line leads from the parables to the crucifixion. By his parables Jesus put his life at stake. He risked his life for the word that could bridge the gap between himself and his opponents and which made possible for them faith and a renovation of their existence [ibid., pp 33-41].

In her concluding section on basic principles of parable interpretation, Linnemann resorts to the familiar insights of form criticism. She points out that in the context of the New Testament we cannot hear the parables as Jesus' listeners did because they have been passed down to us through the tradition of the church. We no longer hear the words of a carpenter and wandering rabbi from Nazareth, but rather the words of the crucified, risen, and exalted Lord. Those who transmitted the parables were not historians and were governed by other interests. Thus they only transmitted the "picture part" of the parable and usually tell nothing about its original historical situation. The church's interest in Jesus' teachings was not historical, but their concern was for the building up of the church, for preaching and teaching, for exhortation and proclamation. Consequently, the church related the parables of Jesus to its own situation. It expected answers and instruction for these concerns from the words of Jesus. For this reason therefore the parables have been transmitted to us with a particular interpretation.

In our discussion of the parables we must always remember that in the context of the Gospels we are dealing with the interpretation of these texts by the church's tradition. In order to hear the parables as Jesus meant them and as his hearers must have understood them, we must use critical methods to go back behind the Gospels. But Linnemann sees another reason for seeking to understand the parables. They were not originally addressed to disciples but to opponents, not to believers but to unbelievers. In a time when the Christian faith is on the defensive and when belief in Jesus as the Christ is beginning to ebb, the parables can perform an apologetic function. Just as Jesus sought to win over his opponents through his parables, so now they have the capacity to pass on the Gospel and to bring contemporary opponents to understand its nature and message [ibid., pp41-47. Following her discussion of the above general principles of interpretation, Linnemann devotes the remainder of her book to an exposition of the individual parables. See pp51-128. The book has extensive footnotes which add up to a significant treatment of contemporary parabolic scholarship].

EBERHARD JÜNGEL

Like Eta Linnemann, Eberhard Jüngel has been a student of Fuchs, and he is identified with the new hermeneutic. While he has not written a book on the parables of Jesus as such, he does discuss them at considerable length in his book Paulus und Jesus (1967). His concern in this work is to investigate the origins of christology by means of a comparison between Paul's justification teaching and the proclamation of Jesus which finds its most significant expression in the parables.

The central idea in the teaching of Jesus was the Kingdom of God, which Jüngel says is brought to speech in the proclamation of Jesus. While Jesus never defined the Kingdom, nevertheless he brought it to speech, and this is most apparent in his parables. But the parables not only occupy the center of Jesus' message, they also give us insight into the person of the proclaimer--into the secret of Jesus himself.

Jüngel begins his section on Jesus' parables by reviewing their past interpretation. He devotes a lengthy section to Adolf Jülicher, whose work was so decisive for subsequent parabolic exposition, and refers to it as the "Aristotelian approach" to the parables. He turns next to Rudolf Bultmann whose method is characterized as the "form critical approach" to the analysis and understanding of the parables. Thirdly, Jüngel describes the "historicizing approach" to an eschatological interpretation of the parables by C. H. Dodd and Joachim Jeremias. Finally, there is the hermeneutical approach to an eschatological interpretation of the parables by Ernst Lohmeyer and Ernst Fuchs. Of the latter two scholars, it is Fuchs of course to whom Jüngel is most indebted and to whom he gives the most attention. He notes that Lohmeyer's essay "Vom Sinn der Gleichnisse Jesu"

had no influence on the progress of New Testament scholarship [Eberhard Jüngel, Paulus und Jesus, 3d ed. (Tübingen:
J. C. B. Mohr, 1967), pp87-135].

Following his review of past parabolic interpretation,
Jüngel makes 12 observations: (1) The proclamation of
Jesus is to be understood as a language-event. We should
not differentiate between an outer form and an inner existential intent as Bultmann does in his program of demythologization. (2) What is true about the message of Jesus in
general is especially true about the parables in particular.
The Kingdom of God is not a theme with which the parables
are concerned. (3) A guiding principle for interpreting the
parables is that the Kingdom comes to speech in parable as
parable, or the parables of Jesus bring God's reign into
language as parable.

(4) The pattern of understanding the parables in
terms of "reality-half, " "picture-half," and "tertium comparationis, " which stems from Jülicher, is misleading because it takes us to the school whereas the parables are
concerned, not to teach us lessons, but to confront us with
ultimacy. (5) The parables have a single point of reference
which is human existence. If the parables are concerned
with the Kingdom of God, then human existence has its point
in the extra nos of the Kingdom of God. (6) Parables are
distinguished from allegories in that they center on one
point which allegories do not. (7) A parable is characterized by both a disclosing and concealing tendency.

(8) The parables are not "halves" in which the
halves are united by the tertium comparationis. Rather they
are language-events in which the entirety of the parable
comes to speech. (9) Insofar as the Kingdom of God exists
as a parable, it preserves the difference between God and
the world. In this sense, the parables of Jesus can be
understood as "contrast parables. " (10) When the Kingdom
of God comes to speech in the parables, we have a significant mode of the Kingdom's coming. But when the Kingdom
appears as a word in Jesus' parables, then we must pay attention to the relationship between this word and the speaker
himself, i. e. , to Jesus himself.

(11) Referring to Fuchs, Jüngel suggests that the
conduct of Jesus is a commentary to his parables. Jesus'
conduct clarifies the will of God and one should read the
parables in this context. The early Christian community

missed this point and supplied their own applications and interpretations, or understood them in terms of a theory of secrecy. (12) The early church tended to put Jesus' parables into a framework and they became part of the tradition, and thus they lost some of their power of analogy. They were handed down because they were ascribed to Jesus, but many must have been lost. One must hope that many of the parables can be viewed in their original context and in the context of their relationship to Jesus as the eschatological category, and that they can recover their analogical power and become meaningful to subsequent generations [ibid., pp135-39].

It appears that Jüngel's key concept regarding the parables of Jesus is that they bring the Kingdom of God to speech or language (zur Sprache) as parable. This is by no means an easy concept to understand, but Jüngel interprets a series of parables from this perspective in a section entitled "The Kingdom of God as Parable" [ibid., pp139-74]. He begins with the parables of the Hid Treasure and the Pearl of Great Price. These parables challenge the hearer to discern the nature of the Kingdom of God by participating in its reality and by discovering that he has been "found" by it. Thus the parables are paradigms of the Kingdom and of God's activity and man's response to God's prior action. Other parables Jüngel discusses are the Dragnet, the Tares, the Seed Growing Secretly, the Mustard Seed, the Friend at Midnight, the Unjust Steward, the Prodigal Son, the Laborers in the Vineyard, the Good Samaritan.

In the parable of the Dragnet the Kingdom of God comes to speech in that the main point of the parable is the gathering and separating. In view of the future separation which characterizes the Kingdom, the people are challenged to decision. Indeed Jesus guarantees his hearers an opportunity for decision. This same eschatological note can be seen in the parable of the Seed Growing Secretly. Jesus is so certain of God's future that he speaks about it in the present. The present of his hearers is free from the past (the time of sowing) and free for the future (the time of harvest). It is a time of hearing and hence an opportunity for decision. In the parable of the Mustard Seed Jesus bids his hearers to consider the present as the time for decision in view of the wonderful future of the Kingdom. The present is a time of the power of the future. The present comes to speech in the parable because the power of the coming Kingdom is already present in this parable. Through

the parable Jesus gathers men together and summons them
to the Kingdom, so that they themselves belong to the beginning of that glorious end.

Let us turn finally to Jüngel's interpretation of the
parable of the Good Samaritan. He regards the parable as
an example-story (Beispielerzählung). The parable deals
with the contrast between the Jews who are without compassion and the Samaritan who is full of compassion insofar as
the man who was in need of compassion and who fell among
the thieves is concerned. The Priest, Levite, and Samaritan all experience the need for love, but the Samaritan is
the only one who responds to it. The contrast between
them is all the more significant when one remembers that,
according to rabbinical teaching, a Jew could not accept a
magnanimous act from a Samaritan because to do so would
impede the redemption of Israel. The parable of the Good
Samaritan relates to both the fulfillment and non-fulfillment
of the Jewish law of loving the neighbor. It shows the
Priest and the Levite, who though bound by the law which
is for them the law of God, not fulfilling it; while the Samaritan, who is not bound by the law, fulfills it as the natural
law of man's conscience. The example-story brings before
us Jesus as the preacher of the law interpreting it as fulfilled in an event of love occasioned by an event of need-for-
love (Liebedürftigkeit). He can do this because he is
speaking from the experience of the love of God as an event.
By its analogical power the example-story confronts us with
the love of God as an event as it draws our attention toward
the need-for-love of our fellow men. The example-story
belongs to the parables of the Kingdom of God because Jesus
announces to his hearers how the future of the Kingdom of
God as a near event of the love of God gives man the opportunity in the present time to love his neighbor. In each
parable there is implicit the eschatological unity of exhortation and demand.

In view of his discussion of the various parables,
Jüngel formulates seven principles for our understanding of
Jesus' proclamation: (1) The proclamation of Jesus is
centered upon the Kingdom of God which comes to speech in
Jesus' message as the near Kingdom of God. (2) The as-
sembling of Jesus' hearers and the proclamation of the
Kingdom of God occur in the proclamation of Jesus as the
language-event of Jesus' parables. (3) The language event
of Jesus' parables brings indirectly to speech Jesus' own
relationship to God. The relationship of Jesus to God becomes explicit in Jesus' conduct toward mankind.

(4) While the Kingdom of God comes to language as parable in Jesus' parables, they are the unifying framework of Jesus' proclamation. From the parables, Jesus' view of God, eschatology, and ethics are understood in their original connection. (5) While the Kingdom of God comes to speech in the parables of Jesus as the near Kingdom of God, it places the future of God in relationship to the present of man. This does away with the question of time as an eschatological theme. Jesus' relationship to God determines man's relationship to the future of God and man's relationship to Jesus.

(6) Jesus is so certain of the Kingdom of God that he can express its future as near the present of man. (7) If the future of God intersects the present of man in the person of Jesus who proclaims the Kingdom of God, then the parables of Jesus point to the future of the act of God in the history of Jesus by pointing to the near future of the Kingdom of God. The parables of Jesus which establish the relationship between the near future of the Kingdom of God and the present of man become the focus of the history of Jesus himself. Quoting Fuchs, Jüngel observes that Jesus' conduct is itself a parable which clarifies the will of God.

Like his mentor, Jüngel is difficult to follow and much of his rhetoric seems unduly opaque. His insistence upon the centrality of the Kingdom of God in Jesus' parables and his claim that they are language-events which bring the Kingdom to speech, indicate that Jüngel takes seriously the integrity of the parable as a literary form. He is not interested in deriving a "non-parabolic" message from them, be it moral, theological, existential, or some other type, but his concern is to have the parables confront us with the Kingdom so that we might participate in its reality.

With this we leave the exponents of the new hermeneutic and turn to three of the leading American interpreters of the parables, viz. Robert W. Funk, Dan Otto Via, and Dominic Crossan.

29   ROBERT W. FUNK

Reviewing the status of parabolic research by the early 1960s, Norman Perrin noted that significant advances had been made in the areas of textual and historical criticism. However, with respect to literary criticism the

situation was very different. He observed that exponents of
the new hermeneutic had brought forth an important new
concept with their claim that the parables are to be understood as language-events. But Perrin held that its inadequa-
cies in literary scholarship and "its passion for the ubiqui-
tous model of the sermon," prevented the new hermeneutic
from making further progress. The way forward, as Perrin saw it, was to return to the literary study of the nature
of metaphor, and it was in this area that Robert Funk made
an "enormously important contribution" [Norman Perrin,
Jesus and the Language of the Kingdom (Philadelphia, Fortress Press, 1976), pp132-33].

Funk's major interpretation of the parables is contained in a chapter entitled "The Parable as Metaphor" in his
book Language, Hermeneutic, and Word of God (1966). As
the title suggests, Funk is convinced that language has become a root problem of contemporary theology. He believes
that by exposing the roots of our linguistic tradition, we may
be able to read that heritage in a wholly new light. Moreover, "new language, or language with new bearings and
power, may well up out of an unpredisposed confrontation
with reality" [Robert W. Funk, Language, Hermeneutic, and
Word of God: The Problem of Language in the New Testament and Contemporary Theology (New York: Harper &
Row, 1966), pp xi-xv].

Funk's book is divided into three parts. In Part I
he examines the theme of "Language as Event and Theology"
in the thought of Bultmann, Heidegger, Fuchs, Ebeling, Paul
Van Buren, Schubert Ogden, and Heinrich Ott. In Parts II
and III he applies his understanding of language and hermeneutic to the parables of Jesus and the letters of Paul.
He begins his discussion of the parables by citing a "clas-
sic definition of the parable" by C. H. Dodd: "At its simplest the parable is a metaphor or simile drawn from nature
or common life, arresting the hearer by its vividness or
strangeness, and leaving the mind in sufficient doubt about
its precise application to tease it into active thought."
Funk sees in this definition four essential clues to the nature of the parable: (1) the parable is a metaphor or
simile which may (a) remain simple, (b) be elaborated into
a picture, or (c) be expanded into a story; (2) the metaphor
or simile is drawn from nature or common life; (3) the
metaphor arrests the hearer by its vividness or strangeness;
and (4) the application is left imprecise in order to tease
the hearer into making his own application [ibid., p133].

Beginning with the fourth point, Funk elaborates these clues which "Dodd has not always followed up." He notes that Dodd is saying that the parable is not closed until the listener is drawn into it as a participant. The application is not specific until the hearer formulates it for himself. Funk, along with Dodd and others, believes that few if any of the parables were originally given applications by Jesus. Through the tradition the church canonized its interpretations along with the parables, and this is regretable because the application may not be in harmony with the intent of the parable. In its strictest sense Dodd's fourth clue means that it is impossible to specify once and for all what the parables mean; for to do so would imply that the parable is expendable once the application has been made and reduced to didactic language. But the parable is not expendable because the church preserved the parable along with the interpretation, and in some cases it preserved the parable without appended interpretation. This leads to a consideration of the nature of parable as metaphor or simile [ibid., pp133-36.].

The distinction between simile and metaphor and particularly the nature of metaphor are the central themes in Funk's analysis of Jesus' parables. Commenting on Jülicher, Dodd, and Jeremias, Funk notes that Jülicher reduces the plurality of allegorical ciphers to single abstract maxims, while Dodd and Jeremias want to refurbish these ideas with historical concreteness. Funk, however, insists that the parables do not transmit ideas. They can only be refurbished by allowing them to become parables again, and that means by taking them metaphorically. "Only so will the almost imperceptible lines in the verbal picture adumbrate the referential totality, the Kingdom of God, which the parables seek to disclose" [Robert W. Funk, "Saying and Seeing: Phenomenology of Language and the New Testament," Journal of Bible and Religion 34 (1966), 206]. In a simile such as A is like B, the less known is clarified by the better known. To say that A is B is a metaphor, and the juxtaposition of two discrete and not entirely comparable entities, "produces an impact upon the imagination and induces a vision of that which cannot be conveyed by prosaic or discursive speech." While comparison or analogy is common to both simile and metaphor, nevertheless the decisive point is the role which the comparison plays. In simile it is illustrative; in metaphorical language it is creative of meaning. In simile as illustration the point to be clarified or illuminated has already been made and can be assumed; in metaphor the point is discovered [Language, Hermeneutic, and Word of God, pp136-37].

With regard to temporal sequence, the metaphor is open-ended. It does not concentrate on a single frame from the film but upon the movement, the flow, the constellation of images which gives presence to the movement. It endeavors to let succeeding persons see what the last ones saw but to see it in individual ways. Thus the metaphor does not foreclose but discloses the future. Funk observes that metaphors may live on indefinitely, since the constellation of meaning which they conjure up depends both on their revelatory power and the perceptive power of the mind which encounters them. They are constantly being refracted in the changing light of the historical situation [ibid. pp142-43].

Closely related to the temporal aspect of the parable is its existential character. In contrast to rational abstraction, the metaphor belongs to the realm of imagination which, unlike abstraction, stands closest to the event. Imagination and its metaphorical vehicle have to do with being or reality in process which they do not merely report but actually participate in. Funk writes:

> The metaphor, like the parable, is incomplete until the hearer is drawn into it as a participant; this is the reason the parables are said to be argumentative, calling for a transference of judgment. Metaphor and parable sustain their existential tenor because they participate in immediacy, an immediacy pertaining to the future as well as to the present and past [ibid., p143].

Funk does not understand the argumentative quality of the parables in terms of debate and controversy, as Cadoux and Jeremias do. He believes that the intention of Dodd's fourth point is to see the parable as precipitating the hearer's judgment. Thus the parable is not an argument in the strict sense, but rather a "revelation" which calls for a response [ibid., pp144-45].

In reviewing the line of parable-interpretation as represented by the "Jülicher-Dodd-Jeremias axis," Funk concludes that their advances were still incomplete. Jeremias had criticized Jülicher because he drew from each parable a single idea of the widest possible generality. Funk notes

that Jeremias and Dodd are still in the same orbit as Jülicher. They also view the parables as a piece of real life
from which a single point or idea is to be drawn. This
point, however, is not a general principle, but one referring to a particular situation within the ministry of Jesus.
Funk writes: "Jülicher's 'broadest possible application' has
been replaced by the particular historical application circum-
scribed by the conditions of the ministry. In other respects
Jülicher's position is unmodified." Both Dodd and Jeremias
believed that Jülicher had failed to appreciate the eschatological orientation of Jesus' parables and that they made this
correction. What has happened therefore, according to Funk,
is that Jülicher's moral point of broadest application has become the eschatological point of particular historical application. The terms have undergone modification, but the
term which remained constant constitutes the problem. That
is, like Jülicher, Dodd and Jeremias derive a set of ideas
from the parables so that the ideational point of Jülicher remains ideational [ibid., pp146-49].

Funk credits Dodd and Jeremias with attaining a degree of success in particularizing the original intent of the
parables. However, Jesus' audience was diverse, so that
the single audience-single idea correlation is fallacious.
Moreover, the parable as metaphor is many-faceted so that
the "historical" interpretation in terms of the leading "idea"
truncates the parable, even for those who originally heard
it. The parable as metaphor has not one but many "points,"
as many points as there are situations into which it is
spoken. And that applies to the original as well as subsequent audiences. "The emphasis on one point over against
the allegorization of the parables was a necessary corrective,
but one point understood as an idea valid for all times is
as erroneous as Jülicher's moral maxims, even if that idea
is eschatological!" The reduction of the parables to a single
idea, whether eschatological or christological, is only a
restricted form of rationalization. "The metaphor must be
left intact if it is to retain the interpretative power" [ibid.,
pp149-52].

In his consideration of the parable as metaphor, Funk
concludes the discussion with an incisive analysis of Dodd's
second and third clues concerning the nature of the parable.
Dodd suggested that the parable is drawn from nature or the
common life and that it arrests the hearer by its vividness
or strangeness. It appears that these two clues present an
irreconcilable paradox. Why should that which is common-

place appear vivid or strange? And why should such a vivid account be controversial so that it precipitates the hearer's judgment or even compels him to decision? As we shall see, it is precisely in this paradoxical situation that the essence of the parable as metaphor adheres.

One might conclude that the realism of the parables illumines man's everyday experiences so that he can affirm, "Yes, that's how it is." But there is more at issue than this. Funk quotes Amos Wilder to the effect that Jesus presents man in such fashion that he shows that man's destiny is at stake in his ordinary creaturely existence, domestic, economic, and social. Thus the everydayness of the parables is translucent to the ground of human existence. The parabolic imagery exposes the structure of human existence that is masked by convention, custom, consensus. The note of ultimate concern is implicit in the everydayness of the parable. But if the experiences of everyday constitute the locus of the parable's intentionality, and if the parable speaks directly about its intention, why then should one be concerned about metaphorical language at all? Funk believes that this dilemma may be resolved by examining the nature of metaphorical language.

Funk refers to Owen Barfield's observation that the literal and nonliteral meanings of a word or sentence can bear various relations to each other. It is the dialectical relationship between the literal and the metaphorical that makes the two reciprocally revelatory. The literal view of the parable never exhausts its intention; the parable is like a picture puzzle which prompts the question, What's wrong with this picture? "Distortions of everydayness, exaggerated realism, distended concreteness, incompatible elements-- often subtly drawn--are what prohibit the parable from coming to rest in the literal sense...." Metaphorical language does not look at the phenomenon, but through it. It seeks to make the world of everyday transparent to another world which is not really different but a strangely familiar one. Moreover, metaphor remains temporally open-ended so that the hermeneutical potential of its vision can continue to make its claim upon the future. It looks through everydayness and allows the world that emerges to encounter the hearer.

It is the superimposition of the everyday with the ultimate, or the familiar with the unfamiliar, which marks the revelatory character of the parable as metaphor. Funk says that the world of the parable is like Alice's looking-glass world: all is familiar, yet all is strange, and the one illuminates the other. However, this situation is not realized unless the parable's realism on everydayness is shattered so that while the hearer can affirm the everydayness of the parables, he is nevertheless shocked to find his familiar world turned inside out or upside down as the parabolic narratives unfold.

In a succinct summary statement, Funk presents the following observations on "the parable as metaphor":

The parables as pieces of everydayness have an unexpected 'turn' in them which looks through the commonplace to a new view of reality. This 'turn' may be overt in the form of a surprising development in the narrative, an extravagant exaggeration, a paradox; or it may lurk below the surface in the so-called transference of judgment for which the parable calls. In either case the listener is led through the parable into a strange world where everything is familiar yet radically different.... It is too little to call the parables as metaphors teaching devices; they are that, but much more. They are language-events in which the hearer has to choose between worlds. If he elects the parabolic world, he is invited to dispose himself to concrete reality as is ordered in the parable, and venture without benefit of landmark but on the parable's authority, into the future [ibid., pp161-62].

With these words Funk concludes his discussion of "the parables as metaphor." He next turns to a detailed examination of two parables--the Great Supper [ibid., pp163-98] and the Good Samaritan [ibid., pp199-222]. Resorting to motifs developed above, Funk notes that the parable of the Great Supper evokes a radically new relation to reality in its everydayness. The auditor discovers that his destiny is at stake precisely in his ordinary creaturely existence. "By means of metaphor, the parable 'cracks' the shroud of everydayness lying over mundane reality." There is in the parable a juxtaposition of the old "logic" of everydayness, but neither can it dispense with it. The metaphorical language brings the old into the new, the familiar into an unfamiliar context and distorts it in order to bring it into a new frame of reference, a new referential totality. Furthermore, the parable is marked by an element of comic criticism: "It exaggerates the situation critically and thus exposes the nerve of the two 'logics.'" Comic criticism opens the way for a radically new orientation toward reality. Funk sets forth the nature and the intention of the parable thus:

> The parable is a narrative (a paradigm of reality, marked by comic criticism) which shifts the outcome of the story to the audience: the auditors are split into two groups, those who resist the new 'logic' and those who enter upon it, who accept the invitation. The choice is made inevitable by the way in which the story unfolds [ibid., p196].

Turning to the parable of the Good Samaritan, Funk rejects the idea that the parable can best be understood in moralistic terms. In all probability the moralistic interpretation does no more than reflect the later interest of the church which happens in this case to coincide with modern interests. Jülicher and others viewed the parable as a Beispielerzählung (example-story) which was in keeping with a moralizing interpretation. Challenging the validity of this designation, Funk centers his attention upon the existential dimensions of the parable. Along with the advocates of the new hermeneutic, he regards it as a language-event rather than an exemplary story. To comprehend the parable, one must grasp how the hearer is drawn into the story and from what perspective the parable is told.

The first sentences of the story of the Good Samaritan are in accordance with everydayness. The "shock" comes with the introduction of the Samaritan. To say that the Samaritan is merely a model of neighborliness is to reduce the parable to a commonplace and to vitiate its impact. Funk again resorts to the dichotomy between the everydayness and the unusual as a key to understanding the parable. The Samaritan is a realistic figure, but the surprising turn of events shatters the realism, the everydayness of the story. The narrative begins with a normal flow of events, but concludes with a factor which is out of kilter with everyday experience. "The 'logic' of everydayness is broken upon the 'logic' of the parable. It is the juxtaposition of the two logics that turns the Samaritan, and hence the parable, into a metaphor" [ibid., p213]. The paradoxical characteristic of the Samaritan is that he is just a Samaritan but also the one the hearers would not expect to see in this story. Therefore the parable which is

both just a story of a good Samaritan and a parabolic metaphor opens before us a new vision of reality which shatters
the everyday view.

Another quality of metaphor is that it gives itself
existentially to unfinished reality. This implies that the
narrative is unfinished until the hearer is drawn into it as
participant. In the case of the parable of the Good Samaritan, the hearer is confronted with a decision as to how he
will comport himself in reference to the story's persona.
But since the parable is temporally open-ended, it resists
ideational crystallization. This means that every hearer
must hear it in his own way. "The future which the parable discloses is the future of every hearer who grasps and
is grasped by his position in the ditch." Each listener
finds himself in the ditch and that is perhaps the reason
that the victim is faceless and nameless. To fathom the
parable one must understand himself as the victim if he is
to be eligible to be drawn to Jesus' side. The victim's
true identity is revealed with reference to his relation to
the three figures who come along the road. "How he views
them determines who he is!" [ibid., p214].

Funk raises the question of the parable's christological significance, and he notes that Jesus does not appear
explicitly. However, Jesus "stands behind the Samaritan,"
not as a messianic figure, but "as one who lives in the
'world,' or under the 'logic,' drawn by the parable." The
hearer of the parable is invited to "see" what the Samaritan "sees" and embark upon his "way." But this is really
an invitation to follow Jesus who himself has embarked
upon this way. In essence the parable is Jesus' permission
to follow him and to launch out into a future that he announces as God's own.

Finally Funk maintains that the focus of the parable
must be upon the sphere of language, and that attention
must be directed away from the Samaritan to those who are
listening to the story. The admonition, "Go and do likewise"
(Luke 10:37) is a call to action which is often interpreted
in moralistic terms. But it calls attention to the event-
character of what happens in the parable and, as a consequence, of what is intended to transpire in the listeners.
The deficiency in the moralistic view is that it does not grasp
the primal world-character of the event. While the Samaritan does not speak, he nevertheless discloses in wordless
deeds the world in which love as event is present. Insofar

as hearers are led to the Samaritan's world, the parable
becomes a language-event that decisively shapes their future
so that the parable's word-character makes it an event of
radical significance. Funk characterizes the nature of the
parable of the Good Samaritan as language-event and its
christological significance as follows:

> The language-event which grounds the Samaritan's
> action precedes the language-event which the para-
> ble may become for its hearers. Only when lan-
> guage-event has taken place, can language-event
> take place. That Jesus belongs to the penumbral
> field of the parable as the one who lurks behind
> the Samaritan and dwells in his world provides
> the justification for reading the parable christolog-
> ically: in Jesus God has drawn near as love,
> which gives Jesus the right to pronounce that
> drawing near upon the world in parable [ibid., p
> 221].

In addition to his discussion of the parable of the
Good Samaritan in Language, Hermeneutic, and the Word of
God, Funk has given a brief exposition of the parable as a
part of the second Society of Biblical Literature's Seminar
on the Parables which was devoted to the parable of the
Good Samaritan. [Proceedings of the seminar were published in the Society's Semeia 2 (1974). Funk's essay entitled "The Good Samaritan as Metaphor" covers pp74-81;
a second essay by Funk, "Structure in the Narrative Parables of Jesus," appears in the same issue on pp51-73.]

In his essay on the Good Samaritan, Funk covers
essentially the same terrain, albeit in briefer compass, as
he did in his book as outlined above. He offers a "reading"
of the parable so that the auditor might hear it "in the appropriate key." In effect Funk takes the reader through the
parable in the hope that it might recreate the effect that
the parable supposedly had on its original hearers.

Funk rejects the view that the parable is an example-
story which offers an example of what it means to be a
good neighbor. The focus is not upon the Samaritan but
upon the man in the ditch. The parable invites the auditor
to be "the victim in the ditch." The "meaning" of the parable is disclosed as the auditors take up roles in the story
and play out the drama. As the hearers are drawn into
the drama, they will discern that its central "meaning" is

that in the Kingdom of God mercy, which one has no right
to expect and which one cannot resist when it comes, is always a surprise.

In a collection of essays entitled Jesus as Precursor
[(Philadelphia: Fortress Press; Missoula, Mont.: Scholars
Press, 1975), pp19-28, 51-72], Funk refers to the parables
of Jesus, and two parables--the Mustard Seed and the Lea-
ven--are treated in separate essays. In his analysis of the
parable of the Mustard Seed Funk moves beyond Dodd and
Jeremias and suggests that the parable must be viewed
against the background of the symbol of the mighty cedars
of Lebanon which inspired Ezekiel's vision in Ezekiel 17:22-
24. The Kingdom referred to in the parable is not a towering empire in the sense of a mighty cedar, but an unpretentious venture of faith (mustard seed). The parable transforms the face of Israel's hope from that of a literal world
(cedar) to a world-transforming faith (mustard seed). It
brings a new hope into view, which unlike the old, is
fraught with risk. The temptation is to convert the mustard
plant back into a towering cedar. However, those who accept Jesus' invitation to "pass through the looking-glass"
will find joy and certainty as "the mighty cedar is brought
low and the humble herb exalted. "

As for the parable of the Leaven, Funk maintains
that the tradition of parabolic interpretation represented by
Jülicher, Dodd, and Jeremias is at an impasse. For Jülicher and his successors parable interpretation is a form of
reduced allegory. Instead of many points corresponding to
a variety of details, there is only one point corresponding
to one, or a pair of details. "The way forward is away-
from-here. "

The road "away from there" for Funk winds through
an analysis and understanding of language. It implies that
"the interpreter must work out of the sedimented tradition
as received by the author of a given text, and into the re-
fraction or deformation of that tradition, as the author in
question brings the tradition to speech afresh" [Jesus as
Precursor, p58]. The basic problem regarding the parables
concerns our ability to recover their original power. In
the course of transmission and interpretation the potential
of the parables to evoke a fresh view of reality was reduced
to a specified meaning, a point, a teaching. "The point
drawn from the parable diverts attention from the parable
itself to what it teaches, and thus from the world onto which

the parable opens to an idea in an ideological constellation, or, as we might also say, in a theology." The loss of the parable as parable means the loss also of the cardinal points on the horizon onto which the parable originally opened. Conversely, the recovery of the parable as parable restores the original horizon. Thus the fundamental question is whether or not it is possible any longer to recover the parable as parable. If this is to happen, the interpreter must be "thrown back upon the text and left there in solitude to confront the text without benefit of conceptual comforts."

Whether the parable of the Leaven, or any other part of the Jesus tradition, is living tradition cannot be answered in advance. Is the foundational language of Jesus and of the Christian faith still alive and meaningful to the proverbial modern man? This, Funk holds, is the only "literacy" that really matters. Moreover, he is convinced that while appropriate criticism can teach one to read texts with larger eyes, it cannot make one "literate." The text alone has that power. "Biblical criticism, like the literary criticism, comes anon to the end of its way: from that point he who aspires to literacy must go on alone" [ibid., p72].

In conjunction with his work and interest in the parables, Robert Funk has been instrumental in the formation and ongoing activity of the Society of Biblical Literature's Seminar on the Parables. It was in June 1972 that Funk, who was then the executive secretary of the Society of Biblical Literature, proposed the formation of a seminar on the parables for scholars with special interest in this topic. He suggested that a parables seminar should succeed the Gospels Seminar whose five-year term was ending that year. He said:

> We have reached, as it seems to me, the end of a first creative burst of activity centering in the study of the parables and are about to embark on a second. Those of us who made contributions to that first effort are now rethinking our positions in an effort to find new directions. Meanwhile, younger scholars have entered the discussions with fresh vigor [Amos N. Wilder, "Semeia: An Experimental Journal for Biblical Criticism: An Introduction," Semeia 1 (1974), 1-2].

Among those who in addition to Funk were involved in the SBL Seminar were Dominic Crossan, James M. Robinson, Norman Perrin, Jack Kingsbury, Dan Otto Via, and Amos Wilder.

Another of Funk's innovations was his proposal to his successor as executive secretary, George MacRae, that an "Experimental Journal for Linguistic and Literary Arts in Biblical Studies" be published. His proposal was approved, and the first issue of Semeia appeared in 1974.

The first meeting of the Society of Biblical Literature Seminar on the Parables was held in 1973 with an anticipated five-year life span. The seminar dealt with the theme of "A Structuralist Approach to the Parables," and the results were published in Semeia 1 (1974). The second year's seminar focused on "The Good Samaritan" with the results published in Semeia 2 (also in 1974). The next meeting of the seminar gave its attention to "The Prodigal Son." Needless to say, the SBL Seminar has provided an excellent forum for American parable scholars to formulate their views and to enter into dialogue and discussion with others. The results of these seminars thus far amply attest to the fact that some of the most creative and innovative work on the parables of Jesus is now centered in this country.

The scope and profundity of Funk's analysis of the parables of Jesus place him clearly among the leading contemporary parabolic interpreters. His analysis of the parables as metaphor and his understanding of them as language-events have caused him to develop insights which are fresh and vibrant, and which have potentiality for further advances. Moreover, in the parables which he analyzes in detail, Funk reflects an admirable synthesis of theory and application. Suffice it to say, Robert Funk has made a noteworthy contribution to present-day parable research, and we can expect further enlightenment on the parables from him.

30   DAN OTTO VIA

Without question, Dan Otto Via is one of the leading American interpreters of the parables of Jesus. His major work on the parables is The Parables: Their Literary and Existential Dimension [Philadelphia: Fortress Press, 1967] in which he develops a methodology that, departing from the Dodd-Jeremias position, has had a noteworthy influence upon contemporary understanding of the parables.

Via contends that we must move away from the methodology of Dodd and Jeremias, which interpreted the parables too narrowly in connection with Jesus' historical situation. As the title suggests, his approach begins at the literary level. The parables must be seen as genuine works of art, real aesthetic objects. A start in this direction has been made by Geriant V. Jones, and Via proposes "a more thorough-going demonstration that a number of Jesus' parables are in a strict sense literary and that because of this they are not just illustrations of ideas and cannot have the immediate connection with Jesus' historical situation which is customarily attributed to them" [ibid., p x]. Via is not suggesting that we should ignore the rich exegetical contributions of the past, but he believes that in the case of certain of the narrative parables the new angle of vision of a more literary approach would enlarge our understanding.

Via begins his discussion with the now familiar distinction between allegory, parable, similitude, and example-story. He proceeds with a criticism of the "one-point" approach to the parables in modern scholarship which has continued to be widely espoused since Jülicher. Via concludes by noting that while the meaning of Jesus' parables cannot be restricted to one central point of comparison, that does not mean that they are allegories. The one-point view is not one of the essential differentiae of a parable. Consequently, Via suggests that we must seek a non-allegorical approach to the parables other than the one-point approach [ibid., pp2-17].

Via turns next to a criticism of the "severely historical approach" which was a reaction to Jülicher's second thesis, viz. that a parable's meaning is to be given the most general possible application. The historical approach as represented by Dodd, Jeremias, and others, held that one can understand the parables only by taking account of their context in Jesus' historical situation. Via recognizes the importance of this approach and the contributions it has made to parable interpretation. However, "some modification of the present tendency seems called for." Consequently, he offers four criticisms of the historical approach.

First, in view of the non-biographical nature of the Gospels it will usually be difficult if not impossible to ascertain in exactly what concrete situation a parable was uttered. The elements from Jesus' ministry or teaching should not be imposed on the parable. The beginning point must be the parable itself.

A second criticism of the severely historical approach is that it ignores the basic human element in the parables. They say something to and about man as man and not just to and about man in a particular historical situation.

Thirdly, some who follow the historical approach seem to leave the parables in the past with nothing to say to the present. While this may not be their intention, nevertheless they do not give adequate attention to the problem of translation. "What is needed is a hermeneutical and literary methodology which can identify the permanently significant element in the parables and can elaborate a means of translating that element without distorting the original intention."

The fourth and perhaps most crucial criticism insofar as Via is concerned is that the historical approach ignores the aesthetic nature of the parables and annuls their aesthetic function. To generalize, the historical approach focuses on the historical context as a clue to the meaning of the parable while a recognition of their aesthetic quality would focus on the parables themselves. The goal of historical and literary criticism is to be able to take any text on its own terms. As for the parables, this goal is better served by recognizing their aesthetic nature than by first of all deriving their meaning from the historical context or by making them illustrations of ideas [ibid., pp21-24; for a further discussion of Via's criticism of the historical method and of his understanding of the parables in general, see Norman Perrin, Jesus and the Language of the Kingdom, pp141-55].

In the first chapter of his book on the parables Via says that the predominant view of the distinction between allegory and parable since Jülicher is inadequate. The difference is not between one point of reference and many, but, rather, the differing ways in which the elements in the story are related to each other and to the real world or world of thought outside of the story. Parables are aesthetic objects, that is, carefully organized, self-contained, coherent literary compositions. This is the reason that the one-point approach is only less allegorizing in degree than the old pre-critical allegorizing because it breaks the internal coherence of the story. The basic difference between allegory and parable is that the features of an allegory are related directly to an outside world and thus are related more or less loosely to each other; while in a parable the events relate first of all to each other within the parable and the structure of connections of these elements is not determined by events or ideas outside of the parable but by the author's creative composition [ibid., pp 24-25].

Before developing his analysis of the parables as aesthetic objects, Via turns to a discussion of the parable and the problems of theological language. He surveys some of the terrain already covered, especially by the exponents of the new hermeneutic. Via accepts the contention of the new hermeneutic that biblical texts must be translated into our historically conditioned language if they are to be understood. However, insofar as the parables are concerned, two qualifications must be made. First, because the parables are aesthetic in nature they are not as time-conditioned as other biblical texts, and therefore the need for translation is not as compelling. And second, because the parables are aesthetic in nature, it is impossible to translate them completely into any other terms. Linguistic aesthetic objects can be interpreted or translated, and the need for clarity justifies this effort. However, Via observes that concomitant with the gain in clarity is a loss of the peculiarly aesthetic function. The paradoxical situation about the parables is that, on the one hand, they need interpretive clarification, while, on the other hand, because they are aesthetic objects they resist complete translation into any other terms [ibid., pp 32-33].

Resorting to a familiar category in present-day parabolic exegesis, Via states that the goal or purpose of translating a biblical text is that it might become a language event. He says that Jesus' parables were a language event in that they introduced a new possibility into the situation of his hearers. They offered a new way of understanding their historical situation. Furthermore, the parables were a language event because they called for a judgment from the hearers. The judgment confronting them entailed a far-reaching decision because they were being asked to decide between their old understanding and the new one that confronted them in the parable. The parable is a language event because it conducts man to the place of decision. The concept of the parables as language events has been central in the work of such exponents of the new hermeneutic as Fuchs and Linnemann. But according to Via they have not sufficiently exploited the event character of the parables because they have not seriously considered how the parables' peculiarly aesthetic function enhances their character as events. It is this deficiency which Via intends to correct [ibid., pp 52-57].

In his chapter "The Parables, Aesthetics, and Literary Criticism" Via continues to formulate his aesthetic view of the parables. He points out that aesthetic experience is non-referential in that it does not point to something beyond itself. In aesthetic experience "the attention is totally engaged by and riveted on the object itself...." A work of literary art is organized in such a way that the parts cohere with each other. Thus the beholder's attention moves from one part to another and not to the outside. "From the aesthetic standpoint, to isolate one element in a literary work for special consideration breaks the unity of the work and obscures the meaning of that element by removing it from the context which provides its meaning" [ibid., pp73-76].

Another mark of a literary work is that it is autonomous because it is fictitious and is an inwardly organized structure capable of attracting non-referential attention. Moreover, it is independent of its author, and although it has links with his life, these are not of crucial importance because they are fused into a new configuration. The revelatory character of a work of literary art cannot be traced to the author's biography or environment. The only important consideration is the internal meaning of the work itself. In a summary statement concerning the aesthetic object, Via writes: "The peculiar function of language used aesthetically is that through its centripetal interlocking of content into form it grasps the attention of the beholder as a total psychomatic unity--including conscious and unconscious aspects--in an intransitive or non-referential way" [ibid., pp77-79].

In reviewing recent literary criticism, Via notes that some critics reject the claim of absolute autonomy and recognize the relevance of biographical, historical, and philosophical factors for interpretation. He refers back to one of his earlier observations that language at its most basic level has an inalienable "pointing" aspect which persists when words are put together aesthetically. The words of a novel, for example, point outward to objects--whether things or concepts--that have a more general meaning than the new, particular meaning given by the form of the novel; and the two meanings are not completely discontinuous. In addition, the aesthetically organized form or pattern of connections has an existential reference in that it contains implicitly a perspective on life or understanding of existence. The reader of a novel will inevitably, at some level of consciousness, relate the implicit understanding of existence in the story to the understanding which he already has. In aesthetic experience our attention moves both within the pattern of connections of the aesthetic object itself and also to the outside as we notice the connection between the implied existential understanding in the form of a novel and our own view of things. Via cites Murray Krieger as one who "has offered a most helpful and fruitful way of relating the literary work to the world of life and thought while protecting its legitimate autonomy." Krieger speaks of the successful literary work operating sequentially as window, mirror, and window. First it is a set of windows through which we see a world we are familiar with. Then the windows become mirrors and the familiar is reorganized so that there is an implicit understanding of existence. Finally the mirrors become windows again giving us a new vision of the world [ibid., pp81-84].

With reference to the parables of Jesus, Via says that the focal attention should be on the whole narrative pattern and somewhat less on the implied understanding of existence. "In aesthetic experience focal attention is on the pattern of happening existence while subsidiary attention is on the implied understanding of existence." As aesthetic objects Jesus' parables are "new configurations of happening existence containing an implied understanding of existence." However, as biblical texts they communicate to us the nature of faith and unfaith; the understanding of existence implied in the plots--in the human encounters and their outcomes-- is an understanding of faith or unfaith [ibid., pp92-95].

Before turning to an interpretation of individual parables, Via proposes "to point out certain connections between the parables and developed literature which justify our treating the former as aesthetic objects." His discussion centers primarily on features belonging to narrative fiction and their bearing upon the parables. Thus narrative fiction depicts the imaginary and the hypothetical. This is also the case with the parables since they are freely invented stories. In the history of Western literature there are two basic kinds of plot movements--the comic and the tragic. In comedy the movement is upward toward wellbeing and the inclusion of the protagonist in a new or renewed society, while in tragedy the plot falls toward catastrophe and the isolation of the protagonist from society. Via believes that in a number of Jesus' parables these two basic plot structures are clearly seen. He cites the Ten Maidens as an example of tragedy and the Prodigal Son as an example of comedy.

Another approach to works of fiction is to classify them according to the protagonist's power of action. Of the various classifications set forth by Via, the parables of Jesus fall into the "low mimetic" or "realistic." According to the low mimetic or realistic mode the protagonist is superior neither to other men nor to his environment but is rather like us. The characters in the parables are people like us who can do about what we can do. The elements of the mythical or romantic are absent. The only tendency toward the high mimetic in which the protagonist may be superior in degree to other men but not to their environment, is in the few cases where a king appears as a character (the Unforgiving Servant, the Wedding Garment), but Via notes that this tendency is not really carried out.

Having considered the parables in relation to various features from the literary tradition, Via suggests that several parables emerge as clearly defined works of narrative literary art and fall into two formal classes. There are those of "low mimetic, realistic tragedy" where we see realistic imagery and ordinary people in dramatic encounters and conflicts moving downward toward catastrophe. In this class are the Talents, the Ten Maidens, the Wedding Garment, the Wicked Tenants, and the Unforgiving Servant. The other class are those of "low mimetic, realistic comedy" where we view realistic imagery and ordinary people in dramatic, face-to-face confrontations moving upward toward well-being. Here are the Workers in the Vineyard, the Unjust Steward, and the Prodigal Son. Since each of the above parables has an identifiable form, Via says that they should be treated as aesthetic objects.

For Via the two chief routes for interpreting the parables are the literary and the existential or literary criticism and theological-existential exegesis. By approaching the parables from the standpoint of literature or as aesthetic objects, one gains fresh insight into their existential and theological dimensions. In the parables one discerns the impingement of the divine upon human existence. Via expresses the relationship between the existential and the aesthetic as follows:

> We may bring together our existential (thematic) and aesthetic concerns by stating that the ontological possibility--possibility in principle--of losing existence is aesthetically the tragic movement, and the ontological possibility of gaining existence

is aesthetically the comic movement.... Since a
parable as an aesthetic object is within limits an
autonomous world, the gain or loss of the one opportunity which is presented in the parable suggests the gain or loss of existence itself [ibid.,
pp95-101].

Having analyzed the parables in reference to their
literary and aesthetic characteristic, Via turns to a discussion of eight of Jesus' parables. As noted above, five
are designated "tragic parables" and three "comic parables."
Each of these parables is discussed in terms of three categories: historico-literary criticism, literary-existential
analysis, and existential-theological interpretation. Via
does not define or explain these terms and the reader is
left to work them out for himself. Norman Perrin has attempted to describe what Via means by this terminology.
He understands "historico-literary criticism" as the effort
to establish the text to be interpreted. This includes the
literary factors involved in a historical understanding. By
"literary-existential analysis" Perrin takes Via to be referring to the total effort to see the parable as an aesthetic,
literary object, with its interrelatedness of plot movement,
activity of the characters involved, the human encounters
and their outcomes, etc., together with the understanding
of existence which these things imply. Finally, Perrin believes that "existential-theological interpretation" refers to
the act of seeing "the parable's understanding of existence
as a pointer to the divine-human relationship." Perrin offers these interpretations with the reservation of "possible
superficiality of understanding" [Perrin, Jesus and the Language of the Kingdom, pp148-49].

As one examines Via's treatment of the individual
parables, it becomes evident that his major concern and
interest lies in the second category--the literary-existential
analysis. Through a literary analysis of the parables'
plots, Via seeks to uncover their existential implications.
As pointed out above, he distinguishes two basic plot move-
ments--tragedy and comedy. The former moves downward
toward catastrophe and isolation while the latter moves upward toward well-being and the inclusion of the protagonist
in a new or renewed society. In the parable of the Prodigal
Son which is a "comic parable" definite existential motifs
can be discerned. "Man is seen as capable of recognizing
who and where he is, particularly of knowing that something is wrong." The issues involved in the parable bring

before us the question of life and death. "The difference between believing that one must merit acceptance and being graciously accepted into a situation of freedom-and-responsibility is the difference between death and life."

Two other examples of Via's literary-existential analysis of the parables must suffice. Both come from the "tragic parables"--the Talents and the Unforgiving Servant. Concerning the servant to whom one talent was given, Via writes:

> The autonomy of the aesthetic object prevents our speculating about what further opportunities he might have had, and the existential implication of this is that the one-talent man's understanding of existence is non-existence.... From the standpoint of the story as a whole, the being rid of his responsibility is at the same time the loss of opportunity, of possibility, of a place to exist meaningfully in the world [Via, The Parables, p120].

As for the literary-existential analysis of the parable of the Unforgiving Servant, Via notes:

> The parable suggests that one may unexpectedley find an openness or receptivity in others which delivers one from a pressing problem and opens up a surprising new possibility for existence. If the new situation is not internalized, however, so that one becomes open to others and can relinquish claims, then the new situation is lost. To accept what is undeserved from others without extending such graciousness dries up the capacity to receive, and one's isolation is thus made complete [ibid., p142; for Via's interpretation of the eight parables cited above, see ibid., pp110-176].

Since the publication of his book in 1967 and the meeting of the first Society of Biblical Literature Parables Seminar in 1973, Via's approach to the parables has changed. The first SBL Parable Seminar was devoted to "A Structuralist Approach to the Parables," and it is evident from Via's contribution to this Seminar that he has made an extensive study of structuralism in the interim since his book on the parables appeared. Instead of his former "literary-existential analysis," Via now speaks of a "literary-structuralist approach." His major contribution to the first SBL

Seminar is an essay entitled "Parable and Example Story:
A Literary-Structuralist Approach, " which is a response to
two articles by John Dominic Crossan [see section 31, fol-
lowing]. Crossan's second essay concerns the parable of
the Good Samaritan and it is primarily this parable that Via
analyzes from a "literary-structuralist" perspective.

He begins by suggesting that narrative exists as two
levels or dimensions: story and discourse. Within the
story level two other levels may be identified and distinguished: plot (sequential analysis), a tightly cohering organic
unity of three episodes which open, maintain, and close the
sequence; and actants (actantiel analysis), a group of not
more than six functions "whose quality is to be the subject
of or participant in a constant action. The actant is usually
a personal character, but it may be an object, institution,
feeling, disposition, condition, etc. According to the actantiel scheme widely held in structural analysis a subject
desires to possess an object or communicate it to a recipient, the object proceeding from an ordainer. In this effort
the subject may be aided by a helper or impeded by an op-
ponent.

Applying the actantiel model to Luke 10:30-35, Via
says that in the story the ordainer and subject are identical.
The Samaritan wants to communicate to the traveler healing
which proceeds from his own (the Samaritan's) will and concern. He is helped in his effort by the oil, wine, donkey,
and innkeeper. The robbers who appear to be the Samaritan's opponents are paradoxically also helpers. They create
the situation in which he can show compassion. If the
priest and Levite are not in the strictest sense the Samaritan's opponents, they are, nevertheless, his opposites.

If one chooses the unit Luke 10:25-37, Via notes that
Jesus wants to communicate to the lawyer from his own
understanding the meaning of "neighbor. " He does this with
the help of the story, but whether the scribe "gets" or accepts the meaning, becomes a real recipient--whether the
opposition posed by the Jewish way of seeing neighborliness
is overcome--remains uncertain [Dan Otto Via, "Parable
and Example Story: A Literary Structuralist Approach, "
Semeia 1 (1974) 107-08, 112-13].

According to Via's "actantiel" analysis, the account
of the Samaritan is either a story about a Samaritan bringing aid and healing to a traveler, or a story in which Jesus

wants to communicate his own understanding of "neighbor" to the lawyer. The conclusion will depend upon whether our unit of concern is the story alone (Luke 10:30-35), or the discourse as a whole (Luke 10:25-37). One of Via's criticisms of Crossan is that he draws the meaning of the parable from an unwarranted juxtaposition of the story and the discourse.

Turning to the problem of metaphor, Via observes that a metaphor is composed of two elements: a vehicle which is relatively well known and a tenor which is less well known. Meaning passes from the vehicle to the tenor. The important factor is the semantic distance or tension between vehicle and tenor which must be overcome through "semantic motion." This motion gives a new vision of reality by evoking a sense of similarity between what were seen as dissimilars: a new vision which comes as a shock, but as a shock of recognition. As for the parables of Jesus, Via concludes, as he did in his book, that there are eight true narrative parables which have a distinct character compared with the rest. The parable of the Good Samaritan, for example, differs from the narrative parables in that the figure who is present throughout and gives the plot its shape is the victim, the actantiel recipient, rather than the actantiel subject as in the narrative parables. In the parable the actantiel subject, the Samaritan, appears only in the last episode. Via concludes that this is the reason why the plot lacks organic unity and thus is not a true narrative parable.

The eight narrative parables are metaphors of the Kingdom of God because "they give a new vision of everyday existence as transacted by the surprising incursion of the transcendent." The metaphoric tenor is the Kingdom of God, and the vehicle is the narrative. Even though the Kingdom of God may not be explicitly mentioned, it is always represented by "the king-master-father figure who is the actantiel ordainer." The king-master-father figure is involved with "a son-servant-subordinate figure who is the actantiel subject." Thus the parable gives "a new vision of human existence as crossed by the divine." "The important point to remember is that the parable is a metaphor of the Kingdom of God because the semantic distance and tension between the divine and the human is supported by the distance between ordainer (king-father) and the subject (servant-son) who are always separate and distinct characters."

In view of the above analysis, Via holds that in the

Good Samaritan there is enough "semantic distance" to make the story a metaphor. However, it is a metaphor, not of the Kingdom of God, but of a new meaning of the responsibilities of neighborliness. Consequently, on this ground it is not a parable.

With regard to the other "four alleged example-stories" (Lazarus and the Rich Man, the Pharisee and the Publican, the Rich Fool, the Wedding Guest), there is not enough semantic tension or distance to be overcome between the two levels for the texts to be regarded as metaphors. Therefore, they likewise are not parables, but remain illustrative examples of what one is to do or not to do.

Via states further that his argument rests largely on formal literary considerations. He differs with Crossan who suggested that the difference between parable and example-story is not one of form and content but rather one of function and intention. Via questions whether this distinction can be easily made. "Can texts which differ so substantially in deep structure, narrative form, and content function in the same way?" While one can make them function in the same way, Via raises the rhetorical question as to whether it is proper to interpret and classify a narrative contrary to its own structurally constituted textuality, its quality of being one form of expression and not another [ibid., pp110, 114-19].

Via's structuralist analysis of the parables represents a fresh and creative approach, one marked by precision and impressive credentials. He is essentially dealing with three separate areas: the distinction between story and discourse, which established the text to be interpreted; the actantiel analysis of the story, which enables us to understand it; and the relationship between the parts of the metaphor and the actants of the story, which makes the story a metaphor of the Kingdom of God. However, in spite of Via's prodigious effort, one must wonder whether the structuralist approach to the parables represents any significant advance in their understanding and interpretation. For the amount of effort expended, the results appear minimal. Moreover, there is a detail to his analysis which makes it quite difficult to follow. One gets the impression that Via is functioning in a "rarefied atmosphere" inhabited by only a few select individuals. Furthermore, one cannot help but speculate as to how the "average" person, inquiring into the interpretation and meaning of Jesus' parables, would react to the labyrinthine character of Via's structuralism.

Having made these observations, one must hasten to
say that Via's contribution to the history of interpretation of
the parables has been significant. Norman Perrin believes
that Via's book is the most important work on the parables
since Jeremias. Via has ushered in a new day, and he is
representative of a growing movement among American parable scholars which takes the problem of language and literary criticism seriously.

31   JOHN DOMINIC CROSSAN

Another leading American interpreter of the parables
is John Dominic Crossan whose expertise spans the fields
of New Testament scholarship and poetry and poetic criticism. He is the one who drew up proposals for the SBL
Seminar on the Parables and was elected by his colleagues
as its chairman. As with Funk and Via, Crossan's work
on the parables is still in progress, and therefore any analysis and evaluation of his work must be tentative.

Crossan's major work on the parables is In Parables:
The Challenge of the Historical Jesus [New York: Harper &
Row, 1973]. It consists of four chapters which originally
appeared as articles in various scholarly journals, and which
now have been "completely rethought, revised, and rewritten for their present integrated presentation." He begins
with a discussion of the form of Jesus' parables and immediately proceeds to an analysis of allegory and parable.
Crossan maintains that the traditional distinction between
allegory and parable as developed by Jülicher is inadequate
and that the entire discussion should be reopened on a more
profound level than the counting of one, more, or main points
of reference. He notes the differences between allegory and
symbolism as expressed by four outstanding poets; Goethe,
Yeats, Coleridge, and Eliot. The upshot of the distinction
as expressed by these poets is that an allegory expresses
that which is intelligible, while a symbol expresses that
which is inexpressible. In view of this distinction, Crossan
raises the question as to where the parables of Jesus are to
be located. Are they allegories in whole or in part, and if
not what are they? [In Parables, pp7-10].

Crossan's next step is to investigate poetic metaphor
to see whether a clearer idea of its identity helps the understanding and interpretation of Jesus' parables. He observes
that metaphor has been used for decoration and adornment of

what could be said in unadorned but equally sufficient prose language. Metaphor can also be used in pedagogic illustration; a good teacher knows the value of metaphor in explaining to students something new to their experience. But there is another dimension to metaphor which can be grasped only within the metaphor itself. Metaphor can articulate a referent which contains a new possibility of world and of language. But one can only experience its reality by risking entrance into it. There are basically two uses of metaphor which Crossan is concerned with. The first are those in which information precedes participation so that the function of metaphor is to illustrate information about the metaphor's reference; but there are also metaphors in which participation precedes information so that the function of metaphor is to create participation in the metaphor's referent. It is in the latter sense that the distinction between allegory and symbol, as cited by Goethe, Coleridge, Yeats, and Eliot, might be interpreted [ibid., pp10-15].

In view of the above distinctions, Crossan proceeds to define the terminology he intends to use. He points out that figurative language has two quite different functions. One is to illustrate information so that information precedes participation. The other is to create participation so that participation precedes information. The former produces allegories and examples which as pedagogic devices are expendable. The latter produces metaphor on the verbal level and symbol on the nonverbal level. They are unexpendable, and even at their worst they are dormant rather than dead. Crossan in his book is only interested in the verbal phenomenon of metaphor, not in symbol. A further distinction is that metaphor can appear as either parable or myth. A parable tells a story which is possible and within normal life experience. A myth, however, tells a story which is neither of these. Crossan offers a succinct definition of parable as "a metaphor of normalcy which intends to create participation in its referent" [ibid., pp16-16].

Crossan compares Jesus' parables to those found in rabbinical literature. He notes that the latter are didactic and pedagogical and are part of a teaching situation very often associated with a very specific text of Scripture or with a very particular problem in ethical living. The parables of Jesus, however, are related to a very different usage. They are not linked to special biblical texts which need explication nor to precise moral situations for which they represent allegorical exemplification. Instead of didactic figures the parables are poetic metaphors which seek to articulate in, by, and through them the presence of the experienced revelation. Quoting Günther Bornkamm, Crossan writes, "Here the parables are the preaching itself and are not merely serving the purpose of a lesson which is quite independent of them." He states further that the entire purpose of his book is contained in Bornkamm's phrase, "the parables are the preaching itself" [ibid., pp19-21].

Crossan goes on to define the boundaries of his categories more carefully. Metaphor should be understood as verbal symbol, while parable is used to denote metaphor structured within normal "reality," as distinct from myth, where normal "reality" can be ignored. Parable may also be included within the context of what Paul Ricoeur terms "symbol." Quoting Ricoeur, Crossan notes: "Unlike a comparison which we look at from the outside, the symbol in fact is the very movement of the primary meaning which makes us share the hidden meaning and thus assimilates us to the thing symbolized, without our being able to get hold of the similarity intellectually." This implies that the experience and the expression have a profound intrinsic unity in the depths of the event itself [ibid., pp21-22].

The subtitle of Crossan's book is "The Challenge of the Historical Jesus." Unlike Via, who has little interest in Jesus as the author of the Parables, viewing them as literary texts to be interpreted, Crossan is much concerned about Jesus and his relationship to the parables. For him there is a creative relationship between experience and expression when one is dealing with metaphor. The fact that Jesus' experience is set forth in metaphorical parables, instead of another linguistic type, implies that these expressions are part of that experience itself. Crossan maintains that there is an intrinsic and inalienable bond between experience and expression that may aid us to understand "what is most important about Jesus: his experience of God." Going on to a discussion of the parables and time, Crossan further underscores their relevance as an avenue to the historical Jesus. "They express and they contain the temporality of Jesus' experience of God; they proclaim and they establish the historicity of Jesus' response to the Kingdom." The parables are not timeless truths, and they do not so much fit into a given historical situation as create and establish the historical situation of Jesus himself. Crossan acknowledges that there is more to Jesus' life than the parables, but the parables express the "ontological ground" of

Jesus' life. They "are cause and not effect of Jesus' other words and deeds.... Jesus' parables are radically constitutive of his own distinctive historicity and all else is located in them. Parable is the house of God" [ibid., pp22, 32-33].

Turning to the interpretation of the parables, Crossan asks where one should begin. He notes that Claude Lévi-Strauss in his study of myths singled out a myth of the Borono Indians of Central Brazil as what he termed his "key myth," or paradigmatic reference myth. Following this structuralist procedure, Crossan begins with three "key parables" of Jesus which "show most clearly the deep structure of the Kingdom's temporality and which contain in themselves the entire parabolic melody: they are key, overture, paradigm; they are above all what Maurice Merleau-Ponty called 'la parole originaire.'" These parables which are to be studied as paradigmatic references are the Treasure (Matt. 13:44); the Pearl (Matt. 13:45); and the Great Fish (Gospel of Thomas 81:28-82:3).

In the three key parables Crossan finds a structural sequence which is paradigmatic of man's experience of the Kingdom of God. Furthermore, in his analysis of these parables, Crossan uses three terms or categories which he regards as basic for an understanding of all the parables and indeed for the whole message of Jesus. These categories are advent, reversal, and action. In the parable of the Treasure a man's normal existence and the future he had presumably planned and projected for himself are rudely but happily shattered. They are totally invalidated by the advent of the Treasure which opens up a new world and unforeseen possibilities. In light of this advent the man willingly reverses his entire past in order to obtain the Treasure. As a result of this advent and this reversal, he obtains the Treasure which now dictates his time and his history. He gets a new world of life and action which he did not have before and could not have programmed for himself. This same advent-reversal-action pattern can be seen in the parable of the Pearl, and to a lesser extend in the parable of the Great Fish in the Gospel of Thomas. Crossan concludes that in their totality the parables proclaim the Kingdom's temporality and that the three simultaneous modes of its presence appear most clearly in the key parables just noted [ibid., pp33-35].

Having delineated the "three key parables" and the "three key categories" for their interpretation, Crossan pro-

ceeds to an analysis of the parables which can be catego-
rized under each of the "three modes of the Kingdom's
temporality:" its advent as gift of God, its reversal of the
recipient's world, and its empowering to life and action.
Some of the parables, such as the Sower, the Mustard Seed,
the Good Samaritan, and the Wicked Husbandmen, are discussed in detail, while each one falls within one of the
above three headings.

The lists are as follows. Parables of Advent: the
Fig Tree, the Leaven, the Sower, the Mustard Seed, the
Lost Sheep, the Lost Coin. Parables of Reversal: the
Good Samaritan, the Rich Man and Lazarus, the Pharisee
and the Publican, the Wedding Guest, the Proper Guests,
the Great Supper, the Prodigal Son. Parables of Action:
the Wicked Husbandmen, the Doorkeeper, the Overseer, the
Talents, the Throne Claimant, the Unmerciful Servant, the
Servant's Reward, the Unjust Steward, the Workers in the
Vineyard.

Beginning with the "parables of advent," Crossan
notes that in the key parable of the Treasure the advent or
finding of the Treasure had ontological primacy. It determined new time and new history for the discoverer. Crossan
says that the parables of advent stress one or another of
three themes: hiddenness and mystery, gift and surprise,
discovery and joy. Hiddenness and mystery are the predominant themes in the parables of the Budding Fig Tree,
and the Leaven; gift and surprise, in the Sower, the Mustard Seed; discovery and joy, in the Lost Sheep, the Lost
Coin.

There are fewer parables of advent than of reversal
and fewer of reversal than action. Whether this emphasis
represents the historical Jesus we cannot tell. However,
Crossan feels that the paucity of parables of advent reflects
the later tradition's needs rather than Jesus' emphasis. The
later tradition which itself experienced God in the cross and
resurrection of Jesus regarded the parables in which Jesus
expressed his experience of God's advent as quite unnecessary. A second factor in Crossan's methodology concerns
the present interpretative settings of the parables within the
gospel texts. These must be bracketed, not because they
are wrong or useless, but because they pertain to later
layers of the tradition and thus are problematic in studying
the historical Jesus.

As noted above, Crossan singles out two parables of advent for detailed analysis--the Sower and the Mustard Seed. For each parable he attempts to trace the history of tradition back to the earliest form of the story. Following this procedure he offers some general conclusions which Crossan believes to be consistent with the parabolic intentionality of Jesus. Thus in the parables of both the Sower and the Mustard Seed there are sharp juxtapositions of two states. In the Sower it is three instances of sowing losses but then three instances of harvest gains, while in the Mustard Seed it is the small seed sown but the large shade of the plant. These parables are not primarily concerned with growth but with miracle, "not organic and biological development but the gift-like nature, the graciousness and the surprise of the ordinary, the advent of bountiful harvest despite the losses of sowing, the large shade despite the small seed. It is like this that the Kingdom is in advent. It is surprise and it is gift" [ibid., pp37-51].

Under the parables of reversal, Crossan gives major attention to the Good Samaritan. As usual, he begins with an analysis of the text to be interpreted. He maintains that Luke 10:25-37 is not an authentic dialogue between a lawyer and Jesus; neither is it two original controversy dialogs in 10:25-28 and 10:29-37 word-linked by "neighbor." A single controversy dialog in 10:25-28 has been very carefully and skillfully expanded into a double one by taking the originally quite separate parable of 10:30-36 and framing it with 10:29 and 10:37. Consequently, the text of the Good Samaritan to be interpreted is 10:30-36 which, according to Crossan, was originally independent of its present context and must be viewed therefore apart from that later framework [ibid., pp 57-62].

What meaning did the parable have for Jesus? As it unfolds the robbers recede and the "clerics follow them into stylistic oblivion." The Samaritan, however, occupies the place of most importance, and "it would be difficult to emphasize the point too much." Moreover, he is a "good" Samaritan who performs the good deed. For Crossan, this is the central point. A Jewish Jesus tells a Jewish audience about a "good Samaritan." The historical context dictated that Samaritans were outcasts with whom Jews have no dealings, "for Jews have no dealings with Samaritans" (John 4: 9). The literal point of the story challenges the hearer to put together two impossible and contradictory words for the same person: "Samaritan" and "neighbor." With impressive insight Crossan notes: "The whole thrust of the story demands that one say what cannot be said, what is a contradiction in terms: Good Samaritan. On the lips of the historical Jesus the story demands that the hearer respond by saying the contradictory, the impossible, the unspeakable." Thus Crossan rejects the general view that the parable of the Good Samaritan is an example-story which teaches the virtue of neighborliness. No, it is a parable of reversal in which good (clerics) and bad (Samaritan) become, respectively, bad and good so that the world is challenged and reversed. To use Crossan's imagery, "When the north pole becomes the south pole, and the south the north, a world is reversed and overturned and we find ourselves standing firmly on utter uncertainty." That is how it is with the parable of the Good Samaritan!

How then was the Good Samaritan changed from a parable to an example-story? Crossan observes that as the gospel moved out into a Gentile environment terms like "Samaritan" had no meaning, and the tendency to convert the parables to example-stories was inevitable. In the parables there is a literal level and a metaphorical level. There is a literal point which stems from the surface level of the story, and a metaphorical one which lives on a much deeper level and appears in a mysterious dialectic with the former point. It is especially easy to remain on the literal level when the protagonist of a parable is performing a morally good action and to then convert the parable into an example. This, suggests Crossan, is exactly what has happened to the Good Samaritan in the course of its transmission.

Thus Crossan concludes that the idea of the Good Samaritan as an example derived from the tradition and not from Jesus. The real purpose of literary creation is to make the "leap" from the literal point to the metaphorical point. The literal point confronted the hearers with the necessity of saying the impossible and having their world turned upside down and radically questioned in its presuppositions. Just so, the metaphorical point is that the Kingdom of God breaks abruptly into human existence and demands a reversal of prior values, closed options, set judgments, and established conclusions. The parables of reversal "portray metaphorically the polar reversal which the Kingdom's advent demands" [ibid., pp62-66, 75].

Under the rubric of the parables of action, Crossan raises the question of the parables and ethics. He points

out that the parables of Jesus seek to draw one into the
Kingdom, and they challenge us to act and to live from the
gift which is experienced therein. But this does not satisfy
most of us because instead of parables we want good precepts and sensible programs. The lonely silences within
the parables frighten us and we experience a haunting in-
security because while they challenge one to life and action
within the Kingdom, they leave that life and that action as
absolute in its call and unspecified in its detail. We seek
moral systems and absolutes which can assure our security,
but the only absolute we keep glimpsing is the Kingdom
"snapping our absolutes like dried twigs. "

    The parables of action are by far the most numerous
and this may reflect more the interest of the primitive
church than the emphasis of the historical Jesus. They portray crucial or critical situations which demand firm and
resolute action, prompt and energetic decision. Sometimes
they depict a situation where the decision is made, other
times where it is not made. Some of them have protago-
nists who succeed, and some fail under the pressure of the
crisis. There is still another set of parables of action
which Crossan calls "Servant parables" which involve a
master-servant relationship at a moment of critical reckoning.

    Crossan proceeds by making a detailed analysis of
the parable of the Wicked Husbandmen and then of the other
eight "Servant parables. " His basis for classifying these
parables is that in their central story-line they contain the
two themes mentioned above: a superior-subordinate relationship and a crisis of reckoning within this relationship.
Crossan discerns a unity in these parables and likens them
to a musical harmony in which no single one is heard adequately until all are heard fully. While these are parables
of action, they are also closely related to the theme of
reversal which is surely one of Crossan's favorite categories. He suggests that in his analysis of these parables
"we shall be watching Jesus slowly developing a parabolic
theme into its own polar reversal. Suffice it to say, Crossan's careful exegesis and his fresh insights surely place
him among the leading contemporary parable scholars.
[For his treatment of these parables, see ibid. , pp79-120].
His concluding paragraph offers a succinct summary to the
parables of action:

        The parables of action all challenge one to life

and action in response to the Kingdom's advent.
But the Servant parable introduces a very disturb-
ing note into all this. The temporality of the
Kingdom appears in the three simultaneous modes
of advent, reversal, and action. But as advent
takes priority over reversal so does this latter
over action. In the eight parables of the Servant
cluster a theme is presented in ordered normalcy
and then is just as carefully reversed and shattered. Like a wise and prudent servant calculat-
ing what he must do in the critical reckoning to
which his master summons him, one must be
ready and willing to respond in life and action to
the eschatological advent of God. But, unfortunately, the eschatological advent of God will always be precisely that for which wise and prudent
readiness is impossible because it shatters also
our wisdom and our prudence [ibid. , pp119-20].

As noted earlier, Crossan has been one of the leaders in the work and deliberations of the Journal of Biblical
Literature Seminar on the Parables. In the first year of
the seminar he contributed a revised and expanded version
of his work on "The Servant Parables" and on "Parable and
Example in the Teaching of Jesus, " the latter being basically a discussion of the parable of the Good Samaritan. His
further interpretations in these articles follow essentially
the course outlined above [see Semeia 1 (1974), 17-62, 63-
104].

The second SBL Seminar was devoted exclusively to
the parable of the Good Samaritan. Crossan developed further a structuralist analysis of the parable in an article
"The Good Samaritan: Towards a Generic Definition of Parable" [Semeia 2 (1974)]. He began with a discussion of
structuralist theory and practice according to various exponents. From these Crossan singled out Algindas Julien
Greimas' actantial method as one "which may prove very
helpful in the present study. " Greimas' model is used as
a structural formula for the parabolic event as polemical
encounter between two contradictory deep structures, that
of the hearer's expectation and that of the speaker's story.
Parable characterizes this story type and is at the opposite
pole from myth. The latter reconciles and mediates contradiction but the former introduces and underlines contradiction. Crossan believes that many of the parables can be
portrayed structurally as a clash between hearer and speak-

er along the axis of communication in Greimas' model. The hearer's expected correlation of Giver/Object/Receiver is reversed either singly or doubly by the speaker's story. Thus the Good Samaritan attacks the hearer's deep structure of expectation and thereby and therein opens one to the possibility of transcendence [ibid., pp82-112].

There follows Crossan's article brief critiques by Robert C. Tannehill and Daniel Patte and Crossan's subsequent rejoinder [ibid., pp113-16, 117-121, 121-28]. For one not schooled in the intricacies of structuralism, the discussion appears quite heady and obscure. However, there can be no doubt that the "American school" of parable interpretation is thriving with vibrancy and innovation. Crossan and his colleagues in the SBL Seminar, through an examination of the linguistic dimensions and implications of the parables, are seeking a fresh way forward. In building upon, and reacting to, Jülicher, Dodd, Jeremias, and the new hermeneutic, they are employing new disciplines and methodologies in order to uncover the parables' genius and power. Where their efforts will lead and whether their contributions will have lasting significance, only the future can reveal. One thing is certain: research into the history of parable interpretation and into their contemporary meaning and present-day relevance can never be the same again.

Part II

The Bibliography

PARABLES IN GENERAL

Aalen, S. "Innbydelsen til Guds Kirke. Belyst ut fra lignelsen om Kongesønnens bryllop." Tidsskrift for Teologi og Kirke 29 (1958), 119-26.

Abineno, Johannes L. C. Sepuluh perumpamaan Tuhan Jesus, tjet. 2. Djakarta: Badan Penerbit Kristen, 1966. 52p.

Adam, A. "Gnostische Züge in der patristischen Exegese von Luk. 15." Studia Evangelica III. Texte und Untersuchungen zur Geschichte der altchristlichen Literatur (Akademie-Verlag, Berlin) 88 (1964), 299-305.

Addison, James T. Parables of Our Lord; Meditations for Lent. New York: Moorehouse-Gorham, 1940. 75p.

Adheran, C. Etudes sur les paraboles de Jésus Christ. Strassburg: 1859.

Adinolfi, M. "L'insegnamento escatologico nelle parabole." Antonianum 36 (1961), 97-111.

_____. "L'interpretazione delle parabole." Rivista Biblica 9 (1961), 97-111, 243-58.

Åkerhielm, H. "Nyare liknelseslitteratur." Svensk Exegetisk Årsbok 3, 47-60.

Aeschimann, André. Pour qu'on lise les paraboles. Paris: Impr. Tournon, 1958. 136p. Also, Paris: Librairie Protestante, 1964. 128p.

Aiken, Warwick. "A Continental Divide in Scripture Interpretation." Bibliotheca Sacra 94 (1938), 219-30.

Albert, Br. B. "Parable Adaptations." Catholic Educator 27 (1956), 192-94.

Alberti, Alb. Parabole e similitudini. Rocca S. Casciano: Cappelli, 1920. 238p.

Alexandre, Jean. "Notes sur l'esprit des paraboles en réponse A. P. Ricoeur." Etudes Théologiques et Religieuses 51 (1976), 367-72.

Algisi, Leone. Gesù e le sue parabole. Torino: Marietti, 1963. 391p.

Alix, Marie. En ce temps-là Jésus parlait du blé. Paris: Permanence Mariale, 1942. 31p.

Allen, Charles L. When the Heart Is Hungry; Christ's Parables for Today. Westwood, N. J.: Revell, 1955. 159p.

Allen, Hattie B. Stories Jesus Told. Illus. by Mariel Wilhoite Turner. Philadelphia: Winston, 1954. 32p.

Almeida, D. I. "L'Opérativité sémantique des récits-paraboles. Sémiotique narrative et textuelle. Herméneutique du discours religieux." Diss., Université Catholique de Louvain, 1976. 485p.

Altenburg. "Gleichnisse Jesu im Lichte der socialen Fragen." Zeitschrift für den Evangelischen Religionsunterricht (1893), 257-72.

Ambrozic, A. M. "Mark's Concept of the Parable; Mark 4:11f. in the Context of the Second Gospel." Catholic Biblical Quarterly 29 (1967), 220-27.

Amthāl al-Injīl. Trans. Amīn Nakhlah. Beirut: 1967. 60p.

Angelini, Cesare. Fatti e parabole. Milano: E. U. Bignami, 1970. 116p.

Angiolini, G. "Lo scopo delle parabole." Palestra del Clero 13, 2 (1934), 49.

Anizan, Félix. La Clef patristique des paraboles. Loudun: La Rayonnement Intellectuel, 1939. 120p.

Anneveld, H. Jezus' gelijkenissen, aan jonge lieden verhaald. Amsterdam: H. W. Willems, 1853.

Anthony, Metropolit. Christus begegnen: Stationen. Übers.

von Helmut Kusterer. Freiburg, Basel, Wien: Herder, 1975. 142p.

Antolin, T. "Las parábolas del Evangelio: Continen una sola o varias lecciones doctrinales?" Verdad y Vida 18 (1960), 117-33; also Semana Biblica Española 19 (1962), 305-18.

_____. "El problema de las conclusiones finales aparentes en las parabolas evangélicas. " Estudios Bíblicos 2 (1943), 3-22.

Antoniazzi, A. "Parábolas de Jesus. " Atual 3 (1972), 79-88.

Anzian, F. Les paraboles de l'Amour. Bruges: Beyaert, 1935. 282p.

Armstrong, April (Oursler). The Tales Christ Told. Garden City, N. Y.: Doubleday, 1959. 256p. (1968, 198p.).

_____. The Tales Christ Told. Phonodisc. Washington, D. C.: Library of Congress; manufactured by American Printing House for the Blind, Louisville, Ky. 1959.

Armstrong, D. H. "The Parables of the Synoptic Gospels, with Special Reference to Modern Interpretation. " Diss., Trinity College, Dublin, 1967/68.

Armstrong, Edward A. The Gospel Parables. New York: Sheed and Ward. Also, London: Hodder & Stoughton, 1967. 219p.

Arndt, Friedrich. Die Gleichnisreden Jesu Christi, 6 Tle. Magdeburg: 1841-47.

Arvidsson, E. Mena något annat: En studiebok om Jesu liknelser. Stockholm: Verbum /Studiebokförlag, 1973. 94p.

Augustin, George. "Les Paraboles de la semence. " Bible et Vie Chrétienne (March 1960), 37-41.

Aussems, A. "Re-writing the Parables in Terms of Modern Life. " Lumen Vitae 14 (March 1959), 64-68.

Ayer, William W. Christ's Parables for Today. New York: Revell, 1949. 173p.

234 / Bibliography

Baagøe, P. H. Jesu lignelser! Hjaelp til bibeltimer med et udvalg af Jesu lignelser som emne. Aalborg: 1954. 40p.

Baarslag, D. J. Gelijkenissen des Heeren, 2dln. 1940.

Bacon, Benjamin W. "The Matthean Discourses in Parables, Mt. 13:1-52." Journal of Biblical Literature 46 (1927) 237-65.

_____. "The Parable and Its Adaptation in the Gospels." Hibbert Journal 21 (1922-23) 127-40.

Baer, Dallas C. Windows that Let in the Light; Sermons on the Parables. Grand Rapids: Zondervan Pub. House, 1940, 132p.

Baguet, Paul M. "The Parabolic Teaching of Christ." Homiletic and Pastoral Review 24 (1923-24) 1241-51.

Bailey, B. An Exposition of the Parables of Our Lord; Showing their Connection with His Ministry, their Prophetic Character, and their Gradual Development of the Gospel Dispensation. With a Preliminary Dissertation on the Parable. London: J. Taylor, 1828, 512p.

Bailey, Kenneth E. The Cross and the Prodigal. The 15th Chapter of Luke Seen through the Eyes of Middle Eastern Peasants. St. Louis: Concordia Pub. House, 1973, 134p.

_____. Poet and Peasant: A Literary-Cultural Approach to the Parables in Luke. Eerdmans, 1967. 238p.

_____. "A Study of Some Lucan Parables in the Light of Oriental Life and Poetic Style." Ph. D. thesis, Concordia Seminary, 1972.

Baird, Edgar M. "An Introduction to the Study of the Parables in the Synoptic Gospels." Ph. D. thesis, Union Theological Seminary (New York City), 1941. 223p.

Baird, J. Arthur. "A Pragmatic Approach to Parable Exegesis: Some New Evidence on Mark 4:11, 33-34." Journal of Biblical Literature 76 (1957) 201-07.

Baljon, J. M. S. "Het doel van Jezus' gelijkenissen. "
Theologische Studiën 15 (1897) 178-94.

Banks, Louis A. Christ's Soul-searching Parables; Evangelistic Sermons on the Parables of Jesus. New York:
Revell, 1925, 187p.

Barclay, William. And Jesus Said; A Handbook on the Parables of Jesus. Philadelphia: Westminster Press,
1970, 222p.

Barella, Giov. Batt. Le parabole evangeliche. Alessandria:
"La Popolare, " 1923, 38p.

Barnett, Albert E. Understanding the Parables of Our Lord.
Nashville: Cokesbury Press, 1940. 223p. Also,
Chicago: A. R. Allenson, 1954.

Barr, A. "The Interpretation of the Parables. " Expository
Times 53 (1941-42) 20-25.

Barretto, Agnelo D. O anúncio do reino de Deus. Re-
flexões sôbre as parábolas. Rio de Janeiro: Edit.
Vozes, 1868, 126p.

Barry, C. "The Literary and Artistic Beauty of Christ's
Parables. " Catholic Biblical Quarterly 10 (1948) 376-
83.

Barry, William. "Parables, " in The Catholic Encyclopedia,
vol. 11. New York: Encyclopedia Press, 1913, 460-
67.

Bartina, S. "Reconstrucción del evangelio por las parábolas. " Estudios Ecclesiásticos 40 (1965) 319-36.

Bastian, Hans-Dieter. "Das Gleichnis im Religionsunterricht
(Hauptschule-Sekundarstufe I). " Linguistica Biblica 2
(1970) 12-13.

Bauckham, Richard. "Synoptic Parousia Parables and the
Apocalypse. " New Testament Studies 23 (1977) 162-76.

Baudiment, L. "La Leçon des paraboles. " Revue Biblique
53 (1946) 47-55.

Bauer, G. L. Sammlung und Erklärung der parabolischen

236 / Bibliography

Erzählungen unseres Herrn. Leipzig: 1782.

Bauer, J. B. "Gleichnisse Jesu und Gleichnisse der Rabbinen." Theologisch-praktische Quartalschrift 119 (1971) 297-307.

Bauer, Karl. Gleichnisse Jesu in 24 Bildern dargestellt. Gütersloh: Bertelsmann, 1931, 24p.

Beardslee, William A. "Narrative Form in the New Testament and Process Theology." Encounter 36 (1975) 301-15. [Reply by T. J. Weeden and B. E. Meland, pp. 316-41].

_____. "Parable Interpretation and the World Disclosed by the Parable." Perspectives in Religious Studies 3 (1976) 123-29.

Behrmann, Georg. Die Gleichnisse unseres Herrn Jesu Christi. In Bibelstunden ausgelegt, 2. Aufl. Hamburg: L. Gräfe & Sillem, 1892, 355p.

Berger, Klaus. "Materialien zu Form und Uberlieferungsgeschichte neutestamentlicher Gleichnisse." Novum Testamentum 15 (1973) 1-37.

_____. "Zur Grage des traditionsgeschichtlichen Wertes apokrypher Gleichnisse." Novum Testamentum 17 (1975) 58-76.

Bergmann, Werner. Die Zehn Gleichnisse vom Reich der Himmel. Lahr-Dinglingen: Verlag der St.-Johannis-Druckerei Schweickhardt, 1976, 103p.

Bernard, R. "La Raison d'être des paraboles." Vie Spirituelle 89 (1953) 347-52.

Beskow, Natanael. Jesu liknelser. Stockholm: Birkagården 1922 (1926). 230p.

Bewer, Julius A. "The Psychological Study of the Words of Jesus, Especially of His Parables." Bibliotheca Sacra 61 (1904) 102-40.

Beyer, Karl. Jesus als Lehrer: Präparationen zu den Gleichnissen und der Bergpredigt nebst Anhang. Berlin: Walter Prausnitz, 1914, 288p.

Bilder helfen hören: Gleichnisworte der Bibel. Hrsg. von Johannes Kuhn. Stuttgart: Quell-Verlag, 1973, 151p.

Bill, Reinhold, and Schmidt, Volker. Gleichnisse -- Handlungen -- Hoheitstitel Jesu. Theologischer Grundkurs für dar 4. -6. Schuljahr. Munchen: Kösel-Verlag, 1974.

Binder, Hermann. "Dieser nimmt die Sünder an. Eine Studie zu Lk. 15 und 16." Diss., Protest. Theol. Institut. Klausenburg (Rum.), 1949.

Birkler, Erik. Jesu lignelser. 17 bibeltimer. København: Spejderforlaget, 1960, 32p.

Biser, Eugen. Die Gleichnisse Jesu. München: Kösel, 1965, 187p.

_____. "Das Gottesreich als Sinn und Thema der Gleichnisse." Hochland 58 (1966) 556-60.

Bishop, E. F. F. "ἀκουέτω -- Mark 4:9, 23." Bible Translator 7 (1956) 38-40.

Black, Matthew. "The Parables as Allegory." Bulletin of the John Rylands Library 42 (1960) 273-87.

Blackman, E. C. "New Methods of Parable Interpretation." Canadian Journal of Theology 15 (1969) 3-13.

Blank, Josef. Die Gleichnisse Jesu. 1. 2. Lebendige Kirche. Bildhefte für christliche Lebensgestaltung. Hrsg. von Ernst Schnydrig und Ernst W. Roetheli. Freiburg i. Br.: Lambertus-Verlag, 1962-63, 12p.

_____. "Marginalien zur Gleichnisauslegung." Bibel und Leben 6 (1965) 50-60.

Bøcker, Anders K. F. Lignelser og Beretninger til Religionstimen. København: Glydendal, 1924-25.

Böhmerle, Theodor. Gleichnisse Jesu. Eine Auslegung in prophetischer Sicht, neu durchges. Aufl. Reutlingen: Philadelphia-Buchh., 1960, 134p.

Bonaiuti, E. "Le parabole di Gesù. Religio 10 (1934) 21-31, 145-52, 209-14, 296-300, 412-17, 525-38; 11 (1935) 16-20.

Bonnard, P. "Où en est la question des paraboles évangéliques? De Julicher (1888) à Jeremias (1947)." Foi et Vie 66, 5 (1967) 36-49.

Bontrager, John. K. "The Story Sermon as a Ministry to Children and Adults in the Light of Psychological Insight and New Testament Understanding of Parable." D. Min. thesis. School of Theology at Claremont, 1977. 105p.

Boobyer, G. H. "The Redaction of Mark IV, 1-34." New Testament Studies 8 (1961) 59-70.

Borsch, Frederick H. "Who Has Ears." Anglican Theological Review 52 (1970) 131-41.

Bosio, E. Le parabole di Cristo brevemente spiegate. Torre Pellice: Libr. Claudiana, 1927. 173p.

Bosley, Harold A. He Spoke to Them in Parables. New York: Harper & Row, 1963. 184p.

Boucher, Madeleine I. "The Mysterious Parable: A Literary Study." Ph. D. thesis, Brown University, 1973, 136p.

_____. The Mysterious Parable: A Literary Study. Washington, D. C.: Catholic Biblical Association of America, 1977. 101p.

Boumard, P. Prêchons l'Evangile, méditonale. T. 1, Les Paraboles. Paris: Bloud et Gay, 1934. 256p.

Bourbeck, Christine. Gleichnisse aus altem und neuem Testament. Stuttgart: Ehrenfried Klotz Verlag, 1971. 336p.

Bourns, Sam. Discourses on the Parables of Our Saviour. London: 1763.

Bouttier, M. "Les paraboles du maître dans la tradition synoptique." Etudes Théologiques et Religieuses 48 (1973) 176-95.

Bover, J. "Las parábolas del Evangelio." Estudios Bíblicos 3 (1944) 229-57.

Bowie, Walter R. "The Parables," in The Interpreter's
   Bible. New York: Abingdon-Cokesbury Press, 1951.
   Vol. 7, pp. 165-75.

Bowker, J. W. "Mystery and Parable." Journal of Theological Studies 25 (1974) 300-17.

Boyer, Ch. Andre. Le Bon Jésus. Illus. by de Calvet-
   Rogniat. T. III, Les Paraboles. Paris: Lethielleux,
   1948, 33p.

Bracco, Luigi. Parabole del Signore. Fossano: TEC,
   1970, 270p.

Bragge, Francis. Practical Discourses upon the Parables
   of Our Blessed Saviour. London: S. Manship, 1710.
   2 vols. , 480p.

Bremond, Arnold. Paraboles de la Table sainte: Commentaire contemplatif de 35 paraboles de Jésus. Lausanne:
   La Concorde, 1944, 80p.

Bring, J. Th. Hvad hafva Jesu liknelser att säga oss?
   Linköping: Östg. Correspis, 1912, 14p.

Brink, Johannes E. van den. Parables of the Kingdom:
   Matthew XIII, 1-52, trans. A. H. Wynd. Bankstown,
   N. S. W.: High Road Publications, 1975, 137p.

Briscoe, Hollie L. "A Comparison of the Parables in the
   Gospel According to Thomas and the Synoptic Gospels."
   Ph. D. thesis, Southwestern Baptist Theological Seminary,
   1966. 198p.

Brooks, A. "The Teaching in Parables." Expository Times
   32 (1920-21) 170-72.

Broughton, Leonard G. The Kingdom Parables and Their
   Teaching; A Study of Matthew XIII. New York: Revell,
   1910, 121p.

Brouwer, Anneus M. De Gelijknissen. Leiden: A. W.
   Sijthoff, 1946, 256p.

Brown, Raymond E. "Parable and Allegory Reconsidered."
   Novum Testamentum 5 (1962) 36-45.

_____. "Parables of Jesus," in New Catholic Encyclopedia. New York: McGraw-Hill, 1967. Vol. X, pp. 984-88.

Brown, S. "The Secret of the Kingdom of God, Mark 4:11." Journal of Biblical Literature 92 (1973) 60-74.

Browne, L. E. The Parables of the Gospels in the Light of Modern Criticism. Cambridge, England: Cambridge University Press, 1913.

Bruce, Alexander B. The Parabolic Teaching of Christ; A Systematic and Critical Study of the Parables of Our Lord. London: Hodder & Stoughton, 1882. 515p. 3rd rev. ed., New York: A. C. Armstrong and Son, 1908. 515p.

Brunn, N. von Das Reich Gottes nach den Lehren Jesu, besonders seinem Gleichnisreden erklärt. Basel: 1816.

Brunner, Heinrich E. Saat und Frucht, zehn Predigten über Gleichnisse Jesu. Berlin: Furche-Verlag, 1938, 127p.

_____. Sowing and Reaping; The Parables of Jesus. Trans. Thomas Wieser. Richmond: John Knox Press, 1964.

Bugge, Christian A. Die Haupt-Parabeln Jesu. Giessen: J. Ricker'sche Verlagsbuchhandlung, 1903.

_____. Jesu Hoved Parabler. Dybwad: 1895, 132p.

_____. Jesu Hoved-Parabler udlagte. København: Gyldendal, 1901, 328p.

_____. Om Jesu Christi Parabler. Christiania: Gyldendal, 1895.

_____. Parablerne om Guds Riges Hemmeligheder. Christiania: 1895.

Buisson, E. Les Paraboles de l'évangile. Genèva: 1848.

Buit, F. M. Du. Le Discours des paraboles: Études synoptiques. Paris: Ligue Cath. de l'Évangile, 1967, 57p.

Bull, N. Stories Jesus Told. London: Evan., 1969, 93p.

Bulman, J. M. "The Parables of Revelation and Judgment."
Review and Expositor 53 (1956) 314-25.

Bungenberg, Theodor. Gleichnisse Jesu: 10 Predigten.
Göttingen: Vandenhoeck & Ruprecht, 1912, 98p.

Burkhart, Jacob P. II. "Rhetorical Functions and Possibilities of the Parables of Jesus." Ph. D. thesis,
Pennsylvania State University, 1972, 161p.

Burkill, T. A. "The Cryptology of Parables in St. Mark's
Gospel." Novum Testamentum 1 (1956) 246-62.

Burnand, Eugène. Die Gleichnisse Jesu. Stuttgart: Verlag
für Volkskunst, 1912, 208p.

_____. Jesu liknelser. Med illustrationer. Stockholm:
Nord. bokh., 1909, 153p.

Buttrick, George A. The Parables of Jesus. Garden City,
N. Y.: Doubleday, Doran; London: Hodder and Stoughton, 1928, 274p.

Buzy, Denis. Introduction aux paraboles évangéliques.
Paris: J. Gabalda, 1912.

_____. Même les miettes: En marge des paraboles.
Paris: Éditions de l'Ecole, 1961. 159p.

_____. Les Paraboles traduites et commentées, 8
ed. Paris: Gabriel Beauchesne, 1932. 701p.

_____. "Les Sentences finales des paraboles évangél-
iques." Revue Biblique 40 (1931) 321-44.

Cadbury, Henry J. "Soluble Difficulties in the Parables,"
in New Testament Sidelights; Essays in Honor of Alexander Converse Purdy. Hartford: Hartford Seminary
Foundation Press, 1960, 118-23.

Cadman, Samuel P. The Parables of Jesus. Illus. by N.
C. Wyeth. Philadelphia: David McKay Co., 1931. 163p.

Cadoux, Arthur T. The Parables of Jesus: Their Art and

Use. London: James Clarke & Co., 1930, 255p.

Calkins, Wolcott. Parables for Our Times; A Study of Present-Day Questions in the Light of Christ's Illustrations, 2nd rev. ed. Boston: Pilgrim Press, 1910, 122p.

Callan, Charles J. The Parables of Christ, with Notes for Preaching and Meditation. New York: J. F. Wagner; London: Herder, 1940, 496p.

Calligaris, Rodolfo. Parábolas evangélicas à luz do espiritismo. Rio de Janeiro: Federação Espirita Brasileira, 1963. 126p.

Cantinat, J. "The Parables of Mercy." Theology Digest 4 (1956) 120-23.

_____. "Les Paraboles de la miséricorde Lc. XV, 1-32)." Nouvelle Revue Théologique 77 (1955) 246-64.

Cardy, Clare E. "God's Purposes for Israel as Presented in the Parables of Christ." Ph. D. thesis, Dallas Theological Seminary, 1956.

Cargill, Robert L. All the Parables of Jesus; An Inspirational Interpretation of the Parables and How They Relate to Life Today. Nashville: Broadman Press, 1970, 127p.

Carlston, Charles E. "Changing Fashions in Interpreting the Parables." Andover Newton Quarterly 14 (1974) 227-33.

_____. The Parables of the Triple Tradition. Philadelphia. Fortress Press, 1975. 249p.

_____. "Positive Criterion of Authenticity." Biblical Research 7 (1962) 33-44.

Carrillo, Alday S. Las parábolas del Evangelio. Mexico: Instituto di Sagrada Escritura, 1972? 180p.

Casá, Félix. "Parabolas y catequesis." Revista Bíblica 38 (1976) 97-111.

Casey, R. P. "An Early Armenian Fragment of Luke

XVI:3-25. " Journal of Theological Studies 36 (1935)
70-73.

Castellani, Leonardo. Doce parábolas cimarronas. Buenos
Aires: Itinerarium, 1959, 173p.

Cavalletti, S. "Il bambino come parabola. " Euntes Docete
25 (1972) 509-14.

Cave, C. H. "The Parables and the Scriptures. " New
Testament Studies 11 (1965) 374-87.

_____. "Les Paraboles et l'ecriture. " Bible et Vie
Chrétienne 72 (1966) 37-49.

Cavedo, R. "Una storia che si fa parabola (Mt. 20:1-16,
21:28-22:14). " Parole di Vita 17 (1972) 335-51.

Cerfaux, Lucien. "La Connaissance des secrets du Royaume
d'après Matt. XIII:11 et parallèles. " New Testament
Studies 2 (1955-56) 238-49.

_____. Er redete in Gleichnissen. Übers. von
Faimund Tschudy. München: Verlag Ars sacra, 1969.
157p.

_____. Mensaje de las parábolas. Tr. by A.
G. Fraile. Madrid: Fax, 1972. 238p.

_____. "Les paraboles de Jésus. " Nouvelle
Revue Théologique 55 (1928) 186-98.

_____. Il tesoro delle parabole. T-Leumann: Elle
Di Ci, 1968. 128p.

_____. O Tesouro das Parábolas. Tr. do francês
por A. Rubim: A Palavra Viva. São Paulo: Ed.
Paulinas, 1973. 150p.

_____. The Treasure of the Parables. Trans. M.
Bent. De Pere, Wis. : St. Norbert Abbey Press, 1968,
143p.

_____. Le Trésor des paraboles, spiritualité biblique.
Paris: Desclée, 1966, 164p.

_____. "Trois rehabilitations dans l'Évangile, " in

Recuil Lucien Cerfaux II. Gembloux: J. Duculot, 1954, 51-59. Also, Bulletin des Facultés catholiques de Lyon 72, 1 (1950) 5-13.

_____ and Garitte, G. "Les Paraboles du Royaume dans 'Évangile de Thomas.'" Le Muséon 70 (1957) 307-27.

Chalendar, Xavier de. Parabolas. Trad. de Florian Diaz de Cerio. Zaragoza: Hechos y Dichos, 1967, 87p.

Chambers, Talbot W. "The Classification of the Parables." Presbyterian Review 8 (1887) 102-15.

Chappell, Clovis G. In Parables. Nashville: Abingdon-Cokesbury, 1953, 153p.

_____. Sermons from the Parables. Nashville: Cokesbury Press, 1933. 220p.

Charles, Howard. The Parables of the Kingdom. Newton, Kan.: Faith and Life Press, 1978, 56p.

Childs, Ann T. Parables to the Point. Philadelphia: Westminster Press, 1963, 106p.

Christie, G. An Exposition of Twenty-Eight Parables of Our Lord. Edinburgh: Church of Scotland Committee, 1934, 140p.

Clark, R. E. D. "Why Speakest Thou in Parables?" Evangelical Quarterly 12 (1940) 129-37.

Clowes, John. The Parables of Jesus Christ Explained in the Way of Question and Answer, 2nd ed. London: Hodson, 1839. 310p. Also, London: Alvey, 1864. Also, London: Speirs, 1882. 359p.

Coates, Thomas. The Parables for Today. St. Louis: Concordia Pub. House, 1971, 73p.

Cogorno, A. Parabole come cronaca. Milan: Ancora, 1972, 119p.

Colacci, M. "Le Parabole del Salvatore e una Profezia di Isaia." Scuola Cattolica 67 (1939) 58-74.

Collyer, William B. Lectures on Scripture Parables. London: Black and Co., 1815, 535p.

Congar, Y. M. J. "The Parables as God's Revelation." Cross and Crown 20 (1968) 10-25.

_____. "Les Paraboles révélatrices du Dieu que vient." Parole et Mission 7, 24 (1964) 19-38.

Conz, C. Phil. Morgenländische Apologen, oder die Lehrweisheit Jesu in Parabeln und Sentenzen. Heilbronn: 1803.

Corell, J. "La problemática de las parábolas a la luz de la historia de su interpretación." Estudios Franciscanos 73 (1972) 5-28; 74 (1973) 5-24.

Cranfield, C. E. B. "Message of Hope; Mark 4:21-32." Interpretation 9 (1955) 150-64.

_____. "St. Mark IV, 1-34." Scottish Journal of Theology 4 (1951) 398-414; 4 (1952) 49-66.

Cronewald, M. Vier Parabeln: Samariter, Jungfrauen, Lazarus, Ungerechter Verwalter. Klosterneuburg b. Wien: Volksliturg. Apostolat, 1930, 42p.

Crossan, John D. "A Basic Bibliography for Parables Research." Semeia 1 (1974) 236-74.

_____. In Parables: The Challenge of the Historical Jesus. New York: Harper & Row, 1973. 141p.

_____. "Parable and Example in the Teaching of Jesus." New Testament Studies 18 (1971-72) 285-307; Semeia 1 (1974) 63-104.

_____. "Parables as Religious and Poetic Experience." Journal of Religion 53 (1973) 330-58.

_____. Raid on the Articulate: Comic Eschatology in Jesus and Borges. New York: Harper & Row, 1976. 207p.

_____. "The Seed Parables of Jesus." Journal of Biblical Literature 92 (1973) 244-66.

_____. "The Servant Parables of Jesus," in Society of Biblical Literature 1973 Seminar Papers, vol 2. Cambridge, Mass.: Society of Biblical Literature, 1973. pp. 94-118. Also, Semeia 1 (1974) 17-62.

_____. "Structuralist Analysis and the Parables of Jesus. A Reply to D. O. Via, J., 'Parable and Example Story: A Literary-Structuralist Approach.'" Linguistica Biblica 25/26 (1973), 21-30. Also, Semeia 1 (1974), 192-221.

Crowe, Charles M. Sermons on the Parables of Jesus. Nashville: Abingdon-Cokesbury Press, 1953. 186p.

Cumming, John. Foreshadows. Lectures on Our Lord's Parables. London: Arthur Hall, Virtue & Co., 1851. 579p. Also, Philadelphia: Lindsay and Blakiston, 1854 (1856) (1863) 379p.

Dabney, R. L. "Of Expounding the Parables." Homiletic Review 33 (1897) 160-65.

Dahl, Nils A. "Gleichnis und Parabel," in Die Religion in Geschichte und Gegenwart, 3. Aufl. Tübingen: J. C. B. Mohr, 1957-65. Vol 2, cols. 1614-19.

_____. "The Parables of Growth." Studia theologica 5 (1951) 132-66.

_____. "The Parables of Growth," in Jesus in the Memory of the Early Church: Essays. Minneapolis: Augsburg Pub. House, 1976, 141-66.

Dale, Aasmund. Liknelser fra Lukas-evangeliet. Oslo: Andaktsbokselskapet, 1956, 18p. (1959) (1967).

Dallmann, William. Short Stories by Jesus. St. Louis, 1943, 219p.

Danieli, G. "Le sette parabole del Regno (Mt. 13, 1-52)." Parole di Vita 14 (1969) 280-95.

Danker, F. W. "Fresh Perspectives on Matthean Theology." Concordia Theological Monthly 41 (1970) 478-90.

Danten, J. "La Révélation du Christ sur Dieu dans les paraboles." Nouvelle Revue Theologique 77 (1955) 450-77.

Darby, J. H. "The Church in the Parables." Irish Ecclesiastical Record 86 (1956) 176-86.

Davidson, William. Sermons on the Parables. Cincinnati:
Western Tract Society, 1876, 445p.

Davis, Joseph L. "The Literary History and Theology of
the Parabolic Material in Mark 4 in Relation to the
Gospel as a Whole." Ph. D. thesis, Union Theological
Seminary (Richmond, Va.), 1966, 199p.

Deever, Philip O. The Kingdom Is.... Nashville: Tidings,
1976, 80p.

_____. Lending the Parables Our Ears: Toward
a Meaningful Experience with the Gospel Parables.
Nashville: Tidings, 1975. 148p.

De Haes, P. "Onze predikatie over de Kerk getoetst aan
de parabels." Collectanea Mechliniensia 47 (1962) 379-
86.

Dehandschutter, B. "Les Paraboles de l'Évangile selon
Thomas; la parabole du Trésor caché (log. 109)."
Ephemerides Theologicae Lovanienses 47 (1971) 199-
219.

Delage, Vincent. Les Paraboles dans la vie. Paris:
Editions ouvrières, 1963, 112p.

Delerue, F. Les Paraboles de l'Évangile. St. Etienne:
L'Apôtre du Foyer, 1924. 2 vols.

Denis, A. M. "De parabels over het koninkrijk (Mt. 13)."
Tijdschrift voor teologie 1 (1961) 273-87. (French
résumé, 287-88).

_____. "Les Paraboles du royaume, révélation de
mystère (Mt. 13)." Communio. Commentarii Interna-
tionales de Ecclesia et Theologia 1 (1968) 327-46.

Denzer, George A. "The Parables of the Kingdom." Ph. D.
thesis, Catholic University of America, 1945, 144p.

_____. The Parables of the Kingdom; A Pre-
sentation and Defense of the Absolute Mercy Theory of
the Kingdom Parables with a Review and Criticism of

Modern Catholic Opinion. Washington, D. C.: Catholic
University of America Press, 1945, 185p.

Derrick, Thomas. The Prodigal Son and Other Parables
Shown in Pictures by Thomas Derrick. New York,
Toronto: Longmans, Green, 1931, 99p.

Desplanques, François. Le Levain du monde; ou, le christi-
anisme pur des paraboles du royaume. Paris: Editions
Spes, 1941, 62p.

_____. Paraboles pour la seconde équipe. Essai
de pédagogie évangélique à l'usage de nos dirigeants.
Paris: Éditions Spes, 1945, 224p.

De Valenti, E. J. G. Die Parabeln des Herrn, für Kirche,
Schule und Haus erklärt. Basel: 1841. 2 vols.

Devrieux, L. La Sagesse selon l'Evangile: méditations sur
quelques paraboles. Avignon: Aubanel, 1924, 174p.

Dew, W. H. "Inductive Reasoning in Science and in the
Parables." Church Quarterly Review 150 (1950) 196-
212.

Diaz, J. M. Anotaciones sobre las parábolas del Evangelio.
Bogotá: Editorial S. Juan Etudes, 1949, 632p.

Dickey, Samuel. "Three Warnings Concerning Jesus' Second
Coming." Biblical World 36 (1910) 268-73.

Dillistone, F. W. "St. Mark II. 18-22: A Suggested Reinterpretation." Expository Times 48 (1936-37) 253-54.

Dillon, R. J. "Towards a Tradition-History of the Parables
of the True Israel (Mt. 21:33-22:14)." Biblica 47 (1966)
1-42.

Dodd, Charles H. "The Gospel Parables." Bulletin of the
John Rylands Library 16 (1932) 396-412.

_____. The Parables of the Kingdom. London:
Nisbet, 1935. 214p. Rev. ed., London: Nisbet; New
York: Scribner's 1961. 176p. (1965, paper). Also
paper, London: Fontana Books, 1965.

_____. Las parabolas del Reino. Trans. A. de

la Fuente Adánez. Madrid: Christiandad, 1974, 180p.

_____. "Une Parabole cachée dans le quatriéme Evangile." Tr. par A. and E. Trocmé. Revue d'histoire et de Philosophie Religieuses 42 (1962) 107-15.

_____. Le parabole del regno. Tr. di F. Ronchi. Brescia: Paideia, 1970. 202p.

Dodd, William. Discourses on the Miracles and Parables of Our Blessed Lord and Saviour Jesus Christ. London: Printed by R. Edwards, for J. Hatchard, 1757 (1809). 4 vols.

Dods, Marcus. The Parables of Our Lord. London: Hodder and Stoughton, 1905. 2 vols.

_____. The Parables of Our Lord. New York: Revell, 1915, 433p.

_____. The Parables of Our Lord. The Parables Recorded by St. Luke. London: Hodder and Stoughton, 1886 (1892) (1902) (1912), 226p.

_____. The Parables of Our Lord. The Parables Recorded by St. Matthew. London: Hodder and Stoughton, 1883 (1885) (1890) (1893) (1895) (1902), 276p.

Doerksen, Vernon D. "The Interpretation of Parables." Grace Journal 11 (2) (1970) 3-20.

Donn, Thomas M. "Discerning the Mysteries of the Kingdom of Heaven." Biblical Theology 4 (1954) 57-62.

Donohue, J. J. "The Parable: Politesse or Pedagogy." The Modern Humanist 13, 2 (1958) 48-58.

Dossin, Andrés. Las parábolas del reino. Rosario: Editorial "Apis," 1954, 56p.

Doty, William G. "The Parables of Jesus, Kafka, Borges, and Others, with Structural Observations," in Society of Biblical Literature 1973 Seminar Papers. Cambridge, Mass.: Society of Biblical Literature, 1973. Vol. 2, pp. 119-41. Also, Semeia 2 (1974) 152-93.

Dräseke, Joh. "Zu den Gleichnissen Jesu." Neue kirchliche

Zeitschrift 3 (1892) 665-69.

Drögmüller, H. P. "Die Gleichnisse im hellenistischen Epos." Diss., Hamburg, 1956, 250p.

Drummond, David T. K. The Engravings of the New Testament; or, the Parabolic Teaching of Christ. Edinburgh: W. P. Kennedy; London: Hamilton, Adams, 1855, 546p. Also published as The Parabolic Teaching of Christ, or the Engravings of the New Testament. New York: R. Carter & Brothers, 1856 (1857) (1872), 440p.

Drummond, James. The Way of Life; New Testament Studies. London: Lindsey Press, 1918. 2 vols.

Drury, John. "The Sower, the Vineyard, and the Place of Allegory in the Interpretation of Mark's Parables." Journal of Theological Studies 24 (1973) 367-79.

Dumas, A. "De l'archétype à la parabole." Vie Spirituelle Supplément 92 (1970) 28-46.

Dunkmann, Karl. Altes und Neues aus dem Schatz eines Hausvaters. Ansprachen an junge Theologen über die Gleichnisse in Matth. Kap. 13. Leipzig: A. Deichertsche Verlh. Nachf., 1911, 117p.

Dupont, Jacques. "El capítulo de las parábolas." Selección de Teologia 7 (1968) 237-46.

_____. "Le Chapitre des paraboles." Nouvelle Revue Théologique 89 (1967) 800-20.

_____. "Le point de vue de Mt. dans le chapitre des paraboles," in L'Évangile selon Matthieu. Rédaction et théologie, pp. 221-59. Gembloux: Duculot, 1972.

_____. Pourquoi des paraboles? La Méthode parabolique de Jésus. Paris: Cerf, 1977. 120p.

_____. "Le Royaume des cieux est semblable à..." Bibbia e Oriente 6 (1964) 15-25.

Eakin, F. E., Jr. "Spiritual Obduracy and Parable Purpose," in The Use of the Old Testament in the New and Other Essays; Studies in Honor of William Franklin Stinespring, pp. 87-109. James M. Efird, ed. Durham, N. C.: Duke University Press. 1972.

Eaton, David. "Professor Jülicher on the Parables of Jesus." Expository Times 10 (1898-99) 539-43.

Edsman, C. M., Föhrer, G., Dietrich, E. L., Dahl, N. A., Frör, K. "Gleichnis und Parabel," in Die Religion in Geschichte und Gegenwart II, 3. Aufl., col. 1614-21. Tübingen: J. C. B. Mohr, 1958.

Eichholz, Georg. Einführung in die Gleichnisse. Neukirchen-Vluyn: Neukirchener Verlag, 1963, 109p.

_____. "Das Gleichnis als Spiel." Evangelische Theologie 21 (1961) 309-26.

_____. Gleichnisse der Evangelien. Form, Überlieferung, Auslegung. Neukirchen-Vluyn: Neukirchener Verlag, 1971 (1975) 239p.

Ellena, Domenico. "Thematische Analyse der Wachtumsgleichnisse." Linguistica Biblica 23 (1973) 48-62.

Ellisen, Stanley A. "The Hermeneutics of the Parables." Ph. D. thesis, Dallas Theological Seminary, 1964, 187p.

Engdahl, E. "Jesu liknelser som språkhändelser." Svensk Exegetisk Arsbok 39 (1974) 90-108.

Englezakis, B. "Markan Parable: More than Word Modality a Revelation of Contents." Deltion Biblikon Meleton 2 (1974) 349-57.

Evans, Christopher F. Parable and Dogma. London: Athlone Press, 1977, 21p.

Evers, M. Die Gleichnisse Jesu. Berlin: Reuther & Reichard, 1893. 24p. (5. Aufl., 1927.)

Ewald, J. L. Der Blick Jesu auf die Natur, Menchheit und sich selbst oder Betrachtungen über die Gleichnisse unseres Herrn. Leipzig: 1786.

Eylert, R. Homilien über die Parabeln Jesu, nebst einer Abhandlung über das Charakterische derselben. Halle: 1806.

Faivre, Nazaire. Jésus, lumière, amour. T. VIII, Les
    Paraboles. Bourg-la-Reine (Seine): L'Auteur, 1947.
    461p. (1955, 471p.)

Farrer, John. Sermons on the Parables. London: F. &
    C. Rivington, 1802. 2 vols. New ed., London: F.
    C. & J. Rivington, 1809, 452p.

Fernandez Ramos, F. El Reino en Parábolas. Madrid:
    Ed. Ce Bi HA, 1963, 152p.

Fevrier, Jacques. Les Paraboles de l'Évangile selon Saint
    Luc et l'enseignement de Jésus-Christ sur la salut et
    la perdition. Neuchâtel: 1938, 74p.

Fiebig, Paul Altjüdische Gleichnisse und die Gleichnisse
    Jesu. Tübingen: J. C. B. Mohr, 1904, 167p.

_____. Die Gleichnisreden Jesu im Lichte der rab-
    binischen Gleichnisse des neutestamentlichen Zeitalters.
    Ein Beitrag zum Streit um die "Christusmythe" und eine
    Widerlegung der Gleichnistheorie Jülichers. Tübingen:
    J. C. B. Mohr, 1912. 284p.

_____. Die Gleichnisse Jesu und die Bergpredigt in
    Verbindung mit rabbinischen Parallelen erläutert für die
    Schüler und Schülerinnen höhrer Lehranstalten. Tübingen:
    J. C. B. Mohr, 1911. 27p.

_____. Rabbinische Gleichnisse. Vokalisierte hebräi-
    sche und aramäische Texte, dargeboten für das Studium
    der Gleichnisse Jesu mit Verzeichnis der nichtbiblischen
    Wörter. Leipzig: J. C. Hinrichs, 1929. 51p.

Filas, Francis L. "The Parables of Jesus." Sponsa Regis
    30 (1959) 135-41.

_____. The Parables of Jesus: A Popular Ex-
    planation. New York: Macmillan, 1959. 172p.

_____. Understanding the Parables: A Popular
    Explanation. London: Burns & Oates, 1960. 168p.

Finders Keepers, Losers Weepers (Filmstrip). Shawnee
    Mission, Kan.: Marsh Film Enterprises, 1975.

Findlay, James A. Jesus and His Parables. London:

Epworth Press, 1950, 158p.

Fink, Ernst. "Die Parabeln Christi über die Zöllner und
Pharisäer, Luk. 15 und 16." Theologische Studien und
Kritiken 7 (1834) 313-34.

Fischer, Erika. Drei Gleichnisse vom Verlorenen. Aus dem
Lukasevangelium. Mit 6 Bildern geschnitten. Berlin: Verlag Haus und Schule; Leipzig: Koeltz, 1947. 8p.

_____. Sieben Gleichnisse vom Himmelreich. In
Scherenschnitten nach Matthäus 13 dargestellt. Berlin:
Verlag Haus und Schule; Leipzig: Koeltz, 1947, 8p.

Fischer, J. A. "Pitfalls in Parables." Homiletic and
Pastoral Review 59 (1959) 1003-08; 60 (1959) 214-18.

Fletcher, J. G. Parables. With Woodcut Frontispieces by
J. J. A. Murphy. London: Paul, 1925, 155p.

Flood, Edmund. Parables of Jesus. London: Ealing Abbey,
1970, 40p.; New York: Paulist Press, 1971, 64p.

Flower, J. Cyril. The Parables of Jesus Applied to Modern Life. London: Lindsay, 1920, 116p.

Fonck, Leopold. Die Parabeln des Herrn im Evangelium
exegetisch und praktisch erläutert, 2. Aufl. Innsbruck:
F. Rauch; New York: F. Pustet, 1904. (1927, 903p.)

_____. The Parables of the Gospel; An Exegetical
and Practical Explanation. Trans. from 3rd German ed.
by E. Leahy. Ratisbon, N. Y.: F. Pustet, 1915,
829p.

_____. Le parabole del Signore nel Vangelo. Tr.
U. Bertine. Roma: Pontificio Istituto Biblico, 1924.
569p.

_____. "Senfkörnlein, Tollkorn, und höhere Para-
belkritik." Zeitschrift für katholische Theologie 26
(1902) 13-32.

Forster, A. Haire. "Parables and their Use." Anglican
Theological Review 46 (1964) 188-94.

Frankemölle, H. "Hat Jesus sich selbst verkündet? Chris-

tologische Implikationen in den vormarkinischen Parabeln. " Bibel und Leben 13 (1972) 184-207.

Frankhauser, Gottfried. Sieben Gleichnisse des Herrn.
Kindern erzählt, 2. Aufl. Basel: Kober, 1920, 173p.

Franklin, Samuel P. "Measurement of the Comprehension
Difficulty of the Precepts and Parables of Jesus. "
Ph. D. thesis, University of Iowa, 1928, 63p.

Fransen, I. "Le discours en paraboles (Mt. 11, 2-13, 53). "
Bible et Vie Chrétienne 18 (1957) 72-94.

Fridrichsen, A. "Liknelser." Symbolae Biblicae Upsalien-
ses 2 (1952) 82-88.

Friedrich, Karl J. Erzählungen Christi. Die Gleichnisse
und Geschichten Christi, aus der Ursprache deutsch.
Worte und deutsche Begriffe von heute volkstümlich
übertragen und mit einem Nachwort versehen. Schwar-
zenberg: M. Helmert, 1916, 40p.

Frothingham, Octavius B. Stories from the Lips of the
Teacher; Retold by a Disciple. New York: G. P. Put-
nam's Sons, 1863. 193p. (6th ed. , 1890.)

Fuchs, Ernst. "Bemerkungen zur Gleichnisauslegung, "
Theologische Literaturzeitung 79 (1954) 345-48. Also in
Zur Frage nach dem historischen Jesus, pp. 136-42.
Tübingen: J. C. B. Mohr, 1960.

Funk, Robert W. "The Narrative Parables: The Birth of
a Language Tradition, " in God's Christ and His People:
Studies in Honour of Nils Alstrup Dahl. Jacob Jervell,
Wayne A. Meeks, eds. Oslo: Universitets-forl. , 1977,
43-50.

_____. "The Parables: A Fragmentary Agenda, " in
Jesus and Man's Hope, D. G. Miller et al. , eds. , pp.
287-303. Pittsburgh: Pittsburgh Theological Seminary,
1971.

_____. "Saying and Seeing; Phenomenology of Language
and the New Testament. " Journal of Bible and Religion
34 (1966) 197-213.

_____. "Structure in the Narrative Parables of

Jesus." Semeia 2 (1974) 51-73.

Furetiere, Antoine. Les Paraboles de l'Évangile traduits
en vers; Avec une explication morale & allegorique
tireé des ss. peres. Paris: Chez Pierre le Petit,
1672, 300p.

Furrer, K. "Die Bildersprache in den drei ersten Evangelien." Zeitschrift für Missionskunde und Religionswis-
senschaft 5 (1890) 112-21.

Gabrieli, G. Le parabole di N. S. Gesu Cristo tradotte e
brevemente spiegate ai piccoli e al popolo. Con le
illustrazioni di E. Burnand. Torino: Lega Ital. Catt.
Editr., 1924, 141p.

Gaeddert, John. Parables of Jesus. Newton, Kan. : Faith
and Life Press, 1978, 85p.

Galama, Gerard. Vier gelijkenissen van den Heiland. Utrecht: Joh. de Liefde, 1891.

Galizzi, D. M. "La Chiesa nel suo mistero (Mt. 13, 1-52)."
Parole di Vita 16 (1971) 4-16.

Gallina, C. Le Parabole di Gesù. Firenze: Libr. Ed.
Fior., 1927, 378p.

Galloway, C. "The Point of Parable." Bible Today 28
(1967) 1952-60.

Gealy, Fred D. "The Composition of Mark IV." Expository Times 48 (1936-37) 40-43.

Geerebaert, V. De God-Mensch: Christus Woorden. T. 1,
De Parabeln. Brussel: Standaardboekhandel, 1929.
579p. Also, Leuven: S. Alfonsus-Boekhandel, 1937.
600p.

Gehreke, O. "Zur homiletischen Behandlung der Gleichnisreden Jesu." Zeitschrift für praktische Theologie 21
(1899) 1-11.

De Gelijkenissen. Geillustreerd door Eugène Burnand.
Met een voorwoord van J. H. Gunning. Leiden: A.
W. Sijthoff's Uitgevers-maatschappij, 1909 (1910) (1926).

De Gelijkenissen van den Zaligmaker, 3e druk. Amsterdam:
W. H. Kirkberger; Utrecht: J. H. van Peursem, 1878.

Genesio da Gallarate, padre. Il regno dei cieli. Brescia:
Franciscanum, 1968, 269p.

George, A. "Paraboles." Dictionnaire de la Bible, Supplément 34 (1960) 1149-77.

Gerhardsson, Birger. "Liknelsen om fyrahanda sädesåker
och dess uttydning." Svensk Exegetisk Årsbok 31 (1966)
80-113.

_____. "The Seven Parables in Matthew 13."
Trans. J. Toy. New Testament Studies 19 (Oct. 1972)
16-37.

Gerlach, P. "Der Sinnzusammenhang der Reich-Gottes-
Gleichnisse bei Matthäus." Deutsches Pfarrerblatt 38
(1934) 185-87, 197-99, 313.

Giblin, C. H. "Structural and Theological Considerations
on Luke 15." Catholic Biblical Quarterly 24 (1962) 15-
31.

_____. "Why Jesus Spoke in Parables: An Answer
from Luke 15." Chicago Studies 7 (1968) 213-20.

Gils, F. -Termes. "Parabola. Parabolas del NT," in
Enciclopedia de la Biblia. vol. 5. Barcelona: Ediciones
Garriga, 1965, 870-78.

Gittermann, R. C. Die Gleichnisse Jesu oder moralische
Erzählungen aus der Bibel. Bremen: 1803.

Die Gleichnisreden Christi. Wien: Wiener Depôt evangel-
ischer Druckschriften, 1877.

Gleichnisreden Jesu aus den vier Evangelien. Stuttgart:
Privileg. Württ. Bibelanst., 1940. Also, Berlin:
Evang. Verlag Anst., 1951. 31p.

Die Gleichnisse des Herrn für Schülern. Mit 30 Originalen
Holzschnitten. Leipzig: Hirschfeld, 1854 (1862), 30p.

Die Gleichnisse des Herrn, nach den Worten der Schrift.
16 Compositionen (in Holzschnitten und Tondrucken) von

Carolifeld, J. Führich, Th. Grosse, etc. Leipzig: A.
Dürr, 1869, 88p.

Gleichnisse für Kinder von einem Kinderfreunde. Frankfurt: Andrea, 1812.

Die Gleichnisse Jesu, 4 Aufl. Illus. Eugène Burnand.
Lahr: Verlag für Volkskunst und Volksbildung, 1930,
208p.

Die Gleichnisse Jesu. Hrsg. von der Gemeinschaft der
Siebenten-Tags-Adventisten in der DDR. Berlin: Union
Verlag, 1957, 30p.

Gleichnisse Jesu. Text nach der Züricher Bibel. Mit 47
mehrfarb. Bildern von Willi Trapp. Locham. Berch-
told-Verlag, 1964, 52p.

Gleichnisse Jesu. Gruppenarbeit unter Jungendlichen über
Bibel und Kirche. Hrsg. von Carl Ernst Sommer.
Zürich: Gotthelf-Verlag, 1960, 87p.

Gleichnisse und Reden Jesu nach der Vulgata. Ausgewählt
von Paul Wetzel. Frankfurt am Main: Diesterweg,
1924, 32p.

Die Gleichnisse und Wunder unseres Herrn, 2 Hfte. Stuttgart: G. Weise, 1887.

Die Gleichnisse vom Himmelreich oder die Unsterblichkeit-
slehre Jesu, im Licht der Ausprüche der Heiligen
Schrift betrachtet und erklärt von einem Bibelforscher.
Bayreuth: C. Giessel, 1891, 195p.

Gleichnisse vom Reich Gottes. Sekundarstufe 1 (6. /7.
Schuljahr). Earb. von Franz W. Niehl. Munchen:
Kösel-Verlag, 1975.

Glen, John S. The Parables of Conflict in Luke. Philadelphia: Westminster Press, 1962, 160p.

Glover, C. H. Messages from the Parables. London:
Independent Press, 1956. Also, Naperville, Ill.: A.
R. Allenson, 1957, 172p.

Das gnädige Recht Gottes und die Freiheitsidee des Menschen, 2 Beiträge aus der Arbeit der Kirchliche Hoch-

schule Wuppertal. Hrsg. von Arnold Falkenroth. Neukirchen-Vluyn: Neukirchener Verlag, 1967, 68p.

Gnilka, Joachim. Die Verstockung Israels. Isaias 6, 1-10
in der Theologie der Synoptiker. Studien zum Alten
und Neuen Testament 3. München: Kösel-Verlag, 1961,
229p.

_____. Das Verstockungsproblem nach Matthäus
13, 13-15, " in Antijudaismus im Neuen Testament?
Abhandlung zum christlich-jüdischen Dialog 2, pp119-
28. Munchen: Kaiser, 1967.

Goebel, Siegfried. "Die Gleichnisgruppe Luk. 15 und 16,
methodisch ausgelegt. " Theologische Studien und Kritiken 47 (1874) 506-38; 48 (1875) 656-707.

_____. Die Parabeln Jesu: methodisch ausgelegt.
Gotha: 1879.

_____. The Parables of Jesus: A Methodical
Exposition. Trans. Professor Banks. Edinburgh: T.
& T. Clark, 1883 (1890) (1894) (1900) (1913), 460p.

Görnandt, Werner. Mancherlei Gleichnisse. Gottesdienste
über 9 Gleichnisse des Neuen Testaments. Berlin:
Kranzverlag, 1933, 163p.

Golenvaux, C. "L'Intelligence des paraboles: la foi. "
Bible et Vie Chrétienne 72 (1966) 50-54.

Good, Charles M. The Parables of Jesus. Boston: Christopher Pub. House, 1961, 142p.

van Goudoever, J. "The Place of Israel in Luke's Gospel. "
Novum Testamentum 8 (1966) 111-23.

Goulder, M. D. "Characteristics of the Parables in the
Several Gospels. " Journal of Theological Studies 19
(1968) 51-69.

Goumaz, Louis. Paraboles et patois vaudois; Essai de tra-
duction en patois vaudois des paraboles de Jésus-Christ
et du Sermon sur la montagne. Lausanne: L'Auteur,
1951, 96p.

Gräbner, Theodor. Jesu Gleichnisreden. Die wichtigsten

Gleichnisse Jesu, für jung und alt erläutert. Mit zahl-
reichen Bildern von Schnorr von Carolsfeld, Führich,
Overbeck, u. a. Reutlingen: Ensslin & Laiblin, 1911
(1921) 64p.

Graffmann, H. "Der Sinn der Gleichnisrede Jesu nach
Matth. 13." Deutsches Pfarrerblatt 39 (1935) 166-68.

Granada, Juan de. Parabolae evangelicae quotquot, ab ecclesia propontur moralibus discursibus explicatae.
1585. 400p.

Granskou, David M. Preaching on the Parables. Philadelphia: Fortress Press, 1972, 129p.

Grant, Frederick C. "A New Book on the Parables." Anglican Theological Review 30 (1948), 118-21 [On Jeremias'
Die Gleichnisse Jesu.]

Graversen, Hans. Jesu Lignelser; Guds Riges Kaar for den
Enkelte og Menigheden. København: Skjern, 1938,
182p.

Gray, Andrew. A Delineation of the Parables of Our Blessed Saviour: To which Is Prefixed, a Dissertation on
Parables and Allegorical Writings in General. Edinburgh: J. Dickson; London: J. Murray, 1777, 505p.

Gray, Ruth S. Stories Jesus Told; The Parables of Our
Lord. Anderson, Ind.: Warner Press, 1958. Unpaged.

Graybill, David J. "The Mystery in What Is Utterly Clear:
Parable as a Model for Understanding the Reality of
God, Church, and Ministry." Ph. D. Thesis. Vander-
bilt University, 1978, 420p.

Greswell, Edward. An Exposition of the Parables and Other
Parts of the Gospels. Oxford: Rivington, 1834-35.
6 vols.

Grimme, Gertr. Die Gleichnisse Jesu. Gladbeck/W.:
Martin-Heilmann-Verlag [Schriftenmissions Verlag],
1952, 42p.

Groenewald, E. P. In Gelijkenisse het Hy Geleer. Pre-
toria: J. L. van Schaik, 1963, 247p.

Gronewald, M. "Porphyrios Kritik an den Gleichnissen des Evangeliums." Zeitschrift für Papyrologie und Epigraphik 3 (1968) 96.

Grossmann, C. G. Comment. historico-exegeticus de procuratore, Parabola Christi ex re provinciali Romanorum illustrata. Lipsiae: 1823.

Grutek, W. "Parabolae Christi. Quibus principiis facilior redditur earum intellectio et usus in institutione." Ruch Biblijny i Liturgiczny 12 (1959) 333-44.

Gryglewicz, F. "The Gospel of the Overworked Workers." Catholic Biblical Quarterly 19 (1957) 190-98.

Guelluy, R. "Divine Love in the New Testament" [as seen in the parables]. Sponsa Regis 35 (Oct. 1963) 40-46.

Güttgemanns, Erhardt. "Die Linguistisch-Didaktische Methodik der Gleichnisse Jesu," in Studia Linguistica Neotestamentica, pp99-183. München: Kaiser, 1971.

_____. "Narrative Analysis of Synoptic Texts." Semeia 6 (1976) 127-79.

Guitton, J. "Little Parables." L'Osservatore Romano (English) 8 (Feb. 23, 1978) 8.

Gutbrod, Karl. Ein Weg zu den Gleichnissen Jesu. Stuttgart: Calwer-Verlag, 1967 (1973) 50p.

Guthrie, Thomas. The Parables Read in the Light of the Present Day. New York: E. B. Treat, 1891, 278p.

Gutzwiller, Richard. De gelijkenissen van Onze Heer. Uit het Duits vert. door J. Krol. Hilversum: Paul Brand, 1962, 165p.

_____. Die Gleichnisse des Herrn. Einsiedeln: Benziger, 1960, 164p.

_____. Die Parabeln des Herrn. Baden: Meierhof-Druckerei; Seelisberg/Schweiz: Schweizer. Kath. Bibelbewegg., 1951. 100p., 2. Aufl., Luzern:

Schweizer. Kath. Bibelbewegg. (SKB), 1957, 102p.

_____. The Parables of the Lord. Trans. Arlene Swidler. New York: Herder and Herder, 1964, 144p.

_____. Le Royaume de Dieu est semblable... Les Paraboles du Seigneur. Trad. par E. Saillard. Mulhouse: Editions Salvator; Paris: Casterman, 1965, 160p.

Hallström, Carl A. Jesu liknelser: Uppåts Bibelstudieplander, 3. Linköping: C. A. Hallström, 1910, 16p.

Hanko, Herman C. The Mysteries of the Kingdom: An Exposition of the Parables. Grand Rapids: Reformed Free Pub. Assoc., 1975, 306p.

Hargreaves, John H. A Guide to the Parables. Foreward by C. H. Dodd. London: Society for Promoting Christian Knowledge, 1968. Also, Valley Forge, Pa.: Judson Press, 1975, 132p.

_____. Las parábolas evangélicas. Tr. by J. Martínez Aduriz. Santander: Ed Sal Terrae, 1973, 216p.

Harnisch, W. "Die Ironie als Stilmittel in Gleichnissen Jesu." Evangelische Theologie 32 (1972) 421-36.

_____. "Die Sprachkraft der Analogie; zur These vom argumentativen Charakter der Gleichnisse Jesu." Studia Theologica 28 (1974) 1-20.

Harrington, Wilfrid J. "Hidden Treasure." Furrow 26 (1975) 523-29.

_____. Hij spraak in parabels. Vert. door J. Verstraeten. Bilthaven: Nelissen, 1967, 144p.

_____. Il parlait en paraboles. Trad. Jacques Mignon. Paris: Cerf, 1967, 153p.

_____. "Key to the Parables." Doctrine and Life (Feb.-May 1963).

_____. A Key to the Parables. Glen Rock, N. J.: Paulist Press, 1964, 160p.

_____. "The Parables in Recent Study, 1960-1971." Biblical Theology Bulletin 2 (1972) 219-41.

_____. "The Parables: Recent Explorations." Doctrine and Life 22 (1972) 395-404.

_____. Parables Told by Jesus; A Contemporary Approach to the Parables. New York: Alba House, 1975, 135p.

_____. "Les Paraboles: études récentes." Bulletin de Théologie Biblique 3 (1972) 219-42.

Harris, Francis B. The Kingdom of God and the Kingdom of the Heavens, as Seen in the Illustrations of the Parables of Our Lord Jesus Christ, Setting Forth the Resurrection of the Dead and the Work of the Future Life, to Its Consummation in Glory, rev. ed. Salem, Ore.: N. D. Elliott, 1913, 267p.

Hauck, Friedrich. "Παραβολή," in Kittel, Gerhard, ed. Theological Dictionary of the New Testament, vol. 5, pp744-61. Trans. Geoffrey W. Bromiley. Grand Rapids: Eerdmans, 1964-69.

_____. "Παραβολή," in Kittel, Gerhard, ed., Theologisches Wörterbuch zum Neuen Testament, vol. V, pp741-50. Stuttgart: W. Kohlhammer, 1933-66.

Haufe, G. "Erwägungen zum Ursprung der sogennanten Parabeltheorie Markus 4:11-12." Evangelische Theologie 32 (1972) 413-21.

Haugg, Donatus. Skizzen zu den Gleichnissen Jesu. Bibelbrief. Stuttgart: Verlag Kath. Bibel-Werk., 1939, 40p.

Heitefuss, Clara. Das Wesen des Reiches Gottes nach den Gleichnissen Jesu. Dinglingen o. J.: St. Johannis-Druckerei, 1916, 56p.

Hendricksen, William. "Preaching from the Parables." The Banner 86 (1951) 295, 310, 327, 343, 359, 374.

Henry, H. T. "Texts and Contexts." Homiletic and Pastoral Review 38 (1938) 906-14.

Hermaniuk, Maxime. La Parabole Évangélique. Vol. 38, series II of Universitas Catholica Lovaniensis. Louvain: Bibliotheca Alfonsiana; Paris: Desclée, 1947. 493p.

Hermant, D. "A Conference on Luke 15." Monastic Studies 10 (1974) 155-63.

Herranz, A. "Las parábolas. Un problema y una solución." Cultura Bíblica 12 (1955) 128-37.

Herz, Johannes. "Die Gleichnisse der Evangelien Matthäus, Markus und Lukas in ihrer geschichtlichen Überlieferung und ihrem religiös-sittlichen Inhalt," in Bekenntnis zur Kirche; Festgabe für Ernst Sommerlath zum 70. Geburtstag, pp52-93. Berlin: Evangelische Verlagsanstalt, 1960.

Heyer, Hermann. Denket um. Überlegungen zu Worten und Gleichnissen Jesu. München: Don Bosco Verlag, 1970, 65p.

Hick, L. "Zum Verständnis des neutestamentlichen Parabelbegriffes." Bibel und Kirche 1 (1954) 4-17.

Hire, R. "Our Catholic Faith: The Parables and Teaching of Jesus." Our Sunday Visitor 63 (Aug. 25, 1974) 6.

Hörtnagel, Hans. Bausteine zu einer Grammatik der Bildsprache, insbesondere der evangelischen Parabeln. Innsbruck: Wagner, 1922, 208p.

Holzmeister, U. "Anmerkungen zur Verwendung der Parabeln des Herrn auf der Kanzel." Theologisch-praktische Quartalschrift 80 (1927) 63-73.

_____. "Vom angeblichen Verstockungsweck der Parabeln." Biblica 15 (1934) 321-64.

Horsfield, Canon. Parables of the Second Coming. London: Marshall, 1924.

Hossbach, W. Predigten über einige Gleichnisreden des Erlösers. Berlin: 1837.

Howard, F. D. Interpreting the Lord's Parables. Nashville: Broadman, 1966, 72p.

Howard, J. K. "Our Lord's Teaching Concerning his Parousia; A Study in the Gospel of Mark. II. Parables and Sayings." Evangelical Quarterly 38 (April-June 1966) 68-75.

Howden, J. Russell. "The Trilogy of Parables in Luke 15." Biblical Review 14 (1929) 331-44.

Hren, D. "Hrvatski prijevod imenice 'parabola.'" Bogoslovskà Smotra 12 (1924) 233-36.

Hubaut, Michel. "Le 'mystère' révélé dans les paraboles (Mc. 4, 11-12)." Revue théologique de Louvain 5 (1974) 454-61.

Hubbard, George H. "The Interpretation of the Parables." Treasury 14 (1896-97) 684-89.

_____. The Teaching of Jesus in Parables. Boston: Pilgrim Press, 1907, 507p.

Hunter, Archibald M. "Interpretation of the Parables." Expository Times 69 (1958) 100-04.

_____. "Interpreting the Parables." Interpretation 14 (1960) 70-84, 167-85, 315-32, 440-54.

_____. Interpreting the Parables. Philadelphia: Westminster Press, 1960 (1961).

_____. The Parables Then and Now. London: SCM; Philadelphia: Westminster Press, 1971, 128p.

_____. P'iyii ch'anshih. Trans. T. C. Wu. Hong Kong: Council of Christian Literature for Overseas Chinese, 1964, 196p.

Huntington, Frederic D. Our Lord's Parables. Lessons for the Instruction of Children in the Christian Life. Boston: E. P. Dutton, 1868, 160p.

Hunzinger, D. -H. "Unbekannte Gleichnisse Jesu aus dem Thomas-Evangelium," in Judentum, Urchristentum, Kirche. Festschrift für Joachim Jeremias. Walther Eltester, ed., pp209-20. Berlin: A. Töpelmann, 1960.

Hurley, N. "Jesus' Parables as Strategic Fiction." Review for Religious 31 (1972) 756-60.

Igarshi, P. H. "Mystery of the Kingdom (Mark 4:10-12)." Journal of Bible and Religion 24 (1956) 83-89.

Improved Question-book and Studies on the Parables and Other Instructions of the Saviour. With the Text. Arranged for Classes of All Ages. Philadelphia, New York: American Sunday-School Union, 1871, 120p.

"L'Interpretation des paraboles évangéliques." Ami du Clergé 36 (1919) 1304-09.

Jacobson, Delmar. "An Exposition of Matthew 13:44-52." Interpretation 29 (1975) 277-82.

Jak, P. Die Parabeln Jesu Christi Sittengeissel. In Predigten. Augsburg: 1804. 2 vols.

Javelet, Robert. The Gospel Paradox. Trans. Donald Antoine. New York: Herder and Herder, 1966, 224p.

_____. Les Paraboles contre la Loi. Fribourg (Suisse), Paris: Editions Saint-Paul, 1962, 192p.

Jentink, Thz. De gelijkenis in den vorm van wonderen en wonderverhalen. Deventer: W. F. P. Enklaar, 1896.

Jeremias, Joachim. De gelijkenissen van Jesus. Vert. uit het Duits door B. Meuwissen. Bilthoven: H. Nelissen, 1968, 174p.

_____. Die Gleichnisse Jesu. Zürich: Zwingli-Verlag, 1947 (1952). Also, Göttingen: Vandenhoeck & Ruprecht, 1954; Berlin: Evang. Verl. Anst., 1955; Göttingen: Vandenhoeck & Ruprecht, 1956 (1958) (1962) (1965) (1970). Gekürzte Ausg., München: Siebenstern Tauschenbuch Verl., 1965.

_____. Jesu liknelser, 2 uppl. Övers. av Stig Lindhagen. Stockholm: Verbum, 1970 (1971), 140p.

_____. The Parables of Jesus. Trans. by S.
H. Hooke from 6th German ed. New York: Scribner's, 1955. 178p. Rev. ed., New York: Scribner's
1963. 248p. 3rd rev. ed., London: S. C. M. Press,
1972.

_____. Las parábolas de Jesús. Tr. de F. J.
Calvo. Estella: Verbo Divino, 1970, 304p.

_____. Le parabole di Gesù. Tr. G. Capra e
A. Colao Pellizzari. Brescia: Paideia, 1967 (1973),
304p.

_____. Les paraboles de Jesus. Trad. de Bruno
Hübsch. Le Puy-en-Verlag: Mappus, 1964, 239p.
Also, Paris: Éditions du Seuil, 1968, 322p.

_____. Rediscovering the Parables. Trans. S.
H. Hooke. London: S. C. M. Press; New York:
Scribner's, 1966, 191p.

_____. "Tradition und Redaktion in Lukas 15."
Zeitschrift für die neutestamentliche Wissenschaft 62
(1971) 172-89.

Jeske, R. L. "Wisdom and the Future in the Teaching of
Jesus." Dialog 11 (1972) 108-17.

Jesu Lignelser. Tagninger af Eugène Burnard. København:
Lohse, 1921, 268p.

Jörgensen, Johs. Tolv av Jesu liknelser. Övers. fran
danskan av J. G. Malmer. Lund: Oversättarens förl.,
1932, 115p.

Jörns, K. P. "Die Gleichnisverkündigung Jesu: Reden von
Gott als Wort Gottes," in Der Ruf Jesu und die Antwort der Gemeinde. Joachim Jeremias zum 70. Geburtstag gewidmet von seinem Schülern. Hrsg. von
Eduard Lohse, Christoph Burchard, Berndt Schaller, pp
157-78. Göttingen: Vandenhoeck & Ruprecht, 1970.

Johansson, Nils. "Τὸ μυστήριον τῆς βασιλείας τοῦ Θεοῦ."
Svensk teologisk kvartalskrift 16 (1940) 3-38.

Johnson, S. E. "King Parables in the Synoptic Gospels."
Journal of Biblical Literature 74 (1955) 37-39.

Jones, Geraint V. The Art and Truth of the Parables; A
Study in Their Literary Form and Modern Interpretation.
London: S. P. C. K., 1964, 250p.

Jordan, G. J. "The Classification of the Parables." Expository Times 45 (1933-34) 246-51.

Joubert, H. L. "Wese en doel van die gelykenis by Jesus."
Nederduitse Gereformeerde Teologiese Tydskrif 14
(1973) 126-31.

Jülicher, Adolf. Die Gleichnisreden Jesu. Freiburg i. B. :
Mohr, 1886 (1888) (1899) (1910). Darmstadt: Wissenschaftliche Buchgesellschaft, 1963 (1969) (1976).

Kahlefeld, Heinrich. Gleichnisse und Lehrstücke im Evangelium. Frankfurt a. M. : Knecht, 1963 (1964), 192p.

_____. Parables and Instructions in the Gospels.
Trans. Arlene Swidler. New York: Herder and Herder,
1966, 174p.

_____. Parables et leçons dans l'Évangile. Trad.
par Georges Bret. Paris: Éditions du Cerf, 1969, 2
vols. , 149p.

_____. Parábolas y ejemplos del Evangelio. Tr. de
R. Velasco. Estella: Ed. Verbo Divino, 1967, 333p.

Karavidopoulos, I. D. "Παραβολή." Θρησκευτική καὶ ἠθική
εγκυκλοπαίδεια 10 (1966) 19-22.

Keach, Benjamin, Exposition of the Parables and Express
Similitudes of Our Lord and Saviour Jesus Christ.
London: W. H. Collingridge, 1856.

_____. Exposition of the Parables in the Parables
in the Bible. Grand Rapids: Kregel Publications, 1974,
904p. [Reprint of Exposition of the Parables and Express Similitudes of Our Lord and Saviour Jesus Christ.]

Kempin, Albert J. The King's Parables. Anderson, Ind. :
Gospel Trumpet Co. , 1938, 128p.

Kennedy, Gerald H. "Nothing without a Parable," in New
Testament Sidelights in Honor of A. C. Purdy, pp10-26.

Hartford Seminary Foundation Press, 1960.

_____. The Parables: Sermons on the Stories Jesus Told. New York: Harper, 1960 (1967), 213p.

Kerr, Hugh T. Children's Parable Story-sermons. New York: Revell, 1945, 128p.

Kessel, Robert. Die Gleichnisse und Bildreden Jesu. Eine Einführung in die Predigt und das innere Leben Jesu, 3. Aufl. Langensalza: H. Beyer & Söhne, 1914, 243p.

Keyes, Nelson B. The Parable. Garden City, N. Y.: Doubleday, 1963, 63p.

Kingsbury, Jack D. "Ernst Fuchs' Existential Interpretation of the Parables." Lutheran Quarterly 22 (1970) 380-95.

_____. "Major Trends in Parable Interpretation." Concordia Theological Monthly 42 (1971) 579-96.

_____. "The Parables of Jesus in Current Research." Dialog 11 (1972) 101-07.

_____. "The Parables of Jesus in Matthew 13: A Study in Redaction-Criticism." Diss., Basel, 1966.

_____. The Parables of Jesus in Matthew 13: A Study in Redaction-Criticism. London: Society for Promoting Christian Knowledge; Richmond, Va.: Knox, 1969. 180p.

Kinkel, Gottfried. Predigten über ausgewählte Gleichnisse und Bildreden Christi. Köln: Eisen, 1842.

Kirk, Edward N. Lectures on the Parables of Our Saviour. New York: J. F. Trow, 1856. Also, R. Craighead, 1857, 506p.; Also, London: J. Blackwood, 1859.

Kirkland, J. R. "The Earliest Understanding of Jesus' Use of Parables: Mark 4:10-12 in Context." Novum Testamentum 19 (1977) 1-21.

Klauck, Hans-Josef. Allegorie und Alleforese in synoptischen Gleichnistexten. Münster: Aschendorff, 1978, 410p.

_____. "Neue Beiträge zur Gleichnisforschung."

Bibel und Leben 13 (1972) 214-30.

Klein, Félix. Les paraboles évangéliques. Paris: Édit.
Spes, 1926. 64p.; Also, Paris: Bloud et Gay, 1933.
56p.

Klemm, Hans G. "Die Gleichnisauslegung Adolf Jülichers
im Bannkreis der Fabeltheorie Lessings." Zeitschrift
für die neutestamentliche Wissenschaft 60 (1969) 153-74.

Klever, Anita. Stories Jesus Told. Illus. by Jo Polseno.
Chicago: Rand McNally, 1967, 45p.

Knap, Czn. Gelijkenissen des Heeren. Schriftoverdenkingen
bij teekeningen van Eugène Burnand. Nijkerk: G. F.
Callenbach, 1919 (1921-23).

Knoch, Otto. Le parabole. Tr. di C. Vivaldelli. Roma:
Città Nuova, 1969, 217p.

_____. Ein Sämann ging aus. Botschaft die Gleich-
nisse. Eine Handreichung. Stuttgart: Katholisches
Bibelwerk, 1963 (1967) (1968), 160p.

Knoke, K. "Jesu Selbstaussage über seine parabolische
Lehrweise, Mark 4, 10-13." Neue kirchliche Zeitschrift 16 (1905) 137-64.

Knox, Ronald A. The Mystery of the Kingdom and Other
Sermons. London: Sheed & Ward, 1928 (1937), 180p.

Koch, Ant. Homiletisches Handbuch. 14. Ergänzungswerk.
T. 2, Homiletische Gleichnissammlung. Bd. 2, Gleichnisse zur katholischen Sittenlehre. Freiburg: Herder,
1954, 491p.

Koch, Carl. Jesu Lignelser, udlagte og belyste. København:
Schønberg, 1905 (1909), 230p. (1915), 396p. (1936);
Also, København: D. B. K., 1960. 295p.; Also,
Arhus: Åros, 1969. 295p.

Koetsveld, C. E. van De Gelijkenissen van den Zaligmaker,
2. Ausg. Schoonhoven: 1869. 2 vols.

_____. De gelijkenissen van het Evangelie, op nieuw
bewerkt tot een huisboek voor het christelijk gezen. Schoonhoven: S. E. van Nooten & Zn., 1886 (1892) (1898).

_____. Die Gleichnisse des Evangeliums, als Hausbuch für die christliche Familie bearbeitet. Leipzig: F. Jansa, 1904, 316p.

Kogel, Julius. Der Zweck der Gleichnisse Jesu im Raumen seiner Verkündigung. Gütersloh: C. Bertelsmann, 1915, 130p.

Kossen, H. B. "Quelques remarques sur l'ordre des paraboles dans Luc XV et sur la structure de Matthieu XVIII, 8-14." Novum Testamentum 1 (1956) 75-80.

Kreuter, J. "Church in Parables." Orate Fratres 8 (1934) 531-34.

La Cava, F. Ut videntes non videant. Il motivo e lo scopo delle Parabole del Vangelo. Roma: Marietti, 1934, 67p.

Làconi, M. "Le parabole in S. Luca." Parole di Vita 6 (1971) 427-36.

Ladd, G. E. "The Life-setting of the Parables of the Kingdom." Journal of Bible and Religion 31 (1963) 193-99.

_____. "The Sitz im Leben of the Parables of Matthew 13: The Soils." Studia Evangelica II, 203-10.

Lagrange, M. J. "Le But des paraboles d'apres l'Évangile selon Saint Marc." Revue Biblique 7 (1910) 5-35.

_____. "La Parabole en dehors de l'Évangile." Revue Biblique 6 (1909) 198-212, 342-67.

Lalien, Mgr. Fleurs de l'Evangile: les paraboles de Jésus. Paris: Lethielleux, 1922, 386p.

Lambrecht, Jan. "Parabels in Mc. 4." Tijdschrift voor Theologie 15 (1975) 26-42.

_____. "Parables in Mt. 13." Tijdschrift voor Theologie 17 (1977) 25-47.

_____. "Revelation and Theology in Mark 4." Bibliotheca Ephemeridum Theologicarum Lovaniensium 34 (1974) 269-307.

_____. "De theologische betekenis van de Parabels. " Bijdragen tijdschrift voor philosophie en theologie 24

_____. "Die vijf parabels van Mc. 4: Structur en theologie van de parabeelrede. " Bijdragen tijdschrift voor philosophie en theologie 29 (1968) 25-53.

Lampo, G. "L'eloquenza del Cristianesimo e le parabole del Vangelo. " Palestra del Clero 14 (1935) 207-11.

Lancelot, John B. Parables of Judgment. London: Church Book Room, 1936? 111p.

Lang, Cosmo G. L. The Parables of Jesus. New York: E. P. Dutton, 1918, 274p.

Lang, G. H. Pictures and Parables. Studies in the Parabolic Teaching of Holy Scripture. London: Paternoster Press, 1955 (1956) 400p.

Laridon, V. "Trilogia parabolarum de Dei misericordia in Lc. 15." Collationes Brugenses et Gandavenses 49 (1953) 310-18.

Lebbe, C. "Puppets, Paint, and Parables. " Living Light 4 (Fall 1967) 29-38.

Lee, R. Similes of Our Lord and His Own. London: Pickering and Inglis, 1930. 2 vols.

Le Frois, Bernard J. Digest of Christ's Parables for Preacher, Teacher, and Student. Techny, Ill.: Divine Word Publishers, 1956, 92p.

Levison, Nahum. The Parables: Their Background and Local Setting. Edinburgh: T. & T. Clark, 1926, 253p.

Lhande, Pierre. L'Evangile par dessus les toits. Paraboles. Paris: Spes, 1933, 114p.

_____. Gleichnisse des Herrn; Radio-Vorträge, ins deutsche übertragen von Otto Koch. Paderborn: Verlag der Bonifaciusdruckerei, 1934, 110p.

Lightfoot, Neil R. Lessons from the Parables. Grand Rapids: Baker Book House, 1965, 184p.

Limburg Brouwer, G. A. van Specimen academicum de Parabolis Jesu Christi. Leiden: 1825.

Lindars, Barnabas. "Two Parables in John." New Testament Studies 16 (1970) 318-29.

Link, W. "Die Gleichnisse des Himmelreichs, Matth. 13, 10-23." Evangelische Theologie (1935) 115-27.

Linn, Samuel. The Seven Parables of the Kingdom. Osage, Iowa: Press of the Woolverton Printing & Pub. Co., 1908, 108p.

Linnemann, Eta. Gleichnisse Jesu. Einführung und Auslegung. Göttingen: Vandenhoeck & Ruprecht, 1961 (1962) (1964) (1966) (1969) (1975), 207p.

_____. Jesus of the Parables; Introduction and Exposition. Trans. John Sturdy. New York: Harper & Row, 1967, 218p.

_____. Parables of Jesus; Introduction and Exposition. Trans. John Sturdy of 3rd German ed. London: S. P. C. K., 1966, 216p.

Lino, Monchieri. Le parabole di Gesù. Brescia: La Scuola, 110p.

Liperovskiĭ, Lev. Chudesa i pritchi Khristovy. Paris: Editions de l'Exarchat Patriarchal Russe en Europe Occidentale, 1962, 177p.

Lisco, Friedrich G. Die Parabeln Jesu, exegetisch-homiletisch bearbeitet. Berlin: 1832 (1835) (1841) (1847) (1861).

_____. The Parables of Jesus Explained and Illustrated. Trans. P. Fairbairn. Boston: Massachusetts Sabbath School Society, 1846, 404p.

Little, James C. "Parable Research in the Twentieth Century: I. The Predecessors of J. Jeremias." Expository Times 87 (1976) 356-60.

_____. "Parable Research in the Twentieth Century: II. The Contribution of J. Jeremias." Expository Times 88 (1976) 40-43.

_____. "Parable Research in the Twentieth Century
III: Developments since J. Jeremias." Expository
Times 88 (1976) 71-75.

Llanos, José María de. Nuestra actualidad en 65 parábolas.
Bilboa: Desclée de Brouwer, 1971, 151p.

Lockwood, Myrna. Jesus Tells a Story; The Parables.
Illus. by Mae Gerhard. New York: Guild Press, 1962,
46p.

Lockwood, William M. The Disputed Parables of Jesus.
Buffalo: Queen City Printing Co., 1913, 27p.

Lönborg, Sven. Jesu liknelser. Studentföreningen Verdandis
Småskrifter 160. Stockholm: Bonnier, 1908 (1927),
34p.

Lohmeyer, Ernst. "Vom Sinn der Gleichnisse Jesu." Zeitschrift für systematische Theologie (1938) 319-46.

Lohse, E. "Die Gottesherrschaft in den Gleichnissen Jesu."
Evangelische Theologie 18 (1958) 145-57. Also in Lohse,
Einheit im NT, pp49-61. Göttingen: Vandenhoeck &
Ruprecht, 1973.

Loisy, Alfred. "Les Paraboles de l'Évangile," in Études
évangéliques, pp1-121; Paris: Alphonse Picard, 1902.
Also, Frankfurt: Minerva-Verlag, 1971.

Long, Roswell C. More Stewardship Parables of Jesus.
New York: Abingdon-Cokesbury Press, 1947, 140p.

_____. Stewardship Parables of Jesus. Nashville:
Cokesbury Press, 1931, 230p.

Lonman, A. D. "Bijdrage tot de critiek der synoptische
Evangeliën. VI. Het mysterie der gelijkenissen."
Theologisch tijdschrift 7 (1873) 175-205.

Luccock, Halford E. Studies in the Parables of Jesus.
New York, Cincinnati: Methodist Book Concern, 1917
(1925) (1928), 131p.

Lumini, L. "Il regno di Dio nelle parabole di Gesù."
Scuola Cattolica 13 (1929) 35-47, 183-96.

Lund, Kristine, and Tange, Jef. Jesu lignelser. Gennemgang for større og mindre børn. (Religions-lærerforeningens skrifter, IV). København: Lohse, 1950, 110p.

_____ and _____ . Jesu liknelser. Metodisk handledning. Övers. från danskan av Einar Lilja. Stockholm: Geber, 1955 (1957), 108p.

McClellan, W. H. "Recent Bible Study" [the Parables]. Ecclesiastical Review 86 (1932) 91-102.

McCool, F. J. "The Preacher and the Historical Witness of the Gospels." Theological Studies 21 (1960) 517-43.

McEvoy, J. A. "Realized Eschatology and the Kingdom Parables." Catholic Biblical Quarterly 9 (1947) 329-57.

McFadyen, Joseph F. The Message of the Parables. London: J. Clarke, 1933, 246p.

Mackay, John A. "Mas yo os digo." Buenos Aires: Editorial Mundo Nuevo, 1927, 245p.

McQuilkin, Robert C. Studying Our Lord's Parables; A Series of Studies. Grand Rapids, Mich.: Zondervan Pub. House, 1935, 168p.

_____ . Studying Our Lord's Parables for Yourself, First Series. Columbia, S. C.: Columbia Bible School, 1929, 80p.

Madsen, Iver K. Die Parabeln der Evangelien und die heutige Psychologie. København: Munksgaard, 1936, 176p.

_____ . "Zur Erklarung der evangelischen Parabeln." Theologische Studien und Kritiken 101 (1929) 297-312; 104 (1932) 311-36.

Magass, W. "Zur Semiotik der signifikanten Orte in der Gleichnisse Jesu." Linguistica Biblica 15 (1972) 3-21.

Maillot, Alphonse. "Introduction aux paraboles." Foi et Vie 74 No. 5-6 (1975) 6-12.

_____ . Les Paraboles de Jésus aujourd'hui. Genève:

Editions Labor et Fides, 1973, 216p.

Maiworm, J. "Umgekehrte Gleichnisse." Bibel und Kirche 3 (1955) 82-85.

_____. "Die Verwalter-Parabel." Bibel und Kirche 13 (1958) 11-18.

Mancini, A. "Di un passo importante di San Luca in rapporto alla gerarchia della Chiesa (Lc. 12, 35-48)." Palestra del Clero 16 (1937) 254.

Manek, J. Ježišova podobenství." Praha: Blahoslav-ÚCN, 1972, 205p.

_____. ...und brachte Frucht. Die Gleichnisse Jesu. Ein Arbeitsbuch für die aus-und Weiterbildung kirchlicher Mitarbeiter. Aus dem Tschechischen von Joachim Dachsel und Ursula Dachsel. Stuttgart: Calwer Verlag, 1977, 120p.

Mangold, W. Populäre Auslegung samtlicher Gleichnisse Jesu Christi in katechetischer Gedankenfolge. 2. Aufl. Cassel: Frenschmidt, 1870, 272p.; 3. Aufl. Leipzig: Hinrichs Verlag, 1878, 304p.

Manson, William. "The Purpose of the Parables: A Re-Examination of St. Mark IV, 10-12." Expository Times 68 (1956-57) 132-35.

Marini, Ach. Le parabole della predicazione. Cremona: t. Provincia, 1901, 13p.

Marshall, I. H. Eschatology and the Parables. London: Tyndale Press, 1963.

Martin, Fernand. Les Paraboles évangéliques. Paris: Spes, 1941, 40p.

Martin, Hugh. Jesu liknelser och deras betydelse för vår tid. Övers. av E. Silen. Stockholm: Kristl. Stud.-Rör., 1938, 303p.

_____. The Parabels of the Gospels and their Meaning for Today. London: Student Christian Movement Press, 1937 (1962). Also, New York: Abingdon Press, 1937, 254p.

Marxsen, W. "Redaktionsgeschichtliche Erklärung der sogenannten Parabel-theorie des Markus." Zeitschrift für Theologie und Kirche 52 (1955) 255-71.

Masson, Charles. Les Paraboles de Marc IV avec introduction à l'explication des Évangiles. Neuchâtel-Paris: Delachaux et Niestlé, 1945, 55p.

Matthews, Shailer. "The Interpretation of Parables." American Journal of Theology 2 (1898) 293-311.

Maturin, Basil W. Practical Studies on the Parables of Our Lord. London, New York: Longmans, Green, 1915; Baltimore: Carroll Press, 1951, 295p.

_____. Practische overwegingen over de parabelen des Heeren, Naar de 5e Eng. uitg. in het Nederlandsch vert. door J. Waterreus. s'Gravenhage: M. Hols, 1910.

May, G. L. He Spoke in Parables. London: Skeffington, 1937, 144p.

Mayr, Igo. So sind sie... die Christen. Bibellesungen aus den Gleichnissen des Herrn. Innsbruck: Rauch, 1952, 127p.

Mecklin, R. W. The Twin Parables, or, the Mysteries of the Kingdom of God: A Series of Expository Sermons on Some of the Leading Parables of Our Lord; To Which Is Appended a Classification of These and Other Developed and Undeveloped Parables or Our Saviour. Richmond, Va.: Whittet & Shepperson, 1892, 135p.

Mees, M. "Die moderne Deutung der Parabeln und ihre Probleme." Vetera Christianorum 11 (1974) 416-33.

Meinertz, Max. Die Gleichnisse Jesu, 2. Aufl. Münster: Aschendorff, 1916 (1921) (1948), 95p.

_____. "Zum Verständnis der Gleichnisse Jesu." Das Heilige Land 86 (1954) 41-47.

Mellon, C. "La Parabole. Manière de parler, manière d'entendre." Recherches de science religieuse 61 (1973) 49-63.

Mendigal, Louis. En marge de l'Évangile. XL. Meditations en marge de quelques paraboles. Paris: Spes, 1941, 158p.

Merell, Jan. Kristova podobenství. Praha: ÚCN, Vyd. Čes. Kat. Charita, 1969, 104p.

Michael, J. Hugh. "Mark 4, 10-12, an Interpretation." Expositor 46 ser. 8, 20 (1920) 311-20.

Michaelis, Wilhelm. Es ging ein Sämann aus, zu säen; eine Einführung in die Gleichnisse Jesu über das Reich Gottes und die Kirche. Berlin: Furche-Verlag, 1938, 280p.

_____. Die Gleichnisse Jesu. Vol. 32 of Die urchristliche Botschaft, 3. Aufl. Hamburg: Furche-Verlag, 1956, 272p.

_____. "Die Gleichnisse Jesu und die Verzögerung der Parousie." Kirchenblatt für die reformierte Schweiz 111 (1955) 193-97.

Middendorff, Friedrich. Neues und Altes. Bilder und Gleichnisse zur Botschaft des Wortes Gottes und zum Leben der Christen. Gesammelt und weitergegeben, 2. Aufl. Wuppertal-Elberfeld: Verlag und Schriftenmission der Evangelischen Gessellschaft für Deutschland, 1962, 192p.

Miguens, M. "La predicazione di Gesù in parabole (Mc. 4; Lc. 8, 4-18; Mt. 13)." Bibbia e Oriente 1 (1959) 35-39.

Milham, Richard. Like It Is Today; Paraphrased Parables. Nashville: Broadman Press, 1970, 127p.

Milligan, William. "A Group of Parables; Luke 16-17." Expositor 4 ser., 6 (1892) 114-26, 186-99.

Millman, William. More Stories Told by Jesus. London: Sheldon Press, 1945, 15p.

Miner, Edmund B. Parabolical Teachings of Christ in Matthew XIII and Luke XV; Or, Old Truths Found in New Places. Boston: Gorham Press, 1915, 138p.

Minihan, J. "Kingdom of Heaven: God's Secret." Homiletic and Pastoral Review 59 (1958) 68-70.

Mitchell, Edward C. The Parables of the New Testament Spiritually Unfolded. With an Introduction on Scripture Parables; Their Nature, Use, and Interpretation. New York: New-Church Board of Publication, 1888; 2nd ed., Philadelphia: W. H. Alden, 1900, 544p.

Miyata, Mitsuo. Kaizaru no mono to kami no mono. Tokyo: Shinkyo, 1971, 234p.

Moffatt, James. "The Ten Best Books on the Parables of Jesus." Expositor ser. 9, 3 (1925) 104-14.

Molland, E. "Zur Auslegung von Mc. 4, 33 Καθὼς ἠδύναντο ἀκούειν." Symbolae Osloenses 8 (1929) 83-91.

Monier, Prosper. Conversations et paraboles. Synthèse de vie chrétienne. Mulhouse: Éditions Salvador; Tournai-Paris: Casterman, 1968, 160p.

Montefiore, Hugh. "A Comparison of the Parables of the Gospel According to Thomas and of the Synoptic Gospels." New Testament Studies 7 (1961) 220-48.

Morel, E. "Jesus au miroir des paraboles." Foi et Vie 55 (1957) 173-94.

Morey, J. J. The Parables of the Kingdom. London: Covenant Press, 1932, 230p.

Morgan, George C. Jesu liknelser. Från engelskan av Gösta Lindahl. Stockholm: Filadelfia, 1952 (1955) 263p.

_____. The Parables and Metaphors of Our Lord. New York: Revell, 1943, 352p.; London: Marshall, Morgan & Scott, 1944, 318p.

_____. The Parables of the Kingdom. New York: Revell, 1907, 221p.

Morgan-Wynne, J. E. "Matthew the Pastor." Baptist Quarterly (London) 26 (1976) 294-304.

Morgenthaler, R. "Formgeschichte und Gleichnisauslegung." Theologische Zeitschrift 6 (1950) 1-16.

Morlet, M. "Bulletin d'Ecriture Sainte. Le chapître des
  paraboles dans l'Évangile de Marc." Esprit et Vie 81

Mortari, Guilliano. Perchè Gesù parlò in parabole? Ve-
  rona: Soc. Ed. Veronese, 1922, 43p.

Moschner, Franz. Das Himmelreich in Gleichnissen. Betrachtungen zu neutestamentlichen Texten. Freiburg:
  Herder, 1953 (1955), 347p.

_____. The Kingdom of Heaven in Parables. Trans.
  David Heimann. St. Louis: Herder, 1960, 326p.

Moses, R. G. The Parables of Our Lord Unfolded and Illustrated. Philadelphia: Hubbard Brothers, 1883, 32p.

Mosetto, F. "Piccola rassegna sul tema: Le Parabole."
  Parole di Vita 16 (1971) 71-76.

Moule, C. F. D. "The Parables of the Jesus of History
  and the Lord of Faith." Religion and Education 28
  (1961) 60-64.

_____. "The Use of Parables and Sayings as Il-
  lustrative Material in Early Christian Catechesis."
  Journal of Theological Studies 3 (1952) 75-79.

Moulton, W. J. "Parable," in Hastings, James, ed., A
  Dictionary of Christ and the Gospels, vol. II, pp312-17.
  New York: Charles Scribner's Sons, 1924.

Mouson, J. "Explicatur parabola de zizania Mt. 13."
  Collectanea Mechliniensia 44 (1959) 171-75.

Mowry, L. "Parable," in The Interpreter's Dictionary of
  the Bible, vol. 3, pp649-54. New York: Abingdon
  Press, 1962.

Mullins, Aloysius. A Guide to the Kingdom; A Simple Handbook on the Parables. Westminster, Md.: Newman
  Press, 1963, 139p.

Mullins, T. Y. "Parables as Literary Forms in the New
  Testament." Lutheran Quarterly 12 (1960) 235-41.

Munk, Kaj. Jesu liknelser återgivna för barn. Övers.

från danskan av Hagb. Isberg. Med illustr. av Rune
Lindström. Stockholm: Diakonistyr., 1944, 69p.

Murphy, Joseph J. "The Parables of Judgment." Expositor
4 ser., 4 (1891) 52-62.

Mussner, Franz. Die Botschaft der Gleichnisse Jesu.
München: Kösel, 1961 (1964), 100p.

_____. Il messaggio delle parabole di Gesù.
Meditazioni teologiche. Tr. di G. Calavero. Brescia:
Queriniana, 1971, 120p.

_____. The Use of the Parables in Catechetics.
Trans. Maria von Eroes. Notre Dame, Ind.: University
of Notre Dame Press, 1965, 107p.

Nehemias, Rogerius. Parabolen oder Gleichnisse der Heiligen Schrift. Ubers. aus dem Englischen ins Deutsche.
Kopenhagen: 1712.

Nelson, Brian A. Hustle Won't Bring the Kingdom of God:
Jesus' Parables Interpreted for Today. St. Louis:
Bethany Press, 1978, 144p.

Nestle, Eb. "Mark IV, 12." Expository Times 13 (1901-
02) 524.

Nevin, Alfred. The Parables of Jesus. Philadelphia:
Presbyterian Board of Publication, 1881, 503p.

Newton, W. L. "Our Lord's Parables; Material for the
Teacher of the Bible." Journal of Religious Instruction
11 (1941) 399-404.

Nichols, A. "Parables for Primaries; A Way to Teach
Little Children." Religion Teacher's Journal 9 (May-
June 1975) 13-15.

Nicolaus Lynckenius. Enige leer en senryke parabelen uit
de Evangelisten Matheus en Lucas. Mit Anm. v. D'
Outrien. Amsterdam: 1725.

Nicoll, Maurice. The New Man; An Interpretation of Some
Parables and Miracles of Christ. New York: Hermitage
House, 1950 (1951), 235p.

_____. De nieuwe mens: Een interpretatie van enige gelijkenissen en wonderen van Christus. Wassenaar: Servire, 1970, 210p.

Nicum, John. Die Gleichnisreden Jesu. Mit 38 Bildern. In den Worten der Heiligen Schrift erzählt und mit Sprüchen, katechismus-und liederangabe, Fragen und Sacherklärung versehen. Reading, Pa.: Pilger-Buchhandlung, 1884, 75p.

Noack, B. "En konstrueret lignelse." Dansk Teologisk Tidsskrift 26 (1963) 238-43.

Noland, Stephen. Special Sermons, and Analyses of Ten of Our Lord's Parables. Nashville: Southern Methodist Pub. House, 1885, 249p.

O'Brien, I. "Seeing, They Do not See." Friar 20 (Dec. 1963) 54-58.

_____. "Three Parables; The Rich Fool, the Barren Fig Tree, the Great Supper." Friar 21 (June 1964) 47-53.

O'Connell, H. "Christ's Parables: Purpose and Meaning." Liguorian 52 (Aug. 1964) 47-52.

O'Connor, Joseph V. The Parables of Our Lord and Saviour Jesus Christ. Philadelphia: J. E. Potter, 1885, 24p.

Oesterley, William O. E. The Gospel Parables in the Light of Their Jewish Background. London: Society for Promoting Christian Knowledge; New York: Macmillan, 1936, 245p.

Ogden, S. M. "Prudence and Grace." Criterion 11 (Aut. 1971) 6-8.

Ohne mich könnt ihr nichts tun. Gleichnisse Jesu nach dem biblischen Wort. Hrsg. von der Pressenstelle der Evang. -luth. Kirche in Thüringen. Mit Bildern von Alf. Wittber. Berlin: Evang. Verlag Anst. (Alleinvertrieb); Jena: [Wartburg-Verlag] Kessler, 1957, 26p.

Ollesch, Helmut. Bilder des Ewigen. Gleichnisse Jesu vom Wesen und Werden des Reiches Gottes und vom rechten

Verhalten der Jünger Jesu. Wuppertal: Aussat Verlag, 1963, 144p.

Ollivier, M. J. The Parables of Our Lord Jesus Christ. Trans. E. Leahy. Dublin: Browne and Nolan, 1929, 421p.

On a Farm in Bible Times (Filmstrip) Eye Gate House, 1963.

Orbe, Antonio. Parábolas evangélicas en San Ireneo. Madrid: La Editorial Católica, 1972. 2 vols.

O'Reilly, Patrick J. The Light Divine in Parable and Allegory; Thoughts for Catholics and Non-Catholics. Chicago: Loyola University Press, 1930, 320p.

O'Rourke, John J. "Jo. 10:1-18: Series Parabolarum?" Verbum Domine 42 (1964) 22-25.

Osborn, Edwin F. The Teaching of the Parables of Jesus Christ. Chicago: Evangelical and Biblical Pub. Co., 1906, 320p.

Osborn, Eric F. "Parable and Exposition." Australian Biblical Review 22 (1974) 11-22.

Osnes, G. "Metaforer och ex-metaforer i det NT." Tidsskrift for Teologi og Kirke 38 (1967) 23-32.

Osten-Sacken, Peter von der. "Streitgespräch und Parabel als Formen markinischer Christologie," in Jesus Christus in Historie und Theologie: Neutestamentliche Festschrift für Hans Conzelmann zum 60. Geburtstag. Hrsg. George Strecker, pp375-94. Tübingen: J. C. B. Mohr, 1975.

Ostmann, R. Die Gleichnisse des Herrn. Für Lehrer und christliche Familien dem Inhalte nach dargelegt. Berlin: 1851.

O'Sullivan, Kevin. Living Parables. Milwaukee: Bruce Pub. Co., 1963, 120p.

Oxenden, A. Nogle af Herrens Lignelser forklarede. Overs. af J. Vahl. København: Prior, 1867.

Palms, J. G. Betrachtungen über die Gleichnisse des
Neuen Testament. Hamborg: 1735.

The Parable Book; Our Divine Lord's Own Stories, Retold
for You by Children; Illustrated with Masterpieces from
Doré, Bida, Hofmann, and Other Artists and with
Numerous Pen Sketches by B. E. Waddell and Bess
Bethel Crank. Chicago: Extension Press, 1921, 213p.

The Parables, Edited by Lyman Abbott, D. D. Illus. by
Arthur E. Becker; decorations by Arthur Jacobson.
New York: D. Appleton, 1907, 193p.

Parables and Proverbs. Philadelphia: Hubbard Brothers,
1880, 12p.

Parables for Boys and Girls. Selected by Marjorie Ingzel.
Camden, N. J.: T. Nelson, 1966.

The Parables from the Gospels. With Ten Original Wood-
cuts Designed and Engraved on the Wood by Charles
Ricketts. London: Sold by Hacon and Ricketts; New
York: John Lane, 1903, 76p.

Parables Jesus Told: God's Love (Filmstrip). Standard
Pub. Co. and Society for Visual Education, 1949.

Parables Jesus Told: The Kingdom (Filmstrip). Standard
Pub. Co. and Society for Visual Education, 1949.

Parables Jesus Told: Right Living (Filmstrip). Standard
Pub. Co. and Society for Visual Education, 1949.

The Parables of Christ (Filmstrip). Catechetical Guild
Educational Society, 1965.

Parables of Our Lord. Claymont, Del.: S. F. Hotchkin,
1863, 40p.

The Parables of Our Lord and Saviour Jesus Christ. Chicago: Baird and Dillon, 1885, 24p.

The Parables of Our Lord and Saviour Jesus Christ. With
Pictures by John Everett Millais; Engraved by the Bro-
thers Dalziel; with a New Introduction by Mary Lutyens.
New York: Dover Publications, 1975, 76p.

"Parables of the Gospels: Artist, Eugène Burnand (1850-1921.)" St. Joseph Magazine 58 (1957) 23-30.

"The Parables of the New Testament." Dublin Review 27 (1849) 181-227.

Parables, Told by Our Lord, Arranged by Nan Dearmer, with Illustrations by Claudia Freedman. London: Faber & Faber, 1944, 27p.

The Parables Told to the People by Jesus of Nazareth as Recorded in the Gospels, with Drawings by Cyrus Le Roy Baldridge. New York: Harper, 1942, 44p.

Les Paraboles. Commentaires de M. Philibert. Ill. de Soeur Christiane-Marie. Paris: Éditions Siloé, 1952.

Les Paraboles de Jésus. Ill. Sherbrook (Canada): Apostolat de la presse, s. d., 32p.

Les Paraboles de l'attente et de la miséricorde. Paris: Ligue Cath. de l'Évangile, 1968, 64p.

Les Paraboles du Christ: fêtes et saisons (Sept. -Oct. 1957) 28p.

Paramo, S. del. "El fin de las parábolas de Cristo y el Salmo 17." Comillas 2 (1967) 95-123. Also, Miscelánea Comillas 20 (1953) 233-56.

Parker, S. A. "Thoughts on the Parables; Sermon." Homiletic and Pastoral Review 52 (1951) 51-54.

Patten, Priscilla C. "Parable and Secret in the Gospel of Mark in Light of Select Apocalyptic Literature." Ph. D. thesis, Drew University, 1976, 247p.

Paulli, Jakob. Jesu liknelser. En uppbyggelsebok. Bemynd. öfvers. af Abraham Ahlén. Stockholm: A. V. Carlson, 1911, 135p.

Pedersen, S. "Er Mark 4 et 'lignelseskapitel?'" Dansk Teologisk Tidsskrift 33 (1970) 20-30.

_____. "Lignelse eller allegori: eksegetiskhomiletiske overvejelser." Svensk Teologisk Kvartalskrift 48 no. 2 (1972) 63-68.

_____ . "Den nytestamentlige lignelsesforsknings metodeproblemer. " Dansk Teologisk Tidsskrift 28 (1965) 146-84.

Peisker, C. H. "Konsekutives ἵνα in Markus 4, 12. " Zeitschrift für die neutestamentliche Wissenschaft 59 (1968) 126-27.

Percy, Ernst. "Liknelseteorien i Mark 4, 11f. och kompositionen av Mark 4, 1-34, " in Professor Johannes Lindblom, Lund, på hans 65-årsdag den 7 juni 1947 (Svensk exegetisk årsbok, XII, 1947), pp242-62; Uppsala: Wretmans boktryckeri A. -B. , 1948. Also, Svensk Exegetisk Årsbok 12 (1947) 258-78.

Perella, G. M. "Le parabole in particolare. " Palestra del Clero 20, 1 (1941) 265-69; 20, 2 (1941) 137-46, 281-88; 21, 1 (1942) 97-98, 129-32, 193-96, 241-46; 21, 2 (1942) 33-40, 97-102, 113-17, 223-27; 22, 1 (1943) 49-52, 65-67, 180-83; 22, 2 (1943) 49-54, 145-50, 209-15, 225-29.

Perkins, Pheme. "Interpreting Parables; The Bible and the Humanities, " in Emerging Issues in Religious Education. Edited by Gloria Durka and Joanmarie Smith, pp149-72. New York: Paulist Press, 1976.

Perrin, Norman. "Biblical Scholarship in a New Vein. " Review of Dan O. Via. , Jr. , The Parables: Their Literary and Existential Dimension. Interpretation 21 (1967) 465-69.

_____ . "The Evangelists' Interpretation of Jesus' Parables. " Journal of Religion 52 (1972) 361-75. Also, Theology Digest 21 (1973) 146-49.

_____ . "Historical Criticism, Literary Criticism, and Hermeneutics; The Interpretation of the Parables of Jesus and the Gospel of Mark Today. " Journal of Religion 52 (1972) 361-75.

_____ . Jesus and the Language of the Kingdom: Symbol and Metaphor in New Testament Interpretation. Philadelphia: Fortress Press, 1976, 225p.

_____ . "The Modern Interpretation of the Parables of Jesus and the Problem of Hermeneutics. " Interpretation 25 (1971) 131-48.

_____. "The Parables of Jesus as Parables, as
Metaphors, and as Aesthetic Objects: A Review Article."
Journal of Religion 47 (1967) 340-46.

Parroy, Henry. Récits évangéliques: Les Paraboles. Lyon,
Paris: Vitte, 1954, 544p.

Peruzzi, Angelo. Studio delle sette parabole in S. Matteo
c. 13, ovvero il regno dei cieli in esse rivelato e sue
fasi. Torre Pellice: Tip. Alpina, 1924, 29p.

Petersen, Norman R. "On the Notion of Genre in Via's
Parable and Example Story: A Literary-Structuralist
Approach." Semeia 1 (1974) 134-81.

Petuchowski, J. J. "La signification theologique de la parabole dans la litterature rabbinique et dans le NT."
Nouvelles Chretiennes d'Israël 23 (1972) 76-87.

_____. "The Theological Significance of the Parable
in Rabbinic Literature and the New Testament." Christian News from Israel 23, 2 (1972) 76-86.

Pewtress, Vera. Jesu liknelser. Övers. av Börje Fors-
berg och Karl-Erik Brattgård. Stockholm: Diakonistyr.,
1961, 32p.

Pfaff, C. M. Commentatio de recta Theologiae parabolicae
et allegoricae conformatione. Tübingen: 1720.

Pfendsack, Werner. Ihr aber seid Brüder. Gleichnisse
des Lukas-Evangelium. Basel: F. Reinhardt, 1962,
127p.

_____. Die Kirche bleibt nicht im Dorf. Gleichnisse
des Matthäus-Evangeliums, ausgelegt für die Gemeinde.
Basel: F. Reinhardt, 1968, 183p.

Pieper, F. "Die Schatzkammer der Gleichnisse Christi."
Chrysologus 32 (1938-39) 137-39.

Pierson, H. Gelijkenissen des Heeren. 's Hage: W. A.
Beschoor, 1891; Amsterdam: W. ten Have, 1919.

Piper, Otto A. "The Understanding of the Synoptic Parables,"

Evangelical Quarterly 14 (1942) 42-53.

Pirot, Jean. Allégories et paraboles dans le vie et l'enseignement de Jésus-Christ. Marseille: Imprimerie
Marseillaise, 1943, 296p.

_____. Paraboles et allégories évangéliques. Le
pensée de Jésus. Les commentaires patristiques.
Paris: Lethielleux, 1949, 508p.

Plummer, A. "Parable," in A Dictionary of the Bible,
James Hastings, ed., vol. III, pp662-65. New York:
Scribner's, 1900.

Poovey, William A. Mustard Seeds and Wine Skins; Dramas
and Meditations on Seven Parables. Minneapolis: Augsburg Pub. House, 1972, 128p.

Poteat, Edwin M. Parables of Crisis. New York: Harper,
1950, 255p.

Poynder, Augustus. "Mark IV, 12." Expository Times 15
(1903-04) 141-42.

Prager, M. "Israel in the Parables." Bridge 4 (1962) 44-
88.

Prins, J. I. "Matth. XIII, 10b: 'Waarom spreekt gij tot hen
in gelijkenissen?'" Theologisch tijdschrift 18 (1884) 25-
38.

Procter, W. C. Scriptural Similes Classified and Considered.
London: Stanley Martin, 1930, 60p.

Provero, Mario. Le Parabole evangeliche ed il loro messaggio. Jerusalem: Franciscan Printing Press, 1974,
171p.

Pryor, J. W. "Markan Parable Theology: An Inquiry into
Mark's Principles of Redaction." Expository Times 83
(1972) 242-45.

Quick, Oliver C. The Realism of Christ's Parables, Ida
Hartley Lectures Delivered at Colne, Lancs., October,
1930. London: Student Christian Movement Press,
1937, 74p.

288 / Bibliography

Quievreux, Francois. Évangile et tradition. T. 1,
Les Paraboles. Paris: Éditions Je sers., 1946,
267p.

Räisänen, H. Die Parabeltheorie im Markusevangelium.
Schriften der Finnischen Exegetischen Gesellschaft 26.
Helsinki, Leiden: Brill, 1973, 173p.

Ragaz, Leonhard. Die Gleichnisse Jesu. Seine soziale-
Botschaft. Bern: Lang & Cie, 1944, 249p. Also,
Hamburg: Furche Verlag, 1971, 212p.

Ramos García, J. "Las parábolas evangélicas. Sentido
literal. " Ilustración del Clero 45 (1952) 381-88.

Randellini, L. "Aspetti formali delle parabole evangeliche. "
Bibbia e Oriente 2 (1960) 1-4.

Rasco, Emilio. "Les Paraboles de Luc XV. Une invitation à la joie de Dieu dans le Christ, " in De Jésus aux
Évangiles. Bibliotheca Emphemeridum theologicarum
Lovaniensium 25, vol. 2, pp165-83. Gembloux: Duculot; Paris: Lethielleux, 1967.

Redding, David A. The Miracles and the Parables; Two
Best Sellers Complete in One Volume. Old Tappan, N.
J. : Revell, 1971, 186p., 177p.

_____. The Parables He Told. Westwood, N. J. :
Revell, 1962, 177p.

Reese, J. "Celebration and Biblical Preaching. " Bible
Today 74 (Nov. 1974) 74-80.

Reese, James M. "Parables: Miracles of Speech. " Our
Sunday Visitor Magazine 66 (June 16, 1977) 14.

_____. "Responding to the Parables. " Catholic
Charismatic 1 (Oct. -Nov. 1976) 10-13.

Reid, John C. Parables from Nature: Earthly Stories with
a Heavenly Meaning. The Parables of Jesus Retold and
Interpreted for Young Minds. Illus. by Reynold H.
Weidenaar. Grand Rapids, Mich. : Eerdmans, 1954,
89p.

Reinhard, L. Institutio theol. parabol. sive de recta ratione interpretand. praecipue C. parab. Lipsiae: 1740.

Reinhardt, K. "Dialektische Aussagen in Jesu Basileia-gleichnissen." Diss., Erlangen, 1968.

Reinhardus, Laur. Intitutiones theologiae parabolicae. Vinariae: 1752.

Renkema, W. B., and Rudolph, R. J. W. De gelijkenissen onzes Heeren Jezus Christus, voor de gemeente verklaard. Rotterdam: D. Bolle, 1905.

Rettberg, F. W. De parabolis J. C. Göttingen: 1827.

Reus, F. J. Meletema de sensu septem parabolarum Matth. XIII prophetico. Copenhagen: 1733.

Richey, Thomas. The Parables of the Lord Jesus According to S. Matthew, Arranged, Compared, and Illustrated. New York: E. & J. B. Young, 1888, 406p.

Ricoeur, Paul. "Biblical Hermeneutics." Semeia 4 (1975) 29-148.

_____. "Listening to the Parables of Jesus; Text Matthew 13:31-32 and 45-46" [sermon]. Criterion 13 (1974) 18-22.

_____. "Listening to the Parables: Once More Astonished." Christianity and Crisis 34 (Jan. 6, 1975) 304-08.

_____. "Royaume dans les paraboles de Jésus." Etudes Théologiques et Religieuses 51 (1976) 15-19.

Riddle, Donald W. "Mark 4:1-34; The Evolution of a Gospel Source." Journal of Biblical Literature 56 (1937) 77-90.

Riegert, E. R. "Parabolic Sermons." Lutheran Quarterly 26 (Feb. 1974) 24-31.

Riesenfeld, Harald. "The Parables in the Synoptic and the Johannine Traditions." Svensk Exegetisk Årsbok 25 (1960) 37-61.

_____. "Les Paraboles dans la predication de Jésus selon les traditions synoptique et johannique." Église et Théologie 22 (1959) 21-29.

Riggenbach, Eduard. Zur Exegese und Textkritik zweier Gleichnisse Jesu. Stuttgart: Calwer Vereinsbuchhandlung, 1922, 17p.

Roberts, Robert E. The Message of the Parables; Some Suggestions as to their Bearing on Present-day Life. London: Epworth Press, 1935, 165p.

Robinson, D. W. B. "The Use of the Parables in the Synoptic Gospels." Evangelical Quarterly 21 (1949) 93-108.

Robinson, J. A. T. "Parable of John 10:1-5." Zeitschrift für die neutestamentliche Wissenschaft 46 (1955) 233-40.

Robinson, James M. "Jesus Parables as God Happening," in Jesus and the Historian: Written in Honor of Ernest Cadman Colwell. Thomas Trotter, ed., pp134-50; Philadelphia: Westminster Press, 1968. Also in A Meeting of Poets and Theologians to Discuss Parable, Myth, and Language, Held at the College of Preachers, Washington, D. C. 1968, pp45-52.

_____. "Jesus' Understanding of History." Journal of Bible and Religion 23 (1955) 17-24.

_____. "Les Paraboles comme avènement de Dieu." Le Point Théologique 3 (1972) 33-62.

Robinson, Maurice A. "Σπερμολόγος: Did Paul Preach from Jesus' Parables?" Biblica 56 (1975) 231-40.

Robinson, Willard H. "The Problem of the Parables of Jesus." Ph. D. thesis, University of Chicago, 1915, 60p.

_____. The Parables of Jesus in Their Relation to His Ministry. Chicago: University of Chicago Press, 1928, 222p.

Rodenbusch, E. "Die Komposition von Lucas 16." Zeitschrift für die neutestamentliche Wissenschaft 4 (1903) 243-54.

Röhr, H. "Buddha und Jesus in ihren Gleichnissen." Neue

Zeitschrift für Systematische Theologie und Religionsphilosophie 15 (1973) 65-86.

Rohden, Huberto. Saberdoria das parábolas; Mística das
beatitudes. São Paulo: Fundação Alvorada, 1974, 239p.

Rohrdantz, T. Gottes Felder. Gespräche über Mt. 13.
Schwerin: Bahn, 1938, 79p.

Rongy, H. "La Journée du lac ou les parables." Revue
Ecclésiastique de Liége 21 (1930) 355-67.

Roorda, A. De gelijkenissen des Heeren toegelicht. Wage-
ningen: Nederbragt & Co., 1904.

Ross, John J. The Kingdom in Mystery; A Study of the
Parables of Our Lord Concerning the Kingdom of
Heaven. New York: Revell, 1920, 379p.

Rossmann, Wilhelm. Der neue Mensch; Der wahre Sinn der
Gleichnisse Jesu. Bremen: G. Winter, 1923, 144p.

Roussel, Alfred. Paraboles évangéliques. Paris: P.
Téqui, 1914, 189p.

Rowlingson, D. T. "How Did Jesus Know God?" Religion
in Life 43 (1974) 294-305.

Ruager, Søren. Guds rige og Jesu person. København:
Aros, 1975, 212p.

Ruf, Karl. Gleichnisse Jesu. Die Bibel dem Volke! Kleine
Bibelhefte für das katholische Volk, Serie 2. Freiburg:
Kanisinswerk, 1941, 57p.

Russell, Elbert. The Parables of Jesus. Philadelphia:
John C. Winston, 1928, 168p.

_____. The Parables of Jesus; A Course of Ten
Lessons Arranged for Daily Study. New York: National
Board of the Young Women's Christian Associations of
the United States of America, 1909, 93p.

Ryfer, E. "Die Gleichnisse Jesu." Schweizerische Reformierten Volksblattes 62 (1928) 188-90, 219-22, 281-84,
376-78, 389-92; 63 (1929) 17-20, 25-27.

292 / Bibliography

S. P. C. "Seis nuevas Parábolas?" Estudios Bíblicos 7 (1935) 51-90.

Sabbatucci, D. "La parabola evangelica. Appunti fenomenologici." Studi e Materiali di Storia delle Religioni 38 (1967) 488-97.

Sabourin, Leopold. "The Parables of the Kingdom." Biblical Theology Bulletin 6 (1976) 115-60.

St. Thomas, Sister. "The Parables Come to Life." Catholic Educator 23 (1952) 156- .

Salm, W. "Beiträge zur Gleichnisforschung." Diss., Göttingen, 1953.

Salmond, Stewart D. F. The Parables of Our Lord. Edinburgh: T. & T. Clark; London: Simpkin, Marshall, Hamilton, Kent, 189-? 122p.

Savignac, Alida de. Paraboles de l'Évangile expliquées et mises à la portée des petits enfants par une mère. Paris: D. Eymery, 1834, 227p.

Schaedel, Heinrich. Das grosse Gleichnis. Lukas 15 und 16. Wüstenrot: Reith Verlag, 1947, 21p.

Schäfer, Jakob. Die Parabeln des Herrn, in Homilien erklärt, 2. Aufl. Freiburg i. B.: Herder, 1911, 576p. (4. Aufl., 1922, 502p.)

_____. Le parabole del Signore: omelie. Trad. di Egido Lari. Firenze: Libr. Ed. Fiorent., 1923. 2 vols.

Schäfers, Joseph. Eine altsyrische antimarkionitische Erklärung von Parabeln des Herrn und 2 andere altsyrische Abhandlungen zu Texten des Evangeliums. Mit Beiträge zu Tatians Diatessaron und Markions Neuem Testament. Münster: Aschendorff, 1917, 243p.

Scharlemann, Martin H. Proclaiming the Parables. St. Louis: Concordia Pub. House, 1963, 54p.

Schelke, K. H. "Der Zweck der Gleichnisreden (Mk. 4, 10-12)," in Neues Testament und Kirche, Festschrift R. Schnackenburg, J. Gnilka, ed., pp71-75. Freiburg i. B.,

Basel, Wien: Herder, 1974.

Scheller, Arndt. Gleichnisse zum Katechismus. Hilfsbuch für den Religionsunterricht in der Schule und für den Konfirmandenunterricht, 2. Aufl. Leipzig: Strübigs Verlag, 1912, 104p.

Schippers, R. Gelijkenissen van Jezus. Kampen: J. H. Kok, 1962, 198p.

Schlatter, Adolf. Die Kirche wie Jesus sie sah. Auslegung seiner drei letzten Gleichnisse Mt. 24, 45-25, 30. Kassel: Neuwerk-Verlag, 1936, 31p.

Schmandt, Henrietta E. Parables of the Master. New York: Vantage Press, 1956, 80p.

Schmidt, Hermann. "Gleichnisse Jesu Grundlage der christlichen Unterweisung." Christliche Welt 10 (1896) 99-103.

Schnackenburg, R. "The Primitive Church and Its Traditions of Jesus." Perspective 10 (1969) 103-24.

Schneider, Gerhard. Parusiegleichnisse im Lukasevangelium. Stuttgarter Bibelstudien 74. Stuttgart: Katholisches Bibelwerk, 1975, 106p.

Schnell, F. "Vom den Gleichnissen des Herrn." Katholische Kirchenzeitung 77 (1937) 186-88.

Schneller, Ludwig. Das Himmelreich; Predigten über die Gleichnisse Jesu, Matthäus 13. Leipzig: H. G. Wallmann, 1930, 162p.

Schnettler, K. "Die modernen Christusgegner und die Gleichnisse Jesu." Kirche und Kanzel 11 (1928) 67-71.

Schoedel, W. R. "Parables in the Gospel of Thomas; Oral Tradition or Gnostic Exegesis?" Concordia Theological Monthly 43 (1972) 548-60.

Scholten, J. J. Diatribe de Parabolis Jesu Christi. Delft, Leiden: B. Bruins et H. W. Hazenberg, 1827.

Schreiner, H. "Wort Gottes und Gleichnis." Zeitwende 15 (1938-39) 222-31.

Schürmann, H. "Die Botschaft der Gleichnisse Jesu." Bibel und Leben 2 (1961) 92-105, 171-74, 254-61.

Schullerus, Adolf. Warum durch Gleichnisse? Referat aus der Pastoralkonferenz des Schenker Kirchenbezirks. Hermannstadt: W. Krafft, 1904, 65p.

Schultze, A. H. A. De parabolarum J. C. indole poetica. Göttingen: 1827.

Schwill, C. A. "Evangelium, Gemeinde und Welt im Lichte der Gleichnisse Jesu." Wahrheitszeuge 52 (1930) 129.

Schyns, M. L'Evangile de Jésus. Son enseignement d'après les Paraboles, 2e éd. Bruxelles: Libr. Evangélique, 1937, 161p.

Seale, Ervin. Learn to Live; The Meaning of the Parables. New York: Morrow, 1955, 256p.

Seedtime and Harvest (Filmstrip). Gospel Slide and Film Service, 1951.

Segbroeck, F. van. "De parabelrede van Mattheus." Ons Geestelijk Leven 47 (1970) 216-25.

_____. "Zonen, wijnbouwers, bruiloftsgasten (Mt. 21, 28-22, 14." Ons Geestelijk Leven 49 (1972) 303-12.

Seim, Turid K. "Nye veier i lignelsesforskningen." Norsk Teologisk Tidsskrift 78 (1977) 239-58.

Sell, Henry T. Studies of the Parables of Our Lord. New York, London, Revell, 1930, 159p.

Sellin, Gerhard. "Gleichnisstruckturen." Linguistica Biblica 31 (1974) 89-115.

_____. "Studien zu den grossen Gleichniserzählungen des Lukas-Sondergutes: die ἄνθρωπός τις --Erzählungen des Lukas-Sondergutes, besonders am Beispiel von Lk. 10, 25-37 und 16, 19-31 untersucht. Diss. Münster i. W., 1973; anerkannt, 1974.

Semeria, G. Le parabole del Signore. Milano: Opera naz. per il mezzogiorno d'Italia, 1940, 146p.

Semiology and Parables: Exploration of the Possibilities Offered by Structuralism for Exegesis. Edited by Daniel Patte. (Pittsburgh Theological Monograph Series, no. 9.) Pittsburgh: Pickwick Press, 1976.

Shafto, G. R. The Lesser Parables of Jesus. London: Epworth, 1939, 160p.

_____. The Stories of the Kingdom: A Study of the Parables of Jesus. London: SCM, 1922, 196p.

Sheppard, John B. "A Study of the Parables Common to the Synoptic Gospels and the Coptic Gospel of Thomas." Ph.D. thesis, Emory University, 1965, 455p.

Die sieben Gleichnisse des Herrn nach dem Evangelium St. Matthäus 13. Kapital. Eine Weissagung auf die Geschichte der Kirche. Gernsbach: Christlicher Kolportagverein, 1890, 36p.

Siegman, E. F. "Teaching in Parables (Mk. 4, 10-12; Lk. 8, 9-10; Mt. 13, 10-15)." Catholic Biblical Quarterly 23 (1961) 161-81.

Signes et paraboles; sémiotique et texte évangélique. Paris; Éditions du Seuil, 1977, 252p.

Simpson, P. "God's Offer of Heavenly Favours." Irish Ecclesiastical Record 93 (1960) 379-85.

Sinclair, T. A. "Note on an Apparent Mistranslation" [Mk. 4:12]. Biblical Theology 5 (1954) 18.

Sineux, Raphaël. Paraboles et paraphrases évangéliques. Bordeaux: L'auteur, 1970, 217p.

Siniscalco, P. Mito e storia della salvezza. Richerche sulle più antiche interpretazioni di alcune parabole evangeliche. Torino: G. Giappichelli, 1971, 222p.

Skovgaard-Petersen, Carl. Jesu Lignelser. København: Lohse, 1922, 132p.

_____. Jesu Lignelser. Til norsk ved Nils Kjøl. Oslo: Indremisjonsforlaget, 1950, 142p.

_____. Jesu Liknelser. Bemynd. övers. från danskan av V. Emanuelsson. Uppsala: Lindblad, 1922, 131p.

Skrinjar, A. "Le But des paraboles sur le règne et l'écon-omie des lumières divines d'après l'Ecriture Sainte." Biblica 11 (1930) 291-321, 426-49; 12 (1931) 27-40.

Smart, Christopher. The Parables of Our Lord and Saviour Jesus Christ. Done into Familiar Verse, with Occasion-al Applications, for the Use and Improvement of Younger Minds. London: W. Owen, 1768, 175p.

Smart, J. D. "A Redefinition of Jesus' Use of the Parable." Expository Times 47 (1935-36) 551-55.

Smith, Bertram T. D. The Parables of the Synoptic Gos-pels. Cambridge: University Press, 1937, 250p.

Smith, Charles W. F. The Jesus of the Parables. Phila-delphia: Westminster Press, 1948, 314p.; Rev. ed., Philadelphia: United Church Press, 1975, 255p.

_____. "Mixed State of the Church in Matthew's Gospel." Journal of Biblical Literature 82 (1963) 149-68.

Smith, Christopher. The Gospel Parables in Verse. New York; Washington: Broadway Pub. Co., 1911, 89p.

Smith, Hay W. "The Fifteenth Chapter of Luke." Union Seminary Magazine 8 (1896-97) 104-10.

Smogór, Casimir R. Wkyżad przypowieści Pana Jezusa w kazaniach. Chicago: Czcionkami i drukiem "Gazety Katolickiej," 1903-05. 2 vols.

Songer, Harold S. "Jesus' Use of Parables: Matthew 13." Review and Expositor 59 (1962) 492-500.

_____. "A Study of the Background of the Concepts of Parable in the Synoptic Gospels." Ph.D. thesis, Southern Baptist Theological Seminary, 1962, 200p.

Sorger, Karlheinz. Die Gleichnisse im Unterricht. Grund-sätzliche Überlegungen. Essen: Hans Driewer Verlag, 1972, 168p.

Soulen, Richard N. "Biblical Hermeneutics and Parable Interpretation in the Writings of Ernst Fuchs." Ph. D. thesis, Boston University, 1964, 388p.

Spanuth, Henrich. Die Gleichnisse Jesu für den Unterricht bearbeitet, 2. Aufl. Osterwieck: A. W. Zickfeldt, 1918, 163p.

Spediacci, M. Parabole di Gesù. Roma: Sales, 1938, 24p.

_____. Parabole di Gesù. Per la gioventù. Roma: Sales, 1941, 22p.

Speyr, Andrienne von. Gleichnisse des Herrn. Einsiedeln: Johannes-Verlag, 1966, 147p.

Spitta, Friedrich. Eugène Burnand als Erklärer der Gleichnisse Jesu. Ein Wort zur Erwägung für Bibelleser und Freunde christlicher Kunst. Strassburg: Strassb. Druckerei und Verlag-Anst., 1911, 39p.

_____. "Die Parabelschnitte Matth. 13, Mark 4, Luk. 8 als typisches Beispiel des Verhältnisses der Synoptiker zueinander." Theologische Studien und Kritiken 84 (1911) 538-69.

Splendori, M. Nel Soprannaturale. Le Parabole di Gesù Cristo. Padova: Tip. Libr. Antoniana, 1925, 188p.

Sprenger, G. "Jesu Säe-und Entgleichnisse, aus den palästinischen Ackerbauverhältnissen dargestellt." Palästinajahrbuch 9 (1913) 79-97.

Spurgeon, Charles H. De gelijkenissen van den Zaligmaker. Twee-en-vijftig leerredenen. Uit het Eng. vertaald door Elisabeth Freystadt. Utrecht: H. ten Hoove: Rotterdam: D. Bolle, 1896 (1909).

_____. Womit kann ich's vergleichen?: 5 Gleichnisse Jesu. Übers. von Manfred Bärenfanger. Stuttgart: Christliches Verlagshaus, 1974, 63p.

Stählin, G. "Die Gleichnishandlungen Jesu," in Kosmos und Ekklesia. Festschrift für Wilhelm Stahlin, pp9-22. Kassel: J. Stauda-Verlag, 1953.

_____. Symbolon. Vom gleichnishaften Denken. Stuttgart: Evang. Verlagswerk, 1958, 515p.

Stanley, D. M. "Pauline Allusions to the Sayings of Jesus."
Catholic Biblical Quarterly 23 (1961) 26-39.

Stedman, Ray C. Behind History. Waco, Tex.: Word
Books, 1976, 166p.

Steinmeyer, F. L. Die Parabeln des Herrn. Berlin:
1884.

Stevens, William B. The Parables of the New Testament
Practically Unfolded. Philadelphia: E. H. Butler,
1855. 336p. (1864, 382p.) Also, Philadelphia: J.
M. Stoddart; Cincinnati: E. Hannaford, 1871. Also,
Philadelphia: Bradley, 1887, 382p.

Stockum, T. C. van. "Idiota cum evangelista Matthaeo
luctans. Nederlande theologisch Tydschrift 19 (Oct.
1964) 15-21.

Stories Told by Our Lord. Illus. by Osborn Woods. Baltimore: Helicon Press, 1960, unpaged.

Storr, Gottlob C. Dissertatio hermeneutica de Parabolis
Christi. Tübingen: 1779.

_____. "Dissertation on the Parables of Christ."
Trans. William R. Whittingham, in The Biblical
Cabinet; Or Hermeneutical, Exegetical, and Philological
Library, vol. IX, pp61-137. Edinburgh: Thomas
Clark, 1835.

Straton, Hillyer H. A Guide to the Parables of Jesus.
Grand Rapids, Mich.: Eerdmans, 1959, 198p.

Summers, R. "Setting the Parables Free." Southwestern
Journal of Theology 10 (Spring 1968) 7-18.

Sutcliffe, E. F. "The Use of Parables." Clergy Review
25 (1945) 207-11.

Svanholm, C. "Hovedproblemene i fortolkningen av Jesus
Lignelser in den nyere Teologi fra Jülicher av." Tid-
skrift for Teologi og Kirke 24 (1953) 164-76.

Swaeles, R. "L'Orientation ecclesiastique de saint Matthieu.

Analyse de trois paraboles: Mt. 21, 33-46; 22, 1-14; 13, 24-30, 36-43." Doctoral diss., Louvain: 1959.

Swann, George B. The Parables of Jesus. Owensboro, Ky.: Progress Printing Co., 1918, 279p.

Swanston, Hamish F. G. "Reading a Parable." Bible Today 32 (1967) 2248-57.

_____. _____. Bible Today 50 (1970) 114-19.

_____. "Reading a Parable II." Bible Today 39 (1969) 2715-22.

Swete, H. B. The Parables of the Kingdom. London: Macmillan, 1920, 213p.

Swint, John J. The Parables of the Kingdom; A Course of Lenten Sermons. Milwaukee: Bruce Pub. Co.; London: Coldwell, 1935, 64p.

Sybel, G. A. Super parab. sacr. Tentamen. Halle: 1767.

Talarico, Nicholas A. "Christopher Smart's The Parables of Our Lord: The Architecture of an Enchiridion." Ph.D. thesis. University of Notre Dame, 1977, 242p.

Tambasco, A. "Celebrating the Kingdom in Parables." Bible Today 74 (1974) 81-87.

Täubl, Anton. Gleichnisse Jesu. Ein theologischer Kurs im Medienverbund. Hrsg. von Dieter Emeis und Werner Rück. Mainz: Matthias-Grünewald-Verlag, 1977, 176p.

Taylor, William M. The Parables of Our Saviour Expounded and Illustrated. New York: A. C. Armstrong & Son, 1886. Also, London: Hodder & Stoughton, 1887, 445p. Also, Garden City, N. Y.: Doubleday, Doran, 1929. Also, Grand Rapids, Mich.: Kregal Publications, 1975.

Te Selle, Sallie M. "Learning for the Whole Person: A Model from the Parables of Jesus." Religion in Life 45 (1976) 161-73.

_____. "Parable, Metaphor, and Theology." Journal

of the American Academy of Religion 42 (1974) 630-45.

_____. Speaking in Parables: A Study in Metaphor and Theology. Philadelphia: Fortress Press, 1975, 192p.

_____. "Trial Run; Parable, Poem, and Autobiographical Story." Andover Newton Quarterly 13 (1973) 277-87.

Theilicke, Helmut. Das Bilderbuch Gottes. Reden über die Gleichnisse Jesu. Gütersloh: Gütersloher Verlagshaus, 1959 (1962) (1963) (1964), 235p.

_____. Guds billedbok. Jesu lignelser. Oslo: Land og Kirke, 1961, 239p.

_____. Le parabole del Signore. Torino: Elle Di Ci, 328p.

_____. The Waiting Father; Sermons on the Parables of Jesus. Trans. John W. Doberstein. New York: Harper, 1959, 192p.

Thiersch, H. W. Die Gleichnisse Jesu, nach ihrer moralischen und prophetischen Bedeutung betrachtet. Frankfurt am Main: 1867 (1875).

_____. Jesu Kristi lignelser i deres moralske og profetiske betydning. København: Schiødte, 1873.

Thiselton, A. C. "Parables as Language Event; Some Comments on Fuchs' Hermeneutics in the Light of Linguistic Philosophy." Scottish Journal of Theology 23 (1970) 437-68.

Thomas, Jesse B. Some Parables of Nature in the Light of Today. Cincinnati: Jennings and Graham; New York: Eaton and Mains, 1911, 95p.

Thomason, Bill G. "The Significance of the Johannine Usage of Parabolic Language in Light of the Hebraic Milieu for the Interpretation of the Fourth Gospel." Th. D. thesis, Southwestern Baptist Theological Seminary, 1973.

Thompson, Robert E. Nature, the Mirror of Grace; Studies

of Seven Parables. Philadelphia: Westminster Press, 1907, 134p.

Thomson, William H. The Parables and Their Home: the Parables by the Lake. New York: Harper, 1895, 159p.

Tinsley, E. J. "Parable, Allegory, and Mysticism," in Vindications: Essays on the Historical Basis of Christianity, Anthony Hanson, ed., pp153-92. London: SCM Press, 1966.

_____. "Parable and Allegory; Some Literary Criteria for the Interpretation of the Parables of Christ." Church Quarterly 3 (July 1970) 32-39.

_____. "The Parables and the Self-Awareness of Jesus." Church Quarterly 4 (1971) 18-27.

Titus, Timothy T. On the Parables of Our Lord. Philadelphia: Lutheran Board of Publication, 1871? 115p.

Tolbert, Mary Ann. Perspectives on the Parables: An Approach to Multiple Interpretations. Philadelphia: Fortress Press, 1978, 144p.

Topel, John. "On Being Parabled." Bible Today 87 (1976) 1010-17.

Torrance, T. F. "A Study in New Testament Communication." Scottish Journal of Theology 3 (1950) 298-313.

Toussaint, S. D. "Introductory and Concluding Parables of Matthew Thirteen." Bibliotheca Sacra 121 (1964) 351-55.

Trapp, Willi. Gleichnisse Jesu mit 47 Bildern. Text nach der Züricher Bibel. Bern: Haller, 1964, 25p.

Trench, Richard C. Notes on the Parables of Our Lord. London: 1841 (8th ed. 1860). Condensed ed., New York: D. Appleton, 1861 (1863). 288p. Also, London: Macmillan, 1882. 526p. (66th ed., 1898). Also, Westwood, N. J.: Revell, 1953. 518p.

Trinquet, J. Les Paraboles de jugement. Paris: Ligue Cath. de l'Évangile, 1967, 63p.

Trocmé, Étienne. "Why Parables? A Study of Mark IV."
Bulletin John Rylands Library 59 (1977) 458-71.

Tue desgleichen: Gleichnisse Jesu. Nach dem biblischen
Wort mit Bildern von Alfr. Wittber. Jena: Wartburg
Verlag, 1953, 26p.

Turton, W. H. "Studies in Texts" [Mk. 4:11, 12]. Theology 20 (1930) 228-29.

Unger, A. F. De parabolarum Jesu natura, interpretatione,
usis scholae exegeticae rhetoricae. Leipzig: 1828.

Unterweise mich, Herr, nach Deinem Wort. Gruppenarbeit
unter Jugendlichen über Bibel und Kirche. Hrsg. von
Carl Ernst Sommer. 13. Gleichnisse Jesu. Frankfurt
am Main: Anker-Verlag, 1960, 87p.

Upjohn, William. Discourses on the Parables. Wells:
1824. 3 vols.

Urmy, William S. Lost and Found. Cincinnati: Hitchcock
and Walden; New York: Nelson and Phillips, 1875,
176p.

Vaccari, A. "Historica veritas in parabolis Christi."
Verbum Domini 28 (1950) 351-54.

_____. "La vita reale nelle parabole evangeliche."
Civiltà Cattolica 102 I (1951) 495-506.

Van de gelijkenissen. Reproducties naar bekende meester-
werken. Maassluis: J. Waltman; Hillegon: Uit. -Mij.
"Editio, " 1919.

Van Wyk, William P. My Sermon Notes on Parables and
Metaphors. Grand Rapids, Mich. : Baker Book House,
1947, 110p.

Vergara Tixera, J. "Significado literal de las treinta y
seis parabolas recogidas en los evangelios." Didascalia
15 (1961) 144-55.

Via, Dan O. , Jr. Die Gleichnisse Jesu. Ihre literarische
und existentiale Dimension. Übers. und mit einem

Nachwort von E. Güttgemanns. Beiträge zur evangelischen Theologie 57. München, C. Kaiser, 1970.

_____. "Matthew on the Understandability of the Parables." Journal of Biblical Literature 84 (1965) 430-32.

_____. "Parable and Example Story: A Literary-Structuralist Approach." Linguistica Biblica 25-26 (1973) 21-30; also Semeia 1 (1974) 105-33.

_____. The Parables; Their Literary and Existential Dimension. Philadelphia: Fortress Press, 1967 (1974), 217p.

_____. "A Response to Crossan, Funk, and Petersen." Semeia 1 (1974) 222-35.

Vincent, J. J. "The Parables of Jesus as Self-Revelation," in Studia Evangelica, pp79-99. Berlin: Akademie-Verlag, 1959.

Vitringa, Campegius. Verklaring van de Evangelische Parabolen. Amsterdam: 1715.

Voaden, T. "Reasons for the Parabolic Method of Teaching in the Scriptures." Canadian Methodist Quarterly 3 (1891) 151-62.

Voeltzel, Rene. Les Paraboles du Royaume. Paris: Commission de l'Enseignement Religieux Protestant, 1960.

Vosté, J. M. De natura et interpretatione parabolarum. Roma: Coll. Angelico, 1926, 80p.

_____. Parabolae Selectae D. N. Jesu Christi. Roma: Coll. Angel., 1930-31 (1933). 2 vols.

_____. "De parabolarum fine." Angelicum 7 (1930) 169-209.

Wachler, Günter. Wenn zwei dasselbe tun. Berlin: Evangelische Verlagsanst., 1967, 15p.

Waelkens, Robert. "L'Analyse des paraboles; deux essais: Luc 15, 1-32 et Matthieu 13, 44-46." Revue Théologique de Louvain 8 (1977) 160-78.

Wallace, Ronald S. Many Things in Parables, Expository Studies. Edinburgh: Oliver and Boyd, 1955. Also, New York: Harper, 1956. 218p.

_____. Many Things in Parables [and] The Gospel Miracles. Grand Rapids, Mich.: Eerdmans, 1963, 161p.

_____. "La Parabole et la predication." Bible et Vie Chrétienne 18 (1957) 36-50.

Wallroth, A. F. Die sieben Gleichnisse des Herrn vom Himmelreich, im 13. Capitel des Evangeliums Matthäi, vorgetragen in neun Predigten. Bremen: Raiser, 1842.

Wanner, Walter. Werkbuch Gleichnisse. Praktische Bibelarbeit. Illus. Giessen: Brunnen-Verlag, 1977, 120p.

Waquim, Carmina, Será o começo do fim? Parábolas de Jesus Cristo. Brasílio: Editorial Itiquira, 1976, 93p.

Ward, Roy B. "C. H. Dodd and the Parables of Jesus." Restoration Quarterly 6 (1962) 34-37.

Watson, John. Lessen over de wonderen en gelijkenissen van den Heere Jezus. Naar het Eng. bew. door E. Banger. (Bibliotheek voor zondags-school-onderwijs, No. 5.) Leiden; Rotterdam: D. A. Daamen, 1897.

Weder, Hans. Die Gleichnisse Jesu als Metaphern: Traditions-und redaktionsgeschichtliche Analysen und Interpretationen. Göttingen: Vandenhoeck & Ruprecht, 1978, 312p.

Wehrli, Eugene S. Exploring the Parables. Boston: United Church Press, 1963, 126p.

_____. The Parables of Jesus; A Couse-book for Leaders of Adults. Boston: United Church Press, 1963, 123p.

Weinel, Heinrich. "Die Bildersprache Jesu in ihrer Beleutung für die Erforschung seines inneren Lebens," in Festgrüss Bernhard Stade. W. Diehl et al., ed., pp49-97. Giessen: J. Ricker'sche Verlags-buchhandlung, 1900.

_____. Die Gleichnisse Jesu, 3. Aufl. Leipzig:
B. G. Teubner, 1910 (1918) (1929), 120p.

_____. Jesu Lignelser tilligemed en Vejledn. til
Forstaaelse af Evangelierne. Oversat. af F. Wandall.
København: V. Pio, 1907, 140p.

Weinholt, Karin. "Om det uløste problem i lignelsestalen i
Mark 4," in Nytestamentlige studier. Redigeret af
Sigfred Pedersen, i samarbejde med Søren Giversen og
Hejne Simonsen, pp73-104. Aarhus: Forlaget Aros,
1976.

Weiser, Alfons. Die Knechtsgleichnisse der synoptischen
Evangelien. Diss., Würzburg, 1970. Published,
München: Kösel, 1971, 312p.

Weiss, Johannes. "Die Parabelrede bei Markus." Theologische Studien und Kritiken 64 (1891) 289-321.

Wendland, H. D. "Von den Gleichnissen Jesu und ihrer
Botschaft," in Die Theologin 2 (1941) 17-29.

Wenger, F. "La Parabole, instrument du mystere du règne
de Dieu, selon l'evangile selon S. Marc 4, 10-12."
Diss., Univ. Neuchâtel, 1944.

Wenham, D. "The Composition of Mark 4:1-34." Diss.,
Manchester, 1969-70.

Werdermann, Hermann. Jesu Gleichnisse im Unterricht.
Frankfurt, Berlin: Heliand-Verlag, 1939, 63p.

Wessenberg, Ign. H. Die Parabeln und Gleichnisse des
Herrn vom Reiche Gottes. Ein Volksbuch für alle Zeiten,
2, Ausg. St. Gallen: Scheitlin, 1845.

Weyers, Klaus. Von Perlen, Salz und einem falschen
Schlips: Nachdenkliches zu Bildern der Bibel. Berlin:
Morus-Verlag, 1975, 31p.

White, Ellen G. Christi Gleichnisse. Battle Creek, Mich.,
Atlanta [etc.]: Review & Herald Verlagsgessellschaft,
1901. Also, Hamburg: Interrat. Traktatgesellschaft,
1914. 436p. Also, Hamburg: Saatkorn-Verlag, 1966,
355p.

_____ . Christ's Object Lessons. Oakland, Cal.,
New York: Pacific Press, 1900, 436p. Also, Washington, D. C.: Review and Herald Pub. Assoc., 1923,
444p. (1941, 398p.)

_____ . Christus kommt wider! Bist Du bereit?
Aus dem Buche "Christi Gleichnisse." Wien: Über-
bacher, 1950, 31p.

_____ . Highways to Heaven. Washington, D. C.:
Review and Herald Pub. Assoc., 1952, 384p. [Previous
editions published under title: Christ's Object Lessons.]

_____ . Kristi Lignelser. Battle Creek, Mich.,
Atlanta [etc.]: Review and Herald forlagsforening, 1901.
Also, Kristiania: Dansk Bogforlag, 1905, 436p.

_____ . Paraboles di Notre-Seigneur. Paris: Dam-
marie-les-Lys, 1933, 448p.

Whittemore, Thomas. Notes and Illustrations of the Parables of the New Testament Arranged According to the
Time in Which They Were Spoken. Boston: The Author,
1832, 277p.

Wiberg, Bertil. "Forhaerdelsestanken i evangelierne."
Dansk Teologisk Tidsskrift 21 (1958) 16-23.

_____ . Jesu lignelser. En gennemgang af lignelsfors-
kningen 1900-1950. København: Gad, 1954, 94p.

Wiersbe, Warren. "Preaching from the Parables." Moody
Monthly 78 (1977) 107-09.

Wiessen. "Die Gleichnisserzählungen Jesu als Predigttexte."
Hannoversche Pastoral-Korrespondenz (1896) 18.

_____ . "Die Hermeneutik der Gleichnisserzählungen
Jesu." Beweis des Glaubens 29 (1893) 41-57, 81-93.

_____ . "Schleiermacher's 'Hermeneutik' und die
Parabelfrage." Beweis des Glaubens 33 (1897) 41-63.

Wiles, M. F. "Early Exegesis of the Parables [in the ante-
Nicene Fathers]." Scottish Journal of Theology 11
(1958) 287-301.

Wilkens, W. "Die Redaktion des Gleichniskapitels Mark 4 durch Matth." Theologische Zeitschrift 20 (1964) 304-27.

Williamson, Ronald. "Expressionist Art and the Parables of Jesus." Theology 78 (1975) 474-81.

Wilson, Ella C. New Testament Parables for Children. Illus. by pictures from the masters and original stories. Boston: Unitarian Sunday School Society, 1884. 52p. Second series, 1886. 67p.

Wilson, Ned M. "Interpretation of the Parables in Mark." Ph. D. thesis, Drew University, 1968, 155p.

Windisch, Hans. "Die Verstockungsidee in Mc. 4, 12 und das Kausale ἵνα der späteren Koine." Zeitschrift für die neutestamentliche Wissenschaft 26 (1927) 203-09.

Winternitz, M., Gunkel, H., Bultmann, R. "Gleichnis und Parabel," in Die Religion in Geschichte und Gegenwart 2. Aufl, II, col. 1238-42. Tübingen: J. C. B. Mohr, 1928.

Wissmann, Erw. Die Bergpredigt und die Gleichnisse Jesu im Unterricht. Berlin: Töpelmann, 1939, 106p.

With the Galilean Fishermen (Filmstrip). Eye Gate House, 1963.

Witzmann, Georg. Präparations-Entwürfe zu den Gleichnissen Jesu. Auf Grund seiner Schrift: "Die unterrichtliche Behandlung der Gleichnisse Jesu" bearbeitet. Dresden: Blehl & Kämmerer, 1906, 60p.

_____. Die unterrichtliche Behandlung der Gleichnisse Jesu. Dresden: Blehl & Kämmerer, 1904, 119p.

_____. Zur Frage nach der unterrichtlichen Behandlung der Gleichnisse Jesu. Jena: 1903, 66p.

Wood, H. G. "The Parables of Jesus," in The Abingdon Bible Commentary, pp914-20. New York: Abingdon Press, 1929.

Zedda, S. "Similitudines Evangelii et similitudines S.

Pauli. " Verbum Domini 24 (1944) 88-95, 112-19, 142-50.

Zeegers, P. De parabels van het Evangelie verklaard voor R. K. priesters, religieuzen en leeken. Vrij bewerkt naar het Duitsch van L. Fonck. Leiden: G. F. Théonville, 1906.

Zehrer, Franz. De boodschap der gelijkenissen I. Over God. Boxtel: Kath. Bijbelstichting, 1974, 103p.

_____. Die Botschaft der Parabeln. Wien, Klosterneuburg, München: Klosterneuburger Buch-und-Kunstverlag, 1965 (1966), 130p.

Zoals er gezegd is over: Gelijkenissen en genezingen. Door N. A. Dodeman, D. Flusser, J. van Goudoever, et al. Hilversum: de Haan; Antwerpen: Standaard, 1967, 162p.

(Part II continued)

INDIVIDUAL PARABLES (See pages xxii - xxiv)

THE BARREN FIG TREE

Bunyan, John. The Barren Fig-Tree; Or, the Doom and Downfall of the Fruitless Professor, Shewing that the Day of Grace May Be Past with Him Long before His Life Is Ended, the Syns also by which Such Miserable Mortals May Be Known. Swengel, Pa.: Reiner Publications, 1968, 76p.

_____. Der unfruchtbare Feigenbaum. Lahr-Dinglingen: Verlag der Sankt-Johannis-Druckerei Schweickhardt, 1976, 87p.

Cousin, H. "Le Figuier désséché; un exemple de l'actualisation de la geste évangélique: Marc 11:12-14, 20-25; Matthieu 21:18-22." Foi et Vie Suppl. issue (May 1971) 82-93.

Derrett, J. D. M. "Figtrees in the New Testament." Heythrop Journal 14 (1973) 249-65.

Faccio, H. M. "Die ficu sterili (Lc. 13, 6-9)." Verbum Domini 29 (1951) 233-38.

Giesen, Heinz. "Der verdorrte Feigenbaum--eine symbolische Aussage: zu Mk. 11, 12-14, 20f." Biblische Zeitschrift 20 (1976) 95-111.

Hiltner, S. "Vine-dresser's Point of View [Lk. 13:6-9]." Princeton Seminary Bulletin 64 (Dec. 1971) 71-74.

Kahn, J. G. "La Parabole du figuier stérile et les arbes récalcitrants de la Genèse." Novum Testamentum 13 (1971) 38-45.

"Parable of a Barren Fig Tree." Extension 60 (Jan. 1966) 44.

Young, Franklin W. "Luke 13:1-9." Interpretation 31 (1977) 59-63.

BLIND LEADING THE BLIND

Brückner, Wilhelm. "Über die ursprüngliche Stellung von Luk. 6, 39. 40=Matth. 15, 14; 20, 24. Ein Beitrag zur Evangelienkritik." Theologische Studien und Kritiken 42 (1869) 616-57.

Wallach, Luitpold. "The Parable of the Blind and the Lame." Journal of Biblical Literature 62 (1943) 333-39.

BUDDING FIG TREE

Dupont, Jacques. "La Parabole du figuier qui bourgeonne (Mc. 13, 28s et par.)." Rivista Biblica 75 (1968) 526-48.

Holzmeister, U. "Ab arbore fici discite parabolam (Mt. 24, 32)." Verbum Domini 20 (1940) 299-306.

Löw, Immanuel. "Zum Feigengleichnis." Zeitschrift für die neutestamentliche Wissenschaft 11 (1910) 167-68.

Schütz, Roland. "Das Feigengleichnis der Synoptiker. (Mk. 13, 28f.; Mt. 24, 32f.; Lk. 21, 29-31)." Zeitschrift für die neutestamentliche Wissenschaft 10 (1909) 333-34.

BURGLAR

Betz, O. "The Dichotomized Servant and the End of Judas Iscariot. (Light on the Dark Passages: Matthew 24, 51 and Parallel; Acts 1, 18)." Revue de Qumran 5 (1964) 43-58.

Holzmeister, U. "Das Gleichnis vom Diebe in den Evangelien und beim hl. Paulus (Mt. 24, 43f.; Lc. 12, 39f.; I Thess. 5, 24)." Zeitschrift für katholische Theologie 40 (1916) 704-36.

Smitmans, A. "Das Gleichnis vom Dieb," in Das Wort Gottes in der Zeit. Fest. Karl Hermann Schelkle zum 65.

Geburtstag dargebracht von Kollegen, Freunden, Schülern. Hrsg. von Helmut Feld und Josef Nolte, pp43-68. Düsseldorf: Patmos-Verlag, 1973.

Thibaut, R. "La Parabole du voleur." Nouvelle Revue Theologique 54 (1927) 688-92.

DEFENDANT

Caird, G. B. "Expounding the Parables. I. The Defendant (Matthew 5:25f.; Luke 12:58f.)." Expository Times 77 (1965) 36-39.

DOCTOR AND SICK

Alonso, J. "La parábola del médico en Mc. 2. 16, 17." Cultura Biblica 16 (1959) 10-12.

DRAGNET

Adinolfi, M. "La parabole delle rete e del lievito nel Vangelo di Tommaso (logia 8 e 96)." Studii Biblica Franciscani Liber Annuus 13 (1962) 33-52.

Quispel, G. "Jewish-Christian Gospel Tradition." Anglican Theological Review. Supplementary Studies 3 (1974) 112-16.

Renié, Jules. "Elegerunt bonos in vasa (Mt. XIII, 48)." Recherches de science religieuse 35 (1948) 271-72.

Vos, Johannes G. "The Parable of the Net Full of Fish." Torch and Trumpet 2 (June-July 1952) 32.

EMPTY HOUSE

Nyberg, H. S. "Zum grammatischen Verständnis von Matth. 12, 44-45." Coniectanea Neotestamentica 2, 22-35.

Plummer, Alfred. "The Parable of the Demon's Return." Expository Times 3 (1891-92) 349-51.

FRIEND AT MIDNIGHT

Bornkamm, Günther. "Predigt über Lk. 11, 5-13." Evangelische Theologie 13 (1953) 1-5.

Bryant, H. E. "Note on Luke 11, 17." Expository Times 50 (1938-39) 525-26.

Buzy, Denis. "L'Ami importun (Lc. 11, 5-10)." Revue Apologétique 51 (1930) 303-20.

Derrett, J. Duncan M. "The Friend at Midnight: Asian Ideas in the Gospel of St. Luke," in Donum Gentilicium: New Testament Studies in Honour of David Daube. E. Bammel, C. K. Barrett, W. D. Davies, eds. Oxford: Clarendon Press, 1978, 78-87.

Dimont, C. T. "Children or Servants." Expository Times 9 (1897-98) 382.

Friend in Need, Your Friend Indeed (Filmstrip). Shawnee Mission, Kan.: Marsh Film Enterprises, 1975.

Güttgemanns, Erhardt. "Struktural-generative Analyse der Parabel 'Vom bittenden Freund' (Lk. 11, 5-8)." Linguistica Biblica 2 (1970) 7-11.

Levison, N. "Importunity? (Lc. 11, 8)." Expositor ser 9, 3 (1925) 456-60.

Magass, W., Güttgemanns, E., Bastian, H. "Material zur Parabel 'Vom bittenden Freund' (Lk. 11, 5-8)." Linguistica Biblica 2 (1970) 3-13.

Martin, A. D. "The Parable Concerning Hospitality." Expository Times 37 (1925-26) 411-14.

Rickards, Raymond R. "The Translation of Luke 11:5-13." The Bible Translator 28 (1977) 239-43.

Souter, A. "Children or Servants." Expository Times 9 (1897-98) 382.

Wilhelmsson, Lars. "Keeping at It." Alliance Witness
112:17 (Aug. 24, 1977) 3-5.

Zerwick, M. "Perseverante orare (Lc. 11, 5-13)." Verbum Domini 28 (1950) 243-47.

GOOD SAMARITAN

Der barmherzige Samariter. Hrsg. von Walter Jens.
Stuttgart: Kreuz-Verlag, 1973, 189p.

Den Barmhjertige samaritan. Illustr. av Kees de Kort.
Overs. av Karen Erika og Birger Mathisen. Oslo:
1970, 18p.

Den barmhjertige samaritaner. Dansk bearb.: Halfdan
Høgsbro og Anker Nielsen. Ill. af Kees de Kort.
København: Haase, 1970, 36p.

Bilderdienst für Christenlehre und Gemeinde. Hrsg. von
der Bibelanstalt Altenburg im Auftrag der Erziehung-
skammer der Evang. Kirche in Deutschland, Berliner
Stelle. A. 22. N.T. Das Gleichnis vom barmherzigen
Samariter. [Umschlagt:] Der barmherzige Samariter.
Berlin: Evang. Verlags-Anstalt, 1956.

Binder, Hermann. "Das Gleichnis vom barmherzigen Samariter." Theologische Zeitschrift 15 (1959) 176-94.

Bishop, Eric F. "Down from Jerusalem to Jericho.'"
Evangelical Quarterly 35 (1963) 97-102.

_____. "People on the Road to Jericho; The Good
Samaritan--and the Others." Evangelical Quarterly 42
(1970) 2-6.

Bolech, P. "Il Buon Samaritano e il suo incontro con
l'uomo sofferente in una situazione-limite." Anime e
Corpi 54 (1974) 383-402.

Bowman, John W. "The Parable of the Good Samaritan."
Expository Times 59 (1947-48) 151-53, 248-49.

Brown, Charles R. Two Parables. Chicago, New York:
Revell, 1898, 250p.

Burri, Eduard. Der barmherzige Samariter. Predigt.
Bern: Pestalozzi-Fellenberg-Haus, 1938, 15p.

Buzy, Denis. "Le Bon Samaritain." Revue Apologétique
50 (1930) 550-69.

Carré, Ezechiel. The Charitable Samaritan. A Sermon
on the Tenth Chapter of Luke, ver. 30-35, Pronounced
in the French Church at Boston. Trans. N. Walter.
Boston: Printed by Samuel Green, 1689, 25p.

Castellino, G. R. "Il Sacerdote e il Levita nella parabola
del buon samaritano." Divinitas 9 (1965) 134-40.

Die Christenlehre, year 3 (1950), part 2; Unterrichtshilfe,
21-28 (Lukas 10. 25-37).

Chuckie Chipmunk (Filmstrip). Cathedral Films, 1956.

Condy, Jeremiah. Mercy Exemplified, in the Conduct of a
Samaritan and Recommended to Universal Imitation; A
Sermon Preached at Boston in the Province of Massa-
chusetts-Bay. Salem: Reprinted and sold by S. Hall,
1769, 16p.

Cramer, R. "'Wer ist denn mein Nächster?'" Schule und
Evangelium 5 (1930-31) 255-57.

Cranfield, C. E. B. "The Good Samaritan." Theology
Today 11 (1954) 368-72.

Crespy, Georges. "The Parable of the Good Samaritan:
An Essay in Structural Research." Trans. John Kirby.
Semeia 2 (1974) 27-50.

_____. "La Parabole dite: 'Le bon Samaritain.'
Recherches structurales." Etudes Théologiques et
Religieuses 48 (1973) 61-79.

Crossan, John D. "The Good Samaritan: Towards a Generic Definition of Parable." Semeia 2 (1974) 82-112.

_____. "Parable and Example in the Teaching of
Jesus." Semeia 1 (1974) 63-104.

_____. "Structuralist Analysis and the Parables of
Jesus, a Reply to D. O. Via, Jr." Semeia 1 (1974)
192-221.

Daniel, C. "Les Esséniens et l'arrière-fond historique de la parabole du Bon Samaritain." Novum Testamentum 11 (1969) 71-104.

Danielou, J. "Le Bon Samaritain," in Mélanges bibliques rédigés en l'honneur de André Robert, pp457-65. Paris: Bloud & Gay, 1967.

De Diego, J. R. "Quién es mi prójimo?" Estudios Eclesiásticos 41 (1966) 93-109.

Derrett, J. D. M. "Law in the New Testament: Fresh Light on the Parable of the Good Samaritan." New Testament Studies 11 (1964-65) 22-37.

Diamond, Lucy. Due racconti di Gesù. Illus. Kenneth Inns. Beatenberg: Edizione Scuola biblica, 1967, 52p.

_____. Zwei Geschichten, die Jesus erzählt hat. Illus. Kenneth Inns. Beatenberg: Verlag Bibelschule, 1967, 51p.

Doherty, J. "Oil and Wine for a Wounded Traveler." Liguorian 51 (Jan. 1963) 44-49.

Dorcy, M. "To Be Samaritans All." Review for Religious 24 (1965) 201-08.

Eichholz, Georg. Jesus Christus und der Nächste. Eine Auslegung des Gleichnisses vom Barmherzigen Samariter. Neukirchen/Krs Moers: Buchhandlung des Erziehungsvereins, 1955, 48p.

Ewing, W. "The Remedies of the Good Samaritan." Expositor 49 ser. 8, 26 (1923) 79.

Eynde, P. van den. "Le Bon Samaritain." Bible et Vie Chrétienne 70 (1966) 22-35.

Funk, Robert W. "The Good Samaritan as Metaphor." Semeia 2 (1974) 74-81.

_____. "How Do You Read?" A Sermon on Luke 10:25-37. Interpretation 18 (1964) 25-37.

_____. "The Old Testament in Parable; A Study of Luke 10, 25-37." Encounter 26 (1965) 251-67.

Furness, J. M. "Fresh Light on Luke 10:25-37." Expository Times 80 (1969) 182.

De Gelijkenis van den barmhartigen Samarien de nood der maatschappij. Met een voorwoord van J. H. Gunning. Groningen: G. J. Reits, 1872.

Gerhardsson, Birger. The Good Samaritan--the Good Shepherd? Conictanea Neotestamentica XVI. Lund: Gleerup; Copenhagen: Munksgaard, 1958.

Ghio, Giac. La parabola del buon Samaritano (Luca X, 25-37). Genova: Tip. della Gioventù, 1913, 59p.

Gholson, Edward. From Jerusalem to Jericho. Boston: Chapman & Grimes, 1943, 122p.

Giavini, G. "Il 'prossimo' nella parabola del buon samaritano." Rivista Biblica 12 (1964) 419-21.

Gollwitzer, Helmut. Das Gleichnis vom barmherzigen Samariter. Neukirchen: Neukirchener Verlag, 1962, 111p.

The Good Neighbor (Motion picture). American Bible Society, 1969? Released by Association Films. Features the felt pen sketches of artist Annie Vallotton.

The Good Samaritan (Filmstrip). Cathedral Films, 1947.

_____. Religious Films, London, 1949.

_____. Church-Craft Pictures, 1953.

_____. Eye Gate House, 1963.

_____. Roa's Films, 1966.

The Good Samaritan (Motion picture). Harmon Foundation, n. d.

_____. Religious Films, London, 1939.

_____. Religious Films, London, 1946. Released in the U. S. by United World Films, 1948.

_____. Loyola Films in cooperation with Cathedral

Films, 1948.

_____ . Broadcasting and Film Commission, 1951.
Made by Everett Parker.

Gordon, James C. "The Parable of the Good Samaritan
(St. Luke X. 25-37)." Expository Times 56 (1944-45)
302-04.

Governanti, G. 'Il Khan del buon Samaritano." Terra
Santa 22 (1947) 49-54.

Grasse, James D. Is that my Neighbor? (16 min.)
Thesis Theological Cassettes 8 No. 11 (Dec. 1977).

Gyllenberg, Rafael. "Den barmhärtige Samariten," in
Svensk Exegetisk Årsbok 12 (1947) 163-74. Also in
Professor Johannes Lindblom, Lund, på hans 65-årsdag
den 7 juni 1947, pp147-58. Uppsala: Wretmans bok-
trycheri A. -B., 1948.

Halévy, Joseph. "Sens et origine de la parabole évangélique dite du bon Samaritain," in Mélanges de critique
et d'histoire, relatifs aux peuples sémitiques, pp234-
40. Paris: Maisonneuve, 1883.

Henry, H. T. "The Good Samaritan." Homiletic and
Pastoral Review 38 (1937-38) 1134-42.

Hermann, I. "Wem ich der Nächste bin. Auslegung von
Lk. 10, 25-37." Bibel und Leben 2 (1961) 17-24.

Heuschen, J. "De parabel van de barmhartige Samaritaan."
Revue Ecclésiastique de Liège 46 (1959) 153-64.

Huber, Max. Der barmherzige Samariter. Betrachtungen
über Evangelium und Rotkreuzarbeit. Nürnberg: Verlag
Die Egge, 1947, 72p.

Imschoot, P. van "Le Bon Samaritain." Collationes Gandavenses 19 (1932) 171-76.

Inman, R. Johnson. "Interpretation through Reading."
Review and Expositor 34 (1937) 315-17.

Jursch, Hanna. Das Gleichnis vom barmherzigen Samariter
in seiner Deutung durch Rembrandt. Berlin: Evang.

318 / Good Samaritan

Verlag Anst., 1952, 16p.

Kahlefeld, H. "'Wer ist mein Nachster?' Das Lehrstück
vom barmherzigen Samariter und die heutige Situation."
Bibel und Kirche 24 (1969) 74-77.

Keller, Gottfried. Das barmherzige Samariter. Büchlein
zum Betrachten und Malen. Geschrieben vom Gottfried
Keller. Gez. von Alfred Kobel. Bern: Blaukreuzverlag,
1957, 8p.

Klemm, Hans G. "Das Gleichnis vom Barmherzigen Samariter. Formkritik auslegungsgeschichte Auslegung."
Diss., Erlangen, 1967.

_____. Das Gleichnis vom barmherzigen Samariter:
Grundzüge der Auslegung im 16. /17. Jahrhundert.
Stuttgart, Berlin, Köln, Mainz: Kohlhammer, 1973,
184p.

Kramer, Janice. The Good Samaritan: Luke 10:25-37 for
Children. Illus. Sally Matthews. St. Louis: Concordia Pub. House, 1964, 32p.

Lambrecht, Jan. "De Barmhartige Samaritaan (Lk. 10, 25-
37)." Ons Geestelijk Leven 51 (1974) 91-105.

_____. "The Message of the Good Samaritan."
Louvain Studies 5 (1974) 121-35.

Leenhardt, F. J. "La Parabole du Samaritain. (Schéma
d'une exégèse existentialiste)," in Aux sources de la
tradition chrétienne. Mélanges M. Goguel, pp132-38.
Neuchâtel-Paris: Delachaux & Niestle, 1950.

Liempd, C. A. von "Parabola boni Samaritani." Verbum
Domini 11 (1931) 262.

Lindijer, C. H. "Oude en eieuwe visies op de gelijkenis
van de barmhartige Samaritaan." Nederlands theologisch tijdschrift 15 (1960) 11-23.

McCorry, V. "The Parable of the Good Samaritan."
America 111 (Aug. 8, 1964) 144.

Maiworm, J. "Der mystische Samaritan (Lk. 10, 33-36)."
Theologie und Glaube (1948) 362-64.

Mann, J. "Jesus and the Sadducean Priests: Luke 10:25-37." Jewish Quarterly Review 6 (1914) 415-22.

Masson, W. J. "The Parable of the Good Samaritan." Expository Times 48 (1936-37) 179-81.

Mattill, A. J., Jr. "The Good Samaritan and the Purpose of Luke Acts. Halévy Reconsidered." Encounter 33 (1972) 359-76.

Maura, Bertram. "Luke X, 25-37." Expository Times 58 (1946-47) 168.

Mazzolari, Primo. Il Samaritano. Brescia: Gatti, 1938, 215p.

Monselewski, Werner. Der barmherzige Samariter. Eine auslegungsgeschichtliche Untersuchung zu Lukas 10, 25-37. Diss. Münster, 1965; Tübingen: Mohr (Siebeck), 1967, 205p.

Mussner, Franz. "Der Begriff des 'Nächsten' in der Verkündigung Jesu. Dargelegt am Gleichnis vom barmherzigen Samariter," in Mussner, Praesentia Salutis, pp125-32; Düsseldorf: Patmos-Verlag, 1967. Also in Trierer theologische Zeitschrift 64 (1955) 91-99.

Nixon, Joan L. Who Is My Neighbor: The Good Samaritan for Beginning Readers: Luke 10:29-37 for Children. Ills. Aline Cunningham. St. Louis: Concordia Pub. House, 1976.

Patte, Daniel. "An Analysis of Narrative Structure and the Good Samaritan." Semeia 2 (1974) 1-26.

_____. "Structural Network in Narrative: The Good Samaritan." Soundings 58 (1975) 221-42.

Pohl, Hertha. Der barmherzige Samaritan. Ein Volksspiel. Freiburg i. Br.: Werthmannhaus: Dt. Caritasverband, 1950, 16p.

Preiswerk, Hans. Der barmhärzige Samariter. Biblisches Laienspiel in Dialekt in 5 Szenen nach Luk. 10, 30-35. Basel: Brunnen-Verlag, 1948, 16p.

Provera, M. "La parabola del Buon Samaritano." Terra

Santa 50 (1974) 109-13.

Rade, Martin. "Der Nächste," in Festgabe für Adolf Jülicher zum 70. Geburtstag. Hrsg. Rudolf Bultmann und Hans von Soden, pp70-79. Tübingen: J. C. B. Mohr, 1927.

Ramaroson, Léonard. "Comme 'Le Bon Samaritain,' ne chercher qu'à aimer (Lc. 10, 29-37)." Biblica 56 (1975) 533-36.

Reicke, B. "Der barmherzige Samariter, in Festschrift für G. Stählin, pp103-09. Wuppertal: Brockhaus, 1970.

Richelsen, John. A Certain Samaritan. New York: Broadway Pub. Co., 1911, 108p.

Runge, Max. Der barmherzige Samariter. Ein biblisches Spiel. München: Kaiser, 1956, 70p.

A Samaritan Helps a Traveler (Filmstrip). Double Sixteen Co., 1966.

Sanchis, Dominique. "Samaritanus ille: L'Exegèse augustinienne de la parabole du bon samaritain." Recherches de Science Religieuse 49 (1961) 406-25.

Schick, Erich. Der Alltag vor Gott. 4. Sei ein Nächster! Eine Besinnung über die Geschichte vom barmherzigen Samariter. Hamburg: Furche-Verlag, 1957, 105p.

Sellin, Gerhard. "Lukas als Gleichniserzähler; die Erzahlung vom barmherzigen Samariter, Lk. 10: 25-37." Zeitschrift für die Neutestamentliche Wissenschaft 65 (1974) 166-89; 66 (1975) 19-60.

Silva, R. "La parábola del buen samaritano (Lc. 10, 29-37)." Cultura Bíblica 23 (1966) 234-40.

Skov, H. "Den barmhjertige samaritaner." Dansk Udsyn 45 (1963) 281-88.

Smith, T. C. "The Parable of the Samaritan." Review and Expositor 47 (1950) 434-41.

Souter, Alex. "Interpretations of Certain New Testament Passages." Expositor 8th ser., 8 (1914) 94.

Spicq, C. "The Charity of the Good Samaritan, Luke 10: 25-37." Bible Today 6 (1963), 360-66; Also in Contemporary New Testament Studies, pp218-24. Collegeville, Minn.: Liturgical Press, 1965.

Stein, Robert H. "The Interpretation of the Parable of the Good Samaritan," in Scripture, Tradition, and Interpretation: Essays Presented to Everitt F. Harrison by his Students and Colleagues in Honor of his Seventy-fifth Birthday. Edited by W. Ward Gasque and William Sanford LaSor, pp278-95. Grand Rapids; Eerdmans, 1977.

Stiefvater, Alois. Der barmherzige Samariter heute. Bonn: Verlag des Borromäus-Vereins, 1946, 24p.

Stockum, T. C. van. "Vijf variaties op een thema; Schiller en de gelijkenis van de barmhartige Samaritaan." Nederlands Theologisch Tijdschrift 17 (1963) 338-47.

Szepánski, L. "'Homo quidam descendebat ab Ierusalem un Iericho' (Lc. 10. 30)." Verbum Domini 1 (1921) 315-17.

Trudinger, L. Paul. "Once again now, 'Who Is my Neighbor?'" Evangelical Quarterly 48 (1976) 160-63.

Vail, A. L. "The Good Samaritan as a Text." Review and Expositor 21 (1924) 309-21.

Via, Dan O., Jr. "Parable and Example Story; A Literary-Structuralist Approach." Semeia 1 (1974) 105-33.

Walter Fish--a Modern Adult Parable (Motion picture). Alba House Communications, 1971. Made by WITF-TV.

Walter Fish: A Parable (Filmstrip). Canfield, Ohio: Alba House Communications, 1976.

Who Is My Neighbor? (Motion picture). Cathedral Films, 1943.

Wilhelm, W. "The New Covenant of Grace; Homily for the Twelfth Sunday after Pentecost." Homiletic and Pastoral Review 64 (1964) 872-74.

Wilkinson, Frank H. "Oded: Proto-Type of the Good Samaritan." Expository Times 69 (1957) 94.

Williams, H. The Good Samaritan: Addresses on the Parable. London: Mowbray, 1926, 50p.

Young, Norman H. "Once again, now, 'Who Is My Neighbor?' A Comment." Evangelical Quarterly 49 (1977) 178-79.

Zerwick, M. "The Good Samaritan." The Furrow 6 (1955) 291-95.

_____. "Homo quidam descendebat ab Ierusalem in Iericho." Verbum Domini 27 (1949) 55-59.

Zimmerman, H. "Das Gleichnis vom barmherzigen Samariter: Lk. 10, 25-37," in Die Zeit Jesu: Festschrift für H. Schlier, pp58-69. Hrsg. G. Bornkamm & K. Rahner. Freiburg, Basel, Wien: Herder, 1970.

HID TREASURE

Bishop, Eric F. F. "Θησαυρῷ κεκρυμμένῳ ἐν τῷ ἀγρῷ (Mt. XIII. 44) σκάψω περὶ αὐτὴν (Lk. XIII. 8)." Expository Times 65 (1953-54) 287.

Charles, R. H. "Two Parables: A Study." Expository Times 35 (1923-24) 265-69.

Dauvillier, J. "La Parabole du trésor et les droits orientaux." Revue internationale des droits de l'antiquité 3e Série. 4 (1957) 107-15.

Derrett, J. D. M. "Law in the New Testament; The Treasure in the Field (Mt. XII:44)." Zeitschrift für die neutestamentliche Wissenschaft 54 (1963) 31-42.

Didier, M. "Les Paraboles du trésor et de la perle (Mt. 13, 44ss)." Revue Diocésaine de Namur 16 (1962) 296-302.

Dupont, Jacques. "Les Paraboles du trésor et de la perle." New Testament Studies 14 (1968) 408-18.

Faccis, Hyac. "De Thesauro abscondito (Mt. 13:44)."

Verbum Domini 28 (1950) 237-42.

Fenton, J. C. "Expounding the Parables: IV. The Parables of the Treasure and the Pearl (Mt. 13:44-46)." Expository Times 77 (1966) 178-80.

Kulp, Hans. "Der Schatz im Acker." Evangelische Theologie 13 (1953-54) 145-49.

Kunze, J. "Das Gleichnis von Schatz im Acker und von der köstlichen Perle." Zeitschrift für den evangelischen Religionsunterricht (1893) 53-59.

Magass, W. "'Der Schatz im Acker' (Mt. 13, 44): Von der Kirche als einem Tauschphänomen--Paradigmatik und Transformation." Linguistica Biblica 21 (1973) 2-18.

Metcalfe, W. M. "The Twin Parables." Expositor 2nd ser., 8 (1884) 54-67.

Noack, B. "En konstrueret lignelse. Refereret og kritiseret." Dansk Teologisk Tidsskrift 26 (1963) 238-43.

Paterson, W. P. "The Parables of the Treasure and the Pearl." Expository Times 38 (1926-27) 261-64, 295-99.

Pousset, É. "Le trésor et la perle." Vie Chrétienne 173 (1975) 12-16.

Rossaro, Piero. "La parabola del tesoro e il diritto orientale." Rivista biblica 8 (1960) 365-66.

Tonkin, S. "The Parable of the Hidden Treasure and of the Pearl Merchant (Matt. 13:44ff.)." Expository Times 33 (1921-22) 330-31.

Weir, T. H. "The Parable of the Hid Treasure." Expository Times 29 (1917-18) 523.

HOUSEHOLDER

Dupont, Jacques. "Nova et Vetera," in L'Évangélique hier et aujourd'hui. Mel. F. J. Leenhardt, pp55-63. Genève: Labor et Fides, 1968.

Hoh, Joseph. "Die christliche γραμματεὺς (Mt. 13, 52)." Biblische Zeitschrift 17 (1925-26) 256-69.

Lüthi, Walter. Das Gleichnis vom Shriftgelehrten. Predigt über Matth. 13, 51-52, gehalten im Berner Münster. Basel: Reinhardt, 1948, 15p.

LABORERS IN VINEYARD

Arvedson, Tomas. "Några notiser till två nytestamentliga perikoper. I. Mt. 20, 1ff." Svensk Exegetisk Årsbok 21 (1956) 27-28.

Aveling, F. W. "The Parable of the Labourers in the Vineyard." Expository Times 5 (1893-94) 549-51.

Bauer, Johannes Bapt. "Gnadelohn oder Tageslohn?" Biblica 42 (1961) 224-28.

Bergmann, P. "Das Gleichnis von den Arbeitern im Weinberge, Mt. 20, 1-16." Katachetische Blätter 30 (1929) 376-409.

Cholmondeley, F. G. "The Parable of the Labourers in the Vineyard." Expository Times 6 (1894-95) 137-40.

Connor, Charles. "The Hire of the Labourers in the Vineyard." Expository Times 21 (1890-91) 261-63.

Couturier, M. A. "Dieu n'est injuste qu'envers luimême." Vie Spirituelle 106 (1962) 421-27.

Curtis, W. A. "The Parable of the Labourers, Matt. XX, 1-16." Expository Times 38 (1926-27) 6-10.

_____. "The Parable of the Labourers," in Festgabe für Adolf Jülicher zum 70. Geburtstag, Hrsg. Rudolf Bultmann und Hans von Soden, pp61-69. Tübingen: J. C. B. Mohr, 1927.

De Raucourt, Gaëtan. "Les Ouvriers de la onzième heure." Recherches de Science Religieuse 25 (1935) 492-95.

Derrett, J. D. M. "Workers in the Vineyard; A Parable of Jesus." Journal of Jewish Studies 25 (1974) 64-91.

De Ru, G. "Conception of Reward in the Teaching of Jesus." Novum Testamentum 8 (1966) 202-22.

Dupont, Jacques. "L'Evangile (du Dimanche de la Septuagésime) (Mt. 20, 1-16): Les Ouvriers de la vigne." Assemblées du Seigneur 22 (1965) 28-51.

_____. "La Parabole des ouvriers de la vigne (Matthieu XX, 1-16)." Nouvelle Revue Théologique 79 (1957) 785-97.

Edwards, W. C. The Parable of the Householder (Mt. 20, 1-16) Prophetically Considered. London: Thynne and Jarvis, 1927, 8p.

Eichholz, Georg. Das gnädige Recht Gottes und die Freiheitsidee des Menschen, 2. Beiträge aus der Arbeit der Kirchlichen Hochschule Wuppertal. Hrsg. von Arnold Falkenroth. Neukirchen-Vluyn: Neukirchener Verlag des Erziehungsvereins, 1967, 68p.

Faust, A. H. In parabolam de operariis in vinea. Cogitationes Helmstadii: 1725.

Feuillet, André. "Les Ouvriers de la vigne et la théologie d l'alliance." Recherches de Science Religieuse 34 (1947) 303-27.

Fonck, Leopold. "Operarii in vinea (Mt. 20, 1-16)." Verbum Domini 4 (1924) 33-40.

Fuchs, Ernst. "Das Wunder der Güte. Predigt über Matth. 20. 1-16," in Glaube und Erfahrung. Gesammelte Aufsätze. III, pp471-79. Tübingen: Mohr (Siebeck), 1965.

Glasswell, M. E. "The Labourers in the Vineyard (Matthew 20:1-16)." Communio Viatorum 19 (1976) 61-64.

The Good Employer (Filmstrip). Roa's Films, 1966.

Gregg, John A. F. "A Study of the Parable of the Labourers in the Vineyard." Expository Times 30 (1918-19) 422-24.

Gryglewicz, F. "The Gospel of the Overworked Workers." Catholic Biblical Quarterly 19 (1957) 190-98.

_____ . "Nauczanie Chrystusa Pana w przypowieŝ-
ciach o robotnikach w winnicy i o synu marnotrawnym. "
Roczniki Teologiczno-Kanoniczne 7

Hassett, J. "Septuagesima Sunday. " Irish Ecclesiastical
Record 103 (1965) 46-48.

Hatch, William H. P. "A Note on Matthew 20:15. " Anglican Theological Review (1944) 250-53.

Hauck, E. "Das Gleichnis von den Arbeitern im Weinberg. "
Pädagogische Warte 39 (1932) 397-99.

Heinemann, H. "The Conception of Reward in Mat. XX, 1-
16. " Journal of Jewish Studies 1 (1948-49) 85-89.

Hill, F. T. "The Parable of the Labourers in the Vineyard. "
Expositor 1st ser. , 3 (1876) 427-32.

Holzmeister, Urban. "Zum Gleichnis von den Arbeitern im
Weinberg (Mt. 20, 1-16). " Zeitschrift für katholische
Theologie 52 (1928) 407-12.

Kiesling, J. R. Dissertatio philogica de procuratione in
vinea Domini ad illustrandam Evang. Mt. XX, 8. Lipsiae: 1740.

Ledrus, M. "Il salario evangelico (nella parabola dei brac-
cianti: Mt. 20, 1-16). " Palestra del Clero 50 (1971)
14-27.

Loeffler, F. S. Explanatio parabolae de operariis in vinea.
Lipsiae: 1726.

McCorry, V. "Christ's Lordship over Man. " America
108 (Feb. 9, 1963) 210.

McIntyre, B. "Septuagesima Sunday; Laborers in the Vineyard. " Homiletic and Pastoral Review 36 (1936) 434-
37.

Mayser, F. P. "The Parable of the Laborers in the Vineyard. " Lutheran Church Review 21 (1902) 388-97.

Mitton, C. L. "Expounding the Parables; The Workers in
the Vineyard (Matt. 20: 1-16). " Expository Times 77
(1966) 307-11.

Mosheim, J. L. Meditatio in parabolam de operariis in vinea. Duisburg: 1724.

Mouson, J. "Explicatur parabola de operariis in vineam missis (Mt. XX. 1-16)." Collectanea Mechliniensia 42 (1957) 611-15.

Nelson, Diedrick A. "An Exposition of Matthew 20:1-16." Interpretation 29 (1975) 288-92.

Oesterley, W. O. E. "The Parable of the Labourers in the Vineyard." Expositor 7th ser., 5 (1908) 333-43.

Orbe, A. "S. Ireneo y la parábola de los oberos de la viña: Mt. 20, 1-16." Estudios Eclesiasticos 46 (1971) 46 (1971) 35-62.

Poort, J. J. De arbeiders in de wijngaard. Utrecht: De Banier, 1967, 89p.

Rupprecht, Johann M. "Die Parabel von den Arbeitern im Weinberge. Matth. 20, 1-16." Theologische Studien und Kritiken 20 (1847) 396-416.

Sanday, W. "The Parable of the Labourers in the Vineyard." Expositor 1st ser., 3 (1876) 81-101.

Schildenberger, J. "Das Gleichnis von den Arbeitern im Weinberg (Mt. 20, 1-16)." Benediktinische Monatsschrift zur Pflege religiösen und geistigen Lebens 25 (1949) 55-58.

Schramm, J. H. Dissertatio de operariis in vinea. Jenae: 1775.

Spies, Otto. "Die Arbeiter im Weinberg (Mt. 20: 1-15) in islamischer Überlieferung." Zeitschrift für die neutestamentliche Wissenschaft 66 (1975) 279-83.

Steffensen, H. "Die Parabel von den Arbeitern im Weinberge." Theologische Studien und Kritiken 21 (1848) 686-90.

Sutcliffe, E. "Many Are Called but Few Are Chosen." Irish Theological Quarterly 28 (1961) 126-31.

Toohey, W. "What Kind of a God Is God? Homily for Septuagesima Sunday." Homiletic and Pastoral Review 65 (1965) 335-36.

Trench, Richard C. On the Parable of the Labourers in the Vineyard: A Letter to the Most Rev. the Lord Archbishop of Dublin. London: Thomas Bosworth, 1866, 15p.

Vargha, Th. "Operarii in vinea (Mt. 20, 1-16)." Verbum Domini 8 (1928) 302-04.

Weiss, Karl. Die Frohbotschaft Jesu über Lohn und Vollkommenheit. Zur evangelischen Parabel von Arbeiterern im Weinberg, Mt. 20, 1-16. Münster: Aschendorffsche Verlh., 1927, 244p.

Wenker, W. "Alcance de Mt. 20, 1-16 en labios de Jesús." Revista Bíblica 26 (1964) 140-45.

Wilke, C. G. "Über die Parabel von den Arbeitern im Weinberg, Matth. 20, 1-16." Zeitschrift für wissenschaftliche Theologie 1 (1826) 71-109.

Williams, W. J. "The Parable of the Laborers in the Vineyard (Matt. XX, 1-16)." Expository Times 50 (1938-39) 526.

Wolf, E. "Gottesrecht und Nächstenrecht. Rechtstheologische Exegese des Gleichnisses von den Arbeiten im Weinberg (Mt. 20, 1-16)," in Gott in Welt. Festgabe für K. Rahner, II, pp640-62. Freiburg, Basel, Wien: Herder, 1964.

Zulich, F. A. Meditatio ad Parabolam de Operariis in Vinea. Jenae: 1740.

LAMP AND BUSHEL

Bover, José M. "Nada hay encubierto que no se descubra.'" Estudios Bíblicos 13 (1954) 319-23.

Dupont-Sommer, A. "Note archéologique sur le proverbe évangélique: Mettre la lampe sous le boisseau," in Mélanges Syriens-Dussaud II, pp789-94. Paris: Geuthner, 1939.

Huby, Joseph. "Sur un passage du second évangile (Marc

IV, 21-25)." Recherches de Science Religieuse 1 (1910) 168-74.

Kennedy, H. A. A. "The Composition of Mark IV, 21-25: A Study in the Synoptic Problem." Expository Times 25 (1913-14) 301-05.

LAST JUDGMENT

Bartlett, David L. "An Exegesis of Matthew 25: 31-46." Foundations 19 (1976) 211-13.

Bligh, P. H. "Eternal Fire, Eternal Punishment, Eternal Life (Mt. 25:41, 46)." Expository Times 82 (1970) 137-42, 83 (1971) 9-11.

Booth, Charles E. "An Exegesis of Matthew 25: 31-46." Foundations 19 (1976) 214-15.

Bornhäuser, Karl. "Zur Auslegung von Matthäus 25, 31-46." Luthertum 2 (1935) 77-82.

Burney, C. F. "St. Matthew XXV, 31-46 as a Hebrew Poem." Journal of Theological Studies 14 (1912-13) 414-24.

Cadoux, A. T. "The Parable of the Sheep and the Goats (Mt. XXV, 31-46)." Expository Times 41 (1929-30) 559-62.

Christian, Paul. Jesus und seine geringsten Brüder: Mt. 25, 31-46 redaktionsgeschichtlich untersucht. Leipzig: St.-Benno-Verlag, 1975, 108p.

Cope, L. "Matthew 25:31-46, 'The Sheep and the Goats' Reinterpreted." Novum Testamentum 11 (1969) 32-44.

Dehn, G. "Das jüngste Gericht. Praktische Exegese von Matth. 25, 31-46." Monatsschrift für Pastoraltheologie 26 (1930) 274-80.

Friedrich, Johannes. Gott im Bruder? eine methoden-kritische Untersuchung von Redaktion, Überlieferung und Traditionen in Mt. 25, 31-46. Stuttgart: Calwer Verlag, 1977, 524p.

Gewalt, D. "Mt. 25, 31-46 im Erwartungshorizont heutiger Exegese." Linguistica Biblica 25/26 (1973) 9-21.

Gross, G. "Die 'geringsten Brüder' Jesu in Mt. 25, 40 in Auseinandersetzung mit der neueren Exegese." Bibel und Leben 5 (1964) 172-80.

Ingelaere, Jean-Claude. "La Parabole du jugement dernier (Matthieu 25:31-46)." Revue d'Histoire et de Philosophie Religieuses 50 (1970) 23-60.

Lago Toinsil, M. "'Allora il re dirà...' Cristo re in Mt. 25, 31-46." Palestra del Clero 47 (1968) 1318-21.

Leitzmann, Hans. "Matthaeus 25, 34 in den Freisinger Denkmälern," in Kleine Schriften II, Texte und Untersuchungen, 68, pp189-90. Berlin: Akademie-Verlag, 1958.

Lock, W. "The Sheep and the Goats." Expositor 5th ser., 10 (1899) 401-12.

McHardy, W. D. "Matthew XXV, 37-XXVI in 074." Journal of Theological Studies 46 (1945) 190-91.

Maddox, R. "Who Are the 'Sheep' and the 'Goats?' A Study of the Purpose and Meaning of Matthew XXV:31-46." Australian Biblical Review 13 (Dec. 1965) 19-28.

Manék, J. "Mit wem identifiziert sich Jesus? Eine exegetische Rekonstruktion ad Mt. 25:31-46," in Christ and Spirit in the New Testament. Edited by Barnabas Lindars and Stephen S. Smalley in honour of Charles Francis Digby Moule, pp15-25. Cambridge, England: Cambridge University Press, 1973.

Mattill, A. J., Jr. "Matthew 25:31-46 Relocated." Restoration Quarterly 17 (1974) 107-14.

Meloni, Gerardo. "Overs et haedi," in Saggi di filologia semitica, pp265-73. Roma: Casa Ed. Italiana, 1913.

Michaels, J. R. "Apostolic Hardships and Righteous Gentiles. A Study of Matthew 25, 31-46." Journal of Biblical Literature 84 (1965) 27-37.

Minear, Paul S. "The Coming of the Son of Man." Theology Today 9 (1953) 489-93.

Mitton, C. Leslie. "Present Justification and Final Judgment; A Discussion of the Parable of the Sheep and the Goats." Expository Times 68 (1957) 46-50.

Nagano, Paul M. "An Exegesis of Matthew 25:31-46." Foundations 19 (1976) 216-22.

Oudersluys, R. C. "The Parable of the Sheep and Goats (Matthew 25:31-46); Eschatology and Mission, Then and Now." Reformed Review 26 (1973) 151-61.

Pikaza, J. "Mt. 25, 31-46 y la teología de la liberación." Cultura Bíblica 31 (1974) 27-28.

Rennes, J. "A propos de Mt. 25, 34-46." Études théologiques et religieuses 44 (1969) 233f.

Robinson, J. A. T. "The 'Parable' of the Sheep and the Goats." New Testament Studies 2 (1956) 225-37.

Smith, T. C. "An Exegesis of Matthew 25:31-46." Foundations 19 (1976) 206-10.

Thebeau, Duane H. "On Separating Sheep from Goats." Christianity Today 16 (1972) 1040-41.

Turner, H. E. W. "Expounding the Parables; The Parable of the Sheep and the Goats (Matthew 25:31-46)." Expository Times 77 (1966) 243-46.

Veldhuizen, A. van "Schappen en bokken (Mt. 25, 32)." Nieuwe Theologische Studiën 6 (1923) 6.

Wilckens, Ulrich. "Gottes geringste Brüder--zu Mt. 25, 31-46," in Jesus und Paulus. Festschrift für Werner Georg Kümmel zum 70. Geburtstag. Hrsg. von E. Earle Ellis und Erich Grässer, pp363-83. Göttingen: Vandenhoeck & Ruprecht, 1975.

Wilcock, John. "St. Matt. XXV, 36; 2 Tim. I, 16-18." Expository Times 34 (1922-23) 43.

Wilkenhauser, Alfred. "Die Liebeswerke in dem Gerichtsgemälde Mt. 25, 31-46." Biblische Zeitschrift 20 (1932) 366-77.

Winandy, J. "La Scène du Jugement Dernier (Mt. 25, 31-

46)." Sciences Ecclesiastiques 18 (1966) 169-86.

LEAVEN

Adinolfi, M. "La parabole delle rete e del lievito nel Vangelo di Tommaso (logia 8 e 96)." Studii Biblica Franciscani Liber Annuus 13 (1962) 33-52.

Aiken, W. "A Continental Divide in Scripture Interpretation (Matthew 13, 33). The Parable of the Leaven." Bibliotheca Sacra 95 (1938) 219-30.

Allis, O. T. "The Parable of the Leaven." Evangelical Quarterly 19 (1947) 254-73.

Didier, M. "Les Paraboles du grain de sénevé et du levain." Revue Diocésaine de Namur 15 (1961) 385-94.

Dupont, Jacques. "Le Couple parabolique du Seneve et du Levain," in Jesus Christus in Historie und Theologie: Neutestamentliche Festschrift für Hans Conzelmann zum 60. Geburtstag. Hrsg. Georg Strecker, pp331-45. Tübingen: J. C. B. Mohr, 1975.

_____. "Les Paraboles du seneve et du levain." Nouvelle Revue Theologique 89 (1967) 897-913.

Funk, Robert W. "Beyond Criticism in Quest of Literacy: The Parable of the Leaven." Interpretation 25 (1971) 149-70.

Jehle, Fr. "Senfkorn und Sauerteig in der Hl. Schrift." Neue Kirchliche Zeitschrift 34 (1923) 713-19.

Kuss, O. "Zum Sinngehalt des Doppelgleichnisses vom Senfkorn und Sauerteig," in Auslegung und Verkündingung I, pp85-97. Regensburg: Pustet, 1963. Also in Biblica 40 (1959) 641-53.

Liese, H. "Fermentum (Mt. 13, 33; Lc. 13, 20s.)." Verbum Domini 13 (1933) 341-46.

Michaelis, Wilhelm. "Die Gleichnisse vom Senfkorn und

vom Sauerteig. " Kirchenfreund 72 (1938) 118-21, 129-
36.

The Mustard Seed and the Leaven (Filmstrip). Roa's Films,
1966.

Pousset, É. "Le sénéve et le levain. " Vie Chrétienne 174
(1975) 13-16.

Straubinger, J. "El simbolismo de la levadura. " Revista
Teologica (La Plata) 2 (1952) 11-21.

Ziener, G. "Das Wort von Sauerteig. " Trierer Theologische
Zeitschrift 67 (1958) 247.

LOST COIN

Cantinat, J. "L'Évangile (du 3e Dimanche après la Pentecôte) (Lc. 15, 1-10): La brebis et la drachme perdues. " Assemblées du Seigneur 57 (1965) 24-38.

Dods, M. "The Lost Sheep and Lost Piece of Money. "
Expositor 3rd ser. , 2 (1885) 16-28.

Dupont, Jacques. "La Brebis perdue et la drachme perdue. "
Lumière et Vie 34 (1957) 15-34.

Engel, J. "Die Parabel vom der verlorenen Drachme (Lk.
13, 8ff.). " Theologie und Glaube 19 (1927) 653-61.

Fonck, Leopold. "Ovis perdita et inventa (Lc. 15:1-10). "
Verbum Domini 1 (1921) 173-77.

Güttgemanns, Erhardt. "Struktural-generative Analyse des
Bildworts 'Die verlorne Drachme' (Lk. 15, 8-10). "
Linguistica Biblica 6 (1971) 2-77.

Kamphaus, F. "'...zu suchen was verloren war,' Homilie zu Lk. 15, 1-10. " Bibel und Leben 8 (1967)
201-04.

The Lost Coin (Filmstrip). Society for Visual Education,
1948.

Piesker, C. H. "Das Gleichnis vom verlorenen Schaf und

vom verlorenen Groschen. " Der evangelische Erzieher 19 (1967) 58-70.

Rodrigues, C. "A Ovelha e a Dracma Perdidas. O Sentido de Duas Parábolas de Lucas. " Atual 3 (1972) 489-97.

Siniscalco, Paolo. Mito e storia della salvezza; ricerche sulle più antiche interpretazioni di alcune parabole evangeliche. Torino: G. Giappichelli, 1971, 240p.

Walls, A. F. "'In the Presence of the Angels' (Luke XV, 10). " Novum Testamentum 3 (1959) 314-16.

LOST SHEEP

Bishop, E. F. F. "The Parable of the Lost or Wandering Sheep. " Anglican Theological Review 44 (1962) 44-57.

Bootsie, the Lamb (Filmstrip). Cathedral Films, 1955.

Bussby, F. "Did a Shepherd Leave Sheep upon the Mountains or in the Desert?" Anglican Theological Review 45 (1963) 93-94.

Buzy, Denis. "La Brebis perdue. " Revue Biblique 39 (1930) 47-61.

Cantinat, J. "L'Evangile (du 3e Dimanche après la Pentecôte) (Lc 15, 1-10): La Brebis et la drachme perdues. " Assemblées du Seigneur 57 (1965) 24-38.

Dods, M. "The Lost Sheep and Lost Piece of Money. " Expositor 3rd ser. , 2 (1885) 16-28.

Dupont, Jacques. "La Brebis perdue et la drachme perdue. " Lumière et Vie 34 (1967) 15-34.

_____ . "Les Implications christologiques de la parabole de la brebis perdue. " Bibliotheca Ephemeridum Theologicarum 40 (1975) 331-50.

_____ . "L'opzione pastorale nella parabola della pecora smarrita (Mt. 18, 12-14), " in Chiesa per il mondo: miscellanea teologico-pastorale nel LXX del card. Michele Pellegrino, vol. I, pp97-104. Bologna: EDB, 1974.

_____. "La Parabole de la Brebis perdue (Matthieu 18, 12-14; Luc 15, 4-7." Gregorianum 49 (1968) 265-87.

Engel, J. "Die Parabel vom verlorenen Schaf." Die Seelsorge 4 (1926) 337-43.

_____. "Die Parabel vom verlorenen Schaf bei Lukas und Matthäus." Theologie und Glaube 20 (1928) 95-101.

Faccio, H. "De ove perdita (Lc. 15, 3-7)." Verbum Domini 26 (1948) 221-28.

Fonck, Leopold. "Ovis perdita et inventa (Lc. 15:1-10)." Verbum Domini 1 (1921) 173-77.

Das Gleichnis vom verlorenen Schaf. Lahr: Ernst Kaufmann, 1965.

God Loves Us (Motion picture). American Bible Society, 1969? Released by Association Films. Felt pen sketches by artist Annie Vallotton.

The Good Shepherd (Motion picture). Salvation Army, 1961.

Gregg, Robert C. "Early Christian Variations on the Parable of the Lost Sheep." Duke Divinity Review 41 (1977) 85-104.

Kamphaus, F. "'...zu suchen was verloren war,' Homilie zu Lk. 15, 1-10." Bibel und Leben 8 (1967) 201-04.

Latourette, Jane. Jon and the Little Lost Lamb: Luke 15:1-7 for Children. Illus. Betty Wind. St. Louis: Concordia Pub. House, 1965, unpaged.

The Lost Lamb (Filmstrip). Double Sixteen Co. , 1970.

The Lost Sheep (Filmstrip). Roa's Films, 1966.

The Lost Sheep (Motion picture). Broadcasting and Film Commission, 1951. Made by Everett Parker.

Luther, Martin. Eine Predigt vom verloren Schaf. Luce

XV. Wittemberg: 1533, 47p.

Monnier, Jean. "Sur la grâce, à propos de la parabole de la brebis perdue." Revue d'histoire et de philosophie religieuses 16 (1936) 191-95; Also in Recherches théologiques par les professeurs de la faculté de théologie protestante de l'université de Strasbourg, No. 1, à la mémoire de Guillaume Baldensperger (1856-1936), pp7-11. Paris: Libraire Félix Alcan, 1936.

The Parable of the Lost Sheep (Motion picture). Cathedral Films, 194-? Edited and released by Blackhawk Films. Eastin-Phelan Corp., 196-?

Peisker, C. H. "Das Gleichnis vom verlorenen Schaf und vom verlorenen Groschen." Der evangelische Erzieher 19 (1967) 58-70.

Rodrigues, C. "A Ovelha e a Dracma Perdidas. O Sentido de Duas Parábolas de Lucas." Atual 3 (1972) 489-97.

Schmidt, W. "Der gute Hirte. Biblische Besinnung über Lukas 15, 1-7." Evangelische Theologie 24 (1964) 173-77.

Seeking the Lost (Filmstrip). Gospel Slide and Film Service, 1951.

The Shepherd and His Sheep (Filmstrip). Society for Visual Education, 1953.

Sweet, J. P. M. "A Saying, a Parable, a Miracle." Theology 76 (1973) 125-33.

Tamsy (Filmstrip). Teaching Aids Service, 1958. Made by Susan McCann.

MARRIAGE FEAST

Bacon, Benjamin W. "Two Parables of Lost Opportunity." Hibbert Journal 21 (1922-23) 337-52.

Ballard, P. H. "Reasons for Refusing the Great Supper." Journal of Theological Studies 23 (1972) 341-50.

Bataillon, L. J. "Un Sermon de S. Thomas d'Aquin sur la parabole du festin." Revue des Sciences Philosophiques et Théologiques 58 (1974) 451-56.

Bauer, J. B. "De veste nuptiale (Matth. 22, 11-13)." Verbum Domini 43 (1965) 15-18.

Beare, F. W. "The Parable of the Guests at the Banquet: A Sketch of the History of its Interpretation," in The Joy of Study. Papers in Honor of F. C. Grant, pp1-14. New York: Macmillan, 1951.

Becker, H. V. Meditationes de Veste nuptiali. Rostock: 1775.

Bover, J. M. "Las dos parábolas de las Bodas reales y de la Gran Cena." Estudios Bíblicos 1 (1929) 8-27.

Bradley, B. "Come to the Marriage; Sermon Outline for the Nineteenth Sunday after Pentecost." Homiletic and Pastoral Review 65 (1965) 1044-46.

Brunec, M. "'Multi vocati--pauci electi' (Mt. 22, 14)." Verbum Domini 26 (1948) 88-97, 129-43, 277-90.

Castellino, Giorgio R. "L'abito di nozze nella parabola del convito e une lettera di Mari (Matteo 22, 1-14)." Estudios Eclesiásticos 34 (1960) 819-24.

Chavannes, H. "Quelques Gloses des évangiles." Revue de Théologie et de Philosophie 42 (1909) 288-310.

Claudel, Paul. La Sagesse; ou, la parabole du festin. Paris: Gallimard, 1939, 61p.

Cripps, K. R. J. "A Note on Matthew XXII, 12." Expository Times 69 (1957) 30.

Derrett, J. D. M. "The Parable of the Great Supper," in Law in the New Testament, pp126-55. London: Darton, Longman & Todd, 1970.

Dillon, R. J. "Towards a Tradition-history of the Parables of the True Israel (Matthew 21:33-22:14)." Biblica 47 (1966) 1-42.

Dormeyer, D. "Literarische und theologische Analyse der

Parabel Lk. 14, 15-24." Bibel und Leben 15 (1974) 206-19.

Dunkerley, Roderic. "The Bridegroom Passage." Expository Times 64 (1952-53) 303-04.

Dupont, Jacques. "In parabola magni convivii (Mt. 22, 2-14; Lc. 14, 16-24)." Actes du Congres International Theol. Vat. II (1968) 455-59.

Fonck, Leopold. "Nuptiae filii regis (Mt. 22, 1-14)." Verbum Domini 2 (1922) 294-300.

Fuchs, Ernst. "2. Sonntag nach Trinitatis. Lukas 14, 15-24," in Göttinger Predigtmeditationen (1961) 190-92.

Giesekke, F. "πολλοὶ γὰρ εἰσὶν κλητοὶ ὀλίγοι δὲ ἐκλεκτοί." Theologische Studien und Kritiken 21 (1898) 344-48.

Glombitza, O. "Das Grosse Abendmahl. Lukas XIV: 12-24." Novum Testamentum 5 (1962) 10-16.

The Great Supper (Filmstrip). Scripture Press, 1955. Made by Beacon Publishers.

The Great Supper (Filmstrip). Roa's Films, 1966.

Haacker, K. "Das hochzeitliche Kleid von Mt. 22, 11-13 und ein palästinisches Märchen. Zeitschrift des Deutschen Palästina-Vereins 87 (1971) 95-97.

Haenchen, E. "Das Gleichnis vom grossen Mahl," in Haenchen. Die Bibel und wir, pp135-55. Tübingen: J. C. B. Mohr, 1968.

Hahn, F. "Das Gleichnis von der Einladung zum Festmahl," in Verborum Veritas. Fest. Gustav Stählin, pp51-82. Wuppertal: Theologischer Verlag Brockhaus, 1970.

Hart, J. H. A. "Possible References to the Foundation of Tiberias in the Teaching of Our Lord." Expositor 8th ser., 1 (1911) 74-84.

Hasler, V. "Die königliche Hochzeit, Matth. 22:1-14." Theologische Zeitschrift 18 (1962) 25-35.

Henry, H. T. "The Great Supper (Luke 14, 16-24)."
Homiletic and Pastoral Review 39 (1938-39) 907-16.

_____. "The Wedding Garment (Mt. 22, 1-14),"
Homiletic and Pastoral Review 39 (1938-39) 1-10.

Hilgenfeld, A. "Das Gleichnis vom Hochzeitmahl, Mt. 22,
1-14." Zeitschrift für wissenschaftliche Theologie 36
(1893) 126-42.

Jeremias, Joachim. "Beobachtungen zu neutestamentlichen
Stellen an Hand des neugefundenen griechischen Hen-
noch-Textes. Lc. 14, 18:Ἀπὸ μιᾶς ." Zeitschrift für
die neutestamentliche Wissenschaft 38 (1939) 118.

Lewis, Agnes S. "Matthew XXII, 4." Expository Times
24 (1912-13) 427.

Liese, H. "Cena magna (Lc. 14, 16-24)." Verbum Domini
13 (1933) 161-66.

Linnemann, Eta. "Überlegungen zur Parabel vom grossen
Abendmahl Lc. 14, 15-24 und Mt. 22, 1-14." Zeitschrift für neutestamentliche Wissenschaft 51 (1960)
246-55.

Loman, A. D. "Bijdrage tot de kritiek der Synoptische
Evangelien. De gelijkenis van het Gastmaal bij Mattheus
(22, 2 vgg.) en Lucas (14, 16 vgg.)." Theologisch
Tijdschrift 6 (1872) 178-200.

Magass, W. "Semiotik einer Tischordnung (Lk. 14, 7-14)."
Linguistica Biblica 25/26 (1973) 2-8.

Maiworm, J. "Die Königshochzeit ausgelegt für Homileten."
Theologisch-praktische Quartalschrift 75 (1922) 105-07.

Merriman. E. H. "Matthew XXII, 1-14." Expository
Times 66 (1954-55) 61.

Michaelis, Wilhelm. Das hochzeitliche Kleid. Eine Einführung in die Gleichnisse Jesu über die rechte Jünger-
schaft. Berlin: Furche-Verlag, 1939, 283p.

Mouson, J. "Explicatur parabola de magno convivio (Mt.
XXII, 1-14; Lc. XIV, 16-24)." Collectanea Mechliniensia 43 (1958) 610-13.

Müller, Friedrich. "Berufung und Erwählung. Eine exegetische Studie." Zeitschrift für systematische Theologie
24 (1955) 38-71.

Musurillo, Herbert A. "'Many Are Called, but Few Are
Chosen' (Matthew 22:14)." Theological Studies 7 (1946)
583-89.

Navore, J. "The Parable of the Banquet." Bible Today
14 (1964) 923-29.

Palmer, Humphrey. "Just Married, Cannot Come (Matthew
22, Luke 14, Thomas 44, Dt. 20)." Novum Testamentum 18 (1976) 241-57.

Parables of the Great Supper (Filmstrip). Religious Films,
London. Released in the U. S. by United World Films,
1950.

Rengstorf, K. H. "Die Stadt der Mörder (Mt. 22:7)," in
Judentum, Urchristentum, Kirche. Festschrift für J.
Jeremias. W. Eltester, ed., pp106-29. Berlin: A
Töpelman, 1960.

Rilling, John W. "A Word in Season." Church Management:
The Clergy Journal 53 (Oct. 1976) 15, 28.

Sanders, J. A. "The Ethic of Election in Luke's Great
Banquet Parable," in Essays in Old Testament Ethics
(J. Philip Hyatt in Memoriam), pp245-71. New York:
Ktav, 1974.

Schlier, H. "L'Appel de Dieu (Mt. 22, 1-14)," in Essais
sur le Nouveau Testament; Lectio Divina, 46, pp255-
62. Paris: Cerf, 1968.

_____. "Der Ruf Gottes. Eine biblische Besinnung zum
Gleichnis vom königlichen Hochzeitmahl (Mt. 22, 1-14)."
Geist und Leben 28 (1955) 241-48. Also in Besinnung
auf das Neue Testament: Exegetische Aufsätze und Vorträge, II, pp219-26. Freiburg, Basel, Wien: Herder,
1964.

Selbie, W. B. "The Parable of the Marriage Feast (Matt.
XXII, 1-14)." Expository Times 37 (1925-26) 266-69.

Sickenberger, Joseph. "Die Zusammenarbeitung verschiedener Parabeln in Matthäusevangelium (22, 1-14)," in Festgabe A. Heisenberg zum 60. Geburtstage gewidmet. Hrsg. Franz Dölger. (Byzantinische Zeitschrift, vol. 30), pp253-61. Leipzig; Berlin: B. G. Teubner, 1929/30.

Silly Excuses (Filmstrip). Cathedral Films, 1963.

Silva, R., Nieto, T. "Estudio critico-literario e interpretación de la parábola de las bodas y de la gran cena (Mt. 22, 2-14 y Lc. 14, 16-24)." Compost 9 (1964) 349-82.

Squillaci, D. "Gesù invitato a cena (Lc. 14, 1-24)." Palestra del Clero 44 (1965) 902-97.

_____. "Parabole delle nozze del figlio del re (Mt. 22, 1-14)." Palestra del Clero 38 (1959) 972-76.

Streefkerk, N. "Waardig en onwaardig (Mt. 22, 1-14)." Homiletica en Biblica 24 (1965) 270-75.

Sutcliffe, E. "Many Are Called but Few Are Chosen." Irish Theological Quarterly 28 (1961) 126-31.

Swaeles, Romain. "L'Evangile (du 2e Dimanche après la Pentecôte) (Lc. 14, 16-24): La Parabole des invités qui se dérobent." Assemblées du Seigneur 55 (1962) 32-50.

_____. "L'Evangile (du 19e Dimanche après la Pentecôte) (Mt. 22, 1-14): La Parabole du festin nuptial." Assemblées du Seigneur 74 (1963) 33-49.

_____. "L'Orientation ecclésiastique de la parabole du festin nuptial en Mt. XXII, 1-14." Ephemerides Theologicae Lovanienses 36 (1960) 655-84.

Trilling, Wolfgang. "Zur Überlieferungsgeschichte des Gleichnisses vom Hochzeitsmahl, Mt. 22, 1-14." Biblische Zeitschrift 4 (1960) 251-65.

Vaccari, Alberto. "La Parabole du festin des noces (Mt. XXII, 1-14). Notes d'exégèse." Recherches de science religieuse 39 (1951) 138-45.

Via, Dan O., Jr. "The Relationship of Form to Content

in the Parables: The Wedding Feast." Interpretation
25 (1971) 171-85.

MASTER AND SERVANTS

Bornhauser, K. "Das Gleichnis von den 'unnützen' Knechten. Bemerkungen zu Lk. 17, 5-10." Pastoralblätter
82 (1939-40) 455-58.

Eichholz, Georg. "Meditation über das Gleichnis von Lk.
17, 7-10," in Kirche, Konfession, Ökumene: Festschrift
für Professor D. Dr. Wilhelm Niesel, Moderator des
Reformierten Bundes zum 70. Geburtstag. Hrsg. von
Karl Halaski und Walter Herrenbrück. pp 25-33. Neukirchen-Vluyn: Neukirchen-Verlag, 1973.

Minear, Paul S. "A Note on Luke 17:7-10." Journal of
Biblical Literature 93 (1974) 82-87.

Moffatt, James. "The Story of the Farmer and His Man."
Expositor 48 ser. 8, 23 (1922) 1-16.

Murphy, J. J. "Unprofitable Servants." Expositor 3rd
ser., 10 (1889) 151-56.

Riggenbach, Eduard. "Ein Beitrag zum Verständnis der
Parabel vom arbeitenden Knecht Luk. 17, 7-10." Neue
kirchliche Zeitschrift 34 (1923) 439-43.

S. E. C. T. "The Dutiful Servant." Expositor 1st ser.,
8 (1878) 365-78.

MUSTARD SEED

Bartsch, Hans-Werner. "Eine bisher übersehene Zitierung
der LXX in Mark 4, 30." Theologische Zeitschrift 15
(1959) 126-28.

Benvenuti, Stan. La parabola del granello di senape: con-
ferenza. Roma: t. Istituto Pio IX, 1907, 68p.

Bowen, Clayton R. "The Kingdom and the Mustard Seed."
American Journal of Theology 22 (1918) 562-69.

Brock, S. P. "An Additional Fragment of 0106?" Journal of Theological Studies 20 (1969) 226-28.

Didier, M. "Les Paraboles du grain de sénevé et du levain." Revue Diocésaine de Namur 15 (1961) 385-94.

Doherty, J. "The Faith that Shelters the World; Parable of the Mustard Seed." Ligourian 52 (June 1964) 47-51.

Dupont, Jacques. "Le Couple parabolique du Sénevé et du Levain," in Jesus Christus in Historie und Theologie: Neutestamentliche Festchrift für Hans Conzelmann zum 60. Geburtstag. Hrsg. Georg Strecker, pp331-45. Tübingen: J. C. B. Mohr, 1975.

_____. "Les Paraboles du sénevé et du levain." Nouvelle Revue Théologique 89 (1967) 897-913.

Fonck, Leopold. "Granum sinapis (Mt. 13, 31s.)." Verbum Domini 1 (1921) 322-27.

Funk, Robert W. "The Looking-glass Tree Is for the Birds; Ezekiel 17:22-24; Mark 4:30-32." Interpretation 27 (1973) 3-9.

Gutzwiller, R. "The Mustard Seed; Excerpt from Parables of the Lord." Way 20 (Nov. 1964) 25-26.

Hertzsch, Klaus-Peter. "Jésus herméneute. Une étude de Mc. 4, 30-32," in Reconnaissance á Suzanne de Diétrich; études et documents recueillis dan le monde à l'occasion de son 80e anniversaire, pp109-16. Paris: Foi et Vie, 1971.

Jehle, Fr. "Senfkorn und Sauerteig in der Hl. Schrift." Neue kirchliche Zeitschrift 34 (1923) 713-19.

Kuss, O. "Zum Sinngehalt des Doppelgleichnisses vom Senfkorn und Sauerteig," in Auslegung und Verkündigung I, pp85-97; Regensburg: Pustet, 1963. Also in Biblica 40 (1959) 641-53.

_____. "Zur Senfkornparabel," in Theologie und Glaube 41 (1951) 40-46. Also in Auslegung und Verkündigung, I, pp78-84. Regensburg: Pustet, 1963.

McArthur, Harvey K. "Parable of the Mustard Seed." Catholic Biblical Quarterly 33 (1971) 198-210.

McCorry, V. P. "Divine Pedagogy: Grain of Mustard Seed." Homiletic and Pastoral Review 56 (Oct. 1955) 53-55.

Mare, W. Harold. "The Smallest Mustard Seed--Matthew 13:32." Grace Journal 9 (Fall 1968) 3-11.

Matthews, Albert J. "The Mustard 'Tree.'" Expository Times 39 (1927-28) 32-34.

Michaelis, Wilhelm. "Die Gleichnisse vom Senfkorn und vom Sauerteig." Kirchenfreund 72 (1938) 118-21, 129-36.

Mussner, Franz. "1Q Hodajoth und das Gleichnis vom Senfkorn (Mk. 4, 30-32 par.)." Biblische Zeitschrift 4 (1960) 128-30.

The Mustard Seed and the Leaven (Filmstrip). Roa's Films, 1966.

Pollard, S. "The Mustard Seed." Expository Times 24 (1912-13) 187.

Pousset. É. "Le Sénéve et le levain." Vie Chrétienne 174 (1975) 13-16.

Ricoeur, P. "Listening to the Parables of Jesus; Text: Matthew 13:31-32 and 45-46." Criterion 13 (Sept. 1974) 18-22.

Schultze, Bernard. "Die ekklesiologische Bedeutung des Gleichnisses vom Senfkorn (Matth. 13, 31-32; Mk. 4, 30-32; Lk. 13, 18-19)." Orientalia Christiana Periodica 27 (1961) 362-86.

Smith, J. Hunter. "The Parable of the Mustard Seed." Expository Times 23 (1911-12) 428-30.

Szímonídesz, L. "Eine Rekonstruktion des Senfkorngleichnisses." Nederlands Theologisch Tijdschrift 26 (1937) 128-55.

Walley, Barbara A. Mustard Seed Faith; An Exposition of the Biblical Mustard Seed. Menomonie, Wis.: Mustard Seed Press, 1968, 3p.

PATCHED GARMENT

Bover, Jose M. "La parabola del Remiendo (Mt. 9, 16; Mc. 2, 21; Lc. 5, 36)," in Metzinger, Adalbertus, ed. Miscellanea Biblica et Orientalia R. P. Athanasio Miller, O. S. B., completis LXX annis oblata, pp327-39. Rome: Herder, 1951.

Ebeling, H. J. "Die Fastenfrage (Mk. 2:18-22)." Theologische Studien und Kritiken 108 (1937-38) 387-96.

Hahn, Ferdinand. "Die Bildworte vom neuen Flicken und von jungen Wein." Evangelische Theologie 31 (1971) 357-75.

Kee, A. A. "The Old Coat and the New Wine; A Parable of Repentance." Novum Testamentum 12 (1970) 13-21.

Klöpper, Albert. "Der ungewalkte Flicken und das alte Kleid. Der neue Wein und die alten Schläuche." Theologische Studien und Kritiken 58 (1885) 505-34.

Lewis, F. Warburton. "New Garments and Old Patches." Expository Times 13 (1901-02) 522.

Lewis, R. R. "'Επίβλημα ῥάκους ἀγνάφου." Expository Times 45 (1933-34) 185.

Synge, F. C. "Mark II. 21--Matthew IX, 16--Luke V, 36: The Parable of the Patch." Expository Times 56 (1944-45) 26-27.

Trudinger, Paul. "Un Cas d'incompatibilité? (Marc 2:21-22; Luc 5:39)." Foi et Vie 72 no. 5-6 (1973) 4-7.

_____. "Word on the Generation Gap: Reflections on a Gospel Metaphor." Biblical Theology Bulletin 5 (1975) 311-15.

PEARL

Burn, J. H. "The Pearl of Great Price." Expositor 2nd ser., 8 (1884) 468-72.

Casel, Odo. "Die Perle als religiöses Symbol." Benediktinische Monatsschrift zur Pflege religiösen und geistigen Lebens 6 (1924) 321-27.

Charles, R. H. "Two Parables: A Study." Expository Times 35 (1923-24) 265-69.

Didier, M. "Les Paraboles du trésor et de la perle (Mt. 13, 44ss)." Revue Diocésaine de Namur 16 (1962) 296-302.

Dupont, Jacques. "Les Paraboles du trésor et de la perle." New Testament Studies 14 (1968) 408-18.

Fenton, J. C. "Expounding the Parables: IV. The Parables of the Treasure and the Pearl (Mt. 13:44-46)." Expository Times 77 (1966) 178-80.

Findlay, George G. "The Parable of the Pearl-Merchant." Expositor 7th ser., 5 (1908) 158-70.

Glombitza, Otto. "Der Perlenkaufmann. Eine exegetische Studie zur Matth. XIII, 45-46." New Testament Studies 7 (1960-61) 153-61.

Hayman, Herbert S. "The Parable of the Pearl Merchant: Matthew XIII, 45, 46." Expository Times 49 (1937-38) 142.

Holk, L. J. van. De kostbare parel. Een fantastische paraphrase van Mattheus XIII:45-46. Rotterdam: Nijgh & Van Ditman's Uitg. Mij., 1927, 70p.

Jacobson, Delmar. "An Exposition of Matthew 13:44-52." Interpretation 29 (1975) 277-82.

Kunze, J. "Das Gleichnis von Schatz im Acker und von der köstlichen Perle." Zeitschrift für den evangelischen Religionsunterricht (1893) 53-59.

Metcalfe, W. M. "The Twin Parables." Expositor 2nd

ser., 8 (1884) 54-67.

Paterson, W. P. "The Parables of the Treasure and the Pearl." Expository Times 38 (1926-27) 261-64, 295-99.

Pousset, É. "Le Trésor et la perle." Vie Chrétienne 173 (1975) 12-16.

Ricoeur, P. "Listening to the Parables of Jesus; Text: Matthew 13:31-32 and 45-46." Criterion 13 (Sept. 1974) 18-22.

Schippers, R. "The Mashal Character of the Parable of the Pearl." Studia Evangelica II, 236-41.

Steffensen, H. "Über Matth. 13, 45. 46. Mit Beziehung auf Wächtlers Erklarungsversuch in den Studien und Kritiken 1846. H 4. 939-946." Theologische Studien und Kritiken 20 (1847) 718-22.

Tonkin, S. "The Parable of the Hidden Treasure, and of the Pearl Merchant (Matt. 13:44ff.)." Expository Times 33 (1921-22) 330-31.

Wächtler, Pfarrer. "Noch ein Wort über die Parabel Matth. 13, 45. 46." Theologische Studien und Kritiken 22 (1849) 416-22.

_____. "Versuch einer Erklärung von Matth. 13, 45. 46. Die Parabel von der köstlichen Perle." Theologische Studien und Kritiken 19 (1846) 939-46.

PHARISEE AND PUBLICAN

Bailey, K. E. "The Pharisee and the Publican, Lk. 18:9-14." [14 min.]. Thesis Theological Cassettes 5 no. 8 (Spring 1974).

Bruce, F. F. "Justification by Faith in the Non-Pauline Writings of the New Testament." Evangelical Quarterly 24 (1952) 66-67.

Dahl, Edward C. "Sinning Saints and Saintly Sinners." New Pulpit Digest 57:425 (May-June 1977) 25-28.

Fernández, J. "La oración del publicano (Lc. 18, 9-14)."

Cultura Bíblica 5 (1948) 193-99.

Fonck, Leopold. "Pharisaeus et publicanus (Lc. 18, 9-14)."
Verbum Domini 1 (1921) 194-99.

Franks, R. S. "The Parable of the Pharisee and the Publican." Expository Times 38 (1926-27) 373-76.

Green, L. C. "Justification in Luther's Preaching on Luke
18:9-14." Concordia Theological Monthly 43 (1972) 732-
47.

Hengel, M. "Die ganz andere Gerechtigkeit. Bibelarbeit
über Lk. 18, 9-14." Theologische Beiträge 5 (1974)
1-13.

Henry, H. T. "The Pharisee and the Publican." Homiletic and Pastoral Review 41 (1940-41) 1065-72.

Hoerber, Robert G. "'God Be Merciful to Me a Sinner'--
A Note on Luke 18:13." Concordia Theological Monthly
33 (1962) 283-86.

Meulenbelt, H. "Lk. 18, 13." Nieuwe Theologische Studiën
2 (1919) 5.

Mottu, H. "The Pharisee and the Tax Collector; Sartrian
Notions as Applied to the Reading of Scripture." Union
Seminary Quarterly Review 29 (1974) 195-213.

Oke, C. Clarke. "The Parable of the Pharisee and the
Publican." Canadian Journal of Religious Thought 5
(1928) 122-26.

The Pharisee and the Publican Pray (Filmstrip). Double
Sixteen Co., 1967.

Rondet, H. "La Parabole du Pharisien et du Publicain dan
l'oeuvre de S. Augustin." Sciences Ecclésiastiques 15
(1963) 407-17.

Scarlett, W. "Two Men: A Meditation." Christianity and
Crisis 14 (1954) 121-22.

Wachler, Günter. Wenn zwei dasselbe tun. Berlin: Evangelische Verlaganstalt, 1967, 15p.

PLAYING CHILDREN

Holzmeister, U. "Unbeachtete Gleichnisse des Evangeliums (Mt. 11, 16-19; Lc. 7, 31-35; Joh. 13, 10)." Theologisch-praktische Quartalschrift 81 (1928) 252-62.

Linton, Olof. "The Parable of the Children's Game." New Testament Studies 22 (1976) 159-79.

Mussner, F. "Der nicht erkannte Kairos; Mt. XI:16-19; Lk. VII:31-35." Biblica 40 (1959) 599-612.

Testa, E. "Un ostrakon sull'elogio funebre e Mt. 11, 16 ss e par." Rivista Biblica 16 (1968) 539-46.

POUNDS

Brightman, F. E. "S. Luke 19, 21 Αἴρεις ὅ οὐκ ἔθηκας." Journal of Theological Studies 29 (1927-28) 158.

_____. "Six Notes." Journal of Theological Studies 29 (1927-28) 158-65.

Candlish, Robert. "The Pounds and the Talents." Expository Times 23 (1911-12) 136-37.

Cremer, F. L. Dissertatio de diverso exitu ac mercede servorum fidelium atque ignavorum. Luc. XIX, 11-27. Harder: 1751.

Dauvillier, Jean. "La Parabole des mines ou des talents et le #99 du code de Hammourabi," in Mélanges dédiés à M. le professeur Joseph Magnol, doyen honoraire de la Faculté de droit de Toulouse, pp153-65. Paris: Recueil Sirey, 1948.

Derrett, J. D. M. "Law in the New Testament; The Parable of the Talents and Two Logia." Zeitschrift für die neutestamentliche Wissenschaft 56 (1966) 184-95.

Didier, M. "La Parabole des talents et des mines," in De Jésus aux Evangiles. Bibliotheca Ephemeridum theologicarum Lovaniensium 25, vol. 2, pp248-71. Gembloux: Duculot; Paris: Lethielleux, 1967.

Dupont, Jacques. "La Parabole des talents (Mat. 25:14-30) ou des mines (Luc 19:12-27)." Revue de theologie et de philosophie 19 (1969) 376-91. Also in Assemblées du Seigneur 64 (1969) 18-28.

Förster, W. "Das Gleichnis von der anvertrauten Pfunden," in Verbum Die manet in aeternum. Festschrift für Otto Schmitz, pp37-56. Witten: Luther-Verlag, 1953.

Herzog, Eduard. Die Parabel von anvertrauten Pfund. Hirtenbrief auf die Fastenzeit des Jahres 1914. Aarau: H. R. Sauerländer, 1914, 15p.

Holdcraft, I. T. "The Parable of the Pounds and Origen's Doctrine of Grace." Journal of Theological Studies 24 (1973) 503-04.

Joüon, Paul. "La Parabole des Mines (Luc 19, 13-27) et la Parabole des Talents (Matthieu 25, 14-30)." Recherches de Science Religieuse 29 (1939) 489-94.

Kamlah, E. "Kritik und Interpretation der Parabel von den anvertrauten Geldern Mt. 25:14ff.; Lk. 19:12ff." Kerygma und Dogma 14 (1968) 28-38.

Lüthi, Walter. "Das Gleichnis von anvertrauten Pfund. Predigt über Lk. 19, 11-27," in Festschrift für D. Albert Schädelin. Das Wort sie sollen lassen stahn, pp207-14. Bern: Verlag Herbert Lang & Cie, 1950.

McCulloch, W. "The Pounds and the Talents." Expository Times 23 (1911-12) 382-83.

Ollivier, Marie-Joseph. "Etude sur la physionomie intellectuelle de N. S. J. C. La Parabole des Mines (Luc XIX, 1-27)." Revue Biblique 1 (1892) 589-601.

Simpson, J. G. "The Parable of the Pounds." Expository Times 37 (1925-26) 299-303.

Stock, Eugene. "The Pounds and the Talents." Expository Times 23 (1911-12) 136-37.

Taylor, C. "Plato and the New Testament, 1. St. Luke XIX, 21." Journal of Theological Studies 2 (1901) 432.

Thiessen, Henry C. "The Parable of the Nobleman and the Earthly Kingdom" Bibliotheca Sacra 91 (1934) 180-90.

Thomson, P. "'Carry on!' (Luke XIX, 13). " Expository Times 30 (1918-19) 277.

Weinert, Francis D. "The Parable of the Throne Claimant (Luke 19:12, 14-15a, 27) Reconsidered. " Catholic Biblical Quarterly 39 (1977) 505-14.

Winterbotham, Rayner. "Christ, or Archelaus?" Expositor 8th ser., 4 (1912) 338-47.

Zerwick, M. "Die Parabel vom Thronanwärter. " Biblica 40 (1959) 654-74.

PRODIGAL SON

Adell, Arvid W. "Nietzsche and a Man with Two Sons. " Religion in Life 45 (1976) 499-504.

Alcott, William A. Story of the Prodigal. Boston: Massachusetts Sabbath School Society, 1836, 59p.

Alonso Díaz, J. "Paralelos entre la narración del libro de Jonás y la parábola del hijo pródigo. " Biblica 40 (1959) 632-40.

Askwith, E. H. "The Parable of the Prodigal Son. " Expositor 8th ser., 7 (1914) 552-57.

Bailey, Kenneth E. "The Lost Son, Luke 15:11-24" [10 min.]. Thesis Theological Cassettes 7 No. 1 (Feb. 1976).

Barry, Phillips. "On Luke XV, 25, συμφωνίας: Bagpipe. " Journal of Biblical Literature 23 (1904) 180-90.

Bauer, Pet. Der Bruder des verlorenen Sohnes. Ein Spiel von Torheit und Tugend in 3 Bildern. München: Höfling, 1951, 32p.

Baumgartner, H. "Christologie, und Parabel vom verlornen

Sohn. " Theologische Zeitschrift aus der Schweiz 5 (1888) 178-99.

Bethge, Eberhard. "Grenzüberschreitung: Eine Paraphrase zu Lukas 15, 11-32. " Reformatio 25 (1976) 68-74.

Black, Harold G. The Prodigal Returns. New York: Revell, 1941, 163p.

Blackwell, George L. The Model Homestead. Three Pointed, Practical and Picturesque Sermons on the Parable of the Prodigal Son. Boston: H. Marshall, 1893, 76p.

Bonus, Albert. "Luke XV, 30. " Expository Times 31 (1919-20) 476.

Bornhäuser, K. "Zum Gleichnis vom verlorenen Sohn. " Dorfkirche 25 (1932) 200-06.

Bostrom, John H. The Prodigal's Brother. Pasadena, Calif. : J. H. Bostrom, 1941. 29p.

Brandenburg, Hans. Das Gleichnis vom verlorenen Sohn, 2. Aufl. Gladbeck: Schriftenmissions-Verlag, 1950, 62p.

Braselmann, Werner. Der verlorene Sohn. Gütersloh: Gütersloher Verlagshaus Mohn, 1975? 16p.

Brendle, Daniel F. The Prodigal Son. Trans. from the German. Philadelphia: Lindsay & Blakiston, 1862, 220p.

Brettschneider, Werner. Die Parabel vom verlorenen Sohn: Das biblische Gleichnis in der Entwicklung der europäischen Literatur. Berlin: E. Schmidt, 1978, 69p.

Broer, I. "Das Gleichnis vom verlorenen Sohn und die Theologie des Lukas. " New Testament Studies 20 (1974) 453-62.

Brown, Charles. "The Great Parable of Grace. " Review and Expositor 16 (1919) 127-35.

Brown, Charles R. Two Parables. Chicago, New York: Revell, 1898, 250p.

Brown, David. "The Elder Brothers of the Prodigal Son."
Expository Times 7 (1895-96) 325-26.

Brown, Robert R. Alive Again. New York: Morehouse-
Barlow, 1964, 151p.

Burr, John. The Prodigal's Progress and the Professor's
Practice; An Analysis of the Parable of the Prodigal
Son and the Elder Brother. London: J. Clarke, 1933,
157p.

Burrell, David J. The Golden Parable; Studies in the Story
of the Prodigal Son. New York, London: Revell, 1926,
159p.

Busch, Wilhelm. Komm heim! Wilhelm Busch spricht über
das Gleichnis vom verlorenen Sohn, 3. veränd. Aufl.
von "Ein Mensch hatte zwei Söhne." Bern: Christl.
Verlaghaus, 1959, 134p.

_____. Ein Mensch hatte zwei Söhne. Stuttgart:
Quell-Verlag, 1949, 143p.

_____. Pastor Wilhelm Busch spricht: Predigten
uber das Gleichnis vom verlorenen Sohn. Stuttgart:
Quell-Verlag, 1976, 144p.

Cabo, Enrique de. Amaneció al regreso; comentario a la
parábola del hijo pródigo. Santander: 1961, 236p.

Carlston, Charles E. "Reminiscence and Redaction in Luke
15:11-32." Journal of Biblical Literature 94 (1975)
368-90.

Chappell, Herbert. The Prodigal Son Jazz. Words by
Tracey Lloyd. London: Clarabella Music; sole selling
and licensing agent for U. S. A. and Canada: E. B.
Marks Music Corp., New York, 1972, 27p.

Chevrot, Georges. Retraite pascale: La Parabole du fils
prodigue. Paris-Bruges: Desclée De Brouwer et Cie,
1939.

Die Christenlehre, year 7 (1954), part 3; Unterrichtshilfe,
37-44 (Lukas 15. 11-32).

Clerc, Charly. Le Mystère du fils prodigue. Montreaux:

Impr. nouvelle C. Corbaz, 1940, 48p.

Coloquio de pastores del hijo prodigo. The Shepherds' Play of the Prodigal Son. A folk drama of old Mexico, edited and translated by George C. Barker. Berkeley: University of California Press, 1953, 167p.

Compton, J. E. "The Prodigal's Brother." Expository Times 42 (1930-31) 187.

Cool, Pz., G. De oudste zoon der gelijkenis. Haarl. I. de Haan, 1871.

Courtois d'Arras, jeu du XIII siècle. Édité par Edmond Faral. Paris: H. Champion, 1911 (1922), 34p.

Courtois of Arras. The Best Seller of the 18th Century, for the First Time in English. By Mag Gentry de Creky. Chicago: Sussman, 1959, 29p.

Cox, Norman W. God and Ourselves. Nashville: Broadman Press, 1960, 139p.

Crespy, G. "Psychanalyse et foi." Études théologiques et religieuses 41 (1966) 241-51.

Dakin, Arthur. "The Elder Brother." Expository Times 19 (1907-08) 141-42.

_____. "The Parable of the Prodigal Son as Literature." Expository Times 35 (1923-24) 330-31.

Daubanton, F. E. De verloren zoon. Bijbelstudie. Amsterdam: Egeling's Boekhandel.; Utrecht: A. Fisscher, 1901.

Dauvillier, Jean. "Le Partage d'ascendant et le parabole du fils prodique." Actes du Congrés de Droit Canonique. 1947 (Paris 1950) 223-28.

Deissmann, Adolf. "The Parable of the Prodigal Son." Religion in Life 1 (1932) 331-38.

Delgado Sánchez, J. "Consideraciones sobre la Parábola del Hijo Pródigo." Cultura Bíblica 39 (1972) 338-41.

Derrett, J. D. M. "Law in the New Testament; The Par-

able of the Prodigal Son." New Testament Studies 14
(Oct. 1967) 56-74.

_____. "The Parable of the Prodigal Son:
Patristic Allegories and Jewish Midrashim." Studia
Patristica 10 (1970) 219-24.

Diamond, Lucy. Due racconti di Gesù. Illus. Kenneth Inns.
Beatenberg: Edizione Scuola biblica, 1967, 52p.

_____. Zwei Geschichten, die Jesus erzählt hat.
Illus. Kenneth Inns. Beatenberg: Verlag Bibelschule,
1967, 51p.

Díaz, José A. "Paralelos entre la narración del libro de
Jonás y la parábola del hijo pródigo." Biblica 40 (1959)
632-40. [Also listed as Alonso Díaz, José]

Dibelius, Otto. Die Rückkehr des verlorenen Sohnes ins
Vaterhaus. Predigt uber Lukas 15, 11-32. Berlin-
Dahlem: Volksmissionarische Abteilung des Centralaus-
schusses für die Innere Mission, 1947, 15p.

Doherty, J. E. "From Rags to Riches." Liguorian 50
(1962) 44-48.

Dürst, Fritz. Ein Vater-zwei Söhne. Vier Predigten über
das Gleichnis vom verlorenen Sohn. Basel: F. Reinhardt, 1968, 62p.

Duncan, Alexander A. "The Prodigal Son." Expository
Times 28 (1916-17) 327.

Duncan, Cleo. Woofy Is Forgiven, and the Prodigal Son.
Illus. Beryl Bailey Jones. Boston: United Church
Press, 1964, unpaged.

Dupont, Jacques. "Le Fils prodigue, Lc. 15, 1-3, 11-32."
Assemblées du Seigneur 17 (1970) 64-72.

Dutcher, Jacob C. The Prodigal Son. New York: E. B.
Tripp, 1870, 125p.

Eichholz, Georg. Die Heimkehr der Verlorenen. Einführung
in Rembrandts Radiergung von 1636 zum Gleichnis vom
verlorenen Sohn. Siegen, Leipzig: Schneider, 1940,
46p.

Elliott, William M. Two Sons. Richmond: John Knox Press, 1955, 62p.

Elmer, Irene. The Boy Who Ran Away: Luke 15:1-2 for Children. Illus. Sally Mathews. St. Louis: Concordia Pub. House, 1964, 32p.

Elsey, Charles W. The Prodigal's Father. Nashville: Broadman Press, 1937, 159p.

Engel, J. "Die Parabel vom verlorenen Sohne innerhalb der neutestamentlichen Theologie." Theologie und Glaube 18 (1926) 54-64.

_____. "Über die Bedeutung der Parabel vom verlorenen Sohn." Theologie und Glaube 19 (1927) 217-30.

The Father's Love (Filmstrip). Roa's Films, 1966.

Favre, Léopold. Parabole de l'Enfant prodigue en divers dialectes, patois de la France. Niort: 1879.

Fischer, Erika. Drei Gleichnisse vom Verlorenen. Aus dem Lukasevangelium. Mit 6 Bildern geschnitten. Berlin: Verlag Haus und Schule; Leipzig: Koeltz, 1947, 8p.

Fisher, Loren R. "Amarna Age Prodigal." Journal of Semitic Studies 3 (1958) 113-22.

Freeman, Winfield. The Prodigal Son. Topeka, Kan.: Capper Printing Co., 1921, 60p.

Frost, Maurice. "The Prodigal Son." Expositor 50 ser. 9, 2 (1924) 56-60.

Fuchs, Ernst. "Das Fest der Verlorenen. Existentiale Interpretation des Gleichnisses vom verlorenen Sohn," in Glaube und Erfahrung. Gesammelte Aufsätze III, pp 402-15. Tübingen: Mohr (Siebeck), 1965.

_____. "Jesu Freude als des Christen Trost und Mut. Predigt über Lukas 15. 11-32," in Predigten für Jedermann. O. Müllerschön, ed. Year 3 (1956) No. 9 Bad Cannstatt: R. Müllerschön Verlag, 1956.

Führich, Josef. Acht Zeichnungen zur Parabel vom ver-

lorenen Sohne. In Kupfer gestochen von Alois Petrák.
Wien: Verlag der Gesellschaft, 1873.

_____. Der verlorene Sohn. Nach den Fürich-
Bildern. Erklärt von Ign. Seipel. Hrsg. von Jak. Schäfer. Wien: Bernina-Verlag, 1949, 28p.

Fürst, A. De gelijkenis van den verloren zoon. Zeven
leeredenen, 2e dr. Amsterdam: Höveker & Zn., 1886.

Gaglio, Antonietta. La parabole del figliuol prodigo. Pa-
lermo: Elianto, 1970, 47p.

Giblet, J. "La Parabola de l'accueil messianique (Lc. 15,
11-32)." Bible et Vie Chrétienne 47 (1962) 17-28.

Gide, André. Die Heimkehr des verlorenen Sohnes. Übertr.
Ferd. Hardekopf. Zeichungen Rud. Fürhmann. Stuttgart: Dt. Verlag Anst., 1951, 49p.

_____. Die Rückkehr des verlorenen Sohnes. Ubertr.
von Rainer Maria Rilke. Wiesbaden: Insel-Verlag,
1950 (1954), 38p.

_____, and De Jong, F. J. De Terngleer van den ver-
loren zoon. Aissen: Van Gorcum, 1928, 48p.

Gioanina, L. "Amore e interesse nella parabola del Figi-
liuol prodigo." Palestra del Clero 37 (1958) 1280-

Das Gleichnis vom verlorenen Sohn. Lahr: Ernst Kaufmann, 1966.

Gnaphaeus, Guilielmus. Acolastus. De filio prodigo comoe-
dia. Lipsiae: N. Faber, 1536, 391.

_____. The Comedy of Aeolastus. Trans. John
Palsgrave. London: Oxford University Press, 1937,
312p.

Görnandt, Walt. Du bist der Gesuchte. (Ein Spiel um das
Gleichnis vom verlorenen Sohn). Berlin: Evang. Verlag
Anst., 1954, 27p.

Goetz, Diego H. Der unsterbliche verlorene Sohn. Wien:
Amandus-Verlag, 1949, 121p.

Goodman, John. The Penitent Pardoned: Or, a Discourse of the Nature of Sin, and the Efficacy of Repentance under the Parable of the Prodigal Son. London: 1679 (1683) (1689) (1694) (1700) (1707) (1713) (1724) (1816).

Gorla, Pietro. Il figliuol prodigo. Milano: t. Lega eucaristica, 1915, 224p.

Graham, Lorenz B. Hongry Catch the Foolish Boy. Illus. James Brown, Jr. New York: Crowell, 1973, 40p.

Greene, Joseph N. The Portrait of the Prodigal; Life Studies in the Experiences of the Prodigal Son. New York: Methodist Book Concern, 1921, 215p.

Grew, Obadiah. Meditations upon the Prodigal Son. London: 1677 (1678) (1684), 264p.

Gubalke, Albr. Rembrandts letztes Wort. Erläuterungen zum 15. Kapitel des Lukas-Evangeliums. Mit Bildern von Rembrandt, Dürer, Bosch und Memling. Siegen, Leipzig: W. Schneider, 1947, 48p.

Guelluy, R. "The Prodigal Son." Sponsa Regis 35 (1964) 279-86.

Hamilton, James. The Parable of the Prodigal Son. Illus. Henry Courtenay Selous. London: J. Nisbet, 1867, 196p.

Harrington, Wilfrid J. "The Prodigal Son." Furrow 25 (1974) 432-37.

Harris, Robert. The Arraignement of the Whole Creature at the Barre of Religion, Reason, and Experience. London: Printed by B. Alsop and T. Fawcet, 1631 (1632), 335p.

Hauser, Karl M. Eine Geschichte vom verlorenen Sohn. Arbou. Berglidruckerei, 1945, 53p.

Heisler, Daniel Y. Life-pictures of "The Prodigal Son." A Gift-book for the Million: Genial, Searching, and Kind. Philadelphia: Printed by Grant, Faires & Rodgers, 1877, 225p.

Henry, Donald M. "The Atonement and the Parable of the

Prodigal Son." Expository Times 17 (1905-06) 523.

Henry, H. T. "The Prodigal Son (Luke 15, 1-32). " Homiletic and Pastoral Review 39 (1938-39) 568-76.

Henry, Matthew. The Parable of the Prodigal Son. New York: American Tract Society, 183-? 8p.

Hilgenfeld, A. "Das Gleichnis von dem verlorenen Sohne, Luc. 15, 11-32. " Zeitschrift für wissenschaftliche Theologie 45 (1902) 449-64.

De historie van den verloren sone, naar den Antwerpschen druk von Godtgaf Verhulst uit het jaar 1655. Uitgegeven door dr. G. J. Boekenoogen. Leiden: E. J. Brill, 1908, 68p.

Hoch, Wilhelm. Der verlorene Sohn. Ein biblisches Spiel in 6 Bildern nach Lukas 15, 11-32. Zürich: Zwingli-Verlag, 1948, 40p.

Holme, Edin. Tonen fra himlen; religiøse smaastykker i tilslutning til Luc. 15, 11-24. Oslo: H. Aschehoug (W. Nygaard), 1926, 168p.

Holmes, John A. The Prodigal Son Ten Years Later. Boston: Pilgrim Press, 1917, 29p.

Huber, Paul. Der verlorene Sohn. Symphon. Gleichnis in 5 Teilen für 2 Sprechstimmen, Soli, Chor und Orchester. Musik von Paul Huber. Dichtung von Georg Thürer. St. Gallen: Tschudy-Verlag, 1954, 39p.

Humburg, Paul. Die ganz grosse Liebe. 28 schlichte Betrachtungen für verlorene Leute über das Gleichnis von den verlorenen Söhnen, 3. Aufl. Neukirchen: Buchhandlung des Erziehungsvereins, 1949. 67p. 4. Aufl., 1957.

Jeremias, Joachim. "Zum Gleichnis vom verlorenen Sohn, Luk. 15, 11-32. " Theologische Zeitschrift 5 (1949) 228-31.

Jorn, Wilhelm. Heimkommen. Eine evangelistische Jugendstunde nach Ev. Lukas 15, 11-32. Stuttgart: Christliches Verlagshaus, 1950, 18p.

Kallensee, Kurt. Die Liebe des Vaters. Das Gleichnis vom verlorenen Sohn in der christlichen Dichtung und bildenden Kunst. Berlin: Evang. Verlag Anst., 1960, 159p.

Kampmann, Theoderich. Ich will mich aufmachen: der verlorene Sohn als Herausforderung. Meitingen, Freising: Kyrios-Verlag, 1973, 31p.

Kelley, Robert L. "The Significance of the Parable of the Prodigal Son for Three Major Issues in Current Synoptic Study." Ph.D. thesis, Princeton University, 1972, 293p.

Klötzli, Wilfried. Ein Mensch hatte zwei Söhne. Eine Auslegung von Lukas 15, 11-32. Zürich, Frankfurt a.M.: Gotthelf-Verlag, 1966, 239p.

Knight, George H. "The Atonement and the Parable of the Prodigal Son." Expository Times 17 (1905-06) 239.

Knoke, K. "Zum Verständnis des Gleichnisses vom verlornen Sohn." Neue kirchliche Zeitschrift 17 (1906) 407-18.

Kruckenmeyer, Erna. And He Came to His Father: Religious Play in One Act. New York, London: S. French, 1927, 25p.

Kühnle, Karl. Das Gleichnis von den zwei Söhnen. Dargestellt in 7 Bildern. Stuttgart: Privileg. Württ. Bibel anst., 1950, 24p.

Lacheman, E. R. "Two Babylonian Parallels to the Prodigal Son Parable." Journal of Biblical Literature 60 (1941) XIII.

Laidlaw, J. "The Parable of the Lost Son: A Study of Luke XV, 11-32." Expositor 3rd ser., 8 (1888) 268-76, 388-99.

Lange, Ernst. Ein Sohn kehrt heim. Laienspiel. Stuttgart: Quell-Verlag, 1954, 63p.

Laros, Matthias. Die drei verlorenen Söhne; oder, von der dreifachen Verlorenheit. Kevelaer: Butzon & Bercker, 1936, 120p.

_____. Die drei verlorenen Söhne--und wir heute?,

3. völlig überarb. Aufl. Frankfurt am Main, Knecht-Carolusdr., 1951, 114p.

Lawet, Robert. Twee zestiende-eeuwse spelen van de ver-looren zoone. Uitg. door Egidius Gerardus Antonius Golama. Utrecht: Dekker & van de Vegt, 1941, 398p.

Le Du, Jean. Le Fils prodigue ou Les chances de la trans-gression. Saint-Orieuc, S.O.F.E.C., 1974, 64p.

Lendrum, John. "Into a Far Country." Expository Times 36 (1924-25) 377-80.

Levinger, Elma C. The Return of the Prodigal; A One-act Play, Based on a Certain Parable in Luke. Boston: Pilgrim Press, 1927, 27p.

Leyburn, John. Hints to Young Men from the Parable of the Prodigal Son. Philadelphia: Presbyterian Board of Publication and Sabbath-School Work, 1888, 183p.

Lindijer, C. H. "Kerk en Israël in de gelijkenis van de verloren zoon?" Nederlands theologisch Tijdschrift 20 (1966) 161-70.

Lohfink, G. "'Ich habe gesündigt gegen den Himmel und gegen dich.' Eine Exegese von Lk. 15, 18. 21." Theologische Quartalschrift 155 (1975) 51s.

Loy, Friedrich. Gottes Vaterhaus. 4 Predigten über das Gleichnis vom verlorenen Sohn. Munchen: P. Müller, 1946, 32p.

Lynch, Charles G. A Sacred Drama, the Prodigal Son, in Five Acts. Easley, S. C.: 1932, 20p.

McConnell, Franz M. After the Feast. Dallas, Tex.: Marshall, 1932, 55p.

McLeod, N. B. "The Parable of the Prodigal Father; A Sermon for Christian Family Sunday." Princeton Seminary Bulletin 64 (July 1971) 43-47.

Madsen, N. P. Tabt og fundet. København: Kirkelig forening for den Indre mission i Danmark, 1910, 101p.

Martin, A. D. "The Word of the Cross and the Parable of

the Prodigal. " Expository Times 24 (1912-13) 526-27.

Martin, Harold S. "The Parable of the Loving Father." Brethren Life and Thought 10 (Summer 1965) 44-49.

"Me levantaré e iré a mi Padre. " Numero especial dedicado a la VIII Peregrinaciòn Universitaria [Cordoba]. Didascalia 17 (1963) 259-335.

Melillo, Michele. Le concordanze dei dialetti di Puglia nelle versioni della parabola del figliuol prodigo. 2 vols. Bari: Università degli studi di Bari, Cattedra di dialettologia italiana della Facoltà di lettere, 1973-75.

_____. Le forme verbali dei dialetti di Puglia nelle versioni della parabola del figliuol prodigo. Bari: Università degli studi, Cattedra di dialettologia italiana della Facoltà di lettere, 1976, 297p.

_____, com. La parabola del figliuol prodigo nei dialetti italiani. I dialetti di Puglia a cura di Michele Melillo. Roma: Archivo etnico linguistico musicale, 1970, 217p.

Melton, William W. The Waste of Sin; A Study of the Parable of the Prodigal Son. New York: Revell, 1922, 170p.

Meulenbelt, H. "Lk. 15, 12. " Nieuwe theologische studiën 2 (1919) 267-68.

Meyer, Karl-Heinz. Der verlorene Sohn. Ein christliches Gemeindespiel nach dem gleichnamigen Gleichnis (Lukas 15, 11-32). Wuppertal: Verlag R. Brockhaus, 1941, 32p.

Modersohn, Ernst. Aus der Fremde in die Heimat. Betrachtungen über das Gleichnis vom verlorenen Sohn. Hildesheim: A. Lax, 1912, 62p.; Freiburg: Fleig, 1923, 40p.

Moon, Robert D. Love's Conquest. Mountain View, Calif. : Pacific Press Pub. Assoc., 1960, 116p.

Moore, G. F. "Συμφωνία not a Bagpipe. " Journal of Biblical Literature 24 (1905) 166-75.

Morgan, George C. The Parable of the Father's Heart. London: H. E. Walter, 1948, 62p.; New York: Revell, 1949, 96p.

Mortari, J. "Parabola de filio prodigo (Lc. 15, 11-32)." Verbum Domini 5 (1925) 289-94, 321-29.

Mott, George S. The Prodigal Son. Philadelphia: Presbyterian Board of Publication, 1863, 143p.

Müller, Michael. Rückkehr zu Gott. Betrachtungen über die Parabel vom verlorenen Sohn. 2. Aufl. Aus dem englischen übersetzt. Freiburg i. B., St. Louis: Herder, 1898, 621p. 1st ed., 1884, has title: Praktische Betrachtungen über die Parabel vom verlorenen Sohn.

Müller, Norbert. Das Gleichnis vom verlorenen Sohn. Ein liturgisches Spiel. Berlin: Evang. Verlag Anst., 1954, 26p.

Nestle, Eb. "The Best Robe." Expository Times 10 (1898-99) 93-94.

Nixon, Joan L. The Son Who Came Home Again: Luke 15: 11-32 for Children. St. Louis: Concordia Pub. House, 1977.

Ollivier, M. J. "Études sur la physionomie intellectuelle de N. S. Jésus Christ. La Parabole de l'enfant prodigue (Luc XV, 11-31)." Revue Biblique 3 (1894) 489-502.

O'Rourke, J. J. "Some Note on Luke 15:11-32." New Testament Studies 18 (1972) 431-33.

Outryve, E. van. "'Een man had twee Zonen,' Lc. 15, 11-32 anders bekeken." Tijdschrift voor Geestelijk Leven 30 (1974) 51-56.

Pailler, J. L'Enfant prodigue. Arras: Brunet, 1924, 392p.

Parker, Mary M. The Prodigal Comes Home, a Biblical Drama in One Act. Chicago: T. S. Denison, 1930, 24p.

Paulo, Salt. Die Geschichte vom verlorenen Sohn. Erzählt. Zeitnahe gezeichnet von Gerh. Olbrich. Jena: Wartburg-

Verlag, 1953, 32p.

Pavel, C. "Probleme morale în parabola Fiului risipitor."
Glasul Bisericii 30 (1972) 268-80.

Peppy, the Pup (Filmstrip). Cathedral Films, 1956.

Pesch, Rudolf. "Zur Exegese Gottes durch Jesus von
Nazaret. Eine Auslegung des Gleichnisses von Vater und
den beiden Söhnen (Lk. 15, 11-32)," in Jesus: Ort der
Erfahrung Gottes, pp140-89. Freiburg im Breisgau,
Basel, Wien: Herder, 1976.

Plotzke, U. De parabel van de barmhartige vader. Brussel:
Jecta, 1971, 106p.

Plumptre, Henry S. Lectures on the Parable of the Prodigal
Son, Delivered in the Parish Church of St. Mary, New-
ington Butts, During the Season of Lent, 1833. London:
J. Hatchard and Son, 1833, 202p.

Poort, J. J. Vader, ik heb gezondigd! Veertien bijbelle-
zingen over de Gelijkenis van de verloren zoon. Dod-
recht: J. P. van del Tol, 1968, 168p.

Price, James J. "Luke 15:11-32." Interpretation 31 (1977)
64-69.

The Prodigal; Chapters by Moorhouse, Moody, Spurgeon,
Aitken, Talmage and Others. Chicago, New York:
Bible Institute Colportage Assoc., 1897, 126p.

The Prodigal Son (Filmstrip). Cathedral Films, 1941.

_____. Concordia Pub. House, 1951.

_____. Church-Craft Pictures, 1953.

_____. Eye Gate House, 1963.

The Prodigal Son (Motion picture). Loyola Films in cooperation with Cathedral Films, 1948.

_____. Harmon Foundation, 1950.

_____. Broadcasting and Film Commission, 1951.
Made by Everett Parker.

The Prodigal Son Returns (Filmstrip). Double Sixteen Co.,
1968.

Prokofiev, Sergei Sergeevich. The Prodigal Son; Ballet
(Phonodisc). Vox PL9310. 1955.

Punshon, William M. The Prodigal Son. Four Discourses
by the Rev. W. Morley Punshon, M.A. Toronto: S.
Rose, 1868, 88p.

Rechenberg, Friedrich G. Der verlorene Sohn. Basel:
Majer, 1948, 72p.

Renger, Konrad. Lockere Gesellschaft. Zur Ikonographie
des verlorenen Sohnes und von Wirthausszenen in der
niederländischen Malerei. Berlin: Mann, 1970, 159p.

Rengstorf, Karl H. Die Re-Investitur des verlorenen Sohnes
in der Gleichniserzählung Jesu Luk. 15, 11-32. Köln
und Opladen: Westdeutscher Verlag, 1967, 78p.

Richardson, C. H. The Mansion, a Poetical Exegesis on
the Prodigal Son. Topeka, Kan.: Kansas Home Pub.
Co., 1890, 28p.

Robertson, W. P. "The Word of the Cross and the Parable
of the Prodigal." Expository Times 25 (1913-14) 181-82.

Robilliard, J. A. "La Parabole du fils aîné: Jésus et
l'amour misericordieux. Vie Spirituelle 106 (1962) 531-
44.

Romano, Armando. La parabola del figlioul prodigo. Lecce:
Lazzaretti, 1904, 6p.

Rose Cecilia, Sr. "Jesus, Revealer of the Father." Cord
14 (1964) 293-300.

Rosenkranz, Gerhard. "Das Gleichnis vom verlorenen Sohn
im Lotus-Sûtra und im Lukasevangelium," in Theologie
als Glaubenswagnis: Festschrift für Karl Heim zum 80.
Geburtstag, pp176-93. Hamburg: Furche-Verlag, 1954.

Rossi, Mario. "Una interpretazione nordica della parabola
del figliuol prodigo." Bilychnis 23 (1924) 21-24.

Rowland, James. Ruin and Restoration; Illustrated from

the Parable of the Prodigal Son. Albany, N. Y.:
Weed, Parsons, 1862, 147p.

Rubsys, A. L. "The Parable of the Forgiving Father," in
Readings in Biblical Morality, C. Luke Salm, ed., pp
104-08. Englewood Cliffs, N. J.: Prentice-Hall,
1967.

Runaway Comes Home (Motion picture). American Bible
Society, 1969? Released by Association Films.

Russell, J. Bonnar. "The Word of the Cross and the Parable of the Prodigal." Expository Times 24 (1912-13)
358-60.

Sanders, J. T. "Tradition and Redaction in Luke 15:11-32."
New Testament Studies 15 (1969) 433-38.

Schell, Herm. Der verlorene Sohn. Luzern: Rex-Verlag,
1944, 102p.

Schniewind, Julius. Das Gleichnis vom verlorenen Sohn.
Auslegung vom Lc. 15. Göttingen: Vandenhoeck &
Ruprecht, 1940, 43p. Also "Das Gleichnis vom ver-
lorenen Sohn," in Die Freude der Busse, pp34-87.
Göttingen: Vandenhoeck & Ruprecht, 1956.

Scholey, Charles H. The Prodigal's Prayer and Fishers
of Men. New York: Revell, 1899, 60p.

Schottroff, L. "Das Gleichnis vom verlorenen Sohn."
Zeitschrift für Theologie und Kirche 68 no. 1 (1971)
27-52.

Schroeder, Frederick W. Far from Home. Philadelphia:
Christian Education Press, 1961, 123p.

Schröder, J. E. De gelijkenis van den verloren zoon met
de gemeente behandeld. Utrecht: C. H. E. Breijer;
Nijkerk: G. F. Callenbach, 1894.

Schultz, Margar. Der verlorene Sohn. Leipzig: St.-Ben-
no-Verlag, 1960, 22p.

Schulze, Georg W. Das Gleichnis vom verlorenen Sohne,
9. Aufl. Braunschweig: C. A. Schwetschke und Sohn,
1888, 382p.

Schweckendiek, Adolf. Bühnengeschichte des verlorenen Sohnes in Deutschland. Leipzig: L. Voss, 1930, 15p.

Schweizer, Eduard. "Antwort an Joachim Jeremias, S. 228-231." Theologische Zeitschrift 5 (1949) 231-33.

_____. "Zur Frage der Lukasquellen, Analyse von Luk. 15, 11-32." Theologische Zeitschrift 4 (1948) 469-71.

Scott, Bernard B. "The Prodigal Son: A Structuralist Interpretation." Semeia 9 (1977) 45-73.

S. E. C. T. "The Prodigal and His Brother." Expositor 1st ser., 9 (1879) 137-50.

Sedgwick, Obadiah. The Parable of the Prodigal... Delivered in Divers Sermons. London: Printed by D. Maxwell for Sa. Gallibrand, 1660, 368p.

Seeking the Lost (Filmstrip). Gospel Slide and Film Service, 1951.

Semper, I. J. "The Return of the Prodigal." Ecclesiastical Review 83 (1930) 142-50.

Senior, Fred. "Luke XV, 30." Expository Times 31 (1919-20) 282.

Silva, R. "La parábola del hijo pródigo." Cultura Bíblica 23 (1966) 259-63.

Simcox, W. H. "The Prodigal and His Brother." Expositor 3rd ser., 10 (1889) 122-26.

Siniscalco, P. "La parabola del figlio prodigo (Lc. 15, 11-32) in Ireneo." Studi e Materiali di Storia delle Religioni 38 (1967) 536-53.

Skovgaard-Peterson, Carl A. Saadan elsker Gud--! En praeken over lignelsen om den fortabte søn. København: J. Frimodt, 1916, 21p.

Sommer, Frederick. The World's Greatest Short Story, a Study of Present-day Significance of the Family Pattern of Life. Oswega, Kan.: Carpenter Press, 1948, 166p.

Souza, Júlio Cesar de Mello e. Romance do filho pródigo; a alegria do peradão divino [par] Melba Tahan. Rio de Janeiro: Conquista, 1967, 286p.

Stewart, Alexander. "The Elder Brother." Expository Times 22 (1910-11) 247-51.

Stickler, H. E. "The Prodigal's Brother." Expository Times 42 (1930-31) 45-46.

Stock, Alex. "Das Gleichnis vom verlorenen Sohn. Strukturale Textanalyse im problemzusammenhang der Pragmatik ethischer Rede," in Ethische Predigt und Alltagsverhalten. Hrsg. Franz Kamphaus und Rolf Zerfass, pp79-87. München: Kaiser; Mainz: Matthias-Grünewald-Verlag, 1977.

Stockum Theodorus C. van. Das Jedermann-Motiv und das Motiv des verlorenen Sohnes im niederländischen und im niederdeutschen Drama. Amsterdam: Noord-Hollandsche Uitg. Mij., 1958, 22p.

Tapman, Lillian S. The Unprodigal Son, by a Wayfarer. Richmond Hill, N. Y.: L. S. Tapman, 1935, 81p.

This My Son (Motion picture). Radio & Television Board, Southern Baptist Convention. Made and released by Family Films, 1955.

Thönen, Ernst. Das Gleichnis vom verlornen Sohn. Lukas 15, 11-32. Zürich: Verlag der Jungen Kirche 1947, 27p.

Tiele, C. P. De gelijkenis van het vaderhuis. Luk. 15:11-32, practisch toegelicht. Rotterdam: P. C. Hoog, 1864; Amsterdam: P. N. van Kampen & Zoon, 1875.

Tolbert, Mary A. "The Prodigal Son: An Essay in Literary Criticism from a Psychoanalytic Perspective." Semeia 9 (1977) 1-20.

Toussaint, Stanley D. "When You Have a Prodigal Son." Kindred Spirit 1 (Fall 1977) 19-20.

Tucker, Louis. When He Came to Himself. Indianapolis: Bobbs-Merrill, 1928, 349p.

Two Sons (Motion picture). Family Films, 1957.

Van der Merwe, Gert J. Die Wonder van die Vaderhuis. Somerset-Wes: N. G. Kerkkantoor, 1969, 52p.

Velte. "Lukas 15, 11-32." Monatsschrift für Pastoraltheologie 26 (1930) 182-91.

Verkuyl, Johannes. Anak hilang; perumpamaan tentang Sang Bapa dengan kedua anaknja, jang bungsu dan jang sulung. Suatu uraian tentang Indjil Lukas 15:11-32. Djakarta: Badan Penerbitan Kristen, 1965, 66p.

De verloren Zoon. Naar teekeningen van Bep. Bijtelaar. 's-Gravenhage: J. N. Voorhoeve, 1930, 11p.

Vernon, Ambrose W. The Loving Father. Boston: Pilgrim Press, 1913, 32p.

Vetter, Ewald M. Der verlorene Sohn. Düsseldorf: L. Schwann, 1955, 36p., 32 plates.

Via, Dan O., Jr. "The Prodigal Son: A Jungian Reading." Semeia 9 (1977) 21-43.

Vincent, Marvin R. The Two Prodigals. New York: A. D. F. Randolph, 1876, 59p.

Vries, Anne de. Der verlorene Sohn. Weinachtsgeschichten. 3. Konst.: Christl. Verlag Anst., 1957. [Trans. of De verloren zoon.]

Waldis, Burkard. Der verlorene Sohn [Ein Spiel]. Erneuert von Alw. Müller. 7. Aufl. München: Kaiser-Verlag, 1950, 47p.

Walsh, Bill. The Prodigal Son. Kansas City, Kan.: Sheed Andrews and McMeel, 1977.

The Wanderer (Filmstrip). Eye Gate House, 1962.

Ward, C. M. The Playboy Comes Home. Springfield, Mo.: Gospel Pub. House, 1976, 107p.

Ward, Richard H. The Prodigal Son: Some Comments on the Parable. London: Gollancz, 1968, 157p.

Wertheim Aymès, Clément A. Die Bildersprache des Hiero-
nymous Bosch. Dargestellt an "Der verlorene Sohn," an
"Die Versuchungen des Heiligen Antonius" und an Motiven
aus anderen Werken. Mit 12 Farbtafeln und 147 Abbil-
dungen. Den Haag: van Goor Zonen, 1961, 118p.

Whitaker, Walter C. The Prodigal Son; Christ's Parable of
Mercy. Jacksonville, Fla.: Church Year Pub. Co.,
1890, 52p.

White, John W. The Runaway. Dallas: Crescendo Publication, 1976, 198p.

Whiting, Thomas A. Sermons on the Prodigal Son. New
York: Abingdon Press, 1959, 111p.

Willcock, John. "Luke XV, 16." Expository Times 29
(1917-18) 43.

Willcox, Giles B. The Prodigal Son. A Monograph. With
an Excursus on Christ as a Public Teacher. New York:
American Tract Society, 1890, 112p.

Williams, G. H. "The Parable of the Elder Brother; Reflections on the Protestant Response to Catholic Ecumen-
ism." Harvard Divinity Bulletin 29 (April 1965) 1-11.

Williams, W. Gray. "The Parable of the Prodigal Son
(Luke XV, 11-32)." Expository Times 26 (1914-15)
141-42.

Witherspoon, Arthur W. "The Atonement and the Parable
of the Prodigal Son." Expository Times 17 (1905-06)
335-36.

Yates, J. E. "Studies in Texts: Sons or Servants? A
Note on Luke XV, 11-end." Theology 49 (1946) 15-18.

Zabriskie, Francis N. The Story of a Soul; Or, Thoughts
on the Parable of the Prodigal Son. New York: A. D.
F. Randolph, 1872, 149p.

RICH FOOL

Birdsall, J. N. "Luke XII, 16ff. and the Gospel of Thomas."

Journal of Theological Studies 13 (1962) 332-36.

Bushy, the Squirrel (Filmstrip). Cathedral Films, 1955.

Derrett, J. D. M. "The Rich Fool: A Parable of Jesus
Concerning Inheritance." Heythrop Journal 18 (1977)
131-51.

Elliott, William M., Jr. "The Man Was a Fool!" Presbyterian Journal 36 (Nov. 23, 1977) 7-8.

Joüon, Paul. "Notes philologiques sur les Évangiles. --Luc
12, 21." Recherches de science religieuse 18 (1928)
352-54.

_____. "La Parabole du riche insensé (Luc 12, 13-
31)." Recherches de Science Religieuse 29 (1939) 486-
89.

Lemeron, Everett G. "Five Follies of the Foolish Farmer."
New Pulpit Digest 56 (1976) 59-62.

Lüthi, Walter. Einer aus dem Volk: Predigt über Lukas
12, 13-21, gehalten im Berner Münster. Basel: F.
Reinhardt, 1976, 8p.

_____. Das Gleichnis vom reichen Kornbauer. Pre-
digt über Luk. 12, 13-21. Basel: Reinhardt, 1945,
11p.

Magass, W. "Zur Semiotik der Hausfrömmigkeit (Lk. 12,
16-21: Die Beispielerzählung vom reichen Kornbauer)."
Linguistica Biblica 4 (1971) 2-5.

Reid, John. "The Poor Rich Fool." Expository Times 13
(1901-02) 567-68.

RICH MAN AND LAZARUS

Alexandre, M. "L'Interprétation de Luc 16, 19-31 chez
Grégoire de Nysse," in Épektasis: mélanges patristiques
offerts au cardinal Jean Daniélou, pp425-41. Paris:
Beauchesne, 1972.

Barth, Karl. "Miserable Lazarus (Text: Luke 16:19-31)."

Union Seminary Review 46 (1934-35) 259-68.

Batiffol, Pierre. "Trois Notes exégétiques." Revue Biblique 9 (1912) 541.

Bishop, E. F. "A Yawning Chasm." Evangelical Quarterly 45 (1973) 3-5.

Bornhäuser, Dr. "Zum Verständnis der Geschichte vom reichen Mann und armen Lazarus. Luk. 16, 19-31." Neue kirchliche Zeitschrift 39 (1928) 833-43.

Browne, Lewis C. Parable of the Rich Man and Lazarus: A Discourse, Delivered in the Universalist Church in Nashua, on Sunday Evening, August 14th. 1842. Nashville: C. T. Gill, 1842, 31p.

Bruyne, Donatien de. "Chasma (Lc. 16, 26)." Revue Biblique 30 (1921) 400-05.

Bunyan, John. The Groans of a Damned Soul. Swengel, Pa.: Reiner Publications, 1967, 108p.

_____. Sighs from Hell: Or, the Groans of a Damned Soul. Discovering from the 6th of Luke, the Lamentable Estate of the Damned. And May Fitly Serve as a Warning-word to Sinners, both Old and Young, by Faith in Jesus Christ, to Avoid the Same Place of Torment. With a Discovery of the Usefulness of the Scriptures, as Our Safe Conduct for Avoiding the Torments of Hell. 17th ed. Boston: Reprinted by John Allen, for Nicholas Boone, at his shop near the corner of Schoolhouse-Lane, 1708, 206p.

Busch, Wilhelm. Der ungerechte Haushalter. (Predigten über Lukas 16, 1-12). Der reiche Mann und der arme Lazarus. (Predigten über Lukas 16, 19-31). Stuttgart: Quell-Verlag, 1948, 128p.

Cadbury, Henry J. "The Name of Dives." Journal of Biblical Literature 84 (1965) 73.

_____. "A Proper Name for Dives." (Lexical Notes on Luke-Acts VI). Journal of Biblical Literature 81 (1962) 399-402.

Cadron, F. Hugh. "'Son' in the Parable of the Rich Man

and Lazarus. " Expository Times 13 (1901-02) 523.

Campbell, Robert C. Heaven or Hell--Which? A Study of the Life Hereafter. New York: Revell, 1931, 159p.

Cave, C. H. "Lazarus and the Lukan Deuteronomy. " New Testament Studies 15 (1969) 319-25.

Cölle, Rudolf. "Zur Exegese und zur homiletischen Verwertung des Gleichnisses vom reichen Mann und armen Lazarus: Luk. 16, 19-31. " Theologische Studien und Kritiken 75 (1902) 652-65.

Cruso, Timothy. Discourses on the Parable of the Rich Man and Lazarus. London: S. Bridge for Tho. Parkhurst, 1697, 188p. Another ed., Sermons upon the Parable of the Rich Man and Lazarus. 1798, 157p.

De Bruyne, D. see Bruyne, Donatien de

Derrett, J. D. M. "Fresh Light on St. Luke XVI:II. Dives and Lazarus and the Preceding Sayings. " New Testament Studies 7 (1961) 364-80.

Dieterle, Samuel. Der reiche Mann und der arme Lazarus. 2 Predigten über das Gleichnis Luk. 16, 19-31. Basel: Evang. Buchhandlung, 1942, 19p.

Dingfield, W. "The Rich Man and Lazarus. " Th. M. thesis, Dallas Theological Seminary, 1954.

Dods, M. "Dives and Lazarus. " Expositor 3rd ser., 1 (1885) 45-59.

Dunkerley, R. "Lazarus. " New Testament Studies 5 (1958-59) 321-27.

Eliade, Mircea. "Locum refrigerii... " Zalmoxis 1 (1938) 203-08.

Evans, Christopher F. "Luke 16:31. Uncomfortable Words V. " Expository Times 81 (1969) 228-31.

Glombitza, O. "Der reiche Mann und der arme Lazarus; Luk. XVI:19-31. " Novum Testamentum 12 (1970) 166-80.

Graf, W. "Dives and Lazarus (Lc. 16, 19-31)." Homiletic and Pastoral Review 38 (1937-38) 1184-85.

Grensted, L. W. "The Use of Enoch in St. Luke XVI, 19-31." Expository Times 26 (1914-15) 333-34.

Gressmann, Hugo. Vom reichen Mann und armen Lazarus. Berlin: Verlag der Königl. Akademie der Wissenschaften, 1918, 90p.

Grobel, K. "'...Whose Name Was Neves.'" New Testament Studies 10 (1963-64) 373-82.

Hafer, R. A. "Dives and Poor Lazarus in the Light of Today." Lutheran Quarterly 53 (1923) 476-81.

Hanson, R. P. C. "A Note on Luke XVI, 14-31." Expository Times 55 (1943-44) 221-22.

Harnack, Adolf von. "Der Name des reichen Mannes in Luc. 16, 19," in Texte und Untersuchungen XIII, 1, pp75-78. Leipzig: Hinrichs, 1895.

Harvey, Theodore L. The Rich Man in Hell: An Awful Mistake of Preachers. With Appendixes Concerning Other Mistakes of Churchmen. Monett, Mo.: C. K. Dow, 1905, 47p.

Haupt, Paul. "Abraham's Bosom." American Journal of Philology 42 (1921) 162-67.

Heckel. "Zu Lukas 16, 19. Der reiche Mann und der arme Lazarus." Monatsschrift für Pastoraltheologie 26 (1930) 177-82.

Heller, B. "Im Schosse Abrahams (Lk. 16, 19-31)." Orientalistische Literaturzeitung 36 (1933) 146-49.

Huie, W. P. "Poverty of Abundance" [from text to sermon on Luke 16:19-31]. Interpretation 22 (1968) 403-20.

Joüon, Paul. "Notes philologiques sur les Evangiles--Luc 16, 30." Recherches de science religieuse 18 (1928) 354.

Klinckhardt, C. G. Super parabola J. C. de homine divite et Lazaro. Comment. exegetico-pract. Lipsiae: 1831.

Königsmann, A. L. Dissertatio de divite epulone immiseri-
cordiae non accusato. Kilon: 1708.

Künstlinger, D. "Im Schosse Abrahams." Orientalistische
Literaturzeitung 36 (1933) 408.

Leenmans, H. A. "Lk. 16:21b." Nieuwe Theologische
Studiën 1 (1918) 104-05.

Lefort, L. Th. "Le Nom du mauvois riche (Lc. 16, 19) et
la tradition copte." Zeitschrift für die neutestamentliche
Wissenschaft 37 (1938) 65-72.

Lorenzen, Thorwald. "A Biblical Meditation on Luke 16:19-
31." Expository Times 87 (1975) 39-43.

Lüthi, Walter. Vom reichen und vom armen Mann. Predigt
über Luk. 16, 19-31. Basel: Reinhardt, 1947, 15p.

Mason, John. Dives and Lazarus. A Sacred Poem in Dialogue. Baltimore: J. B. Piet, 1883? 42p.

Mieses, M. "Im Schosse Abrahams." Orientalistische
Literaturzeitung 34 (1931) 1018-21.

Niedner, C. W. De loco comment. Lucae XVI, 1-13 dissertatio. Lipsiae: 1823.

North, Brownlow. The Rich Man and Lazarus; A Practical
Exposition of Luke XVI, 19-31. London: Truth Trust,
1960, 127p.

Pfeiffer, K. W. Th. "Gleichnis vom 'reichen Mann und
vom armen Lazarus' (Lukas 16, 10-30)." Theologische
Zeitschrift aus der Schweiz 8 (1891) 163-70.

Powell, W. "The Parable of Dives and Lazarus (Luke XVI,
19-31)." Expository Times 66 (1954-55) 350-51.

Renié, J. "Le Mauvais Riche (Lc. 16, 19-31)." L'Année
Théologique 6 (1945) 268-75.

The Rich Man and Lazarus (Filmstrip). Scripture Press,
1955.

Rich Man, Poor Man, Beggar Man, Thief (Filmstrip).
Shawnee Mission, Kan.: Marsh Film Enterprises, 1975.

Rimmer, N. "The Parable of Dives and Lazarus (Luke XVI, 19-31)." Expository Times 66 (1954-55) 215-16.

Rollenhagen, Georg. Georg Rollenhagens Spiel vom reichen Manne und armen Lazaro. Halle (Saale): M. Niemeyer, 1929, 163p.

Sahlin, H. "Lasarus-gestalten i Lk. 16 och Joh. 11." Svensk exegetisk årsbok 37 (1972) 167-74.

Schurhammer, G. "Eine Parabel Christi im Götzentempel." Katholischen Missionen 49 (1920-21) 134-38.

Sommelius, G. Dissertatio in narrationem de divite epulone et Lazaro. Lund: 1768.

Sommerauer, Adolf. Der reiche Mann und der arme Lazarus. Ein Spiel um das Gleichnis Jesu Christi. Stuttgart: Oncken, 1948, 18p.

Standen, A. O. "The Parable of Dives and Lazarus, and Enoch 22." Expository Times 33 (1921-22) 523.

Thurneysen, Eduard. Lazarus und der reiche Mann: Lukas 16, 19-31. Predigt, gehalten am 26. Mai 1940 im Münster zu Basel. Basel: Verlag Evangelische Buchhandlung, 1940, 15p.

Tobler, Gustaf. Reicher Mann und armer Lazarus. Eine immer zeitmässe Botschaft. Zürich: Advent-Verlag, 1949, 29p.

Trudinger, P. "A 'Lazarus Motif' in Primitive Christian Preaching." Andover Newton Quarterly 7 (1966) 29-32.

Wehrli, Eugene S. "Luke 16:19-31." Interpretation 31 (1977) 276-80.

Windisch, Hans. "Over Strekking en Echtheid der Lazarus-Parabel." Nederlands Theologisch Tijdschrift 14 (1925) 343-60.

Das Zürcher Spiel vom reichen Mann und vom armen Lazarus. Die Totenfresser von Pamphilus Gengenbach. Hrsg. von Josef Schmidt. Stuttgart: Reclam, 1969, 63p.

SALT

Coleman, N. D. "'Salt' and 'Salted' in Mark 9, 49 and 50." Expository Times 48 (1936-37) 360-62.

Cullmann, Oscar. "Das Gleichnis vom Salz," in Vorträge und Aufsatze 1925-62, pp192-201. Tübingen: Mohr (Siebeck); Zürich: Zwingli Verlag, 1966.

_____. "Que signifie le sel dans la parabole de Jésus?" Revue d'Histoire et de Philosophie Religieuses 37 (1957) 36-43.

Harris, J. R. "A Further Note on the 'Salt' Section at the End of Mark IX." Expository Times 48 (1936-37) 185.

Hutton, W. R. "The Salt Sections." Expository Times 58 (1946-47) 166-68.

Jacob, C. W. "The 'Salt' Problem in St. Mark." Expository Times 48 (1936-37) 476.

Killermann, S. "Das evangelische Gleichnis vom Salz und eine neue naturkundliche Erklärung." Theologisch-praktische Quartalschrift 92 (1939) 37-41.

Steinkopf, G. "Das Wort vom Salzen Mc. 9, 49: Οὐσία (D) oder Θυσία (k) oder πῦρ (B)?" Theologisches Jahrbuch 8 (1940-41) 93-105.

SEED GROWING SECRETLY

Baltenweiler, H. "Das Gleichnis von der selbstwachsenden Saat (Markus 4, 26-29) und die theologische Konzeption des Markusevangelisten," in Oikonomia-Heilsgeschichte als Thema der Theologie. Festschrift für O. Cullmann. F. Christ, ed., pp69-75. Hamburg-Bergstedt: Herbert Reich, 1967.

Brown, Alexander. "The Ears of Corn." Expository Times 20 (1908-09) 377-78.

Burbridge, A. T. "The Seed Growing Secretly." Expository Times 40 (1928-29) 139-41.

Dupont, Jacques. "La Parabole de la semence qui pousse

toute seule (Marc 4, 26-29)." Recherches de Science Religieuse 55 (1967) 367-92.

Freundorfer, Joseph. "Eine neue Auslegung der Parabel von der 'selbstwachsenden Saat' Mk. 4, 26-29." Biblische Zeitschrift 17 (1925-26) 51-62.

Goebel, Siegfried. "Das Gleichnis Mark 4, 26-29." Theologische Studien und Kritiken 51 (1878) 565-82.

Kilpatrick, G. D. "Mark IV, 29." Journal of Theological Studies 46 (1945) 191.

Kümmel, W. G. "Noch einmal: Das Gleichnis von der selbstwachsenden Saat. Bemerkungen zur neuesten Diskussion um die Auslegung der Gleichnisse Jesu," in Orientierung an Jesus; zur Theologie der Synoptiker. Für Josef Schmid. Hrsg. von Paul Hoffmann, Norbert Brox, Wilhelm Pesch, pp220-37. Freiburg: Herder, 1973.

Manson, T. W. "A Note on Mark IV, 28f." Journal of Theological Studies 38 (1937) 399-400.

Mussner, F. "Gleichnisauslegung und Heilsgeschichte. Dargetan am Gleichnis von der wachsenden Saat (Mc. 4, 26-29)." Trierer Theologische Zeitschrift 64 (1955) 257-66.

Pope, Hugh. "The Seed Growing Secretly." Irish Theological Quarterly 5 (1910) 279-88.

Sahlin, Harald. "Zum Verständnis von drei Stellen des Markus-Evangeliums." Biblica 33 (1952) 53-66.

Strauss, D. F. "Das Gleichnis vom fruchtbringenden Acker bei Marcus 4, 26-29." Zeitschrift für wissenschaftliche Theologie 6 (1863) 209-14.

Stuhlmann, R. "Beobachtungen und Überlegungen zu Markus 4:26-29." New Testament Studies 19 (1973) 153-62.

Weiss, Karl. "Mk. 4:26 bis 29--dennoch die Parabel vom zuversichtlichen Sämann!" Biblische Zeitschrift 18 (1929) 45-68.

_____. Voll Zuversicht! Zur Parabel Jesu vom zuversichtlichen Sämann Mk. 4, 26-29. Münster:

Aschendorffsche Verlh., 1922, 76p.

SERVANT IN AUTHORITY

Turner, C. H. "Notes on the Old Latin Version of the
Bible. 3. A Secondary Feature in St. Cyprian's Text
of Luke XII:47." Journal of Theological Studies 2 (1901)
606-07.

SOWER

Bailey, K. E. "Sower; Discerning the Theological Cluster."
Thesis Theological Cassettes 2 no. 12 (1971).

Bell, C. C. The Sower; A Study of the Parable of Parables.
London: Mowbray, 1928, 167p.

Blei, K. "De gelijkenis van de zaaïer." Vox Theologica,
1956.

Bover, José M. "Problemas inherentes a la interpretación
de la parábola del Sembrador." Estudios eclesiásticos
26 (1952) 169-85.

Bowker, John W. "Mystery and Parable: Mark 4:1-20."
Journal of Theological Studies 25 (1974) 300-17.

Bruner, F. D. "Listening Towards a Theology of Acoustics."
South East Asia Journal of Theology 11 (Autumn 1969) 31-
39.

Bultmann, Rudolf. "Die Interpretation von Mk. 4, 3-9 seit
Jülicher," in Jesus und Paulus. Festschrift für Werner
Georg Kümmel zum 70. Geburtstag. Hrsg. von E. Earle
Ellis und Erich Grässer, pp30-34. Göttingen: Vanden-
hoeck & Ruprecht, 1975.

Cerfaux, Lucien. "Fructifiez en supportant; l'épreuve; a propos de Luc VIII:15." Revue Biblique 64 (1957) 481-91.
Also in Recueil Cerfaux, III (Suppl.) pp111-22. Gembloux: Duculot, 1962.

Courthial, P. "Du texte au sermon; la parabole du semeur
en Luc 8:5-15." Etudes théologiques et religieuses 47
(1972) 297-420.

Dale, R. W. "The Parable of the Sower; Sunday Readings." Good Words (1894) 713-20.

Dalman, G. "Viererlei Acker." Palästinajahrbuch 22 (1926) 120-32.

Didier, M. "La Parabole du semeur," in Au service de la parole de Dieu. Mélanges offerts à Monseigneur André-Marie Charue, pp21-41. Gembloux: J. Duculot, 1969.

_____. "Les Paraboles du semeur et de la semence qui croît d'elle-même." Revue Diocéscaine de Namur 14 (1960) 185-96.

Dietzfelbinger, C. "Das Gleichnis vom ausgestreuten Samen," in Der Ruf Jesu und die Antwort der Gemeinde. Fest. J. Jeremias, pp80-93. Göttingen: Vandenhoeck & Ruprecht, 1970.

Doherty, J. E. "The Sower and the Seed." Liguorian 50 (March 1962) 46-51.

Doncoeur, Paul. "La Parabole du semeur qui sème à'tout terrain." Recherches de science religieuse 24 (1934) 609-11.

Drury, J. "The Sower, the Vineyard, and the Place of Allegory in the Interpretation of Mark's Parables." Journal of Theological Studies 24 (1973) 367-79.

Dupont, Jacques. "Le Chapitre des paraboles." Nouvelle revue théologiques 89 (1967) 800-20.

_____. "Encore la parabole de la Semence, qui pousse toute seule (Mc. 4, 26-29)," in Jesus und Paulus: Festschrift für Werner Georg Kümmel zum 70. Geburtstag. Hrsg. von E. Earle Ellis und Erich Grässer, pp96-102. Göttingen: Vandenhoeck & Ruprecht, 1975.

_____. "L'Evangile (du Dimanche de la Sexagésime) (Lc. 8, 4-15): Le Semeur." Assemblées du Seigneur

_____. "La parábola de la semilla que crece por si sola." Selección de Teologia 9 (1960) 73-78.

_____. "La Parabole du semeur." Foi et Vie 66

no. 5 (1967) 3-25.

_____. "La Parabole du semeur dans la version de Luc." Beihefte zur Zeitschrift für die neutestamentliche Wissenschaft 30 (1964) 97-108.

Egbert, John P. Some Lessons from the Parable of the Sower, the Parable of Growth, and the Law of the Harvest. Buffalo: Ulbrich & Kingsley, 1886, 209p.

Eichholz, Georg. Marc 4, 1-9, 14-20 (Das Gleichnis von Sämann und seine Deutung). Bibelarbeiten ... rhein. Landessynode 1967 in Bad Godesberg. Mühlheim/Ruhr, 1967.

Espey, Albert. Der Sämann, Gleichnisse und Reden nach Heilandsworten den deutschen Menschenkindern in grosser Zeit wiedererzählt. Berlin: Concordia, 1916, 55p.

Finlayson, S. K. "The Parable of the Sower." Expository Times 55 (1943-44) 306-07.

Fonck, Leopold. "Parabola seminantis (Lc. 8, 4-15)." Verbum Domini 2 (1922) 43-48.

George, A. "Le Sens de la parabole des semailles (Mc. IV, 3-9 et parallèles," in Sacra Pagina, II, pp163-69. Paris: Gabalda; Gembloux: Duculot, 1959.

Gerhardsson, B. "The Parable of the Sower and Its Interpretation." New Testament Studies 14 (1968) 165-93.

Giovanni, M. "Sow, Sower, Sow." Ave Maria 101 (Feb. 27, 1965) 14-15.

Grayston, K. "The Sower." Expository Times 55 (1943-44) 138-39.

Guardini, Romano. Wahrheit und Ordnung. Universitäts-Predigten. 7. Das Gleichnis vom Säemann. Wurzburg: Werkbund Verlag, 1956, 24p.

Hall, John. The Sower and the Seed. Philadelphia: Presbyterian Board of Publication, 1856, 127p.

Harwood, Edward. Sermons on the Parable of the Sower. London: 1776.

Hasseveldt, R. "Marginal Musings on the Parable of the Sower." Sponsa Regis 31 (Dec. 1959) 117-20.

Haugg, Donatus. "Das Ackergleichnis. Mk. 4, 1-9; Mt. 13, 1-9; Lk. 8, 4-8." Theologische Quartalschrift 127 (1947) 166-204.

Holzmeister, U. "'Aliud (fecit fructum) centesimum' (Mt. 13, 8. cf. Mc. 4, 8; Lc. 8, 8)." Verbum Domini 20 (1940) 219-23.

_____. "'Exiit qui seminat seminare semen suum' (Lc. 8, 4-15)." Verbum Domini 22 (1942) 8-12.

Irving, Edward. Lectures on the Parable of the Sower, Constituting the Second Volume of His Sermons, Lectures, and Occasional Discourses. London: 1828.

Jeremias, Joachim. "Palästinakundliches zum Gleichnis vom Sämann (Mark IV:3-8)." New Testament Studies 13 (Oct. 1966) 48-53.

Kempf, Georges. Wachet, betet, seid bereit. Ein Evangel-ienspiel nach dem Gleichnis vom Sämann, Matth. 13, 3-9 und 18-23. Paris: Ed. Lutheriennes, 1955, 44p.

Kokot, M. "Znaczenie nasieria w przypowieści o siewcy." Ruch Biblyny i Liturgiczny 26 (1973) 99-107.

Laliberté, J. "Sur la parabole du Semeur (Lc. 8, 5-16)." Revue de l'Université Laval 4, 6 (1950) 475-90.

Lampe, P. "Die markinische Deutung des Gleichnisses vom Sämann; Markus 4:10-12." Zeitschrift für die neutesta-mentliche Wissenschaft 65 (1974) 140-50.

Léon-Dufour, X. "La Parabole du semeur," in Études d'Evangile, pp255-301. Paris: Editions du Seuil, 1965.

Link, Wilhelm. "Die Geheimnisse des Himmelreichs; eine Erklärung von Matth. 13:10-23." Evangelische Theologie 2 (1935) 115-27.

Listening to God (Motion picture). American Bible Society, 1969? Released by Association Films. Illus. Annie Vallotton.

Luck, U. "Das Gleichnis von Sämann und die Verkündigung Jesu." Wort und Dienst 11 (1971) 73-92.

McCool, F. J. "The Preacher and the Gospels." Theology Digest 9 (1961) 145-47.

McDonald, C. "The Relevance of the Parable of the Sower." Bible Today 26 (1966) 1822-27.

Marin, L. "Essai d'analyse structurale d'und récit-parabole: Matthieu 13:1-23." Études théologiques et religieuses 46 (1971) 35-74.

Marshall, I. Howard. "Tradition and Theology in Luke (Luke 8:5-15)." Tyndale Bulletin 20 (1969) 56-75.

Moule, C. F. D. "Mark 4:1-20 Yet Once More," in Neotestamentica et Semitica: Studies in Honor of Matthew Black. E. E. Ellis & M. Wilcox, eds., pp95-113. Edinburgh: T. & T. Clark, 1969.

Muir, George. The Parable of the Sower Illustrated and Applied. London: 1769.

Murray, E. "Hearing Is not Heeding; Homily for Sexagesima Sunday." Homiletic and Pastoral Review 64 (1964) 335-37.

Neil, W. "Expounding the Parables; The Sower (Mk. 4:3-8)." Expository Times 77 (Dec. 1965) 74-77.

Noack, B. "Om Saedemandsparabeln," in Festskrift til Jens Nørregaard den 16. maj 1947. Af N. K. Andersen, et al., pp203-13. København: G. E. C. Gad, 1947.

Pousset, É. "La Parabole du semeur." Vie Chrétienne 170 (1974) 13-16.

Prichard, Harold A. The Sower; Some Suggestions on the Modern Application of a Great Parable. New York: E. P. Dutton, 1923, 219p.

Robinson, W. C. "On Preaching the Word of God (Luke 8: 4-21)," in Studies in Luke-Acts. Essays Presented in Honor of Paul Schubert. Nashville: Abingdon Press, 1966, 131-38.

Ropes, C. J. H. "The Parable of the Field." Biblical World 8 (1896) 20-22.

Schweizer, E. "Du texte à la prédication; Marc 4:1-20." Études Théologiques et Religieuses 43 (1968) 256-64.

Seim, T. K. "Apostolat og forkynnelse; en studie til Mk. 4:1-20." Dansk Teologisk Tidsskrift 35 (1972) 206-22.

The Sower (Filmstrip). Roa's Films, 1966.

_____ (Motion picture). Religious Films, London, 1937. Released in the U. S. by United Films, 1948.

The Sower-seed (Filmstrip). Eye Gate House, 1963.

Stempvoort, P. A. van. "Kerk en Koninkrijk Gods in de gelijkenis van den vierderlei grond." Nederlandsch Theologisch Tijdschrift 1 (1946-47) 347-69.

Stennett, Samuel. Discourses on the Parable of the Sower. London: 1786; Bridgeton, N. J.: J. Davis & J. Bright, 1823, 331p.

Suys, Émile. "Le Commentaire de la parabole du semeur dans les synoptiques (Mat. XIII, 18-23; Marc IV, 13-20; Luc VIII, 11-15)." Recherches de science religieuse 14 (1924) 247-54.

Taylor, Thomas. The Parable of the Sower and the Seed. 3d ed. London: Printed by Thomas Purfoot for John Bartlet, at the Golden Cup, in the Gold-smiths Row in Cheapside, 1634, 354p.

Thiering, B. E. "Breaking of Bread and Harvest in Mark's Gospel." Novum Testamentum 12 (1970) 1-12.

Toohey, W. "Assurance and Challenge; Homily for Sexagesima Sunday." Homiletic and Pastoral Review 65 (1965) 336-38.

Twomey, J. "Sexagesima Sunday." Irish Ecclesiastical Record 103 (1965) 107-08.

Vogels, Heinrich J. "Lk. 8, 8 im Diatessaron." Biblische Zeitschrift 18 (1928-29) 83-84.

Walker, Albert H. "The Parable of the Sower." Preacher's
Magazine 7 (1897) 61-65, 110-13; 8 (1898) 333-36.

Wenham, David. "The Interpretation of the Parable of the
Sower." New Testament Studies 20 (1974) 299-319.

White, K. D. "The Parable of the Sower." Journal of
Theological Studies 15 (1964) 300-07.

Wilder, Amos N. "The Parable of the Sower: Naiveté and
Method in Interpretation." Semeia 2 (1974) 134-51.

The Wind and the Seed (Filmstrip). Cathedral Films, 1955.

TALENTS

Candlish, Robert. "The Pounds and the Talents." Expository Times 23 (1911-12) 136-37.

Chevrot, Georges. L'Eternelle actualité de l'Evangile: La
vie de l'homme nouveau. 3. La parabole des talents.
Le travail et la vie plus féconde. Paris-Bruges:
Descleé De Brouwer et Cie, 1939.

Cobden, Edward. The Parable of the Talents. A Sermon
Preached at the Parish-Church of St. Ann, Westminster,
on Thursday, March the 24th, 1748. London: Printed
and sold by M. Mechell, 1748, 17p.

Dauviller, Jean. "La Parabole des mines ou des talents
et le #99 du code Hammourabi," in Mélanges dédiés
à M. le professeur Joseph Magnol, doyen honoraire de
la Faculté de droit de Toulouse, pp153-65. Paris:
Recueil Sirey, 1948.

Derrett, J. D. M. "Law in the New Testament; The Parable of the Talents and Two Logia." Zeitschrift für die
neutestamentliche Wissenschaft 56 (1966) 184-95.

Didier, M. "L'Evangile (du Commun des confesseurs pon-
tifes) (Mt. 25, 14-30): La Parabole des talents." Assemblées du Seigneur 93 (1965) 32-44.

_____. "La Parabole des talents et des mines,"
in De Jésus aux Evangiles. Bibliotheca Ephemeridum
theologicarum Lovaniensium 25. vol. 2, pp248-71.

Gembloux: Duculot; Paris: Lethielleux, 1967.

Dupont, Jacques. "La Parabole des talents (Mat. 25: 14-30) ou des mines (Luc 19:12-27)." Revue de theologie et de philosophie 19 (1969) 376-91. Also in Assemblées du Seigneur 64 (1969) 18-28.

Ellul, J. "Du texte au sermon; la parabole des talents; Matthieu 25:13-30." Études théologiques et religieuses 48 (1973) 125-38.

Fiedler, P. "Die übergebenen Talente. Auslegung von Mt. 25, 14-30." Bibel und Leben 11 (1970) 259-73.

Ganne, P. "La Parabole des talents." Bible et Vie Chrétienne 45 (1962) 44-53.

"Interpretatio Parabolae Talentorum." Collationes Diocesis Tornacensis 22 (1927) 215-17.

Joüon, Paul. "Notes philologiques sur les Évangiles--Matthieu 25. 21." Recherches de science religieuse 18 (1928) 349.

_____. "La Parabole des Mines (Luc 19, 13-27) et la Parabole des Talents (Matthieu 25, 14-30)." Recherches de science religieuse 29 (1939) 489-94.

Kamlah, E. "Kritik und Interpretation der Parabel von den anvertrauten Geldern Mt. 25:14ff.; Lk. 19:12ff." Kerygma und Dogma 14 (1968) 28-38.

Kramer, Janice. Eight Bags of Gold: Matthew 25:14-30 for Children. Illus. Sally Mathews. St. Louis: Concordia Pub. House, 1964.

McCulloch, W. "The Pounds and the Talents." Expository Times 23 (1911-12) 382-83.

McGaughy, Lane C. "Fear of Yahweh and the Mission of Judaism: A Postexilic Maxim and its Early Christian Expansion in the Parable of the Talents." Journal of Biblical Literature 94 (1975) 235-45.

Matheson, G. "Scripture Studies of the Heavenly State; The Nature of the Heavenly Blessedness (Matt. XXV, 21)."

Expositor 2nd ser., 6 (1883) 204-15.

Miegge, Mario. I talenti messi a profitto. L'interpretazione della parabola dei denari affidati ai servi dalla
Chiesa antica a Calvino. Urbino: Argalía, 1969
142p.

Mombello, Gianni. Les Avatars de Talentum: recherches
sur l'origine et les variations des acceptions romanes
et non romanes de ce terme. Torino: Società editrice
internazionale, 1976. 423p.

Mora, F. L. "Le Refus d'Israël, Mt. 25, 27." Diss.
Studii Biblici Franciscani, Jerusalem, 1970.

Mutch, John. "The Man with One Talent." Expository
Times 42 (1930-31) 332-34.

A Rainy Day Surprise (Filmstrip). Cathedral Films,
1965.

Ravenscroft, John S. A Discourse on the Parable of the
Talents, Delivered before the Episcopal Convention, Held
at Leesburg, Va., May, 1823. Leesburg, Va.: Printed
by B. W. Sower, 1823, 15p.

Schmidt, W. "Die Bedeutung der Talente in der Parabel
Matth. 25, 14-30." Theologische Studien und Kritiken
56 (1883) 782-99.

School Days in the Ocean (Filmstrip). Cathedral Films,
1956.

Stock, Eugene. "The Pounds and the Talents." Expository
Times 23 (1911-12) 136-37.

The Talents (Filmstrip). Roa's Films, 1966.

Talents (Motion picture). Family Films, 1951.

The Ten Talents (Motion picture). Broadcasting and Film
Commission, 1951. Made by Everett Parker.

Tillich, Paul J. "Riddle of Iniquity." Union Seminary
Quarterly Review 13 (May 1958) 3-9. Reprint. Social
Action 25 (Nov. 1958) 20-25.

Walvoord, John F. "Christ's Olivet Discourse on the End of the Age; The Parable of the Talents." Bibliotheca Sacra 129 (1972) 206-10.

TARES

Bunn, Leslie H. "The Parable of the Tares." Expository Times 38 (1926-27) 561-64.

Correll, J. "La parábola de la cizaña y su explicación (Mt. 13, 24-30, 36-43." Pars Diss. Pont. Univ. S. Thomas de Urbe, 62p.; Escritos del Vedat 2 (1972) 3-52.

De Goedt, M. "L'Explication de la parabole de l'ivraie; Matt. XIII: 36-43; création matthéenne, ou aboutissement d'une histoire littéraire?" Revue Biblique 66 (1959) 32-54.

Doherty, J. E. "Should the Church Exclude Sinners?" Liguorian (Sept. 1962) 38-42.

Doty, William G. "An Interpretation: Parable of the Weeds and Wheat." Interpretation 25 (1971) 185-93.

The Fairy Ring (Filmstrip). Cathedral Films, 1955.

Fonck, Leopold. "Parabola zizaniorum agri (Mt. 13, 24-30)." Verbum Domini 6 (1926) 327-34.

Das Gleichnis vom Unkraut unter dem Weizen. Lutherhefte 52-53. Zwickau: J. Herrmann, 1913, 32p.

Heylin, Peter. The Parable of the Tares Expounded and Applied in Ten Sermons Preached before His Late Majesty King Charles the Second, Monarch of Great Britain. To which Are added Three Other Sermons of the Same Author. London: Printed by J. G. for H. Moseley, 1959, 395p.

Homes-Gore, U. A. "The Parable of the Tares." Theology 35 (1937) 117.

Houseman, Hubert G. "The Parable of the Tares." Theology 3 (1921) 31-35.

Jeremias, Joachim. "Die Deutung des Gleichnisses vom

Unkraut unter dem Weizen (Mt. 13:36-43)," in Neotesta-
mentica et Patristica. Festschrift für Oscar Cullmann.
Vol. VI of Supplements to Novum Testamentum. B.
Reicke and W. C. van Unnik, eds., pp59-63; Leiden:
E. J. Brill, 1962. Or Abba. Göttingen: Vandenhoeck
& Ruprecht, 1966, 261-65.

Liechtenhan, R. "Das Gleichnis vom Unkraut unter dem
Weizen." Kirchenblatt für die reformierte Schweiz 99
(1943) 146.

Loman, A. D. "Bijdragen tot de critiek der synoptische
Evangeliën. I. De gelijkenis van het onkruid (Matth.
13:24-30), naar nare oorspronklike redactie en betekenis."
Theologisch tijdschrift 3 (1869) 577-85.

Mouson, J. "Explicatur parabola de zizaniis in agro (Mt.
XIII, 24-30, 36-43)." Collectanea Mechliniensia 44
(1959) 171-75.

Muir, George. The Parable of the Tares, in Twenty-one
Sermons. Paisley: 1771.

Neyländer. "Das Gleichnis vom Unkraut unter den Weizen."
Nach dem Gesetz und Zeugnis 30 (1929-30) 67-70.

Prete, B. "The Wheat and the Cockle." Cross and Crown
4 (1952) 456-65.

Toohey, W. "Men of the Kingdom; Homily for Fifth Sunday
after Epiphany." Homiletic and Pastoral Review 65
(1965) 333-34.

Treier, René. Vom Unkraut unter dem Weizen. Predigt
über Matth. 13, 24-30 und 36-43. Basel: F. Reinhardt,
1948, 13p.

Vanbergen, P. "L'Evangile du 5 ème dimanche après
l'Epiphanie." Paroisse et Liturgie 44 (Jan. 1962) 39-
48.

The Wheat and the Weeds (Filmstrip). Roa's Films, 1966.

Wiches, Dean R. "Note on Matthew 13, 30 and Matt. 6,
30=Luke 12, 28." Journal of Biblical Literature 42
(1923) 251.

TEN VIRGINS

Anderson, Louis J. The Ten Virgins. Chicago: Purdy Pub. Co., 1888, 26p.

Andre, Gustav. Das Gleichnis von den zehn Jungfrauen. In Versen dramatisch dargestellt, 3. Aufl. Berlin: Buchhandlung des Ostdeutschen Jünglingsbundes, 1913, 19p. 5. Aufl., 1927.

Argyle, Aubrey W. "Wedding Customs at the Time of Jesus." Expository Times 86 (1975) 214-15.

Beverley, Thomas. The Parable of the Ten Virgins, with an Apology for the Hope of the Kingdom of Christ within the Approaching Year. London: 1697.

Bornkamm, Günther. "Die Verzögerung der Parusie. Exegetische Bemerkungen zu zwei synoptischen Teste. --Zu Matth. 25, 1-13," in In Memoriam Ernst Lohmeyer, pp119-25. Stuttgart: Evangelisches Verlagswerk, 1951.

Bülow, Gertrud von. Das Gleichnis von den 10 Jungfrauen. Schwerin o. J.: F. Bahn, 1920.

Burkitt, F. C. "The Parable of the Ten Virgins." Journal of Theological Studies 30 (1929) 267-70.

The Busy Bee (Filmstrip). Cathedral Films, 1956.

Buzy, Denis. "Les Dix Vierges." Revue Apologétique 39 (1924-25) 65-84.

Clowes, John. Predigten über das Gleichniss von den zehn Jungfrauen. Tübingen: Verlags-Expedition, 1851. 2 vols.

Cölle, R. "Die Pointe des Gleichnisses von den zehn Jungfrauen." Neue kirchliche Zeitschrift 12 (1901) 904-08.

Coleman, Benjamin. Practical Discourses on the Parable of the Ten Virgins. Being a Serious Call and Admonition to Watchfulness and Diligence in Preparing for Death and Judgment. London: Printed for Thomas Perkhurst, 1707. Also, Boston: Printed and sold by Rogers and Fowle, and J. Edwards, 1747. 344p.

Derrett, J. D. M. "La parabola delle vergini stolte."
Conoscenza Religiosa (1971) 394-496.

Didier, M. "La Parabole des vierges (Mt. 25, 1-13)." La
Foi et le temps 3 (1970) 329-50.

Donfried, Karl P. "The Allegory of the Ten Virgins (Matt.
25:1-13) as a Summary of Matthean Theology." Journal
of Biblical Literature 93 (1974) 415-28.

_____. "The Ten Virgins (Mt. 25:1-13): Cond. from
Journal of Biblical Literature, Sept. 1974." Theology
Digest 23 (1975) 106-10.

Durrwell, F. "Le Désir du salut." Vie Spirituelle 99
(1958) 451-65.

Engler, Karl. Das Gleichnis der 10 Jungfrauen. Witten:
Buchhandlung der Stadtmission, 1920, 16p.; 2. Aufl.
Witten: Bundes-Verlag, 1925, 23p.

Felipe de Fuenterrabia. "La imagen parabólica del matri-
monio y la parábola de las diez virgenes." Estudis
Franciscans 57 (1956) 321-62.

Fels, A. La Parabole des vierges sages et des vierges
folles. Ill. de R. Lecomte. Nancy: Impro. Vagner,
s. d., 16p.

Feuillet, A. "La Parabole des vierges, Mt. 25, 1-13."
Vie Spirituelle 75 (1946) 667-77.

Ford, J. M. "The Parable of the Foolish Scholars; Matt.
25:1-13." Novum Testamentum 9 (1967) 107-23.

Göttler, Fritz. Töricht oder klug? Was bist Du? Gedan-
ken über das Gleichnis von den Jungfrauen, Matth. 25,
1-13. St. Georgen i. Schwarzw.: Jungendbundheim;
Barmen: Deutsche Buchmission, 1927, 16p.

Goudge, H. L. "The Parable of the Ten Virgins." Journal
of Theological Studies 30 (1929) 399-401.

Henrichs, Ludwig. "...Und die bereit waren." Beitrag zur
Auslegung des Gleichnisses von den 10 Jungfrauen.
Giessen: Brunnenverlag, 1921, 32p.; also Leipzig: J.
C. Hinrichs, 1922, 175p.

Heyne, Hildegaard. Das Gleichnis von den klugen und törichten Jungfrauen. Eine literarische ikonographische Studie zur altchristlichen Zeit. Leipzig: H. Haessel, 1922, 121p.

Hilgenfeld, A. "Das Gleichnis von den zehn Jungfrauen Matth. 25, 1-13." Zeitschrift für wissenschaftliche Theologie 44 (1901) 545-53.

Hornschuh, M. "Das Gleichnis von den zehn Jungfrauen in der Epistula Apostolarum." Zeitischrift für Kirchengeschichte 73 (1962) 1-8.

Humpert, Paul. Licht des Lebens, ein Spiel von den klugen und törichten Jungfrauen in einem Vorspiele und drei Teilen mit Gesang und Reigen für die Mädchenbuhne. Warendorf, Westfalen: Genesius Verlag, 1928, 62p.

Huntington, William. The Wise and Foolish Virgins Described. Being the Substance of Two Sermons Delivered at Monkwell-street Meeting, on February 14 and 28, 1797. Boston: Reprinted from the London 2d ed. by True & Parks, 1805, 60p.

Jeremias, Joachim. "Lampades in Matthew 25, 1-13," in Soli Deo Gloria; New Testament Studies in Honor of William Childs Robinson. J. McDowell Richards, ed., pp83-87, 147-49. Richmond, Va.: John Knox Press, 1968.

_____. 'Λαμπάδες, Mt. 25, 1, 3f., 7f." Zeitschrift für die neutestamentliche Wissenschaft 56 (1965) 196-201.

Johnston, Thomas. Christ's Watchword, Being the Parable of the Virgins Expounded. London: J. Bartlet, 1630, 232p.

Keller, Johannes E. Der Bräutigam im Gleichnis der 10. Jungfrauen. Berlin: Verlag von "Weg zur Wahreit," 1922, 99p. Also, Gehlberg: Buchhandlung Haus Geratal, 1940, 214p.

Klempert, Wolfgang. Unsere Bereitschaft aus den kommenden Herrn. Betrachtungen zu Matthäus 25, 1-13, das Gleichnis von den 10 Jungfrauen. Berlin: Evangelische Versandbuchhandlung Ekelmann, 1965, 33p.

Krupka, Ernst. Vor Mitternacht. Eine Bibelarbeit über Matth. 25, 1-13, jungen und alten Bibelfreunden dargeboten. Stuttgart: Verlag der Plakatmission, 1950, 61p.

Lambrecht, J. "Les 'Dix Vierges' (Mt. 25, 1-13)." Revue du Clergé Africain 23 (1968) 225-33.

Leclercq, H. "La Parabole des dix vierges." Dictionnaire d'Archéologie Chrétienne et de Liturgie 176 (1953) 3095-98.

Lehmann, Walter. Die Parabel von den klugen und törichten Jungfrauen. Eine ikonographische Studie mit einem Anhang über die Darstellungen der anderen Parabeln Christi. Berlin: E. Ebering, 1916, 111p.

Maisch, J. "Das Gleichnis von den klugen und den törichten Jungfrauen. Auslegung von Mt. 25, 1-13." Bibel und Leben 11 (1970) 247-59.

Meinertz, Max. "Die Tragweite des Gleichnisses von den zehn Jungfrauen," in Synoptische Studien. München: Karl Zink, 1953, 94-106.

Moore, P. A. "Quinque prudentes virgines." Studies in Comparative Religion 4 (1970) 80-95.

Paul, Jonathan. Das Gleichnis von den 10 Jungfrauen. Mülheim-Ruhr o. J.: Gesellschaft für Mission, Diakonie und Kolportage, 1911, 15p.

Rau, J. G. Quo consilio Jesus Christus parabola de decem virginibus proposuerit anquiritur. Erlangae: 1798.

Reid, James. "The Parable of the Ten Virgins, Matt. XXV, 1-13." Expository Times 37 (1925-26) 447-51.

Ridley, W. D. "The Parable of the Ten Virgins." Expositor 5th ser., 2 (1895) 342-49.

Sabbe, M. "De parabel van de maagden." Collationes Brugenses et Gandavenses 5 (1959) 369-78.

Seiss, Joseph A. The Parable of the Ten Virgins: In Six Discourses. Philadelphia: Smith, English; Boston: Gould & Lincoln, 1862, 189p.

Shepard, Thomas. The Parable of the Ten Virgins Opened and Applied; Being the Substance of Divers Sermons on Matth. 25. 1-13. London: J. H., for John Rothwell, 1660 (1695). 203p. Also, Glasgow: J. M'Aulay, 1796. 2 vols. Also, Falkirk: T. Johnston, 1797. 2 vols. Also, Aberdeen, 1853. 2 vols.

Staats, R. "Die törichten Jungfrauen von Mt. 25 in gnostischer und antignostischer Literatur." Beihefte zur Zeitschrift für die neutestamentliche Wissenschaft 37 (1969) 94-105.

Stonham, Benjamin. The Parable of the Ten Virgins Opened. London: 1676, 316p.

Strobel, Friedrich A. "Zum Verständnis von Mat. XXV, 1-13." Novum Testamentum 2 (1958) 199-227.

The Ten Maidens (Filmstrip). Roa's Films, 1966.

Walvoord, John F. "Christ's Olivet Discourse on the End of the Age; The Parable of the Ten Virgins." Bibliotheca Sacra 129 (1972) 99-105.

Wenthe, Dean O. The Springfielder 40 (June 1976) 9-16.

Wiesen, Pastor. "Das Gleichnis von den zehn Jungfrauen." Theologische Studien und Kritiken 72 (1899) 37-62.

Wintenbotham, R. "The Second Advent." Expositor 1st ser., 9 (1879) 67-80.

Wittkat, Hildeg. Zu spät. Ein Verkündigungsspiel nach dem Gleichnis von den 10 Jungfrauen. Berlin: Evang. Verlag Anst., 1953, 14p.

Zorell, F. "De lampadibus decem virginum." Verbum Domini 10 (1930) 176-82.

TOWER-BUILDER

Jarvis, P. G. "The Tower-Builder and the King Going to War (Luke 14:25-33)." Expository Times 77 (1966) 196-98.

Louw, J. "Lucas 14, 25-33." Nieuwe Theologische Studiën

19 (1936) 144-45.

_____. "The Parables of the Tower-Builder and the King Going to War." Expository Times 48 (1936-37) 478.

Mechie, Stewart. "The Parables of the Tower-Builder and the King Going to War." Expository Times 48 (1936-37) 235-36.

TWO BUILDERS

Bruce, Alexander B. "The Wise and the Foolish Hearer." Expositor 1st ser., 9 (1879) 90-105.

House of the Wren (Filmstrip). Cathedral Films, 1956.

The House that Hunter Built (Motion picture). Radio and Television Commission, Southern Baptist Convention. Made and released by Family Films, 1958.

Jongsma, L. S. "Een huis op een steenrots en... een huis op het zand." Gereformeerd theologisch tijdschrift 9 (1909) 337-43.

Nestle, Eb. "Matt. VII, 25, 27." Expository Times 19 (1907-08) 237-38.

Wagner, Maurice E. "The Heart Contains Its Own Destiny." Psychology for Living 19 (Nov. 1977) 18-19.

Wilson, James P. "In Matthew VII, 25 is προσέπεσαν a Primitive Error Displacing προσέχοψαν ?" Expository Times 57 (1945-46) 138.

TWO DEBTORS

Buzy, Denis. "La Pécheresse et les deux débiteurs." Revue Apologétique 42 (1926) 579-600.

De Urrutia, J. L. "La parábola de los deudores Lc. 7, 39-50." Estudios Eclesiásticos 38 (1963) 459-82.

Hense, Walter. Das Verhältnis zwischen Diatessaron, christlicher Gnosis und 'Western Text.' Erläutert an

einer unkanonischen Version des Gleichnisses vom
gnädigen Gläubiger Materialien zur Geschichte der Peri-
kope von der namenlosen Sünderin Lk. 7, 36-50. Bei-
heft zur Zeitschrift für die neutestamentliche Wissenschaft 33. Berlin: Töpelmann, 1967.

Jüon, Paul. "La Pécheresse de Galilée et la Parabole des
duex Débiteurs (Luc 7, 36-50)." Recherches de Science
Religieuse 29 (1939) 615-19.

Macgregor, W. M. "The Parable of the Money-Lender and
his Debtors (Luke VII, 41-47)." Expository Times 37
(1925-26) 344-47.

Perella, G. M. "La parabola dei due debitors (Lc. 7, 36-
50) e la dottrina della contrizione perfetta." Divus
Thomas 42 (1939) 553-58.

TWO SONS

Boskoop, J. De begenadigede Zondaresse en de Twee naar
den Wyngaard gezondene Zoonen beschouwd in 12 Leerr-
denen. Amsterdam: 1768.

Derrett, J. D. M. "The Parable of the Two Sons." Studia
Theologica 25 (1971) 109-16.

Guy, Harold A. "The Parable of the Two Sons." Expository
Times 51 (1939-40) 204-05.

Macgregor, W. M. "The Parable of the Two Sons." Expository Times 38 (1926-27) 498-501.

Merkel, Helmut. "Das Gleichnis von den 'Ungleichen Söhnen'
(Matth. XXI, 28-32)." New Testament Studies 20 (1974)
254-61.

Michaels, J. R. "The Parable of the Regretful Son." Harvard Theological Review 61 (1968) 15-26.

Riggenbach, E. "Zur Exegese und Textkritik zweier Gleichnisse Jesu," in Aus Schrift und Geschichte. Fest.
Adolf Schlatter, pp17-34. Stuttgart: Calwer Vereins-
buchh., 1922.

Schmid, J. "Das textgeschichtliche Problem der Parabel

Two Sons; Unjust Judge / 397

von den zwei Söhnen," in Vom Wort des Lebens. Festschrift für Max Meinertz. Hrsg. von Nikolaus Adler,
pp68-84. Münster Westf.: Aschendorffsche Verlagsbuchhandlung, 1951.

Schweizer, Alex. "Erklärung der Erzählung Matth. XXI, 28-
32 nach der von Lachmann aufgenommenen Lesart ὁ ὕσ-
τερος S. 31." Theologische Studien und Kritiken 12
(1839) 944-64.

Silva, R. "La parábola de los dos hijos (Mt. 21, 28-32)."
Cultura Biblica 22 (1965) 98-105.

Wiesen. "Das Gleichnis von den beiden Söhnen." Beweis
des Glaubens 29 (1893) 371-86.

UNJUST JUDGE

Buzy, Denis. "Le Juge inique (Saint Luc. XVIII, 1-8)."
Revue Biblique 29 (1930) 378-91.

Cranfield, C. E. B. "The Parable of the Unjust Judge and
the Eschatology of Luke-Acts." Scottish Journal of
Theology 16 (1963) 297-301.

Delling, G. "Das Gleichnis vom gottlosen Richter." Zeitschrift für die neutestamentliche Wissenschaft 53 (1962)
1-25.

Derrett, J. D. M. "Law in the New Testament: The Parable of the Unjust Judge." New Testament Studies 18
(1971-72) 178-91.

De Ru, G. "De gelijkenis van de onrechtvaardige rechter
(Lucas 18:1-8)." Nederlands theologisch Tijdschrift 25
(1971) 379-92.

Deschryver, R. "La Parabole du juge malveillant (Luc 18:
1-8)." Revue d'Histoire et de Philosophie Religieuses
48 (1968) 355-66.

Friend in Need, your Friend Indeed (Filmstrip). Shawnee
Mission, Kan.: Marsh Film Enterprises, 1975.

Huhn, Karl. Das Gleichnis von der "bittenden Witwe,"
Gebetsaufruf Jesu an die Gemeinde der Endzeit. Hamburg:

Verlagbuchhandlung Bethel, 1946, 47p.

Ljungvik, Herman. "Zur Erklärung einer Lukas-Stelle
(Luk. XVIII, 7)." New Testament Studies 10 (1964)
289-94.

Meecham, H. G. "The Parable of the Unjust Judge."
Expository Times 57 (1945-46) 306-07.

Riesenfeld, H. "Zu Μακροθυμεῖ (Lk. 18, 7)," in Neutestamentliche Aufsätze. Festschrift für Josef Schmid, pp214-
17. Regensburg: Pustet, 1963.

Robertson, J. A. "The Parable of the Unjust Judge (Luke
XVIII, 1-8)." Expository Times 38 (1926-27) 389-92.

Sabbe, M. "Het eschatologisch gebed in Lukas 18, 1-8."
Collationes Brugenses et Gandavenses 1 (1955) 361-69.

Spicq, C. "La Parabole de la veuve obstinee et du juge
inerte aux decisions impromptues (Lc. XVIII, 1-8)."
Revue Biblique 68 (1961) 68-90.

Warfield, Benjamin B. "The Importunate Widow and the
Alleged Failure of Faith." Expository Times 25 (1913-
14) 69-72, 136-39.

Wifstrand, Albert. "Lukas XVIII, 7." New Testament
Studies 11 (1964) 72-74.

Wilhelmsson, Lars. "Keeping at It." Alliance Witness
112:17 (Aug. 24, 1977) 3-5.

UNJUST STEWARD

Arnott, William. "The Unjust Steward in a New Light."
Expository Times 24 (1912-13) 508-11.

Bailey, K. "The Unjust Steward." Thesis Theological
Cassettes 2 no. 7 (1971).

Baumann, O. "Praktische Auslegung des Gleichnis von ungerechten Haushalter." Kirchliche Monatschrift (1892)
814-23.

Baverstock, A. H. "The Unjust Steward: An Interpretation."

<u>Theology</u> 35 (1937) 78-83.

Beames, Frederick. "The Unrighteous Steward." <u>Expository</u>
<u>Times</u> 24 (1912-13) 150-55.

Bertholdt, L. L. <u>Comment quo nova parabolae de oeconomo</u>
<u>injusto interpretatio tentatur.</u> Erlangen: 1814.

Bigo, P. "La Richesse comme intendance, dans l'Évangile
à propos de Luc 16, 1-9." <u>Nouvelle Revue Théologique</u>
87 (1965) 267-71.

Bogle, Andrew N. "The Unjust Steward." <u>Expository Times</u>
15 (1903-04) 475-76.

Boyd, William F. "The Parable of the Unjust Steward."
<u>Expository Times</u> 50 (1938-39) 46.

Brauns, Pastor. "Nun noch ein Auslegungsversuch von Luk.
16, 1-14." <u>Theologische Studien und Kritiken</u> 15 (1842)
1012-22.

Bretscher, Paul G. "Brief Studies: The Parable of the
Unjust Steward--A New Approach to Luke 16:1-9." <u>Con-</u>
<u>cordia Theological Monthly</u> 22 (1951) 756-62.

Busch, Wilhelm. <u>Der ungerechte Haushalter.</u> (Predigten
über Lukas 16, 1-12). <u>Der reiche Mann</u> und der arme
Lazarus. (Predigten über <u>Lukas 16, 19-31).</u> Stuttgart:
Quell-Verlag, 1948, 128p.

Caemmerer, R. R. "Investment for Eternity. A Study of
Luke 16:1-13." <u>Concordia Theological Monthly</u> 34 (1963)
69-76.

Camps, G. M. and Ubach, B. M. "Un sentido biblico de
ἄδικος, ἀδικία y la interpretacion de Lc. 16, 1-13."
<u>Estudios Biblicos</u> 25 (1966) 75-82.

Carpenter, W. B. "The Parable of the Unjust Steward."
<u>Expositor</u> 4th ser., 7 (1893) 21-29.

Colella, P. "De mamona iniquitatis." <u>Rivista Biblica</u> 19
(1971) 427-

_____. "Zu Lk. 16:17." <u>Zeitschrift für die neute-</u>
<u>stamentliche Wissenschaft</u> 64 (1973) 124-26.

Collins, R. L. "Is the Parable of the Unjust Steward Pure Sarcasm?" Expository Times 22 (1910-11) 525-26.

Comiskey, J. "The Unjust Steward." Bible Today 52 (1971) 229-35.

Compston, H. F. B. "Friendship without Mammon." Expository Times 31 (1919-20) 282.

Coutts, John. "Studies in Texts: The Unjust Steward." Theology 52 (1949) 54-60.

Davidson, J. A. "A 'Conjecture' about the Parable of the Unjust Steward (Luke XVI, 1-9)." Expository Times 66 (1954-55) 31.

De Klerk, J. A. "Een crux uit Lukas." Vox theologica 3 (1931-32) 127-31.

Del Paramo, S. "La parábola del administrador infiel (Lc. 16, 1-18)." Sal Terrae 32 (1944) 142-48; Comillas 1 (1967) 219-25.

Derrett, J. D. M. "Fresh Light on St. Luke XVI. I. The Parable of the Unjust Steward." New Testament Studies 7 (1961) 198-219.

_____ . "'Take thy Bond...and Write Fifty,' Luke 16:6; The Nature of the Bond." Journal of Theological Studies 23 (1972) 438-40.

Deschryver, R. "La Parabole du juge malveillant (Lc. 18, 1-8)." Revue d'Histoire et de Philosophie Religieuses 48 (1968) 355-66.

Dietzfelbinger, C. "Das Gleichnis von der erlassenen Schuld; eine theologische Untersuchung von Matthäus 18: 23-35." Evangelische Theologie 32 (1972) 437-51.

Double Trouble! (Filmstrip). Shawnee, Kan.: Marsh Film Enterprises, 1975.

Drexler, H. "Zu Lukas 16, 1-7." Zeitschrift für die neutestamentliche Wissenschaft 58 (1967) 286-88.

Eagar, Alexander R. "The Parable of the Unjust Steward." Expositor 5th ser., 2 (1895) 457-70.

Ensfelder, J. Th. "Interprétation de la parabole de l'économe infidèle." Revue de Théologie et de Philosophie
Chrétienne 4 (1852) 182-85.

Feuillet, André. "Les Riches intendants du Christ (Luc
XVI, 1-13)." Recherches de Science Religieuse 34
(1947) 30-54.

Firth, C. B. "The Parable of the Unrighteous Steward
(Luke XVI, 1-9)." Expository Times 63 (1951-52) 93-
95.

Fitzmyer, J. "The Story of the Dishonest Manager (Lk.
16:1-13)." Theological Studies 25 (March 1964) 23-42.

Fletcher, D. R. "The Riddle of the Unjust Steward: Is
Irony the Key?" Journal of Biblical Literature 82
(March 1963) 15-30.

Friedel, L. M. "The Parable of the Unjust Steward."
Catholic Biblical Quarterly 3 (1941) 337-48.

Frith, Harold, and Hooper, Henry T. "The Unjust Steward."
Expository Times 15 (1903-04) 426-27.

Gächter, Paul. "Die Parabel vom ungetreuen Verwalter
(Lk. 16, 1-8)." Orientierung 27 (1963) 149-50.

_____. "The Parable of the Dishonest Steward after
Oriental Conceptions." Catholic Biblical Quarterly 12
(1950) 121-31.

Gander, Georges. "Le Procédé de l'économe infidèle décrit
Luc 16, 5-7 est-il répréhensible ou louable?" Verbum
Caro 7 (1953) 128-41.

Gattlen, J. Die alte, hie neue Deutung der Parabel vom
ungerechten Verwalter und von "Quid mihi et tibi est,
mulier?" Brig (Schweiz): Auctor, 1930, 17p.

_____. Kunsterische Gesichtspunkte in der Parabel
vom ungerechten Verwalter Luk. 16, 1-9. Brig
(Schweiz); Auctor, 1930, 8p.

Gaupp, F. "Die Parabel vom ungerechten Haushalter," in
Tholucks Liter. Anzeiger. 1839.

Gelpke, F. C. Novum tentamen parabolam Jesu de oeconomo injusto interpretandi. Lipsiae: 1829.

Gibson, M. D. "On the Parable of the Unjust Steward."
Expository Times 14 (1902-03) 334.

Grant, John, and O'Neill, F. W. S. "The Unjust Steward."
Expository Times 16 (1904-05) 239-40.

Hampden-Cook, E., and Dutton, F. G. "The Unjust Steward."
Expository Times 16 (1904-05) 44.

Harnisch, Wilhelm. Auch eine Erklärung des Gleichnisses
vom sogenannten ungerechten Haushalter; Luc. 16, 1-13.
Magdeburg: Falckenberg, 1847, 62p.

Hartmann, H. L. Comment. de oeconomo improbo apud
Lc. XVI, 1-3. Lipsiae: 1830.

Hendry, James. "The Parable of the Unjust Steward."
Expository Times 4 (1892-93) 431-32.

Henry, H. T. "The Unjust Steward." Homiletic and Pastoral Review 38 (1938) 1020-30.

Herrmann, J. "Rechtsgeschichtliche Überlegungen zum
Gleichnis vom ungerechten Verwalter (Lk. 16:1-8)."
Jahres-und Tagesbericht der Görresgesellschaft, pp27-
33, Köln: 1969. Also in Tijdschrift voor Rechtsges-
chiedenis. Revue d'histoire du droit 38 (1970) 389-402.

Hölbe, Dr. "Versuch einer Erklärung der Parabel vom
ungerechten Haushalter, Luk. 16, 1ff." Theologische
Studien und Kritiken 31 (1858) 527-42.

Hof, Otto. "Luthers Auslegung von Lukas 16, 9." Evangelische Theologie 8 (1948-49) 151-66.

Hooley, B. A., and Mason, A. J. "Some Thoughts on the
Parable of the Unjust Steward (Luke 16:1-9)." Australian Biblical Review 6 (1958) 49-59.

Hüttermann, F. "Stand das Gleichnis vom ungerechten
Verwalter in Q?" Theologie und Glaube 27 (1935) 739-
42.

Jalland, T. G. "A Note on Luke 16, 1-9," in Studia Evan-

gelica. Texte und Untersuchungen 73. Berlin: Akademie-
Verlag, 1959, 503-05.

Jannaris, A. N. "The Unrighteous Steward and Machiavel-
lism." Expository Times 13 (1901-02) 128-30.

Jensen, K. "Über das Gleichnis vom ungerechten Haushalter,
Luc. 16, 1-13." Theologische Studien und Kritiken 2
(1829) 699-714.

Kaanengiesser, C. "L'Intendant malhonnête (Lc. 16, 1-8a)."
Christus 18, 70 (1971) 213-18.

Kamlah, E. "Die Parabel von ungerechten Verwalter (Luk.
16, 1ff.) im Rahmen der Knechtsgleichnisse," in Abraham
unser Vater. Festschrift für O. Michel. O Betz, et al.,
eds., pp276-94. Leiden, Köln: Brill, 1963.

Kendall, G. "The Parable of the Unjust Steward and Its
Bearing on the Problems of the Early Church." Modern
Churchman 39 (1949) 133-35.

King, Alexander. "The Parable of the Unjust Steward."
Expository Times 50 (1938-39) 474-76.

Kögel, Julius. Zum Gleichnis von ungerechten Haushalter.
Bemerkungen zu Lukas 16, 1-13. Göttingen: C. Bertelsmann, 1914, 36p.

Köster, Friedrich. "Analekten zur Auslegung der Parabel
vom ungerechten Haushalter." Theologische Studien und
Kritiken 38 (1865) 725-34.

Kosmala, H. "The Parable of the Unjust Steward in the
Light of Qumran." Annual. Swedish Theological Institute
3 (1964) 114-21.

Krämer, Michael. "Ad parabolam de villico iniquo (Lc. 16,
8. 9)." Verbum Domini 38 (1960) 278-91.

_____. "Aenigma parabolae de villico iniquo. Lc.
16, 1-13." Verbum Domini 46 (1968) 370-75.

_____. "Das Rätsel der Parabel vom ungerechten
Verwalter. Lk. 16, 1 bis wieweit? Umfang und Sinn."
Diss., Pont. Inst. Biblici, Romae, 1968.

. Das Rätsel der Parabel vom ungerechten
Verwalter: Lk. 16, 1-13; Auslegungsgeschichte, Umfang, Sinn; eine Diskussion der Probleme und Lösung-
svorschläge der Verwalterparabel von den Vätern bis
heute. Zürich: PAS-Verlag, 1972, 303p.

Krüger, Gerda. Die geistesgeschichtlichen Grundlagen des
Gleichnisses vom ungerechten Verwalter, Lk. 16, 1-9."
Biblische Zeitschrift 21 (1933) 170-81.

Larroche, E. "La Parabole de l'économe infidèle (Lc.
16)." Bulletin de Littérature Ecclésiastique (1953) 65-
74.

Ledrus, M. "Il fattore infedele (Lc. 16, 1-9). Stralciato
da uno studio in preparazione sulla modestia (epieikeia)
evangelistica." Palestra del Clero 50 (1971) 978-82.

Liese, H. "Villicus iniquitatis (Lc. 16, 1-9)." Verbum
Domini 12 (1932) 193-98.

Lunt, R. G. "Expounding the Parables; The Parable of the
Unjust Steward (Luke 16:1-15)." Expository Times 77
(1966) 132-36.

. "Towards an Interpretation of the Parable
of the Unjust Steward (Luke XVI:1-18)." Expository
Times 66 (1955) 335-37. Reply. F. J. Williams. 66
(1955) 371-72.

Luther, Martin. Ain Sermon am nächsten Sontag nach Marie
Hymelfart. Augsburg: 1522, 11p.

Maass, F. "Das Gleichnis vom ungerechten Haushalter, Lc.
16, 1-8." Theologia Viatorum 8 (1961) 173-84.

McFadyen, J. F. "The Parable of the Unjust Steward."
Expository Times 37 (1925-26) 535-39.

Marshall, H. S. "The Parable of the Untrustworthy Steward."
Expository Times 39 (1927-28) 120-22.

Marshall, I. H. "Luke XVI, 8--Who Commended the Unjust
Steward?" Journal of Theological Studies 19 (1968)
617-19.

Martin-Achard, R. "Notes sur Mammon et la parabole de

l'econome infidèle. " Études théologiques et religieuses 28 (1953) 137-41.

Middleton, R. D. "St. Luke XVI, 9. " Theology 29 (1934) 41.

Miller, W. D. "The Unjust Stewart. " Expository Times 15 (1903-04) 332-34.

Modersohn, E. De gelijkenis van den onrechtvaardigen rentmeester. Uit het Duitsch door K. Klein. Hilversum: Harkema's Boekh., 1926.

Moore, F. J. "The Parable of the Unjust Steward. " Anglican Theological Review 47 (1965) 103-05.

Murray, George. "The Unjust Steward. " Expository Times 15 (1903-04) 307-10.

Oesterley, W. O. E. "The Parable of the 'Unjust' Steward (St. Luke XVI). " Expositor 6th ser. , 7 (1903) 273-83.

Pargiter, Frederick E. "The Parable of the Unrighteous Steward. " Expository Times 32 (1920-21) 136-37.

Paterson, W. P. "The Example of the Unjust Steward. " Expository Times 35 (1923-24) 391-95.

Paul, Geoffrey. "Studies in Texts: The Unjust Steward. " Theology 61 (1958) 189-93.

Pautrel, Raymond. "'Aeterna Tabernacula' (Luc 16, 9). " Recherches de Science Religieuse 30 (1940) 307-27.

Pfeiffer, K. W. "Gleichnis 'vom ungerechten Haushalter.'" Theologische Zeitschrift aus der Schweiz 8 (1891) 42-49.

Pickar, C. H. "The Unjust Steward. " Catholic Biblical Quarterly 1 (1939) 250-52.

Piper, Thomas S. "Mammon of Unrighteousness. " Good News Broadcaster 35:8 (Sept. 1977) 43-44.

Pirot, Jean. Jésus et la richesse; parabole de l'intendant astucieux (Luc XVI, 1-15). Exégèse traditionelle, étude critique du jeu de mots possible en araméen, utilisation pastorale de la parabole, histoire de son exégèse. Marseille: Impr. marseillaise, 1944, 79p.

Preisker, Herbert. "Lukas 16, 1-7." Theologische Literaturzeitung 74 (1949) 85-92.

Ripon, W. B. "The Parable of the Unjust Steward." Expositor 4th ser., 7 (1893) 21-29.

Rücker, Adolf. Über das Gleichnis von ungerechten Verwalter. Freiburg i. B.: Herder, 1912, 65p.

Samain, P. "Le Bon Usage des richesses en Luc 16, 1-12." Revue Diocésaine de Tournai 2 (1947) 330-35.

Schlögl, Nivard. "Die Fabel vom 'ungerechten Reichtum' und die Aufforderung Jesu, sich damit Schätze für den Himmel zu sammeln." Biblische Zeitschrift 14 (1916-17) 41-43.

Schneider, J. Das Gleichnis vom ungerechten Haushalter. Leonberg/Württemberg: Philadelphia-Verlag, 1952, 16p.

Schreiter, J. C. Historico-critica explicationum Parabolae de improbo oeconomo descriptio. Lipsiae: 1803.

Schwarz, G. "'...lobte den betrügerischen Verwalter?' Lukas 16, 8a." Biblische Zeitschrift 18 (1974) 94-95.

Scott, R. B. Y. "The Parable of the Unjust Stewart." Expository Times 49 (1937-38) 234-35.

Seibert, H. W. Der ungerechte Haushalter. Leipzig: Wallmann, 1930, 23p.

Sibinga, J. Smit. "De onrechtvaardige rentmeester naar het evangelie van Lucas." Vox theologica 26 (1955-56) 112-21.

Simons, Ed. "Die Auslegung der Parabeln Jesu und die Parabel vom ungerechten Haushalter," in Festgabe für Wilhelm Crecelius zum Feier der fünfundzwanzigjährigen Lehrthätigkeit in Elberfeld, pp234-39. Elberfeld: Sam. Lucas, 1881.

Skvireckas, J. "Neteisusis uzvaizdas [villicus, iniquitatis Lk. 16, 8]." Σωτήρ 3 (1926) 43-49.

Spicq, C. La Parabole de l'économe infidèle. Paris: Editions du Cerf, 1947, 16p.

Steele, J. "The Unjust Steward." Expository Times 39 (1927-28) 236-37.

Steinwender, G. L. Über das Gleichniss vom ungerechten Haushalter. Stuttgart: 1840.

Stemler, G. W. "De rentmeester en zijn heer. Luk. 16, 1-9." Theologische studiën 12 (1894) 414-21.

Stoll, R. "The Unjust Steward--A Problem in Interpretation." Ecclesiastical Review 105 (1941) 16-27.

Stone, Edward P. Make Friends; The Unjust Steward and Honesty; A Contrast. Lapeer, Mich.: 1898, 14p.

Šurjanský, A. J. "De condicionibus physicis et socialibus quae in parabole Lc. 16, 1-13 de 'iniusto villico' innuuntur." Theologia Cath. Slovaca 1 (1941) 70-86.

Thielicke, Helmut. Das Gleichnis vom ungerechten Haushalter. Muss die Abgabepflicht nach dem Buchstaben erfüllt werden? (Predigt). Stuttgart: Quell-Verlag, 1950, 11p.

Thomas, W. H. Griffith. "The Unjust Steward." Expository Times 25 (1913-14) 44.

Tillmann, Fritz. "Zum Gleichnis vom ungerechten Verwalter, Lk. 16, 1-9." Biblische Zeitschrift 9 (1911) 171-84.

Topel, L. John. "On the Injustice of the Unjust Steward: Luke 16:1-13." Catholic Biblical Quarterly 37 (1975) 216-27.

"The Unjust Steward." Sign 25 (Nov. 1945) 17-18.

The Unjust Steward (Filmstrip). Eye Gate House, 1963.

Velte. "Das eschatologische Heute im Gleichnis vom ungerechten Haushalter." Monatsschrift für Pastoraltheologie 27 (1931) 211-17.

Vögtle, A. "Das Gleichnis vom ungetreuen Verwalter."

408 / Unjust Steward; Unmerciful Servant

Oberrheinisches Pastoralblatt 53 (1952) 263-70, 286-95.

Volckaert, J. "The Parable of the Clever Steward." Clergy Monthly 17 (1953) 332-41.

Wanset, J. C. "The Parable of the Unjust Steward: An Interpretation." Expository Times 47 (1935-36) 39-40.

Weber, Simon. "Revision gegen die Freisprechung des ungerechten Verwalters Luk. 16, 5-8." Theologische Quartalschrift 93 (1911) 339-63.

Williams, F. J. "The Parable of the Unjust Steward (Luke XVI, 1-9), Notes on the Interpretation Suggested by the Rev. R. G. Lunt." Expository Times 66 (1954-55) 371-72.

Williams, Francis E. "Is Almsgiving the Point of the 'Unjust Steward?'" Journal of Biblical Literature 83 (1964) 293-97.

Wood, C. T. "Luke XVI, 8." Expository Times 63 (1951-52) 126.

Zerwick, M. "Iterum de villico iniquo (Lc. 16, 1-15)." Verbum Domini 25 (1947) 172-76.

Zyro, Fried. "Neuer Versuch über das Gleichnis vom klugen Verwalter, Luc. 16." Theologische Studien und Kritiken 4 (1831) 776-804.

UNMERCIFUL SERVANT

Achenbach, W. Das Gleichnis von Schalksknecht. Predigt über das Evangelium am 22. Sonntag nach Trinitatis. Zwickau: Schriftenverein, 1918, 8p.

Bilderdienst für Christenlehre und Gemeinde. Hrsg. von der Bibelanstalt Altenburg im Auftrage der Erziehungskammer der Evangelischen Kirche in Deutschland, Berliner Stelle. A 13. N. T. Der Schalknecht. Niederdeutsch 16. Jh. Matth. Kap. 18, 21-35. Berlin: Evang. Verlag Anst., 1954.

Breukelman, F. H. "Eine Erklärung des Gleichnisses vom Schalksknecht," in Parrhesia. Festschrift für K. Barth, pp261-87. Zürich: 1966.

Deidun, Thomas. "The Parable of the Unmerciful Servant (Mt. 18:23-35)." Biblical Theology Bulletin 6 (1976) 203-24.

Deiss, L. "L'Évangile (du 21e Dimanche après la Pentecôte) (Mt. 18, 23-35): La Parabole du débiteur impitoyable." Assemblées du Seigneur 76 (1964) 29-42.

Derrett, J. D. M. "Law in the New Testament: The Parable of the Unmerciful Servant." Revue Internationale des Droits de l'Antiquité 3e Série, 12 (1965) 3-19.

Dietzfelbinger, C. "Das Gleichnis von der erlassenen Schuld. Eine theologische Untersuchung von Matthäus 18, 23-35." Evangelische Theologie 32 (1972) 437-51.

Fonck, Leopold. "Servus nequam (Mt. 18, 23-35)." Verbum Domini 1 (1921) 310-15.

Fuchs, Ernst. "The Parable of the Unmerciful Servant (Matt. 18:23-35)," in Studia Evangelica. Texte und Untersuchungen 73, pp487-94. Berlin: Akademie-Verlag, 1959.

Henry, H. T. "The Unmerciful Servant." Homiletic and Pastoral Review 41 (1940-41) 1-10.

Kempf, Georges. Vergebung. Ein Evangelienspiel nach dem Gleichnis vom Schalksknecht, Matth. 18, 23-25. Paris, Strasbourg: Ed. Lutheriennes; Strasbourg: Librairie Oberlin, 1955, 47p.

Komárková, B. "Dluh a vina." Theologická Příloha 30 (1963) 13-16.

The Unforgiving Debtor (Filmstrip). Religious Films, London. Released in the U. S. by United World Films, 1949.

_____ (Motion picture). Religious Films, London, 1939. Released in the U. S. by United World Films, 1946.

The Unforgiving Servant (Filmstrip). Double Sixteen Co., 1968.

Weatherspoon, J. B. "The Spirit of Forgiveness." Review and Expositor 41 (1944) 361-71.

WARRING KING

Jarvis, P. G. "The Tower-Builder and the King Going to War (Luke 14:25-33)." Expository Times 77 (1966) 196-98.

Louw, J. "Lucas 14, 25-33." Nieuwe theologische studiën 19 (1936) 144-45.

_____. "The Parables of the Tower-Builder and the King Going to War." Expository Times 48 (1936-37) 478.

Mechie, Stewart. "The Parables of the Tower-Builder and the King Going to War." Expository Times 48 (1936-37) 235-36.

Thackeray, H. St J. "A Study in the Parable of the Two Kings." Journal of Theological Studies 14 (1913) 389-99.

WATCHMAN

Dupont, Jacques. "La parabole du maître qui rentre dans la nuit (Mc. 13, 34-36)," in Mélanges bibliques en hommage au R. P. Béda Rigaux. A. Descamps & A. de Halleux, eds., pp89-116. Gembloux: Duculot, 1970.

Joüon, Paul. "La Parabole du Portier qui doit veiller (Marc XIII, 33-37) et la Parabole des Serviteurs qui doivent veiller (Luc XII, 35-40)." Recherches de science religieuse 30 (1940) 365-68.

Lövestam, E. "Le Portier qui veille la nuit, Mc. 13, 33-37." Assemblées du Seigneur. Paris: Cerf, 1969 (2, 5) 44-53.

Weiser, A. "Von der Predigt Jesu zur Erwartung der Parusie. Uberlieferungsgeschichtliches zum Gleichnis vom Türhüter." Bibel und Leben 12 (1971) 25-31.

WICKED HUSBANDMEN

Bammel, E. "Das Gleichnis von den bösen Winzern (Mk. 12, 1-9) und das jüdische Erbrecht." Revue internationale des droits de l'antiquité 3e série, 6 (1959) 11-17.

Björck, Gudmund. "Drei Markus-Stellen. --Mc. 12, 4." Conciectanea Neotestamentica I (1936) 1-7.

Blank, J. "Die Sendung des Sohnes. Zur christologischen Bedeutung des Gleichnisses von den bösen Winzern," in Neues Testament und Kirche. Festschrift R. Schnackenburg. J. Gnilka, ed., pp11-41. Freiburg i.B., Basel, Wien: Herder, 1974.

Burkitt, F. C. "The Parable of the Wicked Husbandmen," in Transactions of the Third International Congress for the History of Religions. Vol. II, pp321-28. Oxford: 1908.

Crossan, John D. "The Parable of the Wicked Husbandmen." Journal of Biblical Literature 90 (1971) 451-65.

Dehandschutter, B. "La Parabole des vignerons homicides (Mc. 12, 1-12) et l'Évangélique selon Thomas (logion 65)." Bibliotheca Ephemeridum Theologicarum Lovaniensium 34 (1974) 203-19.

Derrett, J. D. M. "Allegory and the Wicked Vinedressers." Journal of Theological Studies 25 (1974) 426-32.

_____ "Fresh Light on the Parable of the Wicked Vinedressers." Revue internationale des droits de l'antiquité 3e serie, 10 (1963) 11-41.

Dillon, R. J. "Towards a Tradition-history of the Parables of the True Israel (Matthew 21:33-22:14)." Biblica 47 (1966) 1-42.

Doherty, J. "The Murder of the Good Will Ambassadors." Liguorian 51 (July 1963) 48-52.

Dombois, H. "Juristische Bemerkungen zum Gleichnis von den bösen Weingartnern." Neue Zeitschrift für systematische Theologie und Religionsphilosophie 8 (1966) 361-73.

Durand, A. "Life by Death." Sponsa Regis 35 (Sept. 1963) 10-17.

Flemming, G. "Die Sünde der bösen Weingärtner (Mc. 12, 1-12; Mt. 23, 13-33)." Christentum und Wirklichkeit 11 (1933) 70-75.

Fridrichsen, Anton. "Til lignelsen om de onde vingartnere." Svensk Teologisk Kvartalskrift 4 (1928) 355-61.

Gozzo, Serafino M. Disquisitio critico-exegetica in parabolam Novi Testamenti de perfidis vinitoribus. Roma: Pontif. Ateneo Antoniano, 1949, 206p.

Gray, Arthur. "The Parable of the Wicked Husbandmen." Hibbert Journal 19 (1920-21) 42-52.

Hengel, M. "Das Gleichnis von den Weingärtnern Mc. 12, 1-12 im Lichte der Zenonpapyri und der rabbinischen Gleichnisse." Zeitschrift für die neutestamentliche Wissenschaft 59 (1968) 1-39.

Hubaut, Michel. "La Parabole des vignerons homicides." Diss., Louvain, 1974.

_____. La Parabole des vignerons homicides. Paris: Gebalda, 1976, 153p.

_____. "La Parabole des vignerons homicides: son authenticité, sa visée première." Revue Théologique de Louvain 6 (1975) 51-61.

Justus the Ant (Filmstrip). Cathedral Films, 1956.

Klauck, H. J. "Das Gleichnis vom Mord im Weinberg (Mk. 12, 1-12; Mt. 21, 33-46; Lc. 20, 9-19)." Bibel und Leben 11 (1970) 117-45.

Kümmel, W. G. "Das Gleichnis von den bösen Weingärtnern (Mark 12, 1-9)," in Aux sources de la tradition chrétienne. Mélanges M. Goguel, pp120-31; Neuchâtel-Paris: Delachaux & Niestlé, 1950. Also in Heilsgeschehen und Geschichte. Gesammelte Aufsätze, pp207-17. Marbug: N. G. Elwert, 1965.

Léon-Dufour, X. "The Murderous Vineyard-Workers." Sciences Ecclésiastiques 17 (1965) 365-96. Also in Theology Digest 15 (Sept. 1967) 30-36.

_____. "La Parabole des vignerons homicides," in Études d'Évangile, pp303-44, Paris: Éditions du Seuil, 1965. Also in Sciences Ecclésiastiques 17 (1965) 365-96.

Lohmeyer, E. "Das Gleichnis von den bösen Weingärtnern." Zeitschrift für systematische Theologie 18 (1941) 243-59. Also in Urchristliche Mystik. Neutestamentliche Studien, pp161-81. Darmstadt: Wissenschaftliche Buchgesellschaft, 1958.

Mattes, John C. "A Study in Exegesis: The Parable of the Vineyard." Lutheran Church Review 29 (1910) 578-87.

Merli, D. "La parabola dei vignaioli infedeli." Bibbia e Oriente 15 (1973) 97-107.

Miller, Merrill P. "Scripture and Parable: A Study of the Function of the Biblical Features in the Parable of the Wicked Husbandmen and their Place in the History of the Tradition." Ph. D. Thesis. Columbia University (Union Theological Seminary), 1974, 500p.

Mussner, F. "Die bösen Winzer nach Matthaus 21, 33-46," in Antijudaismus im Neuen Testament? Exegetische und systematische Beiträge (Abhandlungen zum christlich-jüdischen Dialog, 2). W. P. Eckert, ed., pp129-34. München: Kaiser, 1967.

Newell, Jane E., and Newell, R. R. "The Parable of the Wicked Tenants." Novum Testamentum 14 (1972) 226-37.

"Parabola de perfidis vinitoribus." Collationes Diocesis Tornacensis 32 (1937) 510-14.

Pedersen, S. "Zum Problem der vaticinia ex eventu; eine Analyse von Mt. 21:33-46 par.; 22:1-10 par." Studia Theologica 19 (1965) 167-88.

Robinson, J. A. T. "The Parable of the Wicked Husbandmen. A Test of Synoptic Relationships." New Testament Studies 21 (1974-75) 443-61.

Silva, Costoya R. "La parábola de los tenteros homicidas. Estudio critico (-literario) e interpretación de Mt. 21, 33-46; Mc. 12, 1-12; Lc. 20, 9-19." Compostellanum 15 (1970) 319-55.

Snodgrass, K. R. "The Parable of the Wicked Husbandmen. Is the Gospel of Thomas Version the Original?" New Testament Studies 21 (1974) 142-44.

Swaeles, R. "L'Authenticité de la parabole des vignerons homicides." Unpublished. Louvain: 1958.

Trilling, W. "Le Jugement sur le faux Israël (Matthieu 21, 33-46)." Lectio Divina 69 (1971) 165-89.

WINESKINS

Ebeling, H. J. "Die Fastenfrage (Mk. 2:18-10)." Theologische Studien und Kritiken 108 (1937-38) 387-96.

Gutzwiller, R. "The Newness of the Kingdom of God; Parable of the Wineskins; Excerpt from Parables of the Lord." Way 20 (Dec. 1964) 17+.

Hahn, Ferdinand. "Die Bildworte vom neuen Flicken und von jungen Wein." Evangelische Theologie 31 (1971) 357-75.

Kee, A. A. "The Old Coat and the New Wine; A Parable of Repentance." Novum Testamentum 12 (1970) 13-21.

Klöpper, Albert. "Der ungewalkte Flicken und das alte Kleid. Der neue Wein und die alten Schläuche." Theologische Studien und Kritiken 58 (1885) 505-34.

Lewis, F. Warburton. "New Garments and Old Patches." Expository Times 13 (1901-02) 522.

Lüthi, Walter. Das Gleichnis vom neuen Wein. Predigt über Luk. 5, 27-39. Basel: Reinhardt, 1947, 12p.

Nagel, W. "Neuer Wein in alten Schläuchen (Mt. 9, 17)." Vigiliae Christianae 14 (1960) 1-8.

Trudinger, Paul. "Un Cas d'incompatibilite? (Marc 2:21-22; Luc 5:39)." Foi et Vie 72 no. 5-6 (1973) 4-7.

_____. "Word on the Generation Gap: Reflections on a Gospel Metaphor. " Biblical Theology Bulletin 5 (1975) 311-15.

Weitbrecht, H. V. "New Wine in New Wine Skins. " Expository Times 19 (1907-08) 142.

INDEX OF SUBJECTS

417

INDEX OF NAMES